Falkland and its People
1901–1913

1. Coat of arms of the Royal Burgh of Falkland

"Azure, on a mount a stag lodged reguardant at the foot of an oak tree, all Proper." The Latin motto, "Learn righteousness and take heed not to despise Christ" is adapted from Virgil, Aeneid vi, 620, "Discite justitiam moniti et non temnere divos" – i.e. "... not to despise the gods". The current Community Council uses the same arms but with a different coronet.

The arms were re-drawn for this book by Frances Crichton Stuart.

FALKLAND

AND ITS

PEOPLE

1901–1913

Research by Thomas Playfair
Edited by Ross Burgess

With a Foreword by Marietta Crichton Stuart

The Falkland Society

First published in Scotland 2020 by The Falkland Society,
Brunton House, Brunton Street, Falkland, Fife KY15 7BQ,
Scottish Registered Charity SC017201

www.falklandsociety.org.uk

A CIP catalogue record for this book
is available from the British Library.

ISBN 978-1-9161504-0-9

10 9 8 7 6 5 4 3 2 1

Selection and arrangement of items by Thomas Playfair.

Editing, Introduction, Notes and Index by Ross Burgess.

Design and typesetting by Ross Burgess.

Foreword by Marietta Crichton Stuart.

Cover image by Peter Jones.

Printed and bound in the UK by
Print2Demand Ltd, Westoning.

Set in Palatino Linotype.

Sponsors

The following have assisted by their sponsorship the publication of this book:

- The Falkland War Memorial Trust

The following individuals:

- Bob Beveridge
- Jack Burgess
- Peter Burman and Ross Burgess
- Julia and Lars Christiansen
- Frances Crichton Stuart
- Marietta Crichton Stuart
- Alan Graham
- Julia Knowles
- David M. Munro
- Bill and Gilli Pagan
- Keith Rennie
- Ann Scott
- John and Josephine Smith
- Ninian C. Stuart
- Dionatas Vargas and Adam Lewis

And three sponsors who wished to remain anonymous.

Contents

Illustrations

Foreword

"The times they are a-changing", Bob Dylan's lyrics could be the anthem for Falkland in the dozen years after the death of Queen Victoria, and, as Noel Coward would later write, we know there were "bad times just around the corner".

A war memorial stands on Falkland's Brunton Green. It lists the names of the 57 men, some full of youthful enthusiasm and plans, others family men, all of whom were to become casualties of the Great War, dying far from Falkland. Two of these names are personal to my family. My grandfather Lord Ninian, who appears throughout this book, was killed in 1915 aged 32 leaving a widow and three children, the youngest being my father Michael, who was just six months old, and like many other children in Falkland had a father he never knew.

Rory Slacke also figures many times in these pages, as Lord Ninian's secretary; one of my grandmother's four first cousins who died, his bleak battlefield grave in France was visited by James Donaldson, the Falkland Bank Manager, another casualty.

Through my researches into the history of Falkland, into the lives of these 57 men and through the pages of this book, I have learned a little of what they left behind going off to destinations unknown to serve King and Country.

The book is the life story of their Falkland community, the families, homes, jobs, entertainment and church; its transformation from a previously almost self-contained town which was creeping into the new century and the new era seeping into the town with the arrival of motor vehicles, electricity, telephones and mechanization, increased travel, the decline of a deferential society and the shift in emphasis from the Estate, its Laird and home-based industry, to factories with a demand for labour and the importation of teenage workers from Kent to keep the machines running. For my own family it is a tale of coming of age, marriage, birth and death.

Nationally there was an end to the Boer war and the decline of the dominance of the British Empire; political upheaval with a struggle to reduce the power of the House of Lords, calls for Irish Home Rule and votes for women, the rise of trade unions and the growth of the working voice. In Falkland the Territorials or Saturday night soldiers, successors to the Volunteers, drilled enthusiastically under the command of Captain Donaldson, whilst in South Wales my grandfather, having become a local MP, took command of a territorial battalion comprised of steel workers.

On a smaller scale, Falkland was changing and the Estate was starting to relax its "No entry" policy. Today many take for granted the open gates of the Estate and free access, but the tramping feet of thousands can, on occasions, be to the detriment of the landscape which had been designed for the few rather than the many. A generation later the House of Falkland at the heart of the Estate was deemed unsuitable by my parents as a family home, preferring the Palace, which, with some alteration, was more manageable and comfortable; it did not stand in splendid isolation on the estate, but was part of Falkland life.

Positions of control still remained in the hands of a small number of men, whilst the Town Council was starting to flex its muscles and the local Masonic lodge thrived. My grandfather felt it was his duty to serve on Fife County Council.

The churches still held sway, albeit there was strife with increasing numbers of Catholics and uproar from some quarters when the school permitted use of a room for "a Popish priest to teach Popery to Popish children". The fitting out of the Palace's Chapel Royal as a Catholic church, and the Memorial Chapel by the Stables on Falkland Estate designed by Reginald Fairlie, a friend and Catholic architect from Auchtermuchty, are tangible outcomes of my own family's faith.

It is hard to imagine a time without television, the internet and mobile phones, but much of the village's entertainment was both home-grown and plentiful; a talk on "Parodies and Parodists" would have an appreciative audience. Numerous clubs and sports thrived including football, golf, cricket, curling – whilst the keeping of birds and flower growing was competitive and Falkland was alive to the sound of music with choirs, brass bands and dancing. The Drill Hall in South Street hosted events ranging from entertainment to political and educational. In an age when women did not have the vote, I learned how my grandmother took an active role in Falkland's political life with its debates, meetings and fund raising, while there was a very real political battle between the Unionists and the Liberals.

Within the Falkland community were distinct groups – the pubs set against the Temperance League with its own hotel and tea rooms; the three churches with differing interactions with the local school; the town and the Estate; the self-employed craftsmen working from home and the factories; the Falkland folk and the incomers.

Having been brought up in the Palace, technically outside the Royal Burgh, and from a family that only came to Falkland in 1887, I perhaps have the perspective and inquisitiveness of an outsider and relative newcomer.

The 1911 census shows 2,356 inhabitants in the parish of Falkland, so hundreds of stories roused my curiosity about jobs such as tenters in the factory, how a family of twelve could live in three rooms in the Balmblae Gasworks or what it would be like to attend a missionary lecture on "Jamaica" with a lantern show with limelight.

Falkland had a plethora of shops and craftspeople, banks, its own doctor and a district nurse who was paid for through charity. Life was often insular, but with the introduction of transport changes and the telephone, the community was reaching out as exemplified by the Light Railway scheme, whilst the village received an increasing number of visitors going on the Palace guided tours.

Despite a local policeman there was petty crime whose perpetrators could be as young as ten: penalties ranged from a hefty £1, five days in prison or, for the under-16s, six strokes of the birch. For many life was unhealthy, precarious and tough; there was an Inspector of the Poor, poorhouses still existed and the needy had to rely on charity, it is not surprising that some local young men sought a new life in the colonies.

It is said that the Victorian era was one when people knew their place and generally stayed close to home; this book vividly depicts Falkland in the succeeding era when it faced change, wider horizons and greater opportunities. However, all the while, we, in hindsight, know what is just around the corner.

Marietta Crichton Stuart

Marietta is the grand-daughter of Lord and Lady Ninian Crichton-Stuart and the official archivist of the Falkland Estate.

Editor's Preface

The Falkland Society's previous major work, *Falkland in the Reign of Queen Victoria, 1837–1900*, gives a fascinating series of snapshots of life in and around the Royal Burgh; but when Tom Playfair told me he was preparing a similar book on the Edwardian era it occurred to me that it could be enhanced by an introduction to set the individual articles in their context, some notes on the people and places mentioned, and above all an index to help you find that particularly interesting passage that you remember reading but now can't locate.

So rather hesitantly I volunteered for what has proved to be a very interesting but very time-consuming task. I have had to explore some of the more arcane and often frustrating aspects of Microsoft Word, and get to grips with software such as GIMP for editing the photographs and QGIS for producing the maps. In the process of editing I have attempted to standardise the punctuation, and correct obvious spelling mistakes, but the nature of the source material means that this can never be completely achieved.

The start of the coronavirus restrictions in March 2020 put a halt to many outside activities, thus giving me more time to work on this book. My husband and I spent many hours just walking round the village and the surrounding landscape, vastly deepening our knowledge and understanding of this beautiful and historic place. With visits to libraries out of the question for the time being, online access to sources such as Wikipedia and the British Newspaper Archive have been invaluable.

In the course of investigating the old buildings of Falkland, many of which (including our own home) are listed as of historic or architectural importance, I discovered that information about local listed buildings is extremely incomplete: in England there was a project to take photographs of every listed building or structure, but nothing similar has been done in Scotland: the Falkland Society's new project, the Falkland Listed Buildings Survey, will fill this gap for our historic parish.

I hope that this book will provoke interest and debate, particularly amongst those who know and love our historic village. If you can point out errors or supply information to fill in the gaps, please contact us at news@falklandsociety.org.uk. Any corrections will be detailed on our website and included in the next impression of this book.

Acknowledgements

I wish to acknowledge the assistance of all the individuals who contributed to the preparation of this volume, including first and foremost Tom Playfair for his tireless researches in the cause of the history of Falkland and its people, also to Peter Jones for his striking cover image, to the Falkland War Memorial Trust and our other sponsors listed on page v for their financial support, and to the Committee of the Falkland Society for supporting this project, and in particular its Chair, my husband Dr Peter Burman, for his forbearance and encouragement during what has proved to be a very long undertaking.

Thanks also to those who gave permission to use photographs and other material, including Jack Burgess (no relation) for his year-by-year chronicle of Falkland News, which has been drawn on extensively, Stewart Thomson for his collection of Historic Images of Falkland, Simon Taylor for the map of parishes of Fife, Frances Crichton Stuart for drawing the Royal Burgh coat of arms for our frontispiece, and others whose ownership of images we have been unable to trace.

Finally special thanks to the Crichton Stuart family for permission to consult and extensively quote from the Falkland Estate Papers in their archives, and to Marietta in particular for not only providing the Foreword, but also for reading the entire book in draft, and contributing many insights which have helped to clarify obscure points and make links between apparently unconnected people and events.

Ross Burgess

Introduction

A new century and a new reign

The turn of the twentieth century and the start of the Edwardian era had little immediate effect on the Royal Burgh of Falkland. The final stages of an overseas war, however traumatic for the South African republics, were having little impact on deeply rural parts of Fife, and gave no hint of the devastation that war was to bring later in the century. The wounding of a single soldier, presented with a gold watch on his return, warranted headlines in the local papers; fourteen years later the papers would be crowded with the deaths of men who had made a mark on local society.

Falkland mourned the old Queen, and celebrated King Edward's coronation, but both were remote figures. Falkland had seen plenty of royalty in Stuart times: James IV and James V created a splendid Renaissance palace on the site of the old castle, and Mary Queen of Scots had some of her happiest days hunting there. But after James VI inherited the English crown, and the court moved south, Falkland Palace became neglected and gradually fell into ruin.

With no royalty at hand it was the Lairds who were the main focus of popular interest and deference. The legacy of the nineteenth-century Lairds of Falkland was and is still very evident – Margaret and Onesiphorus Tyndall Bruce had funded the new parish church and the ornate fountain near the site of the old Mercat Cross, and had built for themselves the magnificent Jacobean-style House of Falkland replacing the old Nuthill House. In 1887 the third Marquess of Bute bought the estate (becoming Hereditary Keeper of Falkland

Palace) so that he could provide a suitable legacy for his second son, Lord Ninian Crichton-Stuart. [1] The Marquess used some of his immense wealth to update and modernise the House of Falkland, and had begun a major restoration of the Palace, improving the accommodation and restoring some of its Renaissance splendour.

On the Marquess's early death in 1900 Lord Ninian was only 17: it was not till 1904 that he came of age and took personal control of the estate. Falkland celebrated this event with banquets, dancing, and public ceremonies. There were similar celebrations when he married, when he and his new wife came to take up residence in the House of Falkland, and on the birth of his son and heir; the funeral when the little boy died was treated with respectful solemnity by the whole community.

Like many Scottish villages, Falkland retained the traditional layout of one main street (the High Street, running east to west), a secondary street running roughly parallel (South Street, Horsemarket, Brunton Street, and South Street West) and several small streets or Wynds at right angles (Cross Wynd, Back Wynd, Mill Wynd). At both ends of the High Street but outside the Burgh boundaries were reminders of the power of the Estate: the Palace gatehouse dominated East Port, and West Port led towards the House of Falkland's lodge gate and stables. The Palace was open to paying visitors, but access through the lodge gate to the park and "policies" of the House of Falkland was strictly controlled, except on special occasions.

Within the historic village, many the people lived in large families in small numbers of rooms, but some of the more affluent had grander houses well outside the main core – Allan Park, Chapelyard, Templelands and the Parish Church's Manse (now Ladywell House) were all in elevated positions on the slopes of the East Lomond Hill.

For Falkland, the Edwardian age represented a change from the certainties of the long Victorian era, and the beginnings of many aspects of what we now see as the modern world. Motor vehicles

---

[1] "Having bound myself to provide landed property of a certain value for my younger sons, Ninian and Colum, I looked for places which I might play with during my own life and leave to them afterwards. Hence Falkland and Pluscarden." (Hunter Blair, page 215)

2. Parish Church and High Street, looking west, c.1938
The large building on the right is St Andrew's House, and the building
beyond it, now called Maspie House, later housed the post office, Beyond that
in turn is the saddlers' house and shop, still called Saddlers House.

began to replace the horse, mains water and sewerage were extended
to Cross Wynd, where the burn would no longer run down the centre
of the street, electric lights began to be installed, and the first telephones came into use, but could be frustrating to use – if you wanted
to get a message to Auchtermuchty it could be quicker to walk the
three or four miles there rather than wait for a phone call to be put
through.

Three Falklands

Falkland at the turn of the twentieth century meant three different
areas: the parish, the estate, and the Royal Burgh.

The parish was the oldest of the three, and with the biggest area,
about seven thousand acres. It was originally the parish of Kilgour:
the settlement of that name (of which little now remains) was the site
until 1620 of the parish church. Parishes in Scotland gradually took
on secular functions, and from 1845 onwards, elected parish councils
oversaw the poor law[1] and subsequently the rudimentary public

---

[1] Some parishes maintained poorhouses, or combined with other parishes to

health service, with Falkland Parish contributing to the fever hospital at Auchtermuchty.

The Royal Burgh of Falkland owed its existence to the royal Palace, and received its charter from James II of Scotland in 1458. It was always something of an honorary Royal Burgh, never for instance sending representatives to the Scottish Parliament. Nonetheless it remained an island of civic administration with its Town Council comprising a provost, two bailies, and nine councillors, plus a Town Clerk and his office. The council met regularly in the Town Hall, providing local government functions that in the surrounding areas were the province of Fife County Council or its Cupar District Committee. It also provided the justification for a settlement of under a thousand people being called a town rather than a village. In 1901 the population of the Royal Burgh was 809, compared with 1,422 for the remaining and much larger "landward" part of the parish.

The Falkland Estate has varied in size as successive Lairds have bought or sold parcels of land, but by 1901 it amounted to over six thousand acres, comprising many separate holdings, some within the parish, some outside it, mostly let out to substantial farmers, plus about a third of the housing in the town of Falkland. This amount of landholding meant that the estate, represented by Lord Ninian's factor, was in constant correspondence with the Town Clerk, representing the Burgh.

There was much interaction during the early years of the century, with the similar-sized neighbouring estate of Lathrisk. Its young laird, whose combination of surnames was inconsistently reported in the newspapers, was very much involved in Falkland, missing its own laird during Lord Ninian's minority. By 1908 however Lathrisk House had been leased to another family, and by 1913 it was sold off to a syndicate and broken.

Echoes of feudalism

Fife in 1901 was a largely industrial county, but geology and geography kept Falkland well away from the shipbuilding and coal mining

form "combination poorhouses" – other parishes provided "outdoor relief" supporting people or families to remain in their own homes.

that dominated the coastal areas. Textile manufacture provided the main alternative to agriculture, with floorcloth and linoleum factories increasing in importance while efforts to maintain the handloom weavers were eventually abandoned.

A few local families occur frequently in the newspaper reports of the times – the Jackson family ran the two factories in the town, and Charles Jackson and his son, Charles Jnr, both served as Provosts. The Bonthrones of Newton of Falkland ran a brewery and were involved in many local activities. Charles Gulland, lawyer and bank agent, was town clerk of Falkland, like his father before him, passing the role over to his son Rowland for a while, until Rowland's untimely death.

Rural Scottish society was deeply hierarchical and patriarchal; indeed feudal, with householders having to pay "feu duties" to their feudal "superiors", generally the major landowners. The movement for women's suffrage had made little headway, although at one point Falkland Palace was closed to visitors because of the fear of damage by militant suffragettes. All the positions of formal power and influence were held by men, with women's involvement largely confined to providing refreshments and entertainment. But women, at least of the middle and upper classes, could express themselves through their clothes in an age when their husbands regularly wore dark suits and ties and working men probably wore a scarf or kerchief round their shirt collar – newspaper accounts of social gatherings gave elaborate descriptions of the colour and cut of the ladies' dresses, while their menfolk were merely listed.

The Church of Scotland was a particular example of feudal arrangements. Having done away with its bishops at the Reformation, it was governed by councils and presbyteries, but continued to be (and referred to as) "the Established Church". In each parish, certain feudal landowners, the "heritors", provided finance in the form of tithes or "teinds", controlled some aspects of the church buildings, and set the minster's salaries using an arcane computation involving "chalders".

In the Disruption of 1843 part of the church had rebelled against this secular interference in church affairs, and in Falkland as elsewhere had swiftly proceeded to build their own church. So in Edwardian times there were two churches in Falkland, the Established Church and the United Free Church. The two were essentially identical in theological terms, and existed strangely in parallel, holding their annual picnics and half-yearly communion services separately but on the same day, and celebrating the progress of their churches' respective missions to Africa. For the annual "kirkin of the council", the Provost and councillors attended one church in the morning, the other in the afternoon.

The third Marquess of Bute had converted to Roman Catholicism on coming of age in 1868, and the Palace and the House of Falkland were kept as Catholic establishments. There was a home for Catholic orphan boys in St Andrew's House, and a Catholic school in Brunton House, but by 1911 the Catholic children attended the local "Public School" (using that term in the Scottish sense of a school open to all, controlled by an elected school board) and received lessons once a week from a visiting Catholic priest, a practice that reignited old anti-Catholic feeling in some quarters.

In politics Falkland was staunchly Liberal, and the East Fife MP was the Liberal Prime Minister H. H. Asquith. Issues of the day included Home Rule (for Ireland, not yet for Scotland) and Tariff Reform versus Free Trade. Lord Ninian and his circle were Conservative (described in Scotland as "Unionist": the party nationally is still officially the Conservative and Unionist Party), but the local people irrespective of party congratulated him on being elected, at the second attempt in 1910, as MP for the hitherto Liberal seat at Cardiff.[1]

Temperance was still a local issue, and the Band of Hope tried to persuade people to sign the pledge to abstain from alcohol. As well as several regular hotels and public houses there were two temperance hotels, but the Ness family, who owned one of them, would clearly have liked to drop the temperance label, as they applied without success for a liquor licence.

The social scene

Local societies of various sorts flourished. The most prestigious were perhaps the Freemasons, and the very similar B.O.A.F.G. (British

---

[1] The South Wales coalmines and the Cardiff Docks had been the source of much of the family's wealth. Lord Ninian's father had restored Cardiff Castle at vast expense, and had served a year as Mayor of Cardiff.

Order of Ancient Free Gardeners). Both of these were for men only. There were flower shows and bird shows, popular lectures, and a literary society. For younger people there were the Y.M.C.A, the Boy Scouts, and the Young Women's Guild. The Cricket Club and Golf Club played regularly, and the Curling Club played whenever there was enough ice on the pond.

The annual Falkland Market was held in June, but had ceased to be a market in any real sense, being given over to games, dancing, and entertainment. In 1902 it was promoted as "highland games" and in 1911 it was postponed for a week to coincide with the Coronation. Another annual event, favoured more perhaps by the upper classes, was the race meeting and ball in Perth in September.

Crime in Falkland was generally of a minor nature, and dealt with by the local Burgh Court, with the Provost and Bailies acting as magistrates, or more often by the Sheriff in Cupar, the county town, with penalties such as £1 or five days in prison, or for the under-16s six strokes of the birch.

Falkland then and now

More than a century on from the Edwardian era, there are fewer shops than before catering to local needs, but gift shops and cafés cater for day visitors. Many of the older houses have been upgraded, but others, for instance in Balmblae and Brunton Street, have been demolished. Council housing started to appear after the Great War with Lomond Crescent, and new residential streets have appeared to the south of the village. The Falkland Estate is run by a trust, the House of Falkland has been a residential school for more than 70 years, and its stables have become a café, visitor centre, and art gallery. The lodge gates are now open for all to visit the park and the Maspie Den. The Palace still has a Crichton Stuart (without the hyphen) as its Hereditary Keeper, but the National Trust for Scotland was appointed Deputy Keeper in 1952 and they now manage the Palace. The Bonthrones' old brewery at Newton has found a sympathetic new use, but the Jacksons' old floorcloth and linoleum factory (St John's Works), later used for making paper bags, has been demolished, leaving a big empty space to the south of the village.

The Town Council, Parish Council and School Board have all been swept away; the County Council has been replaced by the new Fife Council, and a Community Council has been set up, with consultative functions only, covering much the same area as the old parish.[1] The two churches have been reunited (the former United Free church is now a private house) but the ministers, no longer occupying the old Manse, are not the influential leaders of society that they clearly were in Edwardian times. The Chapel Royal in Falkland Palace still serves the local Catholic community. The flow of water from the fountain has been temporarily suspended, but the Town Hall clock (installed in 1858) still chimes the hours.

---

[1] But excluding Freuchie. Its official name – the "Royal Burgh of Falkland and Newton of Falkland Community Council" – references the old Royal Burgh which covered only a small part of the Community Council area.

1901

2 January 1901

A negligent mother

Before Sheriff Gillespie on Friday, Rachel Thomson, Mill Wynd, was charged at the insistence of the School Board with a contravention of the Education Act, she having failed to provide efficient elementary education for her illegitimate child, Alex Reid, twelve years. Accused admitted the offence, remarking that the boy had a sore foot and could not go to school. The woman had been cited at least four times, and had been warned more than once, but without any good result. Accordingly the Board had been obliged to prosecute her.[1] From 8th September until 15th December the boy had only made 27 attendances out of a possible 136. Accused was fined 10s with the alternative of four days imprisonment. (FH)[2]

3 January 1901

Concert

A popular concert promoted by the Ornithological Society was held in the Drill Hall[3] last night, and was very largely attended. Mr James

---

[1] Mr J. L. Anderson, solicitor, appeared on behalf of the School Board, and said the case was a bad one. (FFP, 5 January)

[2] For an explanation of these references, see the "Sources" chapter.

[3] For more about this and other local venues, see the "Places Mentioned" chapter.

Cusin presided A first rate programme was sustained by the follow-ing artists: Miss Jessie Stark, soprano; Miss Jemima Haig, soprano; Miss M. Mitchell, violinist; Miss Janet Kennedy, Highland Dancing; Mr Charles Mitchell, tenor; Mr Andrew Rintoul, bass; Mr Charles Cameron, comedian. Miss A. Mitchell was the accompanist. A dance followed. (DC)

3 January 1901

Poultry and pigeon show

The forty second annual show of the Falkland Ornithological Society was held in the Drill Hall yesterday. This year the canary classes were cancelled and the total entries only numbered 272, a considerable fall-ing off compared with last year. Withal it was a good show. Mr John Laing, Auchtermuchty, who was an outstanding winner in the Dorking[1] classes, secured, among other honours, the special for the most points in the show, and the cup for the best bird in the show, which having been won three times now becomes his own property. There was a good attendance of visitors during the day. (DC)

4 January 1901

Cruelty to a horse

In front of Sheriff Armour,[2] Cupar, Robert Spence, carrier, Falkland, acknowledged having worked a bay horse while it was suffering from two raw sores, one under the saddle and the other under the collar. He said that the saddle was chambered, and that on the day on which the charge was made against him the sores were dry. He had been working the horse ever since, and, in fact, it was standing at the front door of the Courthouse.

Inspector Walters was told to examine the horse and report. The inspector said there was a scar on the rear side of the back, but he was of opinion that the horse was not suffering any pain. His Lordship, in

---

[1] The Dorking is one of the oldest breeds of British chicken, originating from the Surrey town of that name, and sometimes said to date back to Roman times.

[2] Samuel Beveridge Armour, Advocate, was Sheriff-Substitute of Fifeshire. In 1910 he changed his surname to Armour-Hannay. (CFUK)

view of the respective statements, limited the sentence to a fine of £1, or five days imprisonment. (DC)

5 January 1901

Trooper Bonthrone

We regret that this well-known trooper was dangerously wounded at Nooitgedacht,[1] where the Fife Yeomanry suffered so severely. The War Office has issued the following.

"20th Company Imperial Yeomanry: 912b Corporal D. Bonthrone, reported severely wounded, is now said to be dangerously wounded." (FFP)

10 January 1901

Hermit millionaire's strange life

Thirty years ago George Johnston, millionaire and laird of the Fife Isle estate, near Dundee,[2] vowed that no man should see his face again, and kept his vow. But now he is dead. A Dundee correspondent wires this story:

His father was an army officer, and then Indian tea planter. He accumulated a huge fortune and settled on the Fife Island estate. Although hard and morose, strange in habit, and violent in temper, he fell in love with Jean Douglas, the daughter of a peasant, and married her. She bore him a son, and died. That was a bad day for George Johnston's father. He brooded, they say, over his loss. His temper became ungovernable; his son's was hardly better.

One day the son tied his father into a carpet, threw him into a room, and decamped to the woods. The police caught him, and he was sent abroad. Thirty years ago the father died, and the son returned to live a solitary, sordid life, without the touch of romance which redeemed his father's. Never once did he set foot across the threshold of the dilapidated manor house. A maid cooked his scanty meals, but never saw him. She would lay the food down, ring a bell, and withdraw.

---

[1] A battle at Nooitgedacht, in the Transvaal, resulted in a British defeat by the Boer forces (13 December 1900).

[2] Actually the Lathrisk Estate, near Falkland! The Dundee correspondent seems to have been very unreliable.

Only then would Johnston come out of his den.

He had a craze for purchasing the tops of all the hills in the county. The Marquis of Bute proposed to construct a railway from Falkland Palace[1] to the town of Falkland, partly through Johnston's ground, but Johnston would have none of it.

When he died a box of 40,000 sovereigns was found, and bank notes innumerable stowed away in odd corners. He never married, and his fortune, computed at five millions, is said to go to his nephew, Lieut. Maitland-Makgill-Crichton, of the Seaforth Highlanders, now serving in the Soudan. (LEP)

11 January 1901

A wealthy man of Fife

A good deal of excitement has been occasioned in Fife concerning the estate of the late Mr George Johnston of Lathrisk, who died on the 29th ult. It has been stated that Mr Johnston died fabulously wealthy, and particulars more or less of a sensational nature have been circulated, which purport to describe the supposed peculiar habits of the deceased. It has been stated that the estate was worth several millions, but inquiry at a well-informed source has proved this estimate to be grossly exaggerated.

The story which has created most sensation in the neighbourhood of Falkland, however, relates to the alleged discovery of a "miser's hoard" in Lathrisk House. The details of the story are circumstantially told to the effect that Mr Charles Gulland, the law agent of the deceased, while conducting a search for a will among the repositories at Lathrisk, came upon a heavy oak, iron-bound chest, containing £40,000 in gold, besides bundles of Western Bank of Scotland five pound notes.[2] The actual facts of the case are that Mr Gulland, in company of Mr Henry Murray of Balmungo, who will inherit the movable estate, made the customary search among Mr Johnston's documents for a will. The immediate object of the search proved un-

---

[1] Perhaps a mistake for Falkland Road.

[2] These if they had existed would have been worthless, the Western Bank having collapsed in 1857.

successful, and no will has yet been found.[1] The only money that was found was a sum of £600.

Those who were acquainted with Mr Johnston's strict business habits quickly discredited such an imaginative story of a "glittering pile" hoarded away in an oaken chest, but it has undoubtedly caught the public fancy, and all sorts of wild rumours are now current in the "Kingdom" as to the enormous wealth of the deceased. It may be computed that Mr Johnston drew annually about £14,000 from the valuable estates to which he succeeded at his father's death. These estates consist of Lathrisk, Rossie, Largo, and Urquhart, in Fifeshire; Bavelaw in Mid-Lothian, and Monzie in Perthshire. Besides, he succeeded to a large amount of movable estate, and his fortune has been accumulating since. In financial speculation Mr Johnston took no part, choosing rather to invest his revenues in heritable securities.

Up till the last he took a keen interest in the management of his various estates, and while he preferred to live a life of seclusion, the statements as to his habits in that respect that have appeared are grossly exaggerated. It has been said, for instance, that not only did he shut himself up from his servants, but that he even refused to see his commissioner, and that all communication had to be done in writing. This is entirely without foundation. Mr Gulland paid a visit regularly to Lathrisk once a week, or oftener when occasion demanded it, and in discussing business the laird evinced a lively interest in everything. He was a well-educated man, and he had spent twenty years of the earlier part of his life on the Continent, visiting in turn Paris and the fashionable resorts on the Mediterranean. On the subject of his travels he was always ready to speak, and a return to the Continent was a contemplation he often discussed. While he came little in contact with the outside world, he was a most diligent reader of the newspapers, and he spent a large part of his time in reading *The Times*, and *The Scotsman*, while he was also well supplied with the illustrated papers. Mr Johnston had also some skill as an artist, and painting and music were recreations in which he fondly indulged. Mr Johnston was by no means a miser of his great wealth. He gave liberally to

---

[1] A "will" was in fact discovered during 1901, apparently sewn into a silk dress, but it was soon revealed as an unconvincing forgery, and the perpetrator was sentenced to eighteen months in prison.

charity, and his servants were well treated.

Until an inventory is made, the exact amount of his heritable and moveable estate will not be known, but it is believed that it will probably exceed a million. The heir-at-law, to whom the estates go, is Lieutenant Makgill Crichton Maitland, 78th Seaforth Highlanders, who is a grandson of a cousin of the deceased;[1] while Mr Henry Maitland of Balmungo, St Andrews, a full cousin, will fall heir to the movable property. There are a number of relatives on the maternal side, and two were present at the funeral. (TS)

11 January 1901

Home-coming of the young heir

Lieutenant Charles Julian Maitland Makgill Crichton, of the 78th Highlanders, the heir to the late Mr Johnston of Lathrisk, is on his way home from Cairo, where his regiment is presently stationed, and is expected to reach Charing Cross on Sunday evening. He will come off at once for Scotland, and is expected to arrive on Monday at Lindores, where his mother and sister, Mr Lewis Maitland, and other friends, will receive him. (SAC)

12 January 1901

Death

At Horsemarket on the evening of the 4th inst., Isabella Glendinning, aged 11 years 9 months second and dearly beloved daughter of James Forsyth, builder. (FFP)

16 January 1901

Good news

Mr A. Bonthrone, Newton of Falkland, has received a telegram regarding his son, who was dangerously wounded in the Fife contingent Imperial Light Horse, giving a very assuring message of the excellent progress he is making. The ball, which entered his right side, has been located, and he is otherwise doing well. (DC)

---

[1] See under "Johnstons of Lathrisk" in the "Falkland's People" chapter.

26 January 1901

Queen Victoria

Great regret was felt here on Wednesday when the news of the Queen's death was known. The town and church bells were tolled with short intervals at ten, twelve and two o'clock. (FN)

28 January 1901

Farmhouse theft

Before Hon. Sheriff-Substitute Gray at Cupar today, George Dowie, labourer, of no fixed residence, was charged with having on 22nd inst., from the dwelling-house at Denside Farm, Falkland, occupied by William

3. Queen Victoria

Dowie, farmer, stolen a gun and powder flask, and also with having on 26th January, from the barn at Denside Farm, stolen a bridle and hedge bill. He pleaded guilty. Five previous convictions for theft were recorded against accused, and his last sentence of sixty days' imprisonment was repeated. (DET)

28 January 1901

Proclamation of the King

The Provost mentioned that the Magistrates' seat in the Parish Church had been draped in black. The Town Council then proceeded to Falkland Cross where Charles Gulland, the Town Clerk, was asked by Provost Page, in presence of the public, to read the Royal Proclamation, and he read the Proclamation of the new king as Edward the seventh, King of the United Kingdom and Emperor of India. On the return of the Council to the Town Hall, all present took the oath of allegiance to King Edward, which was duly administered by Charles Gulland, the Town Clerk, and they severally subscribed the roll to that effect. Signed in the name in presence and appointed by, William Page, Robert Miller, Bailie. (FTCM)

30 January 1901

Church service

At the close of the service in the Established Church on Sunday the Dead March in "Saul" was played by Mr Spence, organist, in memory of Her Majesty the Queen. The congregation remained standing. (FH)

6 February 1901

Memorial service

A special memorial service was held in the Established Church on Saturday afternoon at 3 o'clock. The hour fixed being a most suitable one, the attendance was large and thoroughly representative of all classes in the community. A procession was made from the Town Hall to the Church by the under mentioned bodies. The local Volunteers, The Provost and Magistrates, the members of the Masonic Lodge and Free Gardeners. Much interest was manifested in the procession, which was witnessed by a large gathering. In the Church special seats were allotted to them, and the impressive service, which was conducted by the Rev. Mr Johnston began with the 23rd Psalm being sung. (FH)

15 February 1901

Amateur skating championship

The results of the various competitions yesterday were as follows:
  1st medal, the Gulland, won by Mr W. Peggie, 30 points.
  2nd medal, the Bruce, won by Mr George Lumsden, 25 points.
  3rd medal won by Major Cusin.
  4th medal won by Mr William Ewan.
Second Competition:
  Silver biscuit box won by Mr George Morgan.
  Drawing medal was won by Dr Mackay.
  Highest aggregate, Johnston Silver Bowl, won by Mr W. Peggie with 69 points. (DET)

20 February 1901

Illness of Lord Ninian

In a letter from Mr Pitman, Edinburgh, he states Lady Bute is presently in Russia looking after Lord Ninian who has had an attack of typhus fever, but is now getting well.[1] (FEP)

23 February 1901

Death

At the Bruce Arms, on the 18th inst, after a lingering illness, Thomas Hardie, hotelkeeper, in his 47th year. (FFP)

7 March 1901

Property for sale

Letter to J. & F. Anderson, Edinburgh

Dear Sirs,

I enclose a letter received from Mr Gulland about a tenement opposite the Palace, situated between the gardener's house and the low thatched cottages on the east. Were the trustees allowed to purchase this would be a desirable acquisition to the property, as all the houses in front of the Palace would belong to Lord Ninian Crichton-Stuart, who could preserve them in their present form or improve them at any future period he might find convenient.

Yours Faithfully, William Wood. (FEP)

11 March 1901

Curling Club dinner

The annual dinner in connection with this club took place on Friday night in the Town Hall. Mr Charles Gulland, town clerk, presided over the large attendance. Dr McKay being croupier. A most enjoyable evening was spent. Provost Bonthrone, Auchtermuchty, and Mr Tod, Cash, were present as representatives of Stratheden Club. Among the new members made was the Laird of Lathrisk, Lieutenant Maitland Makgill Crichton Johnston, who kindly paid the expenses of the dinner. (DC)

11 March 1901

Assault on gamekeeper

Before Sheriff Armour, in Cupar Sheriff Court today, Charles Birrell,

---

[1] This was actually in Kiev, now in Ukraine.

of no occupation, Cross Wynd, was charged with having, on Sunday, 10th February, in a field named the Hillpark, on the farm of Kilgow-rieknowe, assaulted Andrew McQueen, gamekeeper, East Conland, by seizing his left hand and severely twisting and pulling the fourth finger, and striking him a severe blow on the right shoulder with a stick. Accused pleaded guilty, and it was explained that the game-keeper was trying to take a rabbit from accused when the assault was committed. A fine of £2 or twenty-one days imprisonment was imposed. (DET)

11 March 1901

The Lawson boys

Before Sheriff Armour in Cupar Sheriff Court today three brothers named Heriot, Alexander, and William Lawson, sons of and residing with Jessie Lawson, Balmblae, Falkland, were charged with having on Sunday 3rd March:

(1) at the stable at East Port, occupied by William Burgon,[1] fish dealer, stolen a key;

(2) at the Co-operative Society's bake-house, broken into the said bake-house, and stolen from a tin box 9d in money;

(3) at South Street East, broken into the Drill Hall and stolen seven watches, a revolver, eight watch chains, two brooches, a brass pan, a bracelet, three rings, a shaving brush and two pipe mouthpieces.

The three boys, the oldest of whom was 12, and the other two were twins of 10 years of age, pleaded guilty. Their father is a soldier serving in South Africa. Mr Brown, Procurator-Fiscal, said there was a good deal of sympathy with the mother. It seemed that the boys had discovered that the key of the stable would open other doors, and they had thus got into the bake-house and the Drill Hall. In the latter a travelling jeweller had been having a sale, and the boys literally stuffed their pockets, evidently thinking it was a grand haul. He understood that the boys had been in similar mischief before, although there had been no complaint. The property had been practically all

---

[1] Mr Burgon had a fishmonger's shop at the far end of Eastport. His son William was killed in WWI.

recovered, and he thought that in the case the First Offenders Act[1] might be applied.

The Sheriff, addressing the boys' mother, asked if she did not think it advisable that the boys should receive a few strokes with the birch rod.

Mrs Lawson, I think so.

The Sheriff said that he was glad she had taken such a sensible view of the matter. He ordered the boys to receive four strokes each with the birch rod, and expressed the hope that it would have the effect of keeping them out of mischief. (DET)

18 March 1901

Bruce Arms

Letter to Mr Anderson, Castle St., Edinburgh

Dear Sir,

I beg leave to forward an application for the lease of these subjects, from the widow of the late Mr Hardie who died recently. She has got a transfer of the licence from the burgh authorities with the aid of her daughter and son in law she will carry on the business satisfactorily. I enclose last grants to Thomas Hardie who having taken too much of his trade supplies, was in recent years rather a hindrance than a help to his wife, and I did not consider it judicious to press him to take a new lease after Whitsunday 1896.

The widow will take the lease for three or four years, as you may consider most suitable. Should the lease be granted she approves all the terms and conditions contained in the old one which I have read over and explained to her. She will require a national copy.

Yours faithfully, William Wood. (FEP)

20 March 1901

Agricultural fraud

John Mackenzie, flesher, Cross Wynd, denied at Cupar yesterday, having between 3rd and 10th November, falsely represented to

---

[1] The Probation of First Offenders Act 1887 allowed for offenders with no previous convictions to be spared imprisonment, on condition that they kept out of trouble thereafter.

Robert Duncan, that he was authorised by his father to purchase potatoes for him, thereby inducing Duncan to give him 14 cwt. of potatoes, which Mackenzie appropriated to his own use. Mackenzie was defended by Mr J. Welch.

Duncan, cross-examined, admitted that Mackenzie said he would pay him for the potatoes some day, and never said his father would pay for them. John Bonthrone, carting contractor, Auchtermuchty, said he was at Mairsland farm roup in October, when he heard Mackenzie ask Duncan if he could sell one of the pits he had bought to his old man. Accused's brother paid the potatoes. John Mackenzie, snr, said he never gave an order for potatoes to his son. In cross-examination he said that in October last his son came to him and asked him if he required any potatoes.

His Lordship found the charge proved, but, looking to the nature of the whole offence, he thought the ends of justice would be met by dealing with Mackenzie under the First Offender's Act, if he would give an undertaking to come up for sentence any time within the next six months under a penalty of £1. (DC)

27 March 1901
Bruce Arms Inn
Dear Major Wood,

With reference to your letter of the 13th inst. You do not mention whether in your opinion the present rent of £19 for the Inn, and £6 for the garden is sufficient.

We assume that no expenditure by the landlord will be asked for and that Mrs Hardie will accept the premises in their present condition.

Yours faithfully, J. & F. Anderson. (FEP)

28 March 1901
Bruce Arms
Letter to Mr Anderson, Castle St, Edinburgh
Dear Sir,

Your letter of 27th inst. I consider the rent now paid for this subject, fair and as much as we can look for from a free tenant, who has no right to name his successor and get a bounty in name of goodwill. The landlord has full power to let the premises to whom he likes and this should be retained. The two previous tenants to Mr Hardie. Though they had the place at the same rent, went bankrupt in three or four years.

The only expenditure on the building will be 2s.6d for repair of decayed wooden facings of the porch at front door, which Mrs Hardie proposes to have painted imitation marble at her own expense.

Yours faithfully, William Wood. (FEP)

2 April 1901

Tutor to Lord Ninian

Letter to William Wood

Dear Sir,

Lord Bute has engaged a certain Mr Armstrong as tutor to Lord Ninian for three months from Monday next.[1] Part of the arrangement is that Mr Armstrong is, in addition to his fee, to receive a payment of £2 per week, out of which he has to find his own board and lodgings.

There was a great deal of difficulty at first in connection with the settlement of terms between her Ladyship and Mr Armstrong and the matter was eventually put into my hands.

He has raised difficulties about the nature of accommodation he is likely to be able to get in Falkland, and I told him that the late Lord Bute's private secretary and former tutors had been able to find suitable accommodation, but in order to make matters run smoother I ventured to say that you would doubtless be ready to help him find quarters.

You will probably hear from Mr Armstrong tomorrow morning and I shall be very much obliged if you can give him advice about rooms. I told him that personally I had put up at the Commercial Hotel for two days during the winter and suggested that he might do the same until he finds suitable lodgings.

Yours faithfully, J. Pitman. (FEP)

---

[1] Mr Armstrong had actually been the tutor since summer 1900, and had been with Lord Ninian in Kiev when Lord Ninian fell ill.

5 April 1901

Tutor to Lord Ninian

Letter to Mr Pitman Edinburgh

Dear Sir,

I have your letter of 2nd inst. and I shall be pleased to assist Mr Armstrong in getting lodgings when he comes to Falkland. I have not yet spoken to any of the householders, of whom there are two or three eligible parties, if the tutor is not too fastidious. I have not yet heard from Mr Armstrong, and I think he should act on your suggestion to take a day or two at the Inn till he looks about for suitable quarters.

Yours faithfully, William Wood. (FEP)

13 April 1901:

The Bruce Hotel

Letter from Charles Gulland

Dear Major Wood,

The Sanitary Committee of Falkland ask me to call your attention to the state of the stream that passes through the hotel gardens, the property of the late Marquis of Bute, and of the other streams below, and perhaps you will make an early inspection with the view to the stream being cleaned. I have not been in the hotel garden myself for some years, but the Committee have sent me a note as Clerk of the Local Authority.

Yours faithfully, Charles Gulland. (FEP)

30 April 1901

Palace staircase decoration

Letter to Mr Pitman, 48 Castle St, Edinburgh

Dear Sir,

The well of the staircase in my quarters was cemented five years ago, and got a slight coat of blue paint, window recesses white. It was left in this unfinished state to allow the acids of the cement to exudate. The cement is now quite dry but covered with particles of a white floury substance which looks very bad and unclean. My wife has asked me to get the stair repainted by the time she finishes her spring cleaning, and I beg leave to submit an estimate of cost, £5 2s., which I trust you will authorise me to expend for this necessary sanitary work.

Yours faithfully, William Wood. (FEP)

1 May 1901

Palace staircase

Letter to William Wood

Dear Major Wood,

With regard to the well of the staircase at the Palace I quite approve of the painting being done as proposed at the estimated cost of £5 2s. I return Mr Ross's estimate.

Yours faithfully, Pitman. (FEP)

21 May 1901

Cross Wynd reconstruction

It was agreed unanimously seeing that the Cross Wynd is at present open in connection with the laying of the sewerage and water mains to ask the proprietors on each side of the street to have their building connected now by the services pipes with these mains and the Clerk was instructed to write to them accordingly. And it was further agreed that should any of such proprietors delay to do so these service pipes should be laid by the council and the individual proprietors charged with the expense. The Clerk was asked to point this out to the proprietors when writing them with this recommendation, and to request a reply from them before Monday the 27th inst., at 4 o'clock pm.

It was further agreed to ask the Gas Company Committee to meet the Town Council on as early a day as may be found suitable with a view of the gas pipes being put into a state of repair or renewed by the company where necessary.

Bailie Miller pointed out to the meeting that the agreement of William Duncan as to the street manure man and the carting thereof had been terminated at Whitsunday last, and it was agreed that Bailie Miller should wait upon Mr Duncan and ask him to engage for another year on the same conditions, failing which it was decided to advertise for offers as usual.

The Clerk was instructed to advertise for offers for furnishing metal

The Falkland Society Photo Arch[...]

4. Cross Wynd before reconstruction
with the burn still running down the middle of the Wynd
towards the Parish Church and the Fountain.

for the Burgh roads for the ensuing summer, the usual quantity to be supplied, also for offers to keep the roads and lay on the metal for the year to Whitsunday 1902.

Mr Jackson reported to a letter which had been sent to him by the Clerk stating that a complaint had been lodged alleging a nuisance by the outflow on the road at his house of foul water and other effluence from his cesspool. Mr Jackson stated that he was quite prepared to do as other proprietors did in the neighbourhood and said that in order to do this he would disconnect the pipes of his closet so that no obnoxious matter could be discharged. (FTCM)

22 May 1901
Water mains
Letter to Major Wood
Dear Sir,

At a meeting of the Town Council held last night I was instructed to write to several owners of property in the Cross Wynd requesting them, seeing that the street is at present open in connection with the laying of water and sewerage mains, to connect their houses with such mains. I shall be glad to hear from you before Monday 27th inst at 4 o'clock afternoon, that you agree to do this forthwith, of course at your own expense. I was further asked to state that in the event of there being any delay or refusal on the part of proprietors, the work would be performed by the council in virtue of their statutory powers, and that the proprietors delaying or refusing would be charged with the expense.

Yours Faithfully, Charles Gulland. (FFP)

25 May 1901
Drains
A large staff of workmen, employed by Mr Strachan, the contractor, are at present busy laying down the water and sewerage pipes in Cross Wynd. (FFP)

1 June 1901
School
The sum collected for the war fund by the scholars of the Public School amounts to £2 6s.

The Government Inspector, reporting on Falkland School, says the school continues to be very ably and faithfully taught, and has in all respects a highly satisfactory appearance. It shows the great perseverance of Mr Richardson and his assistants. (FFP)

20 June 1901

Town Council meeting

Provost Page, in reference to the necessary road metal for the Burgh, that Mr C. Johnston of Lathrisk has kindly granted the required metal for this season from Bridgend Quarry, and the Clerk is directed to take in offers for supplying the metal broken to 4 ounce or thereby, this does not apply to the laying on of the metal, which is performed by the Burgh roadman, but it applies to providing breaking and carting the metal.

An offer by William Duncan, High Street, dated the 7th current for carting manure and rubbish from depots and for ground stance, for the year ending Whitsunday 1902. William Duncan asks for £11. The Clerk is directed to accept this offer.

An application from Mr Christopher Brunton, Butcher, Falkland, dated the 20th inst., for a Slaughter House Licence on the former stance was considered. The meeting agree to grant the application, but the Clerk is directed to inform Mr Brunton that this is only granted on condition that the premises shall be better kept and made and continue wholesome and sweet, and they recommend him to provide a cement floor for the premises.

The necessary procedure anent licences for slaughter houses shall be carried out forthwith. (FTCM)

26 June 1901

Showman sent to prison

A Burgh Court was held in the Town Hall on Saturday. Provost Page and Bailie Harvey on the bench. Two showmen were accused of having stolen 9 shillings from a grocer's till in the town on Friday evening, and one of them was sent to prison for fourteen days without the option of a fine. (FH)

29 June 1901

Church choir outing

On Saturday the members of the Established Church choir enjoyed their annual outing. The rendezvous this year was St. Andrews, where, being favoured with beautiful weather, a most enjoyable day was spent. (FFP)

29 June 1901

Refreshments

Picnic parties visiting Falkland can be supplied with teas and refreshments at Moderate Rates at Watterson's Palace Bakery, Horsemarket Wynd. (FFP)

9 July 1901

Cross Wynd

Bailie Miller stated that certain members of the Council had met with Councillor James Forsyth, proprietor of certain subjects in the Cross Wynd, and seeing that in the reconstruction of the Wynd, his outside stair leading up to one of his dwelling houses projects a few steps.[1] A readjustment of said stair was proposed. After deliberation it was agreed that the stair shall be run up the front wall of the house so as to remove the projecting steps, and James Forsyth shall do this at his own expense, on receiving the sum of £2 10s, to which sum he limits his estimated share of the half expense. Further the Council agree to continue the street to the foot of Alexander Lawson's stair, but no further, and that at scheduled rates.

Bailie Miller further stated that certain of the Council had inspected the stream of the Mill Wynd opposite or near to the property belonging to Henry Wright, who suggests the strand to be re-laid, and offers the sum of £2 10s towards this object. On condition that Henry Wright contributes £2 10s the Council decided to relay the gutter at a higher level to their own satisfaction, and to in-cut a grate at a central point

---

[1] Many of the houses in Cross Wynd at this period had forestairs – outside staircases to a separate apartment on the first floor. The houses in question have since been demolished, but forestairs are a feature of many houses in Falkland to this day.

at the top of the Mill Lade. (FTCM)

11 July 1901

Ordination

Ordination of Rev. James H. Morrison of Perth to the United Free Church at Falkland. Cupar United Free Presbytery held an open-air meeting in the church grounds at Falkland. (FN)

16 July 1901

Street lighting

It was suggested by the officer who attends to the street lighting, he should be provided with a torch for the lighting, but as it appears that this would necessitate an adjustment of the lamps, the matter is remitted to the lighting committee to ascertain the expense of all and sundry and to report. (FTCM)

19 July 1901

Foresters' holiday

Dear Sir,

We are favoured with your letter of yesterday mentioning the request of the forester's men and other labourers that they should be allowed a holiday to go to the Kinross Games and should have an allowance of £2 14s to pay for a brake to take them there. Mr Pitman is presently from home, and we have not been able to get his instructions on the subject, but we think that, in the circumstances explained by you, we may take it upon ourselves to agree to the request made. You may therefore do so, and make the allowance of £2 14s.

Yours faithfully, J. & F. Anderson. (FEP)

20 July 1901

Volunteer killed on the Lomonds

A peculiarly sad fatality befell a young volunteer who was engaged as marker at the Purin Hill range on the East Lomond Hill on Saturday afternoon. The annual shooting match between the Falkland and Leslie Companies of the 6th V.B.R.H. Volunteers. was almost concluded, there being only four men left to fire at the last distance, when one of the two markers, Alexander Bonthrone, aged 18, and employed as an apprentice mechanic in Eden Valley Factory, Freuchie, was shot in the forehead, the bullet grazing the skull and reappearing again at the back of the head. How the accident happened is not known; but it is conjectured that Bonthrone had ascended the pit and exposed his head above ground. He was noticed lying bleeding from the head by the other marker, who had his attention called to the fact that something was wrong by the signalling from the firing point of "stop-firing". This signal was the outcome of there having been no response from the target at which Bonthrone was stationed after the shot had been delivered from the firing point in the usual manner.

Captain Lumsden, who was in charge, assisted by Sergt-Instructor Ford of the Falkland Coy., and Sergt-Instructor Sylvestor of the Leslie Coy., summoned Surgeon-Captain Mackay of the Falkland Coy., who dressed the wound and saw the unfortunate fellow taken home to Freuchie on an improvised stretcher. The wound was on the left side of the head, and a part of the skull was shot away.

Bonthrone died on Monday forenoon, never having regained consciousness. Much sympathy is felt for his brothers and sisters and for his mother, who is a widow. The fatality has caused a great gloom among the Falkland Company, and in Freuchie, where the deceased was highly respected, his death is deeply lamented. The remains were interred on Wednesday with military honours.[1] (FN)

20 July 1901

Organ from Mr Carnegie

Mr Andrew Carnegie has been bestowing organs lavishly on churches throughout Scotland within the last few weeks. In many cases he has been gently approached and has at once "done the generous", usually however, on condition of the congregations themselves raising a certain portion of the cost. It was, however, with extreme pleasure, that the congregation of the Falkland United Free Church learned at their social meeting last week in connection with the ordination of their new pastor, the Rev. James H. Morrison, that

---

[1] In Falkland Cemetery there is an obelisk to Private Alexander Bonthrone, 6th Bn Black Watch, died 15 July 1901, aged 20, that was erected by the Volunteers.

Mr Carnegie was to present an organ to the church, paying all the cost himself. This gratifying announcement was made by Mr Hew Morrison, librarian of Edinburgh Public Library, who is a personal friend of Mr Carnegie, and enjoys his confidence on many matters. As the gift was entirely unsolicited, the intimation which Mr Morrison was able to make was a great surprise to the congregation. (FN)

24 July 1901

Burgh Court

The Burgh Court was held on Monday, the Provost and Magistrates on the bench, when three men from Dundee pleaded guilty of a theft of eleven pints of ale from the Stag Inn. Sentence of ten days imprisonment or 7s 6d was imposed. The fines were paid. (FH)

5. Andrew Carnegie (1835–1919)

Born in Dunfermline, he emigrated to America with his parents aged 12. He invested in steel and other industries, made a vast fortune, and gave most of it away to charitable causes.

25 July 1901

Presentation

Corporal David Bonthrone, who recently returned from South Africa, where he had served with the 20th Company Imperial Yeomanry, was entertained in the Town Hall on Tuesday by the members of the Falkland C.C., and was presented with a handsome gold watch. Mr Charles Gulland, town clerk, presided. The presentation was made by Mr Crichton Johnston of Lathrisk. (DC)

26 July 1901

Tenancy of the Bruce Arms Inn

Letter to Mrs Hardie

Dear Madam,

I beg leave to offer my condolences on the loss of your husband, who has been taken from you recently.

I regret having to write you so soon on business matters but think it right to come to some understanding with you as to the occupation of the Inn after Whitsunday next. Your late husband's lease expired at Whitsunday 1896. He did not apply for a new lease but occupied as a yearly tenant thereafter. If you can see your way to carrying on the Inn on same terms. I will be glad to treat with you personally. You should not introduce any third party for a transfer of the business without the consent and approval of the landlord's trustees.

Yours faithfully William Wood. (FEP)

27 July 1901

Drains

The contractor, Mr Strachan, is making rapid progress with the water and drainage scheme, and a great improvement on the Cross Wynd is thereby effected. (FFP)

27 July 1901

Falkland Road Station

A daring burglary was committed early yesterday morning at the booking office at Falkland Road Station. Admission to the office was gained by picking the lock, and the burglars smashed open the safe with some of the surface men's tools, with which they had possessed themselves. Fortunately, the safe only contained £2 odds.

Between three and four o'clock the stationmaster, who resides at the station, thought he hears a noise as if someone was moving about, and he at once got up and made an inspection of the premises. He found the booking office door open, and the safe standing open with the cash gone. Proceeding to the signalman's cabin he got into telegraphic communication with Cupar. Information reached Mr C. Hunter, deputy chief constable, about 4 o'clock yesterday morning, and that indefatigable officer lost no time in having his men on the job. Learning that four suspicious characters had been seen about New Inn the previous night, and suspecting that the gang were from

6. Falkland Palace from The Pleasance

Kirkcaldy, the country between Falkland Road and the Lang Toon[1] was scoured with the utmost vigilance. At Markinch the local constable came across a couple of men of the suspicious class, and he took them into custody. About half the amount of the missing money was found in their possession. Inspector Bisset left for Markinch in the morning. A sharp lookout is being kept for the other pair of suspects. It is conjectured that this is the same gang that burgled Kinghorn Station a few days ago. (DC)

5 August 1901

Access to the Palace and grounds

Letter to William Wood

Dear Sir,

I am led to believe that Mr Mackenzie, my predecessor was granted the privilege of access to the Palace and grounds. I do not know if it was granted to him as minister or for personal reasons, but I should esteem it a very grateful however if you could see your way to extend

---

[1] Kirkcaldy was one of the places known popularly as the "Lang Toon" or "Lang Toun" (long town).

the same privilege to myself. If you cannot do so kindly forgive my boldness in making the request.

Yours sincerely, J. Morrison, United Free Manse. (FEP)

10 August 1901

Proposed new works

It is reported that a movement is on foot for the erection of floorcloth works[1] in the neighbourhood of Falkland, and that a company has been formed for the carrying out the objects in view. The industry would prove a great boon to the Howe of Fife, not only in giving labour to men and boys, but in affording female workers for the factories, which are gradually finding greater difficulty in getting hands in these rural districts for power-looms. (DC)

17 August 1901

Thunderstorm

A terrific thunderstorm visited this district on Saturday. Rain fell in torrents and considerably laid the crops. The flower show was ruined. (FFP)

17 August 1901

Burgh roads

A meeting of the Town Council was held on Friday night to look over the offers for the carting of the metal for the burgh roads. Mr James Hamilton was found to be the lowest offer. 5s.6d.per cubic yard. (FTCM)

17 August 1901

Falkland Floorcloth Company

The Falkland Floorcloth Company, for the manufacture of floorcloth and linoleum, are to commence building operations immediately. (FN)

---

[1] Floorcloth was a type of hard-wearing canvas painted on both sides, used as a floor covering. It was popular in the eighteenth and nineteenth centuries, being easy to keep clean, particularly in places where spillages might occur, but was superseded by linoleum. (Gilbert 1987, pp 101–105)

9 September 1901

Cart driver asleep

At a JP Court, John Lumsden, a carter, residing at or near Burn Mill, Leven, was charged with having, on Friday 2nd August, on the public highway about 400 yards northward of the junction of the Falkland and Strathmiglo road and Falkland and Dunshalt road, allowed a cart of which he had the charge to travel on the said highway without having some person to guide the horse drawing the cart. The accused pleaded guilty. Chief Constable Bremner[1], who prosecuted, said that the accused had stated to the constable that he was to plead not guilty, and the result was that the witnesses had been brought. The constable had met two single carts and horses, the drivers of which were in the first cart, and both asleep. He could make no charge against the driver of the first cart, for the reason that sleeping in a cart, he was sorry to say, was not an offence under the Road Act. The horse yoked in the second cart was quite unattached. Accused remarked that he was in the first cart, but had the reins in the cart. The bench imposed a modified fine of 10s 6d, with 15s 6d of expenses, the alternative being five days imprisonment. (DET)

28 September 1901

Factory workers entertained

On Saturday afternoon the employees of the power-loom factories in Falkland and their friends were handsomely entertained to tea and refreshments at Lathrisk House through the kindness of Mr Maitland Johnston and Mrs and Miss Maitland. Auchtermuchty Brass Band were present, and supplied dance music for several hours. Mr Jackson, manufacturer, on behalf of the workers thanked Mr Johnston and Mrs and Miss Maitland for the handsome manner in which the company had been entertained, and called for a hearty vote of thanks to the host and hostesses, which was enthusiastically given. (FFP)

---

[1] Captain James Fleming Bremner was Chief Constable of Fife and Kinross from 1863 to 1903. His retirement was shortly followed by his death, aged 78. —*Edinburgh Evening News*, 16 November 1903.

28 September 1901

Presentation

The office-bearers of the United Free Church waited on Rev. Mr and Mrs Morrison at the manse on Wednesday evening, and presented them with a beautiful afternoon tea and coffee service as a marriage gift from the congregation. (FFP)

5 October 1901

Cricket Club

At a meeting of the Cricket Club, held on Thursday, it was decided to discontinue the hiring of the Reading Room, as the maintenance was a heavy drain on the funds of the club. (FFP)

5 October 1901:

Handlooms

At Falkland several handlooms are again in operation. They have been furnished up by the Marchioness of Bute, and provide employment for a few people. Her ladyship finds a ready outlet for work done on the handloom, for which there is evidently a growing demand, and the hope is entertained that this is but the beginning of some revival, in however modest a way, of the ancient industry, which once on a time kept all the Fifeshire villages busy. (FFP)

10 October 1901

A voice from Falkland

To the Editor of The Courier.

Sir,

   the time for the election of commissioners to serve on the Burgh Council is drawing nigh. In the old Royal Burgh of Falkland the same party has been in office for many years. There have been few changes among the Magistrates, and our present civic rulers seem to imagine that their office expires when they expire.

   Let us show them that there is still stamina among us, and that we wish our grand old town, with its many historical associations, to be kept abreast with the times.

   J. B. (DC)

7. Brunton Street

Brunton House is on the left. The houses on the right have been
demolished and replaced by Brunton Green.

14 October 1901

Brunton Street

It was proposed in reference to the paving operations of the Burgh
streets that the portion in Brunton Street adjoining that part which
was recently paved right on to South Street West, at the junction with
the main or principal street, should be repaired as the street is in a
very rough condition. (FH)

23 October 1901

Lawson twins

Before Bailie Armour at Cupar yesterday, Alexander Lawson, and
William Lawson jun., residing with their mother, Jessie Lawson, Falk-
land, acknowledged having, on 8th October at West Kilwhiss Farm,
Auchtermuchty Parish, broken into the ploughmen's bothy there and
stolen a white metal Albert chain and a white metal Albert watch.
Both boys aged ten years, had been previously convicted. The boys'
mother, who was in Court, said her husband was a soldier in South
Africa. She had eight boys, and did her best for them. The Sheriff said

he thought the boys should have more consideration for their mother. The circumstances were rather lamentable, and he thought it would be best for them if they got six strokes each with the birch rod. (DC)

30 October 1901
Mrs Robb's property
Letter to William Wood
Dear Sir,

We thought we had heard the last of the matter, but it has come up again. We had a letter sometime ago from Messrs Walker & Orr, complaining that notwithstanding their former letter question nothing has been done to protect Mrs Robb's property from the encroachment of the Mill Dam. In your letter of 7th February you state that if Mrs Robb could produce any Feu contract from Mrs Tyndall Bruce, she may be in rightful possession of the roadway. On asking for a title there has been sent to us a disposition by Harry Hope, Writer in Falkland, in favour of David Wishart, which bears to convey a piece of ground of nine feet breadth lying south of the Mill Dam brae on the north side of David Wishart's yard. It rather looks as if it had been found that Mr Hope had no title to convey the bit of ground, because a homologation[1] thereof by Mrs Tyndall Bruce and her husband was got shortly thereafter. We enclose copy of this disposition and shall be glad to hear from you again after you have perused it and reconsidered the matter.

There may be a technical objection to the terms of this deed, but if it can be reasonably inferred that Mrs Robb is entitled to the site of this old road, we do not know that Lord Bute's Trustees would be inclined to raise any question about it. Beyond any expenses there may be in protecting the property from the encroachments of the Mill Dam. We understand that the site of the road is not of any value to the estate.

Yours faithfully, J. & F. Anderson (FEP)

---

[1] See Glossary.

1 November 1901

Mrs Robb's property

Letter to J. & F. Anderson, Edinburgh

Dear Sirs,

I have perused your letter of 30th ult. and copy of disposition by Harry Hope, in favour of David Wishart and his heirs of the nine foot road south of the Mill Dam Brae and north of Wishart's yard. Had this document been produced earlier there would have been no controversy over the matter. I would propose to build a retaining stone wall to the height of one foot above the highest level of the water at the proper season, now if the frost keeps off, or next spring. The expense will not be great if we get favourable weather. There are plenty rough suitable stones in the Mill Quarry to do the task.

Yours faithfully, William Wood. (FEP)

9 November 1901

Town Council election

The election took place on Tuesday for the election of Town Councillors. There were five seats and eight candidates.

The result of the poll was declared about 9 o'clock as follows: Successful – Mr Michael Reekie, farmer (102); Mr Thomas Sutherland, tailor (100); Mr David Reid, shoemaker (98); Mr Charles Jackson, jun., manufacturer (96); Mr John Angus, innkeeper (78). Unsuccessful – Mr Alex Fraser, joiner (68); Mr George Hardie, clothier (57); Mr John Fernie, mason (45); The only new Councillor is Mr Charles Jackson, jun. There was a great crowd at the declaration of the poll, who seemed well pleased with the result. (FN)

23 November 1901

Public meeting

A public meeting was held in the Town Hall on Friday night to discuss the formation of a Bowling Club and a Golf Club. Provost Page presided. There was a large attendance, and both schemes were favourably received. Committees were formed to deal with the separate Clubs, and Mr Jackson and Mr Rowland Gulland were appointed conveners. (FFP)

23 November 1901

Concert in Drill Hall

The annual concert under the auspices of the Falkland Cricket Club was held in the Drill Hall here on Saturday evening. The Laird of Lathrisk, Mr Crichton Johnston occupied the chair. A first class vocal programme was ably sustained by the following ladies and gentlemen: Miss Arnot, Newton of Lathrisk; Misses Smith and C. Miller, Edinburgh; Captain Wemyss, Lathrisk;[1] Dr Anderson, Strathmiglo; and Messrs Carswell, Ladybank and Dandie, Edinburgh. A violin selection was given by Mr D. Cooper, Cupar. The accompaniments were played by Miss Makgill Crichton; Mrs Tarbolton and Misses Smith, Edinburgh; and Mr Rennie, Edinburgh. There was a very large attendance. (FFP)

14 December 1901

Town Council meeting

At a meeting of Town Council on Wednesday night, a petition was read from the Golf Committee asking to be allowed to utilise the Myre as a golf course. The matter was discussed at some length, and it was ultimately agreed to grant the request. (FN)

---

[1] Captain Wemyss was later married to Mary Makgill-Crichton of Lathrisk.

1902

11 February 1902

New linoleum factory

A new factory at Falkland, for the production of floorcloth and lino-leum is nearing completion, and operations are expected to commence within the next few weeks. (DET)

11 February 1902

Death of Major Wood, Falkland

Major Wood died at his residence, the Palace Falkland, on Sunday, after a few weeks' illness, the result of a chill. He was factor for Mr A. Hamilton, and also for the late Lord Bute. He had been on the Falkland estate above 30 years. He was in the Black Watch, and went through the Indian Mutiny and also the Crimean War. Deceased was above 70 years of age, and has left wife, four daughters, and five sons. He will be greatly missed by many in the district, as he was a generous giver to the poor. (DET)

14 February 1902

Funeral of Major William Wood

The funeral of Major Wood, Falkland Palace, who for more than 30 years was factor on Falkland Estate, were interred [*sic*] in Falkland Cemetery yesterday (Thursday) amidst signs of universal sorrow.

Previous to the conveyance of the remains of the deceased from Falkland Palace a funeral service was held in the Parish Church, when

8. Major William Wood

Factor to the Falkland Estate for
many years

the officiating clergymen were the Rev. Mr Johnston, the Rev. Mr Fraser, Freuchie and the Rev. D. N. Hogg, Auchtermuchty. At the conclusion of the service the organist played the "Dead March" in "Saul." There was a large assemblage in the church, representing all classes of the community.

At half-past two o'clock the town bell began to toll, and the hearse conveying the coffin left the Palace en route for the cemetery. Immediately behind the hearse walked a detachment of the Black Watch from Perth, of which regiment deceased gentleman was formerly an officer. Following the regulars were the local company of volunteers, under the command of Captain Lumsden, the employees on the estate, and the general public. On arriving at the entrance to the cemetery the coffin was removed from the hearse and carried to the grave on the shoulders of the representatives of the Black Watch. The pall-bearers were the four sons of the deceased, Mr J. Todd (son in law), and Mr Todd, Jun, grandson.

Among those present at the grave were: Mr Charles Gulland, town clerk; and the Provost and Magistrates; Major Cusin; Mr Jackson; Messrs Lumsden,[1] Freuchie; Mr Williamson; Mr Lawrie; Mr Morgan, Kilgour; Mr Morgan, Nochnarie; Mr Lawson, Falkland Wood; Dr Bell, Kingskettle; Dr Mackay, Falkland; Mr Todd, Cash Mill; Mr Todd, Pardovan; Mr Sheriff, Falkland; Mr Bell, Lundie Mill; Mr Ritchie, Plains; Mr Amos, Drumdreel; Mr Todd, East Brackley; Mr Howe, Pleasance; Councillor Cant, Auchtermuchty; Councillor Simpson,

---

[1] The Lumsdens were a well-known family in Freuchie, where the Lumsden Memorial Hall, still stands; it was left in Trust by Helen Lumsden in 1883 in memory of her husband Thomas Lumsden, Linen Manufacturer, for the benefit of the inhabitants of Freuchie.

Auchtermuchty; Mr Ritchie, Cashmill; Mr Walker, town clerk, Auchtermuchty; Mr T. Ferlie, Auchtermuchty; Mr Stocks, postmaster, Auchtermuchty; Mr Ritchie, Dunshalt; Mr Walker, Demperston; Mr Henderson, Reedieleys; Mr Rae, Urquhart; Mr Smith, Dunshalt; the Rev. D. N. Hogg, Auchtermuchty; Mr Rae Arnott, Lochieheads; Rev. Mr Gordon, Kingskettle; Rev. Mr Fraser, Freuchie; Rev. Mr Johnston, Falkland; Mr Meiklejohn, Newton of Falkland; Mr A. Bonthrone, Newton of Falkland; Mr D. Bonthrone, Newton of Falkland; Messrs Galloway, Falkland; Mr Angus, Commercial Hotel; Mr Swanson, Bruce Arms Hotel; Mr Duncan, Kilgowrieknowe; Mr Leven, Auchtermuchty; ex-bailie Clark, Auchtermuchty; Mr Reekie, Falkland; Mr Bryce, Falkland.[1] (DC)

15 February 1902

Major William Wood

By the death of Major William Wood, which took place at his residence, Falkland Palace on Sunday night, Falkland has lost one of its best known and highly respected citizens. It had been known for some weeks that he was in a rather critical condition from the effects of a chill contracted some time ago, and earnest hopes were entertained that the excellent medical skill with which he was attended might manage to pull him through, but these hopes were not realised.

When a young man he enlisted in the 42nd Royal Highlanders (Black Watch) and went through the Crimean campaign and also the Indian Mutiny. He rose from the ranks, and after being Sergeant-Major for a short time, he received his commission to the rank of Major. As the result of his services in the trying ordeals through which his regiment passed, he was the possessor of a number of medals, which he prized after his retirement from active service, among them being the Crimean medal, the Turkish medal, and Indian Mutiny medal. Thirty two years ago he came to Falkland as factor to Mr Andrew Hamilton Tyndall Bruce, when that gentleman came into possession of the extensive estate of Falkland and Nuthill. When these properties were acquired by the late Lord Bute the Major was retained as the factor and in the discharge of his duties he was looked

---

[1] It was not the custom at this time for women to attend the graveside.

upon as a gentleman of sterling integrity, and was very much respected by the late Lord Bute.

Possessed of a fine physique and a comely bearing, his frank manner was greatly admired by all he came in contact with. He was possessed of more than ordinary intellectual abilities, and was not only a pleasant conversationalist, but could acquit himself well on the platform. He leaves a widow, five sons, and four daughters, who have the sympathy of a very wide circle of friends and acquaintances. None will miss him more than the poor of the district to whom he was most liberal. The Major had attained the ripe age of 74 years. (FFP)

5 March 1902

New publication

A series of papers on Scottish Coronations by the late Marquis of Bute has just been published in book form. The cloth in which the volume is bound was woven by Lady Margaret Bute's[1] handloom weavers at Falkland. (FH)

6 March 1902

House in Cross Wynd

Letter to J. Anderson WS, Edinburgh:
Dear Sir,

You would observe in the statement of arrears of rent at end of each month, the name of Elizabeth Hyslop, an old woman who was without means or relatives. The Town Officer called yesterday to hand in the key of her room, and to report that the woman died in the poorhouse on Thursday the 27th, the day after she was taken there. He reported that the inspector and committee visited the house, one room of which was occupied by the deceased. One room, upstairs is tenanted by an old widow woman, Mrs L. Reekie, and the other two rooms have been unoccupied for some time. The local Authority will endeavour to clean the room, which is very dirty and will charge the proprietor for doing so.

What little furniture is in the house falls to the proprietor, but it is in such a state of dirt and decay that it is only fit to be burned. There

[1] More correctly referred to as Lady Margaret Crichton-Stuart.

is one chest full of some stuff which the inspector is afraid must be in the same condition as the table and chair, but he cannot touch it without caution.[1] Will you kindly send instruction what is to be done.

Your faithfully, p.p. William Wood.[2] (FEP)

11 March 1902
Palace guide
Letter to Mr Pitman, Edinburgh

Dear Sir,

Mr D. Campbell, groom and Palace guide, wishes to know definitely if any change will be made with him this Summer, or if he will be kept on as guide, for if a change is to be made it is time he were looking about for some other employment. This also you might perhaps be able to decide when next over here.

Yours faithfully, p.p. William Wood. (FEP)

15 March 1902
Proposed branch railway

Investigations are at present afoot, writes a correspondent, as to the feasibility of bringing in a railway line from Falkland Road Station to Falkland. An interested party has during the past week interviewed several of the leading traders of the district on the subject, and a few local gentlemen are also working with the view of bringing the proposed scheme to a successful issue. There is no doubt that the introduction of the railway into Falkland would be a great boon to the inhabitants and district. Falkland has until now stood, in the matter of railway facilities, isolated from the outer world, notwithstanding the fact that a considerable tonnage in linens, malt and farm produce has to be carted so far a distance.

Then there is another industry, the manufacture of floorcloth and linoleum about to be started, which will yield a very large annual tonnage, and it is this fact which has given the question its present

---

[1] George Baxter, Town Officer, was paid 6s for removing refuse from the house in Cross Wynd.

[2] Letters from the estate office continued being signed "p.p. William Wood" for some time after Major Wood's death.

prominence. The railway will be hailed with delight by the townspeople, as it will mean to them so many advantages which have hitherto been denied. It is to be hoped nothing will be left undone to secure its completion. (FN)

21 March 1902
Palace guide
Letter to Mr Pitman
Dear Sir,

I received your letter of the 19th inst. regarding Campbell, the groom and guide. I did not know till yesterday that he had written to you and thanked you on my behalf for so kindly considering his request. He brought your letter to me and asked me to express his gratitude to you for the kindness shown him and to explain to you that he has got another situation so will know his present position on 14th April, as at first arranged. When the manufacturer Mr Jackson heard that Campbell was leaving he sent for him on Wednesday and offered him the post of warehouseman in his factory here. This being a good offer and most suitable work for him Campbell accepted without delay. He has got a house in the village, just now vacant, so will be able to leave entirely on 14th or 15th April. In the meantime Campbell is very useful to me going messages in connection with the office work, as I have not been able to do much walking lately, then he attends to the general tidying up about the gateway of the Palace.

Yours faithfully, p.p. William Wood. (FEP)

25 March 1902
House for overseer
Dear Sir,

When talking to you about a residence for the new overseer[1] you mentioned a house belonging to Mr Gulland as the only one you know of in Falkland to let. I presume the house you referred to was Lomondside House as advertised in the *Scotsman*. Please let me know

---

[1] The "overseer" in question would have been George Gavin – he took over administration of the Falkland Estate after Major Wood's death, but was not officially given the title of Factor until 1904.

where about this house stands and whether you think it would be suitable for the estate overseer to live in.

John Pitman. (FEP)

16 March 1902

Lomondside House

Letter to Mr Pitman, Edinburgh

Dear Sir,

I am in receipt of your letter of 25th inst. Lomondside House [1]belonging to Mr Gulland is the only one of any size to let in the place just now. It is situated off Back Wynd only a few yards beyond Mr Gulland's bank premises and a few minutes walk from here. It has a very good garden attached and this lies immediately beyond the Bruce Arms, Inn garden. The rent I believe has been £25 per year. Dr Mackay occupied this house a few years ago until he moved into his present one as being more suitable for him. There are two good sized public rooms but the bedrooms are small, however for an ordinary sized family it would be a very good house.

Yours faithfully, p.p. William Wood. (FEP)

To Let in Balmblae

House, Three Apartments, Stable, Washing House, Garden
Apply George Baxter. Falkland.

(DC, 31 March 1901)

---

15 April 1902

Lomondside House

Letter to J. & F. Anderson, Castle St, Edinburgh

Dear Sirs,

---

[1] Lomondside House had been occupied by Charles Fernie a widower aged 91 in 1901, along with his two unmarried daughters Amelia and Agnes, aged 52 and 51 and general servant, Barbara Jane Hardie aged 29.

I think you will find Thomas Ross, painter,[1] will do the work required for this house in a very satisfactory way and extremely moderate. He is the only painter in the place and has always done what work has been required for the estate in this district. He lives next to Lomondside, his house and shop being just on the same entrance off the Back Wynd.

Yours faithfully, p.p. William Wood. (FEP)

26 April 1902

Palace guide

Letter to J. & F. Anderson

Dear Sirs,

Since Mr D. Campbell left, Andrew Hillock has been working about the place tidying up passages, cellars and places which are shown to the public, and has been attending to the few visitors who have come lately, as the old man Reekie is too lame to walk much or to go up and down stairs. There have been few visitors as yet but more may come now as the season is advancing, and a guide would almost be necessary here. In the meantime Hillock can do all that is required. He has the old man working at the sand pit and doing any odd jobs about the estate.

Yours faithfully, George Gavin. (FEP)

1 May 1902

Coronation Day

Seeing that the Coronation Day of His Majesty King Edward is fixed for Thursday the 26th June[2] and that it has been recommended that the following day, Friday, be also observed as a general holiday, the Town Council appoint both days 26th and 27th June as holidays on this great occasion, but under the reservation, and they decide as

---

[1] Account from Thomas Ross for painting Lomondside House. £3 16s 6d. Lomondside House was sold by Mrs Gulland, Millfield in 1920 to the War Memorial Committee for £800.

[2] The coronation planned for 26 June had to be postponed at short notice because the King was suffering from appendicitis. It was finally held on 9 August.

follows: Namely the 26th the Coronation Day, to be a close holiday and the 27th shall be observed as a holiday at the pleasure of this community, subject to the approval of the community.

This Council hereby arrange to have the Falkland Market on Friday 27th and to vote towards a treat to the children on the 26th, and towards games at the market on the 27th. The sum of £10 out of the "Common Good" in or as nearly as may be in equal sums for the treat and games. The arrangements of details is left to the Town Council. (FTCM)

13 May 1902

Coronation Day

Dear Mr Pitman,

As mentioned in my letter written earlier today I have this evening looked at the field for permission to hold the local coronation celebrations in, which has been asked. It lies immediately to the south east of Falkland House and to the south of the burn. The field, which is shown in the estate plan as originally divided into three is bounded on the south by the old Leslie Road and is let as part of Westfield Farm. It is proposed that the school children of Falkland should, in charge of their teachers, walk in procession to the field on the 26th June about noon and spend the day engaging in games. The committee would like also permission to hang swings on the branches of a row of trees in one part of the field. They also intended that the procession of children should enter by the Lodge Gate. There is however a gate entering the field from the Leslie Road, and I suggested to the members of the committee who accompanied me to it that if permission were given I thought it could only be on their using this entrance, he said they would be quite agreeable to that. A meeting of the committee is to be held on Monday first and they would like to know before then whether their request will be granted. Of course the consent of the tenants of Westfield is necessary but the committee are to arrange as to this themselves. If permission is granted I shall make the usual stipulations as to gathering up papers, that no broken glass or other objectionable articles be left, and the children are not allowed to wander.

Yours faithfully, George Gavin. (FEP)

16 May 1902

Coronation festivities

Dear Mr Gavin,

Referring to your letter of 13th. As to the application that has been made by the committee who are getting up games and sports in connection with the Coronation festivities, that they might have permission to use a portion of the Falkland Policy Park, my brother writes from London that he has spoken to Lady Bute on the subject. Lady Bute grants permission for the committee to use the field on 26th June for the purpose and on the conditions mentioned in your letter, as to the entrance by the gate on the

9. King Edward VII

Leslie road, gathering up all papers etc, and not allowing the children to wander through the grounds. Lady Bute also agrees to the hanging of swings on the trees, provided the forester is satisfied that this can be done without injuring the trees. [1]

Yours very truly, John Pitman.

P.S. The ropes of the swings are very carefully fixed to the branches. I should think there would be great risk of the friction of the ropes cutting through the bark of the branches. (FEP)

17 May 1902

Opening of new golf course

On Saturday 10th May the new golf course was opened with befitting ceremony.

In the absence of Mr Maitland-Makgill-Crichton of Lathrisk, Miss Daisy Gulland, one of the local champion players drove the first ball – and a splendid shot it was. The course has been laid out by Mr James Philp, Freuchie, and is situated partly on the common land to the eastward of the ancient burgh locally known as the "Myres", and partly

---

[1] Wages for men erecting swings for coronation festivities, 5 shillings.

on the Lathrisk estate, in two fields kindly granted by the present popular laird, who has taken an exceedingly keen interest in the movement.

The course is very rough as yet, but this is not to be wondered at when it is remembered in what condition it was when a commencement was made to lay it out. At the present time there are no want of hazards, natural and otherwise. After some months' play matters will be greatly improved and the greens should be in fine condition. The course will prove an attraction to the numerous summer visitors who frequent the locality every season.

Mr Charles Gulland, town clerk, after his daughter had struck off the first ball, spoke a few words congratulating the Club on their acquiring such a suitable course, and wished them every success. A number of interesting singles were thereafter played amongst the members and visitors, when some good scores were chronicled. Mr Makgill-Crichton of Lathrisk is patron of the Club, Mr Rowland Gulland, captain, and Mr James Forsyth, secretary, George Baxter being green-keeper. Among those present were – The Rev. George Lowe, Freuchie; the Rev. Charles Fraser, Freuchie; the Rev. Mr and Mrs Johnston; the Rev. Mr and Mrs Morrison, Falkland; Mr J. L. Lumsden, Freuchie; Mr Charles Gulland; Mr Rowland Gulland; Mr Bonthrone and Mr D. Bonthrone, Newton of Falkland; Mr Christopher Morrison, Monifieth; Mrs Gulland; Mrs Mackie; and Misses Lumsden, Freuchie. The weather was all that could be desired, and a most enjoyable time was spent.

The opening of the course marks an important advance in the sporting life of the community, which, thanks to the facilities placed at its disposal by Mr Bonthrone in the free use of suitable ground, has long held a good reputation in out-of-door pastimes.

The following is a description of the course: Two good drives and an iron shot should reach the first green, which is encircled by sand dunes. Five is par play. The second hole requires to be very carefully played. Rough territory lies on the left, and whins on the right; but, with decent luck, four should suffice. The third hole presents no difficulties, the green being reachable from the tee. The ball, however, must be kept straight, as a pulled drive may find lodgement among trees, or at the foot of a dyke. Three is good play, though four in the rough state is not amiss. Going to the fourth hole, which is on the

Lathrisk estate, a strip of beech trees has to be negotiated. Four is par value. No. five is plain sailing; and at the sixth, the player has the option of driving round a rough square or of taking the hazard right away. This and the succeeding hole should be manipulated in four strokes each. To the inexperienced golfer, the seventh is the most trying hole, owing to whins and a number of lint[1] holes in which the natives of old, making use of a small burn that whimpers by, steeped their lint – grown at one time very extensively in Fife. The eighth hole is also difficult, a sliced drive running the chance of being trapped in a bunker. If a good line is kept, the hole may be managed in three. The home hole is placed in the old curling pond, with a reserve green beside it. Here also four suffices; and anything about 40 for the round may be considered excellent play. (FN)

24 May 1902

Coronation celebrations

Dear Mr Pitman,

With reference to the accompanying two letters handed to me yesterday by Mr Galloway and which I now return, and to the conversation with him I have now seen the secretary of the local committee, the treasurer and one or two of the members. I find that they have at present collected a sum of about £40 by house to house visitations, and that they did not expect to get very much more. With the funds available it is intended to give some three hundred children a mug each and refreshments, and to apply any surplus in the purchase of tea and sugar for the poor of the town, and probably give the elderly people who might accompany the children some refreshments also.

I took care not to promise anything, but indicated that Lord Bute's trustees might yet assist. Those of the committee I saw were highly grateful at this prospect and said that if a sum were given it would be able then to do something more for the poor, as they were afraid that after providing for the entertainment of the children and those accompanying them there would not, with the funds presently in hand, be much to devote to this deserving part of the day's proceedings. A large committee was appointed to canvas the districts, Provost Page,

---

[1] i.e. flax.

builder, is convener, Mr John Sheriff, (formerly Managing Clerk to Mr Gulland, and is now retired) is secretary, and Mr Walter Peggie, slater, is treasurer.

Yours faithfully George Gavin. (FEP)

29 May 1902

Post office

Dear Sir,

We cannot agree to Miss Reekie's request to have new windows put in, but are willing that the painting should be done.

Yours faithfully, J. & F. Anderson. (FEP)[1]

2 June 1902

Fatal accident

A young man named Alexander Lumsden, residing in Gallatown, Kirkcaldy, met his death on Saturday evening under distressing circumstances. It appears that Lumsden, who was in the employment of Mr Collins, posting master, Gallatown, left in charge of a picnic party bound for Falkland. The party was duly landed at their destination, and it would seem that the deceased had been requested to mount his machine and set off for home. This he declined to do, and one of the party, by way of persuading him to start, drove off in a homeward direction. Immediately Lumsden saw this he ran after the machine, apparently with the intention of stopping it or mounting the box. In any case, the unfortunate young fellow, who was under the influence of drink, stumbled and fell in front of the brake, and, the wheels passing over him, he received such an injury that he died soon after. Dr Mackay was at once summoned, but the lad was beyond human aid. He was twenty two years of age, unmarried. His remains were removed to the Bruce Arms, Hotel and were taken home last night. The inquiry stated when he was knocked over the wheels passing over his chest fractured all the ribs on the left side and

---

1 Jane Reekie was Sub Postmistress, aged 33. She lived with four unmarried sisters. Jessie, Grocer and Shopkeeper aged 30. Emily, Towel Machinist, aged 24, Davina, Post Office assistant, aged 21, Margaret, Telegraph Messenger, aged 18. The Post office at this time seems to have been at the bottom of Cross Wynd in a building that no longer exists, next to the pillar box.

crushing the lungs into pulp. Death was instantaneous. (DC)

4 June 1902
Boer War surrender
The news was brought here by a company of Freuchie youths, who arrived about 3.o'clock on Monday morning, blowing horns and making a considerable din. On arrival of the mail cart with conformation the bells were rung and flags were soon displayed throughout the town. The local Flute band turned out in the evening and paraded the principal streets. [1] (FH)

12 June 1902
Request for site for flower show
Dear Sir,

We have now heard from Lady Bute[2] with reference to the request of the Falkland Horticultural Society referred to in your letter of 4th inst. Her Ladyship objects most strongly to the football proposition, but would be willing to allow the flower show to be held in the park. Lady Bute says that the actual spot can be decided later or probably when Her Ladyship comes to Falkland, but she is doubtful about giving entrance by the Lodge Gate. This however can be arranged with her Ladyship who will no doubt be at Falkland before the time of the show. If you find it necessary to write again upon this matter you had better communicate with Lady Bute direct. We are afraid the Trustees have no power to give a contribution to the flower show.

Yours faithfully, J. & F. Anderson. (FEP)

---

[1] The surrender was on 31 May 1902.

[2] From his father's death until his own coming of age in 1904 the estate was managed by Trustees on Lord Ninian's behalf, hence Lady Bute being consulted.

Games and Dancing

Falkland Gymnastic Games and Dancing
Myre of Falkland.
On Friday 27th June 1902.
Games to Commence at One o'clock p.m.

PROGRAMME

		1st Prize	2nd	3rd
1.	Running Long Leap.	5s	3s	2s
2.	100 yards Race.	7s 6d	5s	2s 6d
3.	Sword Dance.	7s	6s	5s
4.	Sack race, once round (local)	3s	2s	1s
5.	Half Mile Race.	8s	5s	2s 6d
6.	Running High Leap.	6s	3s	2s
7.	300 yards race for Boys under 16years (local).	3s	2s	1s
8.	Highland Fling.	7s	6s	5s
9.	One Mile Race.	10s 6d	6s	3s
10.	Girls Race under 16 years of age (local).	3s	2s	1s
11.	Sailors' Hornpipe.	7s 6d	5s	
12.	Hurdle Race, twice round 3 feet Hurdles.	7s 6d	4s	2s 6d
13.	Three-Legged Race (local)	3s	2s	1s
14.	Irish Jig.	7s 6d	5s	
15.	Race for men 50 years and Above, once round (local).	3s	2s	1s
16.	Bicycle Race, at 7 p.m.	Time-piece	Silver Cigarette Case	Silver Badge, Gold Centre

LOCHGELLY PRIZE BRASS BAND will perform select pieces of music during the games. (FFP, 21 June 1902)

21 June 1902

Marquis of Bute's coming of age

Through the generosity of Lady Bute, the employees of Falkland estate were entertained to a cake and wine banquet in the Bruce Arms, Hotel. Mr George Gavin of the estate office presided over a company of about 50. The toast of "The health of the Marquis of Bute" was proposed by the chairman and enthusiastically pledged.

Other toasts were – "Lady Bute," "Lady Margaret," and "Lord Ninian".[1] The purveying was in the capable hands of Mr Hardie. The following telegram was dispatched by the Provost and Magistrates to the Marquis,

"The Provost and Magistrates and Town Council of the Royal Burgh of Falkland hereby offer hearty congratulations, on behalf of themselves and the community, to the most noble the Marquis of Bute on his attaining the years of majority. They sincerely trust that the Marquis will have a long life, happiness and prosperity."

The employees on the estate sent the following congratulatory telegram to his Lordship:

"Workmen on Falkland estate send hearty congratulations on this auspicious occasion." (DC)

2 July 1902

Malicious mischief

Yesterday before Sheriff Armour at Cupar Andrew Lawson, labourer, Victoria Place, was charged with having, on 22nd June, on the public highway leading from Falkland to New Inn, maliciously broken the shafts of four small hammers used for breaking stones, and stole a hammer. Accused pleaded guilty to the charge of malicious mischief alone, which was accepted, and he was fined £1, with the alternative of five days in prison. (DC)

---

[1] The toast of The Marchioness of Bute was proposed by Mr E. McCallum, forester, that of Lady Margaret, by Mr E. Macpherson, Palace Gardens, that of Lord Ninian, the future laird, by Mr Hillock, Palace guide, and that of Lord Colum, by Mr M. Smith. A vote of thanks to the chairman terminated the proceedings. (FFP, 28 June)

5 July 1902

Market and games.

This annual event was held on Friday in delightful weather. This year the games were under the patronage of the Provost, Magistrates, and Town Council, and were highly successful. Friday also saw the celebration of the old-established "market", and the Royal Burgh was *en fête*; while there were many visitors present for the occasion.[1]

The games took place in the Common or Myre, which is a suitable park for the purpose. Early in the forenoon the school children were presented with Coronation mugs, and after Lochgelly Brass Band had paraded through the town, the sports programme was entered upon, and continued till well on in the afternoon.

The arrangements were admirably carried out by Mr John Sheriff, secretary; and Provost Page; Mr Charles Jackson, manufacturer; Mr Charles Jackson, jnr; Bailie Miller; Mr David Bonthrone, Newton of Falkland; Councillor Forsyth, members of committee; and Mr Walter Peggie, treasurer. Bailie Miller, Mr Jackson and Councillor Jackson officiated as judges.

Later in the day dancing was engaged in. The band played selections after the games at Millfield House, and were entertained by Mr and Mrs Gulland. Mr Angus, Commercial Hotel, who also saw to the comfort of the band, called for a vote of thanks to Mr and Mrs Gulland, which was cordially given. (FN)

9 July 1902

Cattle sale

Thursday 10th July 1902. Sale of cattle and horses at Westfield Farm

Fat Bullocks; 72 two years old Bullocks, a large number of them in

---

[1] The substantial prizes offered brought out a fine field of competitors from various parts of the county and from Leith, Dundee, Forfar and Perth. The day being observed as a holiday in the district, there was a large attendance of visitors including Mr and Mrs Gulland and party, Millfield; Mr Jackson, manufacturer; Dr and Mrs Mackay; Major Cusin; Mr John Lawson, Falkland Wood. What is known locally as "The Market" was also celebrated yesterday and located in the Myre was a fair representation of the "show" fraternity with Aunt Sallys, hobby-horses, sweetie and try-your-luck stands. (DC, 28 June). The event was also described as "Highland Games".

Forward Condition; 12 Six-Quarter Stirks; 1 Calving Cow, four years old; 1 Bay Driving Mare, eight years old, about 16 Hands high; 1 grey Horse, eight years old, suitable for Van or Farm work; 1 Brown mare, fit for heavy work; 1 Dog cart; 1 Gig. A large number of the cattle are home-bred.

Luncheon at 3 o'clock: Sale immediately after.

Brakes will leave the Auction Mart, Ladybank, at 2.30 p.m., to Convey Intending Purchasers to the Sale.

Terms of Sale: two Months credit or Discount for Cash. (DC)

11 July 1902
Old house opposite Palace
Dear Mr Gavin,

We have your letter of 9th forwarding plans of proposed new house to be erected on the site of this old house, and estimating the cost of re-building at about £400. We do not observe any mention of painting or papering which we presume would have been added to the £400, even if the £400 would include everything we are afraid that the expenditure is one which could not be undertaken by the Trustees, looking to a very small estimated return of £10 per annum. On referring to Messrs Page and Miller's report we see that they make two suggestions. One, a house of two stories and the other for two houses of one storey, each on the site of the old house and the washing house. We fear that this latter alternative could not be carried out at a cost that would yield a reasonable return for the expenditure.

Yours faithfully, J. & F. Anderson. (FEP)

12 July 1902
George Baxter
Sanitary Inspector, account for cleaning and disinfecting Elizabeth Hislop's[1] house, Cross Wynd, 14 shillings. (FEP)

18 July 1902
Returned from the front
Sergeant William Lawson, 1st Cameron Highlanders, who has served

---

[1] Or Hyslop.

in South Africa for fully two years, arrived in Falkland on Tuesday night. During his stay in South Africa he took part in many striking episodes. (AJ)

15 August 1902

Old House opposite Palace

My Dear Sir,

Lord Bute's Trustees at their last meeting had before them a memo as to this old house. They decided that looking to the very small rent expected to be received if the house were re-built as proposed, they could not as estate management expend money on re-building. The question of re-building therefore must be delayed until the estate is handed over to Lord Ninian on his attaining majority. As the house is reported by experts to be in a dangerous condition the Trustees have authorised the pulling down of the house so far, taking off the roof and leaving the front wall standing to a height of say 6 or 7 feet, and building up windows and doorway. Will you please arrange to have this done, and as the house is in a conspicuous place in the main street of Falkland please see that a neat job is made of the wall which to be left standing.

I understand that the house, or a portion of it is occupied by a man Smith who works on the estate. You will have to give him some notice before turning him out. Will it be necessary to find another house for him?

Yours truly, John Pitman. (FEP)

16 August 1902

William Wood memorial

There is a very imposing memorial about to be erected in Falkland Cemetery to the memory of the late Major Wood, so long the factor of the Falkland estate, and who was held in very high esteem throughout the district. The monument is the outcome of a spontaneous desire on the part of the tenantry and friends to perpetuate in a tangible way the memory of one who endeared himself to all with whom he had come in contact. The memorial will show a figure in Carrara marble placed upon a massive granite pedestal. The design is by Mr A. Murdoch, sculptor, Kirkcaldy. (FFP)

10. William Wood's
monument in Falkland
Cemetery

Coronation

The royal ancient burgh was gay with bunting and flags in honour of the auspicious event, [1] and admirable arrangements had been made by the Coronation Committee. The community responded well, and the Committee were placed in possession of ample funds to carry out the day's celebrations in fitting style.

When, unfortunately, it was found necessary, owing to the King's illness, to postpone the children's treat and other functions then arranged for, it was thought well to present to the school children the handsome Coronation jugs which had been purchased for them, and this was done at the time in the Public School.

The day was observed as a holiday, and beautiful weather favoured the celebrations. Through the kindness of the Marchioness of Bute, the park within the beautiful grounds of Falkland House was put at the disposal of the Committee.

---

[1] The coronation was held on 9 August, the original planned date of 26 June had to be abandoned because of the King's illness. Lord Ninian was a "Gold Staff Officer" at the coronation and received a coronation medal. The role involved marshalling the coronation procession inside Westminster Abbey.

Swings had been erected and a racecourse laid out. At noon the children headed by the Falkland flute band, under the leadership of Mr Michael Reekie, marched from the Public School to the field, and refreshments were then served. The programme of sports arranged was during the afternoon successfully carried through. The flower show was held in the same field, and old and young accordingly mixed freely. The day's entertainment was greatly enjoyed. The Committee and those gentlemen who so ably took charge of the sports are to be congratulated upon the success which attended the celebrations. (FN)

16 August 1902

Children entertained

The special feature of the day was a treat to the children, and seldom, if ever, has there been a prettier sight seen in our streets than their march from Public School to the park at Falkland House. There they were entertained. A long programme of games was gone through, including an exhibition of physical drill, under Sergeant Ford. The local flute band did yeoman service, and contributed in no small degree to make the day one to be long remembered. (FFP)

30 August 1902

Service in Town Hall

Two lady pilgrims conducted a service in the Town Hall on Sunday night, there was a good attendance. (FFP)

30 August 1902

Harvest

The harvest, it is expected, will be fully three weeks later than last year, for, with the exception of a field of barley here and there, the crops are still very green, and the ripening seems yet a long way off. (FFP)

12 September 1902

Balmblae Burn

Dear Mr Gavin,

I shall come over on Monday for the meeting. As there are a good many things at Falkland to see after, I think it will be best for me to spend nearly the whole day there. If it is a fine day I shall not require the trap to be sent to meet me as I shall bicycle from the station. I shall come by the train arriving at Ladybank at 10.50 a.m. and so should arrive at Falkland at 11.45.a.m. If it is a wet day I shall take the slower train arriving at Falkland Road Station 11.36.a.m. I certainly think that it would be advisable for the Burgh to be represented at the Balmblae Burn meeting. Please therefore try and arrange this.

Yours faithfully, John Pitman. (FEP)

16 September 1902
Balmblae Burn
Dear Mr Gavin,

When you are seeing the tenant of the Mill about the proposal to put some water down the Balmblae Burn in dry weather you should point out to him that it was alleged that he or his men had been raising the dam on the Maspie and so preventing any water getting down the burn. I shall be interested to hear what he says as to this and the proposal to periodically flush the Balmblae Burn.

Yours truly, John Pitman. (FEP)

17 September 1902
Balmblae Burn
Dear Mr Gavin,

We have your letter of 16th inst. and are glad to learn that Mr Galloway, the tenant of the mill[1] is agreeable to the proposal that water should be allowed down the bye-pass into the Balmblac Burn for one hour every day and that if a sluice is erected they will undertake to turn on and off the water. Please therefore arrange to have the necessary sluice put in. We agree with you that there should be no delay in carrying out the arrangement. We are also glad to hear that the Town Council have agreed to assist in cleaning the burn. Mr

---

[1] The Turning Mill was driven by water from the Mill Burn, which fed a pond to the north of West Port and was then taken via a mill lade (partly in tunnel) to drive Galloway's wood-turning machinery, before discharging into the Balmblae Burn. The mill has since been demolished, and the site is now occupied by Mill Green.

Gulland has not yet communicated with us on the subject, but we shall let you know exactly what they agree to do, as soon as we hear from them. If Mr Gulland does not soon write, we shall at some time call upon the Burgh to strictly enforce its bye-laws as to laying filth and refuse in the burn. We shall also call upon the County Authorities to see that no refuse is thrown in from the Balmblae side.

Yours faithfully, J. & F. Anderson. (FEP)

24 September 1902

Balmblae Burn

My Dear Gavin,[1]

Mr Gulland has written intimating that the Burgh has agreed to share in the cleaning out of the burn, but for this year only as various questions require to be elucidated, such as the proprietorship of the burn. He goes on to make the suggestion that the estate should put in an engine at the mill and thus economise the water. We have acknowledged the intimation to the cleaning out of the burn, and we have told him of the arrangements made for the construction of a sluice and the turning of water over the bye-pass for a hour in the evenings in dry weather. In view of the trouble likely to be raised by Mr Gulland in the future we have taken care to say that the above arrangement about the sluice and turning water over the bye-pass has been made without prejudice to the right of the properties of Falkland Estate or others to the water.

Yours faithfully, John Pitman. (FEP)

27 September 1902

Dressmaking

A dressmaking class was opened on Tuesday night, under the auspices of the County Council, in the Public School, under the superintendence of Misses Aitken and Noble. The attendance was good. (FN)

---

[1] George Gavin, addressed on letters at this time as "The Overseer, Estate Office, Falkland" had moved into Lomondside House, and lived there with his family until Whitsunday 1906 when he moved to the Palace, having been appointed principal factor in 1904. He had previously worked at the Moncreiffe Estate near Bridge of Earn.

Allowances for Lomondside House

Paid Falkland Gas Co. for gas for Overseer's House at Lomondside
   from 5th may to 24th Sept. 1902. £1.18s.6d.

Paid Charles Gulland half years rent £12.10s.

Paid G. Gavin, allowance for upkeep of bicycle £3.

Thomas Love & Sons, Perth for removal of Overseer's furniture
   here from Moncreiffe. (FEP)

---

30 September 1902

Lomondside House

Dear Mr Gavin,

   We have this morning received a letter from Mr Gulland, who is rather indignant at having been written to, however he states that he has given Mr Page instruction to at once place a pipe in the ditch and fill it in. Mr Gulland however says that he understood from you that we were to do a similar work through the Bruce Inn garden adjoining, and states that Provost Page has informed him that you have only authorised the putting in of a few pipes in the garden and not throughout the whole length of the burn. He asks whether this is true. In reply, we are informing Mr Gulland that we only thought it necessary to carry the pipe a short way into the Bruce Arms, garden and not cover in the rest of the burn as there were no buildings in that garden, but that we would do whatever the Sanitary Inspector insists upon. If therefore the Sanitary Inspector insists upon laying the whole of the ditch with a pipe, we think you should have this done as it cannot be a very expensive matter, and will save further trouble in the future.

   Yours faithfully J. & F. Anderson, Edinburgh. (FEP)

30 September 1902

Balmblae Burn

Dear Sir,

   The new sluice is now on course of being fitted up by the joiner, but before its erection on the day it would be well the cleaning of the burn should be done. I have written to Mr Gulland that I am ready to do this work and asking him when it would be convenient for him to send two men on behalf of the Burgh.

Yours faithfully, George Gavin. (FEP)

8 October 1902
Balmblae power
Dear Sir,

The clearing out of the burn was completed yesterday. The sluice at west end of dam is finished and tomorrow Messrs Galloway will begin to put the sluice water daily down the burn, Perhaps you will accordingly write to the Clerk of the District Committee informing him that everything agreed out and asking that the regulations as to putting filth into the burn by any Balmblae people should be strictly enforced, and similar letter to the Town Clerk as regards those residents on the Burgh side of the burn. It is for consideration whether you should ask them specifically what preventative measures they will take in the Burgh at least beyond posting notices prohibiting these practices. Yours faithfully, George Gavin. (FEP)

15 October 1902
Balmblae Burn
Dear Mr Gavin,

We have today written both to the Town Clerk and to the Clerk of the District Committee reporting that the arrangement regarding the sluice, cleaning of burn, and turning water down the burn has now been carried out, and we have asked them both to take steps to enforce regulations to prevent further pollution.[1] We have also said to Mr Gulland that we were disappointed at the town not having sent men to help in the cleaning of the burn and you will submit to them an account of the cost of the work and ask for payment of half thereof.

Yours Faithfully, J. & F. Anderson. (FEP)

[1] James Forsyth, builder, was paid £8 6s 1½d for repairing dam. Robert Miller, joiner, was paid £1 4s 10d for fitting up new sluice. James Forsyth, mason, was paid 4s 3d for stone work of new sluice.

21 October 1902

The Fountain

It was decided at a meeting that the Town Fountain be allowed again to run all night free and after this date and that the valves of both cisterns be regulated, so that the overflow shall become the same from both cisterns. (FTCM)

15 November 1902

Kirkin of the Council

The annual ceremony of the "Kirkin" of the Council took place on Sunday. The members assembled in the Town Hall, and headed by the Town Officer, marched to the Parish Church, where the pulpit was occupied by the Rev. A. L. Johnston, who conducted the service. In the afternoon the Council proceeded to the U.F. Church, where the Rev. Mr Morrison officiated. (FN)

22 November 1902

Parish Council

A meeting of the Parish Council was held in the school on Friday night, Mr Jackson in the chair, for the purpose of electing a medical doctor in place of Dr Mackay, who has left the district. Dr Jack was appointed by six votes to three for Dr Hardie. (FFP)

November 1902

Bruce Arms Inn

William Page was paid £2 2s 8d, for covering an open ditch in front of Bruce Arms, Inn. (FEP)

5 December 1902

Town rubbish

A letter dated 4th December 1902 was read from James McLeish, the carter of the collecting in the Town's Depots. Mr McLeish complains that he objects to so much rubbish being mixed with the dung. It was explained that Mr McLeish's principal objection was that garden rubbish, thorn and hedge cuttings, and it was decided that hand bills be positioned throughout the Burgh forbidding any such material being emptied into the depots, and the officers were also instructed to prevent as far as in their power any objectionable matter being put in. (FTCM)

23 *December 1902*
Alleged theft of porter
David Anderson, labourer, Back Wynd, was today charged, before Sheriff Armour with having between 13th and 15th December, in High Street, broken into the cellar of the house occupied by David Lumsden, publican, and stolen twelve pint bottles of porter. Accused pleaded not guilty. (DEP)

1903

6 January 1903

Death of Rowland Gulland

We regret to announce the death of Mr Rowland Gulland, only son of Mr Charles Gulland, town clerk, which took place at Millfield, Falkland, on Sunday fore-noon. Mr Gulland contracted a bad cold about a week ago, which developed into pneumonia. He was about 30 years of age, and was engaged in business as a lawyer and banker along with his father. A fine cricketer and tennis player, he oftentimes assisted Cupar clubs in their matches, and he was an enthusiastic Volunteer, being a member of A Squadron of the Fife and Forfar Imperial Yeomanry. Much sympathy is expressed for Mr and Mrs Gulland in their sore bereavement. (DC)

10 January 1903

Rowland Gulland's funeral

On Sunday morning the inhabitants of Falkland were startled by the news of the death of Mr Rowland Gulland, only son of Mr Charles Gulland, lawyer and banker, Falkland. Mr R. Gulland was a strong, athletic young man, who had just lately been associated with his father as joint agent of the British Linen Bank, and had also been appointed Town Clerk of Falkland. He was an adept in all manly sports. The cause of death was a severe attack of influenza, culminating in brain fever. The sympathy of the whole parish and district is with his parents and sisters in this sudden calamity that has come upon them.

11. Rowland Gulland

Died 1903, aged about 30, having briefly succeeded his father as Town Clerk of Falkland

The remains of deceased were interred in Falkland cemetery on Wednesday amid signs of universal regret. The hearse containing the coffin, which was of polished oak, was followed to the grave by a large cortege. Alongside the hearse walked a detachment of A. Squadron Fife and Forfar Imperial Yeomanry of which corps deceased gentleman was a member under the command of Sergeant-Major Vine, while among those in the rear was a deputation of the local lodge of B.O. Free Gardeners, of which lodge the deceased was an honorary member. The town bell was tolled, while all along the route through which the funeral cortege passed window blinds were drawn down out of respect for the memory of deceased. On arriving at the cemetery the coffin was carried to the grave side by the members of the Imperial Yeomanry, while previous to the coffin being lowered into the grave a funeral service was conducted by the Rev. Mr Johnston.

The pall-bearers were: Mr Charles Gulland (father of the deceased); Mr D. Ballingall, Blair Drummond, Stirling (cousin of the deceased); Dr A. Macintosh, Bridge of Allan (brother in law); Mr Harold Tarbolton, architect, Edinburgh (brother in law); and Mr Conrad Howell, London.

The members of the Imperial Yeomanry who took part in the funeral solemnities were: Sergeant-Major Berwick, Sergeant Stewart, trumpeter Mckenzie and Troopers A. and J. Morgan, D. Scott, Carswell, Scott, Andrews, Pringle, Birrel, Campbell, Dawson, Adamson. A large number of wreaths were sent by friends of the deceased. (FFP)

10 January 1903

Child burnt in Falkland

A little girl, named Jeannie Anderson, was severely burned on Tuesday evening. She was playing with other children of the house when her clothes caught fire, and serious injuries were sustained before the flames could be extinguished. (FFP)

10 January 1903

Y.M.C.A. social

The Y.M.C.A. social was held on Thursday night in the Town Hall, Mr Walter Peggie, president, in the chair. The programme, which comprised solo singing, part singing, recitations and games, were gone through with great spirit, and the large company gave every sign of having enjoyed a most pleasant evening. (FFP)

22 January 1903

Industrial progress

The burgh at present is in a thriving condition. The value of the property in the burgh is slightly over £3000, and the population, according to the last census, is 2,229.[1] A couple of linen factories give employment to about one hundred hands, and the recently introduced linoleum industry affords employment for about a score of workers. (DEP)

22 January 1903

Weaving

Lady Bute, the widow of the late Marquis, who takes much interest in the welfare of the local people, has given a fillip to the old hand-loom weaving industry, and in about a dozen homes her Ladyship has introduced looms, which are worked by her protégés.

Her Ladyship has also established homes for orphan Catholic boys and girls, several of the former being hired out to farmers in the district. (DEP)

---

[1] This is surely the population of the parish, not of the burgh.

7 February 1903

Vacancy for certifying surgeon

The Chief Inspector of Factories gives notice that in consequence of the resignation of Dr Hardie, an appointment as certifying surgeon, under the Factory and Workshop Act at Falkland, is vacant. (FN)

10 February 1903

Theft from a Fife hotel

Today, at Cupar Sheriff Court, William Skinner, labourer, Well Brae, was charged with having, on Saturday 24th January, within the bar-room in the Lomond Hotel, Freuchie, occupied by Mrs Jane Middleton, hotelkeeper, stole a parcel containing one pair of drawers and a tweed cap. A plea of guilty was tendered, and Mr James Welch, Cupar, appeared for accused. Sheriff Armour imposed a fine of £1, or seven days imprisonment on condition that the accused would pay the value of the articles stolen. (DEP)

12 February 1903

Use of the Palace Chapel in the evening

Letter to J. & F. Anderson

Dear Sirs,

In a letter I received today from Lady Bute she says "The priest is anxious to use the Palace Chapel on Saturday evenings in Lent for a series of sermons or lectures." I have spoken to one of the trustees and he sees no reason against it. I am writing to Father Wolfenstan to this effect, and her Ladyship added, "I am reminded that there is no light and thus I cannot go to any expense." I write at once in order that a definite decision may be given on this point. The Chapel has no gas nor light of any kind and would thus be unsuitable. I am afraid for many reasons it would not to be wise to hold public meetings in the Drawing-room. There is also the difficulty that there are no seats, and there is the question of opening the Palace Gates at night for meetings. The guide would also require to be in attendance to close up the place.

I am your obedient servant, George Gavin. (FEP)

12 February 1903

Nuisance at Brunton House

Extract from Lady Bute's accounts

By Geo. Baxter. Wages of men cleaning out closets at Brunton House[1] on request to complaints by Sanitary Inspector as to there being public nuisance. 11s 6d (FEP)

13 February 1903

Repair to thatched roof

Letter to John Bett Thatcher, Auchtermuchty

Dear Sir,

A considerable time ago I wrote asking you to go over the thatch roof of the game-keeper's house at Chancefield, but you have never done so nor replied to my letter. Water is again coming through the roof and I would like to know whether you will go and repair it. Be good enough to write me on receipt.

Yours truly, George Gavin. (FEP)

24 February 1903

Boyish prank

Heriot Bain Lawson (14) floorcloth worker, Alexander Lawson (12) schoolboy, High Street West, admitted before Sheriff Armour at Cupar today: Having between 12th and 13th February, at the west end of Horsemarket, broken into the shop occupied by John Chisholm, baker, and stolen nine pies. Accused had been previously convicted. Heriot was ordered to receive six strokes with the birch rod and Alexander four. (DEP)

11 April 1903

Presentation

On Saturday evening a number of friends met in the Bruce Arms

---

[1] 1901 census for Brunton House: Romond Aboad de Lazeu; Spanish; age 27, elementary and science teacher; Rachel Graham boarder age 9; Ayrshire; Annie Higgins; boarder age 9 Hawick; Sarah Higgins boarder age 6 Hawick; Agnes O'Brien boarder age 8 Glasgow. The "closets" were presumably water closets.

Hotel for the purpose of entertaining Sergeant Ford, who is leaving the district to fill an appointment under Kinross School Board. He has now completed his time in the Army Reserve, and for the last five years he has been Sergeant-Instructor to the Volunteers here. Councillor Hardie presided, and at an interval during the evening presented the Sergeant, in name of the subscribers, with a handsome easy chair. The Councillor passed a high compliment on Sergeant Ford for the assiduity displayed in the Volunteer movement in the district. He was sure that the Sergeant had the best wishes from numerous friends for his success in his new sphere of labour. The recipient made a feeling reply, thanking them heartily for the kindness and for the quite unexpected mark of their esteem. He could assure them that he highly appreciated the sentiment which had prompted them in their present action. With song and pleasing sentiment an enjoyable hour was spent. (FN)

28 April 1903
Collecting of town rubbish
It was agreed to advertise for cart-man for the removal of the town's manure and rubbish. The depots to be discontinued and the manure and rubbish lifted throughout the whole of the Burgh. It was arranged that the cart would require to go twice a week round the Burgh during the month of May to the middle of October and once a week during the other months. Offers to be taken for a period of one year from 18th May 1903. It was also agreed that material such as tins, paper to be collected only once a month on the last Friday. When the manure is being removed twice a week it was decided that it would require to be Tuesdays and Fridays, as early in the morning as possible.

It was decided to advertise in the *Peoples Journal* on 2nd May. (FTCM)

9 May 1903
Falkland's wicked twins
Before Sheriff Armour in Cupar Sheriff Court today, Alexander Lawson and William Lawson junior, both 12 years of age, sons of William Lawson, labourer, High Street West, Falkland, were charged with having:

(1) on Friday 1st May, in High Street, broken into the shop occupied

by the Falkland Co-Operative Society with intent to steal; and
(2) also on 1st May, in New Road broken into the killing-house
occupied by C. C. Brunton, butcher, and stolen one and a half
pounds of beef, half a pound of liver and one pound of fat.

The boys pleaded guilty, and Alexander admitted three previous convictions, and William admitted two previous convictions, on which occasions they were birched. Mr Brown, Procurator Fiscal, said that the boys had been committing thefts of this kind for a lengthened period. He thought the proper course was to send them to a reformatory, but they could not get that done until they had an undertaking from the public authority to contribute to their maintenance. He suggested that his Lordship should simply record their plea, and continue the case for sentence. He would allow the boys to go home, and their father would look after them. The Sheriff continued the case until Tuesday 26th May. (DET)

22 May 1903

Burglarious twins strike again

Alexander Lawson and William Lawson, both 12 years of age, sons of William Lawson, labourer, High Street West, were charged, before Sheriff Armour, at Cupar yesterday with having on May 15th in New Road, Falkland, broken into Kinross Cottage,[1] occupied by Isabella Henderson and Susan Henderson, factory workers, and stolen one penny of money and two apples; and second on 16th May, at Lathrisk, broken into cottage occupied by Arthur Ross, gardener, and stolen two pounds weight of bread and one pound weight of honey. The boys pleaded guilty, and Alexander admitted three previous convictions and William two. The Fiscal said that at the time these two housebreakings were committed the accused were actually waiting sentence on another charge of housebreaking. He asked his Lordship to adjourn the case for sentence until Tuesday. He had written twice to the Town Clerk of Falkland upon the question of contributing towards the cost of the boys' maintenance in a reformatory, but had received no reply. The Sheriff expected Falkland Town Council would have the matter under consideration. The father and mother

---

[1] Actually Kinnes Cottage, as confirmed by other press articles.

of the boys were most respectable people.

The Fiscal said the boys when sent messages were perfectly honest and never money or anything was missed from their home. The boys one weak point seemed to be housebreaking. The Sheriff adjourned the case for sentence until Tuesday. (DET)

26 May 1903

What to do with the terrible twins?

The Falkland twins, Alex and William Lawson, aged 12, against whom there are two charges of housebreaking, and who had previously confessed their guilt, came before Sheriff Armour at Cupar today for sentence.

The Fiscal said that neither the Parish Council nor the Town Council of Falkland would undertake to pay the weekly sum of 2s towards the boys' maintenance in Rossie Reformatory, so that the hands of the Court were practically tied. The lads seemed to have a perfect mania for housebreaking, and the articles they stole were principally food and things of practically little value.

The father of the boys said the beginning of their crime was the playing of truant. For staying away from school he punished them so hard that they were frightened to come home, and stayed out all night, and he supposed it was more for food than for anything else that they broke into these places. It would be much better if the boys could be separated for the one had a great influence over the other.

The Sheriff said he was satisfied it would be for the boys' advantage if they were both sent to a reformatory,[1] but after what had been said by the Procurator-Fiscal it was apparently impossible that he could take that course. He thought it certainly a great blot upon the criminal system. He hoped that this might reach the proper quarter, and that something might be done with the view of remedying that state of

---

[1] Rossie Reformatory near Montrose holds a legacy dating back to 1857 when it opened its doors as a reformatory with the purpose of reclaiming "young offenders". Part of the purpose of the reformatory was to provide safety to young people who had faced adversity, committed offences or faced a hostile home environment. Rossie Reformatory aimed to provide help in recovery and to eradicate any chances of re-offending, helping young people become useful members of the community.

matters. His Lordship then ordered the boys each to receive eight strokes with the birch rod. (DEP)

30 May 1903

In Memoriam

In loving memory of my dear son Alexander Lumsden, who was accidentally killed at Falkland on 31st May 1902, in his twenty first year.[1]

> Had we but seen his panting look,
> Or watched his dying bed,
> We think our hearts would not have felt
> The bitter tears we shed.
> On earth there's strife, in Heaven rest,
> They miss him most who loved him best.

Inserted by his sorrowing mother. (FFP)

6 June 1903

Presentation cup for Golf Club

Falkland golfers may rejoice in having so generous a patron as Mr Makgill-Crichton of Lathrisk. It was largely owing to his generosity, not only in the matter of finance, but in giving the use of a portion of his own lands so as to allow of an extended course, that the Falkland Golf Club had its inception. And now although Mr Makgill-Crichton is not at present resident in the district, his interest in the Club has, apparently, not abated. He has presented the Club with a magnificent silver cup which is now on view in the window of Mr Thomas Williamson, saddler, Falkland, and agent for Messrs. R. Forgan & Son, golf club makers, St Andrews. The inscription on the cup is as follows:

"Presented by C.J. Maitland-Makgill-Crichton of Lathrisk To The Falkland Golf Club For Annual Competition 1903."

The cup is being very much admired. In view of the fact that Mr Makgill-Crichton takes such an interest in the Club, and in Falkland matters generally, it is gratifying to think that, as has recently been reported, Mr Makgill-Crichton intends shortly to make Lathrisk his

---

[1] See page 54.

chief residence. (FN)

13 June 1903

Advertisement

Commercial Hotel. Falkland.

John Angus, Proprietor.
FIRST CLASS ACCOMMODATION FOR VISITORS.
PICNICS AND EXCURSIONS CATERED FOR.

The above Hotel is provided with every convenience, including a Large Hall adjoining Hotel, specially Erected for Excursion Parties; also, Four Bedrooms, Parlour, and Kitchen, with W.C. (FN)

27 June 1903

Market and Games

The annual market and games at Falkland were held on the Myre on Friday. There was a large attendance of spectators. Dancing was heartily engaged in until dusk, splendid music being supplied by Largo Brass Band. (FN)

13 July 1903

Church Sale of Work

A pretty Sale of Work, promoted by the Women's Guild of Falkland Parish Church for church purposes, was held in the Parish School on Saturday.

At the head of the movement was Mrs Johnston, the Manse, president of the Guild, and Mrs Dun, Woodmill, hon. Secretary, and it was mainly to the indefatigable labours of these ladies and the enthusiasm they invoked that the bazaar was in every respect an unqualified success. The schoolrooms presented a bright and animated appearance from the opening until the close of the day's proceedings.

Within the larger room there were three stalls tastefully decorated and adorned with a great variety of useful and ornamental goods. At the Manse Stall Mrs Johnston presided, and was assisted by Miss Hardie, Miss A. Maxwell, Miss Page, and Dr Alex Grieve. Here a beautiful bedspread, the work of the members of the Guild, was much admired. Mrs Dun had for her assistants her daughters (Miss Madge L. Dun, Miss Harry J. Dun) and Miss Williamson, Miss Stalker and

Mr George Robertson. This stall contained a lovely assortment of work, and included contributions from Lady Gilmour; set of china from Mr Alexander Bonthrone, Newton of Falkland; drawing-room easy chair from Mr John Sheriff, Falkland; large piece of Falkland linoleum from Mr Jackson, manufacturer; a nice selection of Wemyss ware; a soda water bottle containing 560 three-penny pieces collected by the Misses Dun.

The refreshment stall literally groaned under its weight of good things, and Mrs and the Misses Morgan, Nochnary, had a busy time supplying the wants of their numerous customers. In the adjoining room tea was served by Miss Duncan, Miss Annie Duncan, and Miss Reekie. Not the least interesting part of the bazaar was the entertainments got up by Mrs Dun and her talented daughters. The stage effects were most complete. There were two performances of the charming sketch "A Kiss in the Dark," the dramatis personæ being Miss Madge Dun, Miss Harry L. Dun, Miss Lily Leburn, Gateside, Mr A. Marshall Stewart and Mr Walter Mitchell, St Andrews. These ladies and gentlemen also took part in the concerts, along with Dr Anderson; Mr Beveridge, Kettle; and Mr George C. Leburn. Miss Kate H. Carswell, Blackety-side, Leven, was a most efficient accompanist. The various entertainments were thoroughly enjoyed by large audiences.

There was a large attendance at the opening ceremony, including Rev. A. Lyon Johnston, minister of the parish, who presided; Mr and Mrs F. L. Maitland, Lindores; Mrs D. Maitland Makgill Crichton, Lathrisk; Rev. Charles Fraser, Freuchie; Mr George Dun, Woodmill; Mr A. Bonthrone. Newton of Falkland; Mr John Sheriff; and Mr Richardson, Schoolhouse.

After prayer had been engaged in by the Chairman, Mr George Dun introduced Mr and Mrs Maitland, who had kindly consented to open the bazaar. Mr Maitland, who was received with applause, said it always gave his wife and himself great pleasure to take part in any movement connected with the Church of Scotland. The Women's Guild was one of the chief branches of its general organisation, and it was doing a work which should be encouraged in every possible way. (Applause) Falkland appeared to almost lead that branch of the Church's work in the Presbytery of Cupar, and it was very gratifying to see evidences of such zeal, pains, and trouble in the cause they were that day espousing. He had pleasure in declaring the bazaar open and in wishing it every success. (Applause)

Rev. Lyon Johnston called for a hearty vote of thanks to Mr and Mrs Maitland for coming over to Falkland and opening their bazaar. They were very much indebted to them.

Business was then proceeded with, and a brisk day's buying and selling experienced, the total drawings amounting to £118 17s 9d. Mrs Dun is to be congratulated on the excellence of the arrangements and the great success of the undertaking. (DC)

29 August 1903
Accident to local doctor
Dr Jack met with a cycling accident on Tuesday while doing his rounds. He has had to keep indoors since, but it is hoped he will soon be alright. (FFP)

5 September 1903
Property sales
The property of the late Mrs James Smart, Falkland, has been sold by auction in Mr Gulland's office. Mr Taylor, Kinghorn, bought the house and garden at Loanfoot for £85; Mr James Robertson, Falkland, bought the house in Cross Wynd, Falkland, for £7 10s; and Mr John Steedman, Falkland, bought the house (in ruins) in Dunshalt, for £5 10s. (FN)

12 September 1903
Presentation
On Friday evening, Mr Ewan Macpherson, head gardener at Falkland House, was entertained on the occasion of his leaving for Edinburgh, by a large company of well-wishers, in the Bruce Arms, Hotel. In the course of the evening, Councillor George Hardie, in an appreciative speech, presented Mr Macpherson, on behalf of a large number of subscribers, with a handsome Albert in case and a beautifully-equipped travelling bag. Mr Macpherson suitably replied, and a happy hour was spent in mirth and song. (FN)

19 September 1903

Advertisement

Hand Printer Wanted: To a man with family of sons and daughters.
  Constant employment will be found for all.
  Apply Falkland Floorcloth Coy. (FFP)

31 October 1903

Town Council nominations

Six nominations for four vacancies, viz: Bailie Miller, and Messrs.
Charles Jackson, John Angus, Walter Peggie, Thomas Williamson and
Alexander Fraser. The first three are retiring members. Provost Page,
who also comes out just now, declined re-nomination. (FN)

7 November 1903

Municipal elections

Successful: R. Miller, 113 votes; T. Williamson, 97; J. Angus 90; A.
Fraser, 88. Unsuccessful: C. Jackson, 75; W. Peggie, 74. (FN)

November 1903

Ex-Provost Page

Mr William Page, who retired from the civic chair of Falkland last
November after twenty-four years of public service, is one of the few
still with us who can tell many an exciting tale of life at the Australian
and New Zealand "diggings" fifty years ago. Brought up to the
mason trade, like his uncle,[1] who built the fine Parish Church of
Falkland, he sailed for Melbourne when a young man of 19, and for
twelve years might be said never to have known what it was to dwell
under any covering more substantial than a canvas tent. He partici-
pated in the smiles and frowns of fortune peculiar to the digger's life,
and was ever ready, where might was often regarded as right, to keep
and to hold by the strength of his own right arm. He returned to this
country 37 years ago, and resumed his former calling as a builder in
Falkland, where, under the direction of the late Marquis of Bute, he

---

[1] William Page's uncle was George Page. In addition to the kirk, he built the
Fountain and the Temple of Decision.

effected an extensive restoration of the old historic Palace. He has proved himself a worthy and useful citizen of the ancient burgh, and is followed into retirement by the best wishes of many friends. (FNA)

14 November 1903

New Provost

A meeting of Town Council was held on Friday, when Bailie Miller was elected Provost; Mr Thomas Sutherland, Senior Bailie; and Mr William Lawrie, Junior Bailie. (FN)

26 November 1903

Bruce Buildings

Letter to J. & F. Anderson:

Dear Sirs,

Yesterday evening Andrew Mitchell, who sometime ago took the house occupied by Miss Kilgour, as from the 28th inst., called here and explained that he had been dismissed from his employment in the Linen Factory, and would in consequence require to leave Falkland. He was, he said, accordingly very anxious if he could be relieved of the house. As it so happened the tenant of the adjoining house, William Lawson, told me a few day ago that he regretted very much having given up his house as, while he then contemplated leaving Falkland, he had changed his mind and had resolved to remain and assist his father, the tenant of Falkland Wood. I told Andrew Mitchell that if Lawson would take the house which he had taken he would be relieved. Having seen Lawson I found he was only too glad to do so and he will accordingly remove out of the one part of the house into the other.

The kitchen of both houses are papered but are in a very dirty condition, with a great deal of torn paper. It is by no means economical to paper the walls of the kitchens and as something must be done to these two houses. I have asked the painter[1] to have them size coloured as the parties take possession on Saturday, of which I hope you will approve.

Yours faithfully, George Gavin. (FEP)

---

[1] Thomas Ross was probably the painter.

12. Old house in process of demolition

The site is now the Palace Pantry. The house to its left is now the convenience store and Post Office (next door to an earlier Post Office), and the house with the columns has since been extended to two storeys.

26 December 1903

The late Rev. John Barrack

It was learned in the end of last week with great regret that the Rev. John Barrack, senior minister of Falkland Parish, had died at Maida Hill, London, on Thursday. It is a good many years since Mr Barrack's health first began to fail; but until the summer of 1898, he persevered bravely with his ministerial duties.[1] Then, however, he felt called on to ask relief, and arrangements were made for the election of a colleague and successor – the congregation's choice ultimately falling on the present minister, the Rev. A. Lyon Johnston. (FN)

26 December 1903

Falkland – A link with the past

The phrase "sitting under his own roof-tree" has not now the literal significance it had in days gone by; but a look at the undernoted

---

[1] Rev. Barrack was ordained in 1853, and was minister at Falkland from 1866 to 1898.

photograph will help to bring out the old meaning. It shows what is generally supposed to have been the oldest house in the burgh of Falkland. This dwelling stood opposite the Palace of Falkland, until recently, when it had to be demolished. On the thatch and divots being removed, the old "roof-trees" supporting the roof were exposed as shown. These were the oak limbs set into the ground and brought up and "tied" by cross pieces firmly fixed by oak pins, the whole erection resembling the framework of the hull of a ship. The age of this old house cannot have been less than a couple of centuries, and may probably have been a great deal more. The oak when taken out was as fresh as the day when the hewers felled it in the adjoining forests of Falkland, and these interesting relics have wisely been preserved in one of the rooms of the old Palace. Until a few years ago, these "roof-trees" had sheltered Falkland Post Office as far back as the oldest inhabitant could remember. The house immediately adjoins the existing remains of the gate pillars of the "East Port" of Falkland, and it is not an unreasonable conjecture that it was at one time the abode of the keeper of that gate. The late Marquess of Bute, to whom the house belonged, evinced the keenest interest in the old building. Recently, however, it gave unmistakeable signs of decay, and its demolition became a regrettable necessity in the interests of public safety. (FNA)[1]

---

[1] This article was also reprinted in the *Illustrated Guide to Falkland* (reprinted 1915)

1904

5 March 1904

Business to let

To be Let, with Entry at Whit-Sunday next, the Old Established LICENSED GROCERY BUSINESS for many years conducted by the late Mr David Reekie, Postmaster, Falkland, and latterly by Miss Jessie Reekie. The business has a Good Trade, and There is ample scope for improvement.

For further particulars apply to the Proprietor, Charles Gulland, Writer, Falkland. (DC)

1 April 1904

Address to Lord Ninian

Dear Mr Gavin,

I have been asked to draw up an address by the Falkland Estate tenantry to Lord Ninian Crichton-Stuart on the occasion of his coming of age and entering into possession of the estate. I am quite willing to do what I can; but the difficulty is I know so little about him. Can you come to my aid? Lord Ninian is, of course a young man yet with his history all to make; but you may be able to suggest a sentence on what would be appropriate and complimentary. I must also make special reference to his late father and his mother. I have a few facts about the Marquis but not much about the Marchioness and perhaps here again you might be helpful. In fact any hint you may be able to give will be thankfully received. I seem always to be begging when I write you but your readiness to oblige at all times is, I am afraid very much the

83

case. You will kindly treat this letter as confidential meantime. Mr Dun, Woodmill, is the party who has applied to me, but I do not wish the proposal to get ventilated through anything I may say.

Yours faithfully, George Innes. (FEP)

12 April 1904

Catering for coming of age

Dear Mr Gavin,

Mrs Johnston does her catering very well. I have employed her several times and have been to quite a lot of functions. You need have no hesitations about pressing for her being engaged.

Yours faithfully, William. D. Patrick WS, Notary Public. (FEP)

30 April 1904

Offering a band for coming of age

Dear Mr Gavin,

I had a letter from Mr Innes, about a dance to be held in Falkland on 16th May. I will be pleased to supply you with a band for said dance. Band of four instruments, namely piano, violin, clarinet, and cornet. This makes a nice quartet. Mr Innes mentions in his note to violin, cornet, clarinet and double bass. This is not a good combination. The band I mention would cost £5 5s, that includes railway fare and hotel expenses as we will have to stay all night. I can get you hire of piano from Mr Diggle at very reasonable terms. Please let me know at your earliest convenience as my men are all in the theatre in Dundee and have to find deputies for the night.

Yours faithfully, D. G. Maule, Bandmaster, Cupar. (FEP)

30 April 1904

Invitation cards for coming of age

Dear Mr Gavin,

As promised I enclose copy of text of the address to Lord Ninian. I suppose our manager would as I instructed send you proofs of the three invitation cards today. I propose to print them in gold, except the smallest one, the extra cost is trifling and it enriches them very much.

Yours faithfully, George Innes, Fife Herald, Cupar. (FEP)

30 April 1904

Sunday drinking

It seems that more than a merely passing notice in the papers is necessary to put down the Sunday drinking here. Things cannot long continue as they have been for some time without the proper authority being called upon to deal promptly with this abuse. (FFP)

30 April 1904

Band of Hope treat

The Band of Hope children enjoyed their annual treat in the Drill hall on Saturday night. The young people presented a very happy appearance, and after disposing the contents of a well filled bag, went into a programme of song and recitation, which they carried through with much ability. An important feature of the evening was the presentation by the Rev. Mr Johnston of a splendid gentleman's dressing-case to Mr Alexander Sutherland. Mr Sutherland has taught the class for some years, but has had to sever his connection with it, having been lately transferred by the British Linen Company Bank to their Glasgow office. Before separating the usual votes of thanks were given in proper children style. (FFP)

6 May 1904

Band and programme for rejoicing

Dear Mr Gavin,

I enclose your draught of programme, if not suitable just make any alterations you think will be suitable and I will amend to it. Are you having no band at banquet in the afternoon? As a rule there is always a band playing during dinner, and also to the toast list. If you think of having one I will be pleased to play a selection of music during the dinner, and we could do it very reasonable. For playing selections it would be a great improvement to have a double bass. I only mention this as I have supplied music for a great many banquets of the same as your are having, and they always have music. I went to see Mr Innes yesterday morning, but did not see him. I tried the piano and found it down in pitch and slightly out of tune. I told the boy to let Mr Innes know to get it tuned, and put up to pitch So as to make the music as brilliant as possible.

Yours faithfully, D. G. Maule, Provost Wynd, Cupar. (FEP)

9 May 1904

Town Council

At a meeting of the Council, Provost Miller presiding, it was resolved, by a majority of one, to present Lord Ninian with the freedom of the burgh on his coming of age, which takes place on 16th inst. This was agreed to, on the understanding that no expense will be incurred by the Common Good or the ratepayers. (DC)

9 May 1904

Wine for the dinner

Dear Mr Gavin,

We write to advise you that we are sending off today, by goods train, some cases of wine, five in number, for the entertainments on Monday the 16th inst. We understand that Messrs J. & F. Anderson have arranged with you to take charge of the cases, until you hand them over to our cellar-men on Monday morning. They will travel to Falkland by the 7.35 a.m. train from Edinburgh. Please therefore have the cases carted from the station to the place they have to lie till Monday.

Yours faithfully, Mr Cockburn Campbell, 32, St Andrews Square, Edinburgh. (FEP)

12 May 1904

Drink for the rejoicing

Dear Sir,

Your kind note to hand. The whisky will be ready on Friday morning. There are a few small things for Mrs Johnston I am taking the liberty to send along with the whisky. Could I trouble you to take charge of same till Mrs Johnston comes. Trust the whisky will give satisfaction.

Yours faithfully, A. B. Keddie, 13 Bonnygate, Cupar. (FEP)

12 May 1904

Piano for band

Dear Mr Gavin,

I have your note of hand of the 9th inst. I have seen Mr Innes and arranged about the lending of a piano. Mr Innes is to send on the programmes as soon as they are printed. I have to meet the rest of the band at Ladybank at 5 p.m. If you have conveyance at that train we will be in Falkland about 6 p.m. Trusting it will be grand weather.

Yours faithfully, D. G. Maule. (FEP)

13 May 1904
Food for the rejoicing
Letter to George Gavin
Dear Sir,

In reply to yours of the 10th. I beg to thank you for the guaranteed numbers. I expect to be in Falkland tomorrow about 3 o'clock, would you readily arrange to have the kitchen fire lit for me. I feel sure before coming that everything will be perfectly arranged, look forward to seeing you tomorrow. With best regards to Mrs Gavin.

Yours faithfully, Isabel Johnston, Argyll House, St Andrews. (FEP)

13 May 1904
Photographs
Dear Mr Gavin,

I will leave here (St Andrews) on Monday on one o'clock train arriving at Falkland Road Station at 2.15 p.m. I should be glad if you will meet me there with trap, if quite convenient for you, so that I may be in time to receive your instructions from the Marchioness of Bute. I hope the day will be fine for the photographs and also for the rejoicings tomorrow of Lord Ninian Crichton-Stuart.

Yours faithfully, George B. Rodger. (FEP)

15 May 1904
Coming of age
Dear Mr Gavin,

I am sorry that I will not be able to be at the dinner at the Palace tomorrow to show my respects to Lord Ninian Crichton-Stuart on his coming of age.

Yours faithfully, ex Provost Page. (FEP)

16 May 1904

Coming of age celebrations

Today the town of Falkland is *en fête* consequent on the coming of age of Lord Ninian Crichton-Stuart, second son of the late Marquis of Bute. The weather is charming and the House of Falkland gay with bunting. A series of interesting presentations took place, the first of which was at noon, when a deputation from the tenants presented his lordship at the House of Falkland with an illuminate address containing congratulations on the attainment of his majority and on entering into possession of the Falkland Estate. The address proceeded:

"The historic traditions of the estate, apart from its extent and natural beauty, render it doubly precious to a son of the most noble Marquis of Bute, of revered memory, and the high office now conferred upon you of hereditary keeper of the royal and ancient Palace of Falkland will, we feel sure, be most worthily fulfilled, in view of your late father's services to the nation."

13. Lord Ninian Crichton-Stuart aged 21

Following this came the presentation of a silver cigarette box from the estate employees, and thereafter the freedom of the royal burgh of Falkland was conferred upon his lordship. On his entering Falkland Palace, the children from Lady Bute's Private School presented his lordship with a basket of flowers. Within the Palace grounds Lord Ninian entertained the tenants and tradesmen to dinner. (EEN)

16 May 1904

Interesting presentations

A series of interesting functions took place to-day on the occasion of the coming of age of Lord Ninian Crichton-Stuart, second son of the late Marquis of Bute. At twelve o'clock his Lordship was presented at Falkland House by a deputation representing the tenantry with an address setting forth that the historical traditions of the estate, apart from the extent and natural beauty, rendered it doubly precious to a son of the most noble Marquis of Bute. Thereafter his Lordship was presented by the estate employees with a silver cigarette box. This ceremony was followed by the presentation of the freedom of the burgh. At one o'clock Lord Ninian entertained the tenantry at dinner at Falkland Palace. Lord Ninian presided over a company numbering about 150. The rejoicings were carried out in beautiful weather. (DET)

16 May 1904

Fire

The Fire Brigade was summoned on Saturday afternoon. The cause of the alarm was the burning of a rick of straw adjacent to one of Mr Jackson's works. When the engine arrived the straw was consumed. The factory escaped damage. (DC)

17 May 1904

Coming of age

Lord Ninian Crichton-Stuart, second son of the late Marquis of Bute coming of age was celebrated at Falkland yesterday. Speaking at a dinner, Lord Ninian said that at present he was at Oxford working for an army examination, and with luck and some hard work he hoped by November to be a member of his majesty's forces. It would be an honour to him to be that, because he would be the first of his family to be a member of the forces of the Empire, and because he would be able after he came back to Fife, to take even more interest than at present in the Volunteers and the Yeomanry. (EEN)

16 May 1904

Dinner invitations

Letter to A. F. MacDonald, Solicitor, Elgin

Dear Sir,

I am favoured with your letter of the 4th inst. and have pleasure in enclosing herewith invitation cards issued for the dinners on the occasion of the coming of age of Lord Ninian Crichton-Stuart. The large card was issued to the tenantry, the small one being sent out to the estate workmen.

The dinner to the tenantry (among whom, I may say were included the principal tradesmen) was held at one o'clock, at which Lord Ninian personally presided. The toast list was as you will observe a very short one, it was made so in order that the proceedings might not be unduly protracted.

The dinner to the estate workmen was held in the evening at which I occupied the chair. The invitation to the tenantry dinner did not extend to wives and daughters, but a dance was given to certain of the tenant's and workmen's wives and daughters after the workmen's dinner in the evening.

Yours faithfully, George Gavin. (FEP)

2 June 1904

Falkland Police Station

Dear Mr Gavin,

Referring to recent conference at Falkland in regards to Police Station, my committee are not in favour of continuing the present Police Station, but would very much prefer to acquire the site which was looked at on the south side of the Main Street and opposite the Palace. I shall be glad to know whether the proprietor of that site is willing to sell and if so on what terms. I hope you may be able to let me know before the 14th curt. To save time I send a copy of the letter to Messrs J. & F. Anderson.

Yours faithfully, W. Patrick, County Clerk. (FEP)

8 June 1904

Victim of Lomond Hill tragedy

The intelligence which reached Perth last night that the unfortunate victim of the Lomond tragedy was none other than William Alexander Glass, son of Mr Glass, chemist, Perth, caused a feeling of profound sorrow in the Fair City.

As was reported in the Courier on Monday, the dead body of a respectably dressed young man was found lying on the East Lomond Hill by a paper worker hailing from Leslie. In the near vicinity of the corpse a small phial labelled poison was also discovered, and the natural surmise was that the unfortunate lad had succumbed to carbolic poisoning.

Mr Glass, the father of the deceased, it is understood, had perused the paragraph in Monday's paper, but at the time he had no idea that the contents had such a close relation to his own family. Yesterday, however, he learned that his son had left Edinburgh, where he was employed as a chemist's assistant, on a week-end trip, and had not reappeared at his customary duties at the commencement of the week. Mr Glass became perturbed, and on noticing that the body found on the Lomond Hills had not been identified, a strong presentiment came over him that the deceased might be his son William. Proceeding to Falkland yesterday he found that his surmise was only too true.

Deceased was quite a young man, being only in his twenty-second year. It is thought that he had been studying for an examination, and that his mind had in consequence become unhinged. The news of his sad end came as a very severe blow to his relatives, who are widely known and highly respected in Perth. (DC)

13 June 1904

St Andrew's House

Dear Mr Gavin,

It has perhaps already been informally brought within your notice that a committee of the Town Council visited on Saturday afternoon the house in High Street, known as St. Andrews House, and now the property of the Lady Margaret Crichton-Stuart, where the causeway blocks have recently been uplifted. The committee considered that the Burgh rights had thereby been infringed, no doubt thoughtlessly, as they have the street right up to the wall of the house, but would be willing if the causeway is replaced to allow a layer of earth to be put

14. St Andrew's House in 2020
The "causeway" now used for car parking.

on the top to a depth of five or six inches, in which flowers could be grown if desired, and provided the edging were put on the straight, but this always at the pleasure of the Town Council. The party in charge of the house made reference to the cripple child's[1] love of flowers as being the reason for the wish to lay out the flower beds on the street, but I am sure if the subject should come within the review of the Lady Margaret, Her Ladyship will recognise that although the foundation of my own house occupied by Mrs Campbell, against the wall of which a rockery has been placed might be materially affected by dampness. I would indeed personally be one of the last to prevent the alleviation of the pain of suffering. If you think it necessary you can communicate the contents of this letter to Her Ladyship.

Yours faithfully, Charles Gulland. (FEP)

---

[1] The "cripple child" was George Quilter, son of Gertrude Quilter, matron of St Andrew's Home. Mrs Quilter received £3 15s she had paid for bath chair for her son, in accordance with Lord Ninian's instructions.

14 June 1904
Causeway at St Andrew's House
Letter to Mr Charles Gulland

Dear Sir,

I am favoured with your letter of yesterday with reference to the uplifting of the causeway in front of St. Andrew's House. I regret that the Burgh rights had in consequence been infringed, and I have today arranged for the blocks being replaced to the satisfaction of your committee.

Yours faithfully, George Gavin. (FEP)

14 June 1904
Golf Club

Dear Mr Pitman,

I have your letter of yesterday. The secretary and treasurer of the Golf Club is Mr George Robertson, West Port. The entry money is 10s.6d. and annual subscription 10s.6d.

Yours faithfully, George Gavin. (FEP)

18 June 1904
Annual market and games

High holiday was observed in the ancient and Royal Burgh of Falkland yesterday, the occasion being the annual market and the games. The market has long ceased to be numbered with the things of the past, but the games have continued through many centuries, and yesterday, in fine weather, a goodly gathering of townsfolk and visitors witnessed a fine programme of dancing and athletic events at the Myre, which lies within the shadow of the historic Palace of Falkland. Lochgelly Temperance Band was engaged for the day, and their labours began at noon, when they led the games procession through the principal streets of the town. The band, in addition to playing selections at internals, provided the music for the dancing competitions, and in the evening for the tripping of the light fantastic. The dancing at the Myre is quite a feature of the market, and last night it was heartily engaged in by quite a large assemblage of lads and lasses. At the sports the entries, particularly in the step dancing, were larger than usual, and competition was fairly keen. (DC)

4 August 1904

Burying Ground

Letter to J. & F. Anderson, Edinburgh

Dear Sirs,

I had a call the other day from the Rev. Mr Johnston, the Parish Minister, and Mr Alex Bonthrone, one of the heritors. They explained that there had been a complaint as to the untidy condition of the Burying Ground, situated you will recollect, on the south side of the main road in the town leading to the approach gates, and that the minister, who explained that the grass was high, proposed to have it cut, they further explained however that the tenant of the property on the west side of the entrance gate to the Burying Ground, belonging to Falkland Estate and tenanted by Mrs George Ramsay, had a hole in the garden wall through which a large number of hens kept by her passed into the Burying Ground, and they wished this hole shut up. They further, I gathered, wished a gate which leads from the inside of the Burying Ground entrance to the garden of the property shut or secured.

Yours faithfully, George Gavin. (FEP)

17 August 1904

Butcher shop

Dear Mr Gavin,

As I have mentioned to you on previous occasions I am anxious to have built for myself a new shop and house, I would be glad to know if Lord Ninian Crichton-Stuart would be willing to erect suitable premises on the vacant site opposite the Palace if a rent acceptable to him were given.

Yours faithfully, Christopher Brunton. (FEP)

18 August 1904

Butcher shop

Dear Mr Gavin,

I have your letter enclosing a letter from Mr C. Brunton, butcher, Falkland. There is no legal difficulty which would present Lord Ninian from building on the vacant site opposite the Palace if he cared to do so. However I feel sure that Lord Ninian would never agree to

15. C. C. Brunton with his horse and cart

put up a butcher shop in such a conspicuous place. It would quite spoil the look of the old street opposite the Palace. It is not worth while troubling Lord Ninian in the matter and Mr Brunton shall just be informed that his proposal cannot be agreed to. [1]

J. Pitman, Edinburgh. (FEP)

20 August 1904

Gamekeeper assaulted

Andrew Morgan, forester, Annfield[2] was charged at Cupar Sheriff Court on Thursday with having on 22nd July assaulted Joseph McKay, gamekeeper, Chancefield, by seizing him by the breast and by the throat, compressing his throat, throwing him to the ground and striking him several severe blows on the body. Accused pleaded guilty, remarking that he had received provocation from the gamekeeper, who, he said, had circulated rumours about him.

Sentence, £1 or ten days imprisonment. (FFP)

---

[1] The little shop next to the Bruce Hotel did become a butcher shop.

[2] Annfield was one of the cottages along the Kilgour Road past the Pillars of Hercules. Chancefield is a bit further up the Kilgour Road.

13 September 1904

Well-known Fife factor retires

It is understood that Mr Charles Gulland, factor on the Lathrisk Estates has intimated his retiral from the factorship. The news will be learned with regret by a wide circle, and especially in Central Fife, where for many years Mr Gulland, who has also acted as solicitor and bank agent in Falkland, has been a well-known figure. In a letter to the tenants intimating the termination of his connection with the estate, Mr Gulland says,

"The estate connection with my late father and with myself has been a very lengthy one, extending in my father's case as far back as about the year 1822. As factor I wish you farewell and in doing so have to thank you for the courtesy and kindness you have always shown to me." (DET)

16 September 1904

Electricity for House of Falkland

Dear Mr Gavin,

We have arranged with Mr Chancellor, the electrical engineer, to visit Falkland House and stables on Thursday next the 22nd, with a view to reporting to Lord Ninian the probable cost of putting in an electric light installation. Will you kindly show Mr Chancellor round the house and give him all the information he may require, and also discuss with him as to the best site for putting up oil or gas engine and dynamo. Mr Chancellor proposes to arrive at Falkland Road Station at 9.18 a.m. Please see that he is met.

Yours faithfully J. Anderson. (FEP)

20 September 1904

Electricity for House of Falkland

Dear Mr Gavin,

Thanks for your letter. When it was arranged that Mr Chancellor should report on the electric lighting of Falkland House, and that he should go over on Thursday I was unaware that Lady Bute would be in occupation of the mansion house. However I have written to Lady Bute explaining and no doubt she will be quite agreeable to Mr Chancellor going through all the rooms of the house.

16. The House of Falkland
Showing the formal gardens

I had forgotten that a Glasgow and London firm had given a similar report and estimate some years ago for the late Lord Bute, but as we intended now to take competing estimates, the figures given by the firm you refer to will be of great assistance (Messrs Paterson & Cooper, Kirkcaldy).

Kindly send me the specifications. You need not mention this to Mr Chancellor. With regard to the use of water power, we thought that it would be advisable to leave that alone, seeing that there had been difficulty about the water supply. I therefore suggested to Mr Chancellor the use of a gas or oil engine. Of course before putting the estimate before Lord Ninian I intended asking Mr Carfrae what he thought about the use of water power to drive the dynamo.

Yours faithfully J. Pitman, 48 Castle St. Edinburgh. (FEP)

24 September 1904
Property sales
For sale by public roup within the Bruce Arms, Hotel, Falkland, on Wednesday 5th October 1904 at one o'clock afternoon. The following subjects belonging to Mr Alex. Page, Spirit Merchant.

1. That property, situated in Back Wynd, consisting of two tenements of two storey dwelling houses, stone built and slated, with large walled-in garden. Rental £19 5s. Upset Price £220.
2. That property, situated at Balmblae, consisting of a two storey dwelling house and weaver's shop, stone built, part tiled and slated, with garden ground. Rental (when occupied) £6 5s. Feu-duty Nominal. Upset Price £35.
3. That four acres, Scots Measure,[1] of Arable Land fronting the road from Kirkcaldy to Falkland. Rental £12. Upset Price £200.

For further particulars, apply to Messrs Gibson & Spears, Solicitors, Kirkcaldy, who have the titles and articles of roup. (FFP)

25 October 1904

Post Office

Letter to George Gavin

Dear Sir,

Your note to hand today about shop in Post Office. Seeing you are to repair floor in back shop and white wash the roofs, also that the coal bunker is all right. I am quite satisfied to the agreement as stated.

Yours faithfully, George Hardie, Pleasance. (FEP)

25 October 1904

Turning mill

Letter to J. & F. Anderson, Edinburgh

Dear Sirs,

Last week Mr D. Galloway called to say that suddenly and without any indication of any kind the shaft of the water wheel has broken asunder causing of course a total stoppage of the work.

Being confined to the house I was unable to go and examine it, but I had a telegram at once sent to Mr Melville, engineer, Kirkcaldy to come and review the danger. I told Mr Galloway that I was not aware whether the cost of this work, which will be a good few pounds, fell on him or upon the proprietors.

Yours faithfully, George Gavin. (FEP)

---

[1] A Scots acre was about half a hectare, or 1.3 English (Imperial) acres.

7 November 1904

Bruce Arms Hotel

Dear Mr Gavin,

We have received the lease of the above subjects, in favour of Mrs Hardie. We note the conversation which you have had with Mrs Swanson and are prepared to allow the matter to lie over until 15th approx, by which time she should be able to say definitely whether she wishes to leave at Whitsunday 1905.

Yours Faithfully, J. Anderson (FEP)

15 November 1904

Fatal accident

Robert Mill, factory worker, fell down the stair of his dwelling-house on Saturday night and received injuries on the head, from the effects of which he died early yesterday morning. (DC)

24 November 1904

Bruce Arms urinal

Dear Mr Gavin,

At a meeting of the Town Council held on the evening of Tuesday last, this Council had under consideration the report of the Burgh Sanitary Inspector regarding the unsanitary condition of the urinal at the back of the Bruce Arms, Hotel. The inspector condemned this urinal as a public nuisance, and the Council decided that its removal should be instructed forthwith.[1] Kindly give this matter your immediate attention.

Yours Faithfully, Charles Gulland, Bank Building, Falkland. (FEP)

29 November 1904

Bruce Arms Hotel

Letter from Anderson, Castle St. Edinburgh.

Dear Mr Gavin,

I note that Mrs Hardie, the tenant is dead. I enclose the lease for

---

[1] Payment to William Page, builder, for demolishing outside urinal by order of Burgh Sanitary Authorities. 15s.8d.

your inspection, you will see that the tenancy is from year to year terminable on six months notice prior to any term of Whitsunday. The lease is to Mrs Hardie and her heirs. It will be impossible therefore to bring the lease to a close before Whitsunday 1906. I think however you should take the first opportunity of informing Mrs Hardie's representatives that Lord Ninian intends to give them notice to terminate the lease at Whitsunday 1906, but if they wish to give up the place next Whitsunday Lord Ninian will be willing to take it off their hands. It is possible that they may wish to give it up when they know that there is no chance of them being allowed to remain on after 1906. Clause "Third" gives certain powers for immediately terminating the lease in the events mentioned, but I suppose these events are not likely to take place.

Yours Faithfully, J. Anderson.(EP)

10 December 1904
Bruce Arms Hotel
Dear Sir,

We regret to learn that there is a chance of the license, being withdrawn. It is provided in the lease that in the event of forfeiture, withdrawal or refusal of the license, the proprietor may immediately bring the lease to a termination, and enter into possession of the premises without any process of law or proceedings of any kind other than a letter addressed and delivered or posted to the tenant at the premises let.

Yours Faithfully, J. Anderson. (FEP)

20 December 1904
Streets
Letter from Melville & Lindsay, 110, George St. Edinburgh
Dear Mr Gavin

We enclose notice sent out by the Town Clerk of Falkland relative to the register of streets which is being prepared. From this we gather that it is proposed to fix the width of the streets. Can you please tell us what is proposed will in any injurious way affect Lady Margaret's property of St. Andrew's House. You will probably have received similar notices for other properties. Will you kindly examine the plans in Mr Gulland's office and let us hear if any protest is required. We enclose copy of description from the titles. We understand that the house stands back from the street and that the ground in front of it is not enclosed, but notwithstanding this the ground in front, or part of it may really belong to Lady Margaret, and if this be so the plan in Mr Gulland's office should, if it is not so already be got marks to show that the ground in front does belong to Lady Margaret.

Yours Faithfully, Melville & Lindsay. (FEP)

28 December 1904

New factor

Mr George Gavin, Falkland Estate Office, Falkland Palace, has been appointed principal factor on the Falkland estates. Mr Gavin has since the death of Major Wood, nearly three years ago, acted as resident factor on the estate. After a preliminary period in the Sheriff clerk's office, Aberdeen, Mr Gavin received his early training in estate management in the estate office of the Earl of Wharncliffe at Newtyle, in Strathmore, under the then factor, Mr Andrew Whitton of Couston, and latterly under Mr J. W. Barty, Dunblane, who succeeded to the factorship. After having experience in the management of large landed estates in West Perthshire and Stirlingshire, he received the local management of the Moncreiffe and Trinity-Gask estates in Perthshire, belonging to Sir Robert Moncreiffe, Bart. Subsequently he received his appointment to the Falkland Estate. (DC)

30 December 1904

Death of octogenarian

Mr Robert Sharpe died at his residence, West Port, a little before one o'clock yesterday, in the 88th year of his age. He has been very frail for some time, but was always able to move about a little, and it was only about mid-day that he began to feel not well. Medical aid was summoned, but the end came almost immediately. Deceased acted as correspondent to the *People's Journal* for a great number of years, and when it happened in that quiet village that there was no item of news for the weekly column, he used to feel it very much. Robert leaves a son, the Rev. J. Sharpe, Heatherlie, Selkirk, and two daughters to mourn his loss. Mrs Sharpe died in June of the present year. (DET)

1905

7 January 1905

Concert

It is rarely the good fortune of a country audience to be treated to a concert such was given here on Thursday last. A varied programme of instrumental and vocal music was sustained throughout, with an ability and goodwill on the part of all the artistes which not only reflects the highest credit on everyone of them, but places the good folks of Falkland under a debt of thanks, which is given with one consent and without stint. Mr Charles Jackson, jun., Lomondvale, occupied the chair with much acceptance. (FFP)

23 January 1905

Lease of Bruce Arms Hotel

Dear Sir,

We have received your letter of 20th inst, enclosing the lease of the Bruce Arms, Hotel in favour of the late Mrs Hardie, and we note that Mr Gulland, acting on behalf of Mrs Swanson, has intimated that his client is willing to resolve the lease as at 28th May next on certain conditions, and that after consultation with Lord Ninian you have agreed to the renunciation being accepted on the terms proposed. We think it is desirable that all conditions relating to the arrangement for the termination of the lease should be embodied in the renunciation. And we shall be obliged if you will favour us with full particulars. We shall be glad to know whether Mrs Swanson is the sole surviving child of the late Mrs Hardie, or is sole executrix and representative

17. The Bruce Arms
With the Town Hall clock in the background

under a will by the deceased. Kindly also say in whose name the licence is at present, whether in Mrs Swanson's, her husband's or joint names.

Yours faithfully, J. & F. Anderson. (FEP)

25 January 1905

Bruce Arms Hotel

Letter from J. & F. Anderson

Dear Mr Gavin,

We have prepared and now send for approval draft remuneration of lease of the subjects, which we think should be granted by Mrs Swanson. You will observe that we have taken the proprietor bound to pay the sum of £45 in respect of goodwill, and also to take over the fitting at valuation. It will, therefore, fall upon the proprietor to make his own arrangements as to these with the incoming tenant, and by doing so, he will be in a position, in the event of the way-going tenants being found insolvent, to place the half year's rent against any sum which may be found to be due by him. We would also draw your attention to the special clause, which, looking to the substantial price paid to the retiring tenants in respect of goodwill, we have thought it desirable to introduce, in order to prevent them entering into competition with their successors in the premises. As the bargain with Mr Gulland is now completed, we think you may advertise the premises. We presume you will, in the event of a new tenant not being obtained prior to the date when the applications for licences must be lodged, see that the necessary steps are taken to ensure that the license will not be allowed to drop.

Yours faithfully, J. & F. Anderson. (FEP)

28 January 1905

Proposed light railway

A meeting of gentlemen interested in the construction of a light railway between Falkland Road Station on the main line of the North British Railway and the Royal burgh of Falkland, was held in the Public School, Falkland, on Saturday (26th).

Among those present were: Mr Alexander Lawson of Annfield;[1] Mr Alexander Bonthrone, Newton of Falkland; Mr J. L. Lumsden, Eden Valley House, Freuchie; Messrs Jackson, manufacturers, Falkland; Major Cusin, Falkland; Mr James Carr, factor for Mr Makgill Crichton of Lathrisk; Mr George Gavin, factor for Lord Ninian Crichton-Stuart of Falkland; Mr George Dun, Woodmill; Mr David Bonthrone, Newton of Falkland; Mr Thomas Aitken MICE, Cupar; Mr W. D. Patrick, county clerk, Cupar; Mr J. L. Anderson, town clerk, Cupar; Mr John Sheriff, Falkland etc.

On the motion of Mr Bonthrone, Mr Lawson of Burnturk was called to the chair. Mr Lawson explained that the Sub-Committee of the Cupar District Committee appointed to consider the matter had obtained a report from Mr Aitken CE, the road surveyor, upon the subject, which the County Clerk read to the meeting, and from which it appeared that the cost of constructing the railway three and a half miles long would be about £10,500 exclusive of the land. Mr Lawson

---

[1] This is Alexander Lawson of Annfield and Burnturk (near Kings Kettle) not to be confused with Annfield Farm near Falkland.

proceeded to state that the local people could not expect the County Council to take the initiative and to promote the scheme. At the same time the Act permitted the County Council to advance money to any light railway company, and the question of making the advance, if necessary in the present case, would be duly considered at the time. Mr David Bonthrone, Newton of Falkland, submitted a report dealing with the amount of traffic likely to pass over the line, which was computed to be 19,089 tons per annum, and passenger traffic 27,000 per annum. The figures have been carefully compiled from information supplied by the manufacturers, farmers, and other traders in the district.

The Chairman then called upon Mr J. L. Anderson, town clerk, Cupar, who, along with Mr Bonthrone and others, had taken an interest in this question for some time, to explain the procedure to be followed in getting the necessary Order empowering the promoters to construct the line. Mr Anderson proceeded to explain the provisions of the Light Railway Act 1896, and stated that assuming that none of the local authorities through whose districts the railway passed would act as petitioners for the Order, it would be necessary, and, indeed, was the usual practice for a company to be incorporated to instruct the line. Powers might then be taken in the order allowing the County Council or District Committee and also the Town Council of Falkland to make such loans to the light railway company or to take such portion of the stock of the company, as might be mutually arranged. Mr Anderson explained the conditions requiring to be fulfilled before a loan could be obtained from the Treasury, and also explained the procedure which had been adopted in the case of the Lauder Light Railway Company and other similar companies in Scotland. After a general discussion, it was decided that a local Committee be formed to make all the investigations and arrangements necessary in the preliminary stages of the proposal.

The following gentlemen were appointed members of Committee: Mr J. L. Lumsden, Freuchie; Mr A. Bonthrone, Newton of Falkland; Mr Charles Jackson, Falkland; Provost Miller, Falkland; Mr Dun, Woodmill; Mr Gavin, Falkland; Mr Lawson, Burnturk; Mr Makgill Crichton, Lathrisk; Mr Curr, Largo; Mr J. W. Jackson, Falkland. Mr John Sheriff, Falkland was appointed Secretary of the Committee, and Mr Charles Jackson, Convenor. (FN)

3 February 1905

Bruce Arms Hotel

These well-known and old established licensed premises known as the Bruce Arms, Hotel, together with stabling and large garden are, owing to the death of the tenant, to be let, with entry at 29th May 1905. The hotel occupies one the best sites in the Royal Burgh of Falkland, and is in close proximity to the Palace of Falkland. For further particulars apply to George Gavin, Factor, Estate Office, Falkland Palace, who will receive offers till 25th February 1905. (DC)

18 February 1905

Public House for sale

The premises presently occupied by, and belonging to Alexander Page, and the goodwill of the business. For further particulars apply to Messrs Gibson & Spears, who will receive offers up to 22nd February. (FFP)

18 February 1905

New joint-stock company

Last week the following new Joint-Stock Company was registered: Charles Jackson & Sons (Limited), Pleasance Works, Falkland, capital £45,000, in £10 shares, which the public are not asked to subscribe for; to acquire and carry on the business of linen manufacturers carried on by Charles Jackson & Sons, and the floorcloth manufacturing business carried on by Mr Jackson under name of the Falkland Floorcloth Company. Signatories: Charles Jackson, John W. Jackson, and Charles Jackson jnr., linen manufacturers; James Jackson, floorcloth manufacturer; William Jackson, civil engineer; and Mrs Euphemia Jackson, Lomondvale, Falkland; and Thomas Jackson, commercial traveller, 52 Glebe Park, Kirkcaldy. (FN)

23 February 1905

Bruce Arms

Letter to Mr John Page

Dear Sir,

    I regret that I missed seeing you when here. I duly received your

18. The floorcloth and linoleum factory (St John's Works)
Date unknown: probably post 1933.

letter of the 15th inst. and also received Mr Mason's offer. I am to see him with reference to it in Perth on Saturday with regards to your own letter in which you mention that should he be the successful party you would become security for the rent. Perhaps you would kindly as a matter of business either give me a reference to your banker or get him to write me a letter in order to keep matters in form.

Yours truly, George Gavin. (FEP)

25 March 1905

Fire

Fire broke out in a shed at Dovecot Farm, tenanted by Mr William Duncan, on Tuesday evening, but happily the flames were extinguished before any serious damage was done. (FN)

25 March 1905

Lord Ninian and his Durham estates

Lord Ninian Stuart, brother of the Marquess of Bute, who attained his majority last year, and came into possession of his Durham county

estates, has visited Tantobie, Dipton, and Burnopfield this week. Accompanied by his agent, Mr Armstrong of Newcastle, he inspected
the three acres of land purchased from him by the Tanfield Urban
Council, for conversion into allotment gardens for working men.
Lord Ninian expressed satisfaction with the action of the Council, and
stated that he would afford every encouragement to miners to culti-
vate their gardens. Proceeding from Tanfield to Burnopfield, the
party passed Bryan's Leap, a beautiful dene bordering each side of
the new road, and his Lordship encouraged the hope that he will
favourably consider a proposal that he should give the dene to the
public as a park and recreation ground. (YP)

25 March 1905
Accident
While James Heatherwick was unloading a cart at the Floorcloth
Works on Tuesday, a slight hitch occurred, and the cart shafts came
down heavily upon his leg. Dr Jack, who was summoned, found that
the leg was broken above the knee. (FN)

3 April 1905
Bruce Arms wallpaper
Letter to Hayes & Finch[1]
Dear Sirs,
   I regret that I was unable to call upon you on Saturday as to the
wall paper for the Bruce Arms, Inn. I have no doubt, however that
you will have made up your mind as to suitable patterns and if you
will kindly return the pattern book I shall order the papers.
   Yours faithfully, George Gavin. (FEP)

4 April 1905.
William Page
Early in April 1905 the death occurred of ex-Provost William Page at

---

[1] Hayes & Finch still exist, and are one of the world's finest manufacturers
and suppliers of church furnishing.

his residence, The Terrace[1], Falkland, in his 75th year. The late Mr Page retired from the civic chair of Falkland in November 1903, after 24 years of public service. (FN)

11 April 1905

Old chest

Dear Mr Gavin,

When Lord Ninian visited Duraway[2] Estates the other day he arranged with Mr Armstrong that a certain old iron chest belonging to his ancestor Lady Windsor, and an old oak table, should be sent to Falkland. Mr Armstrong is to despatch these to Falkland Road Station, sending you a letter of advice. When they arrive will you please have them placed in Falkland Palace.

Yours faithfully, J. Anderson, Castle St. Edinburgh. (FEP)

15 April 1905

Funeral of Ex-Provost Page

The funeral of ex-Provost Page took place to Falkland Cemetery on Friday 11th. Prior to the removal of the remains, service was conducted by the Rev. A. Lyon Johnston, parish minister.

The pall-bearers were: Messrs William Page, James Page, Thomas Page, and George Page (sons); Mr James Philp, Markinch (son-in-law); Mr Peter Kinnear, Letham, Forfar (brother-in-law); Mr James Clark, Brechin (brother-in-law); and Mr Alexander Page, Falkland (nephew).

Among those who attended the funeral were: Mr Charles Gulland; Mr Alexander Bonthrone, Newton of Falkland; Mr George Dun, Woodmill; Mr James Tod, Easter Cash; Mr John Sheriff; Mr George Gavin, factor; Mr Charles Jackson; Mr James Jackson, Jnr; Mr Charles Henderson, Balbirnie Gardens; Provost Millar;[3] Mr Lawrence Reid; Mr George Angus, Commercial Hotel; Mr George Morgan, Nochnarie; Mr David Reid; Mr Walter Forsyth; Mr David Bryce; Mr

---

[1] Also, and now usually, called Royal Terrace.

[2] Apparently a typo for Durham; see page 113.

[3] The Provost's name was certainly "Miller", but the spelling "Millar" occurs in several sources.

Thomas Williamson, saddler; the Rev. Morrison; Bailie Lornie; ex-Bailie Sutherland;[1] Mr Davidson, British Linen Bank. (FN)

19 April 1905

Licensing Court

Andrew Ramsay, 3 Viewlands Terrace, Milnathort, applied for a transfer of the public house certificate in Falkland at present held by Alexander Page.

On the motion of Provost Millar the license was granted, on the understanding that a back door would be closed.

19. Provost William Page
Proudly wearing the Provost's Chain of Office with the arms of Falkland.

An application by William Mason, waiter, Henderson's Buildings, High Street, Perth, for a transfer of the certificate for Bruce Arms, Hotel, at present in the name of Mrs Swanson, was unanimously granted. (DC)

20 April 1905

Bruce Arms Inn

Dear Lord Ninian,

The licensing board took place in Cupar on Tuesday last, and I am glad to say that the transfer of licence was granted to the new tenant.

Your Lordship will observe under the heading of licensing courts in this weeks *Fife Herald* what took place at the court. There is no doubt that the hotel, has unfortunately been allowed to fall into a state, not only of dirt, but of disrepair, and this seemed to be known to a few of the Justices. I had however prior to the court in Cupar seen a number of the Justices and explained to them personally what your Lordship means to do for the improvement of the place.

Your Lordship will observe, that in the end the licence was granted,

---

[1] Thomas Sutherland was still Bailie at this time, and for several more years.

under the proviso that the repairs are carried out to the satisfaction of the Chief Constable and Provost Millar. Licensing Judges nowadays are prone to take advantage of a chance to have licences abolished, that one cannot be too careful in handling a matter of this kind.

Your obedient servant, George Gavin. (FEP)

22 April 1905
New licence

Much interest was evinced locally at the application for a new licence and transfers of licences in the burgh. An application for transfer of licence made by Mr Wm. Mason, waiter, Perth, new tenant of Bruce Arms, Hotel, was unanimously granted. It was stated that the premises were to be considerably altered and improved by the landlord Lord Ninian Crichton-Stuart. A sum of at least £200 was to be spent on the premises. It was remitted to the Chief Constable and Provost Millar to see that the plans were carried out. While an application by Mr Robert Ness for a new licence was unanimously refused. The public-house licence formerly held by Wm. Page has been granted to A. Ramsay, Milnathort, on the understanding that the back entrance should be closed. (FN)

22 April 1905
Reason for refusal of licence

Robert Ness, coach-hirer, Liquorstane, applied for a new certificate for the licence for premises belonging to Mrs Catherine Ness. The Chief Constable repeated that in his opinion there was no necessity for the licence in the burgh. There was a licence to each 116 inhabitants. Mr T. W. Davidson, solicitor, who appeared for the applicant, submitted a petition signed by about a hundred male householders in Falkland in support of the application. Provost Edwards, Newburgh, and Provost Millar, Falkland, both opposed the application on the ground that there were sufficient licences in the district already, The license was unanimously refused. (FFP)

25 April 1905
Bruce Arms Inn

Dear Mr Gavin,

We have now prepared and sent herewith draft lease in favour of William Mason, the new tenant of the above premises. No notice is specified in your notes with regard to the mutual break, but we have stipulated for six months notice. Kindly say if this is satisfactory. Only one dresser is mentioned in your notes. We have included among the articles to be taken over by the tenant at entry two large dressers, which in accordance with the bargain with Mr Gulland as expressed in the remuneration of the present lease. Probably, however, the arrangement has been altered since the remuneration was signed.

J. Anderson, 48, Castle St. Edinburgh. (FE P)

26 April 1905

Falkland House and shootings

To Let.

The mansion House of Falkland with Policies, Garden, Offices, to let from Whitsunday next. [1] The House which is beautifully situated at the foot of the Lomond Hills is six miles from Ladybank Junction and three miles from Falkland Road Station, both on the main line of the N.B. Railway. It is fully furnished and contains three public rooms, two suits of rooms consisting respectively of sitting-room with bedroom and dressing room off. Billiard room, thirteen bedrooms and four dressing rooms, three bathrooms, kitchen and servants accommodation.

The Stable accommodation consists of sixteen stalls; two horse boxes; two coach houses; harness room; coachman's house (furnished) and grooms' rooms. The shootings extend over 6.000 acres; 360 being moor-land and the remainder excellent low ground and coverts, fully stocked with game.

For further particulars apply to George Gavin, factor, Falkland Palace. (FEP)

---

[1] The House of Falkland was let to Sir John Murray, the famous Scottish-Canadian oceanographer. Whit Sunday in 1905 was 11 June. The lease was extended to a second year.

28 April 1905

Bruce Arms Inn

Letter to William Mason, Victoria Hotel, Perth

Dear Sir,

I am favoured with both your letters of yesterday enclosing one from Mr Gulland, which I return. There is doubt Mrs Swanson is being put to some inconvenience but things are progressing so well that I think you will find that the bulk of the dirty work will be over by your entry. We have had to put new windows entirely into most of the upstairs back rooms. The masons have slapped out and built up the new large window in both rooms, also built in a new grate.

The walls had to be broken for new gas fittings, and restored by the plasterer portions of walls where lathed and plastered. All this will be finished very shortly and I think accordingly that you might wait and see how Mrs Swanson gets on with her arrangements. There will not be very much to do to the house in any case after you come in. I am paying Mrs Swanson for cleaning up after the men.

As I may not be able to see you for some days and as the principal copy of the lease had better be signed before 15th May, I send you the draft for your approval kindly send it on to Mr Page for his approval, also if you might let me have it back within a few days.

Yours faithfully George Gavin. (FEP)

29 April 1905

Cricket Club

The members of the Falkland Cricket Club have again been granted the use of a park within Falkland House grounds. The ground, although a trifle rough, has the making of a good pitch, and members have already had several practices in preparation for their opening match against Kirkcaldy 2nd XI tomorrow (Saturday) on the latter Club's ground. (FN)

13 May 1905

Presentation

On Wednesday of last week the employees of the Falkland Floorcloth Factory held a meeting in the Lomond Tavern for the purpose of presenting Mr Page with a handsome umbrella as a token of their esteem and respect. The female staff presented Mrs Page with a gold brooch of much beauty. An enjoyable evening was spent, Mr James McCall making the presentation. (FN)

17 May 1905
Falkland House
Falkland House and Shootings, the property of Lord Ninian Crichton-Stuart, has now been let for one year to Sir John Murray, of Challenger Expedition fame. (FH)

18 May 1905
Visitors to Palace
Dear Sir,

You are quite right in assuming that the palace is open daily to visitors. The admission for a party of the size indicated, will be the lowest charge: 3d per head.

A guide is kept for showing visitors over the Palace. Visitors sign his book and the amount of entry money is taken by him.

Yours faithfully, George Gavin. (FEP)

20 May 1905
The proposed light railway
As will be seen from our advertisement columns today, an application is intended to be made to the Light Railway Commissioners for an Order to incorporate a Company to construct and run a light railway connected with the N.B.R. line between Kettle, Freuchie and Falkland, there being five lines in all. The promoters are Messrs Charles Jackson, manufacturers, Lomondvale, Falkland; John Lawson, farmer, Falkland Wood; George Dun, Woodmill, Auchtermuchty; and Alexander Fraser, joiner, Falkland. The solicitors for the order are Messrs Robertson, Dempster and Co., Town and County Bank Buildings, Methven Street, Perth. (FN)

25 May 1905
The light railway
Letter to John Pitman WS Edinburgh.
Dear Sir,

I have this morning received a letter from Lord Ninian in reply to mine regarding the proposed Light Railway and opposition thereto. The following is what His Lordship says regarding the matter.

"The Light Railway business is causing me great annoyance, and the whole proceedings will have to be watched most carefully. I of course absolutely refuse to have anything what ever to do with it and shall obstruct it in anyway in my power. But care must be taken not to allow the Falkland and District population to think I am doing so against their interests."

Having in view what His Lordship says makes a little difficulty in knowing how to act. There is no doubt that, if the railway is to be an accomplished fact, and if there be no other organised opposition to the scheme, it would be impolite on Lord Ninian's part to oppose. However, there is yet plenty of time to study the whole phases of the matter, and I shall be glad to hear from you again, when you have discussed the matter with your brother.

Yours faithfully, George Gavin. (FEP)

26 May 1905
The light railway
Dear Lord Ninian,

I note what Your Lordship says regarding this most troublesome matter, which as Your Lordship says must be watched most carefully, as I find, that sometime will elapse before an enquiry is held, there is time to consider and to watch the development of events. I have come to think that, if others do not oppose, and if there be no organised active opposition to the scheme by others, it might be impolite on Your Lordship to oppose in case it maybe thought, that Your Lordship was doing so against the interests of the public at large.

Your obedient servant George Gavin. (FEP)

2 June 1905
Falkland Estate
To Let at Martinmas, 1905.

The desirable Houses at Fiddlehall, with 17½ acres of land, lying adjacent to the Burgh of Falkland, as presently occupied by Mr James Clark.

For further particulars apply to George Gavin, Factor, Falkland Palace. (DC)

17 June 1905
Cricket
On Saturday (10th), before a large number of spectators, Falkland Cricket Club met the members of Leven Y.M.C.A. under ideal weather conditions. The home team took the wicket first, and compiled 58 runs for 8 wickets. The visitors only managed to score 17 runs for 7 wickets, and as "time" was up the match was declared drawn. Special mention may be made of the batting of Messrs Bryce and Grieve for the home team, and also for the bowling of Mr T. S. Michie, to whom fell 5 wickets for 13 runs. (FN)

17 June 1905
The proposed light railway
At a meeting of the School Board held in the Public School on Friday evening (16th) – Mr Alexander Bonthrone presiding – plans were submitted in connection with the proposed light railway into Falkland showing the amount of ground belonging to the School which would be required for the proposed scheme, also the ground the promoters of the railway offer in lieu of what is taken. It was agreed, by 5 votes to 2, that the Board give an assent to the proposals. (FN)

23 June 1905
Bruce Arms Inn
Letter to Mr W. Mason
Dear Sir,
  I am assured with your letter of this date, informing your willingness to cede possession of the wine cellar, presently forming part of the subjects let to you, on your receiving a change of rent of £4 per annum. On behalf of the proprietor I agree to the arrangement and the cellar will hereafter form part of the butcher's premises.
  Yours faithfully, George Gavin. (FEP)

23 June 1905

Rent for butcher's shop

Letter to Mr Christopher Brunton, Butcher

Dear Sir,

I have received your letter of this date containing an offer of £8 10s of yearly rent for the Butcher's Shop, presently occupied by you, with the addition of the cellar behind, and as allowed and approved of, to sort your business on behalf of the proprietor I accept the offer and agree to your subletting the shop. [1]

Yours faithfully, George Gavin. (FEP)

1 July 1905

Golfing exhibition

On Thursday of last week, the members of Falkland Golf Club were treated to an exhibition of golf by the present amateur champion, Mr A. G. Barry, and his brother, Mr C. Barry. Play took the form of a four-some, the champion being partnered by Mr C. J. M. Makgill-Crichton of Lathrisk, and his brother by Mr D. McMillan. The latter couple had the best of matters throughout, and won the match by three holes. As the weather was bright, there was a large turn-out of members and friends. (FN)

4 July 1905

Telephone installation

Letter to Secretary of the General Post Office, Edinburgh

Dear Sir,

I duly received your letter of the 10th June last, with quotation of rentals for the installation of telephone at House of Falkland and Falkland Palace, which I at once communicated to the proprietor Lord Ninian. I have only today received his Lordship's instruction.

He is now prepared in accordance with the quotations given by you

---

[1] Payment to J. Paterson, Newton of Falkland, for mason work of Butcher Shop. £1 13s 3d. Payment to J. C. Rolland & Sons, Markinch, for painting pantry interior white enamel and outside wood work. £7 16s 7d. Payment to Walter Peggie, plasterer, for cement work, new cement floor under new arrangement of tenancy. £9 18s 4d.

at the £30 rental, with the message rate of course, in addition for an exchange circuit between Falkland Post Office and Falkland Palace with an extension to House of Falkland.

Yours faithfully, George Gavin. (FEP)

4 July 1905

Telephone

Letter to Sir John Murray

Dear Sir John

I have at last heard from Lord Ninian regarding various matters including telephones. I am glad His Lordship has agreed to go with the scheme and I am today writing to the secretary of the Post Office, asking him to send the engineer here on an early date, in order that we may fix the line of poles along the approach so that they may be concealed as far as possible. I have sent men today to attend to the fountains. (FEP)

8 July 1905

Telephone system

Arrangements are being made for introducing a system of telephones into Falkland Palace, with an extension to House of Falkland. The work, which is to be carried out by the Post Office authorities, will be under the supervision of their engineer, and operations will be commenced on an early date. (FN)

8 July 1905

New publication: *Guide to Falkland*

There has just been issued by Messrs J. & G. Innes, *Fife News*, Cupar, an Illustrated *Guide-Book to Falkland*[1] – the first of its kind for that

---

[1] The book contains on its title page a poem by Charles Gulland:

> *Falkland! A stronghold and a refuge prized*
> *By virtue of her guardian Lomond Hills,*
> *And doubly prized in easy times of peace*
> *For pleasantrie and glee and active sport.*

The second edition, undated but presumably published in 1915, contains a tribute to Lord Ninian on his death, with photograph.

historical burgh. The booklet, which is published at sixpence, gives with considerable detail, the story of Falkland's Royal Palace, and contains much interesting matter about the town and district. Among its illustrations, two of special note are quaint photos of the Palace and town, as they appeared about a hundred years ago. (FN)

8 July 1905

Cricket

Playing on the home pitch last Saturday (1st), the members of the local Cricket Club defeated the St Johnston XI from Perth. The visitors were all disposed of for 35, and with two wickets in hand, the home team had run up a score of 43. Messrs Dobson and Lawson each contributed 9 "not out", the former having to retire owing to a slight mishap. (FN)

11 July 1905

Bruce Arms alterations

Letter to David Stewart, 8 High St, Perth

Dear Sir,

I am favoured with your letter of yesterday enclosing sketch plan of proposed alterations at Bruce Arms, Hotel. I am afraid it will require some modification for the reason that access from the kitchen to front door can only be had by going through bar parlour. The tenant seems now to think that he would give up the idea of a bar parlour if this would permit, probably, of a bar longwise instead of across and would also probably allow for a passage to kitchen being more easily got.

Yours faithfully, George Gavin. (FEP)

15 July 1905

Sale of Work

A biennial Sale of Work in connection with the Parish Church Women's Guild was held in the Public School on Saturday (8th) at 2.00 p.m. The proceeds of the sale are to be applied towards defraying the cost of introducing a system of hot water pipes into the church, and on this account, exceptional interest and enthusiasm has, for a considerable time past, been evinced by the lady members of the congregation, as doubtless they fully realised that so much depended upon the fruit of their labours. The schoolroom, with its stalls laden with useful and ornamental work, presented a most striking appearance.

The opening ceremony was performed by the Rev. A. Lyon Johnston, minister of the parish, who, after a short prayer, said that he was greatly pleased to welcome such a large number of the congregation. He would not weary them with a long speech, and thought that, on such an occasion, the best advice he could give was contained in the old Scottish saying, "Fa' tae."

There were, in all, three stalls – The Guild Stall, the Congregational Stall, and the Produce Stall, over which presided their respective holders ably assisted by many willing helpers. The tea-room was a source of considerable income, and thanks were due to the contributors to this department.

A musical programme was tastefully carried through in the afternoon by the Misses Dun and Bryce and Mr Spence, organist. In the evening, the entertainment included a dramatic sketch, entitled "Boxing the Compass", which reflected great credit upon the performers – Misses Hood and Mr Bruce.

The winners in the prize-drawings were: Chair: Miss Hardie, Temperance Hotel; bedspread: Miss Gulland, Millfield; quilt: Mrs Joseph Duncan, Lomond Cottage; reading lamp: Miss C. Bisset, Pleasance; set of china: Miss K. Lawson, Victoria Place; ham: Mrs F. Kilgour, West Port; cheese: Mr D. Dun, Woodmill. Prizes were presented by Mrs Johnston for best dressed dolls, and these were awarded to (1) Miss J. Livingston, and (2) Mrs A. Harris.

The sale proved to be an unqualified success, the total drawings amounting to £113 11s. As this does not fall much short of the desired sum, the members of the Guild, who worked so earnestly in the interests of the sale, have reason to feel that their efforts have been amply rewarded, and that they have earned the gratitude of all interested in the improvement of the Parish Church. (FN)

19 July 1905

Telephone

Letter to Lord Ninian, Chelsea Barracks

Dear Lord Ninian,

The Post Office engineer came here two days ago and I went over with him the line to be taken by the poles and wires for the telephone. I am glad to say that the poles will be completely hidden from the moment they enter the Lodge Gates. I have also arranged to have a private telephone fitted up between the house and stables by an electrical engineer in Kirkcaldy at a cost not exceeding £9. As it is of importance to Sir John Murray that the work should be proceeded with as soon as possible, perhaps your Lordship will return the agreement with the Post Office as until that agreement is in their hands I do not expect that they will commence the work.

Your obedient servant, George Gavin. (FEP)

28 July 1905

Pig-keeping

Dear Mr Gulland,

I am favoured with your letter of 27th inst with reference to the complaints to the keeping of pigs by Mr Alex Douglas, Horsemarket. I shall take an early opportunity of examining the premises again, with a view to seeing what can be done either to mitigate or remove any nuisance which may exist.

Yours faithfully, George Gavin. (FEP)

29 July 1905

Motor car accident

A serious motor accident took place at the old bridge at Guardbridge on Wednesday afternoon (26th).

A motor car belonging to Lady Murray, House of Falkland, on the way to St Andrews, dashed into a cart, smashing it to pieces. The horse was very badly injured, while the driver of the cart, E. J. Turner, Tayport, was much cut about the head, and received other injuries. A boy who was with him escaped unhurt. One of the occupants of the motor car, an elderly American lady, Mrs Johnston, at present a guest of Lady Murray, jumped out of the car in order to save herself, when she was violently thrown to the ground. She was at once removed to the house of Dr Smyth, who attended to her injuries. It was found that Mrs Johnston had had her left arm fractured, and, besides suffering from shock, had received a severe contused wound on the forehead. Two of Lady Murray's daughters, who were in the car, along with their tutor, escaped unhurt. Later on Mrs Johnston was driven home to Falkland. The injured man, Turner, after having his injuries attended to, proceeded home by rail. (FN)

29 July 1905

Town Council

At a meeting of Town Council held in the Town Hall on Tuesday (25th), Mr John Burnett, Kirkcaldy, was selected from a large number of candidates to be Inspector of Works over the sewage system scheme about to be carried out. (FN)

5 August 1905

Parish Church

Operations in connection with the installation of the new heating system – hot water pipes – in the Parish Church have now been commenced, and the work is expected to be completed before the end of next week. (FN)

5 August 1905

Cricket

Playing in Upper Scroggie Park last Saturday (29th July), Rothes inflicted a crushing defeat on the local players. Notwithstanding heavy rain in the early part of the day, the pitch proved to be in very fair playing order. The visitors, who had first innings, early showed signs of first-class form, and after giving the members of the home team plenty of "leather hitting", were dismissed with a total score of 93. The Falkland eleven only managed to secure 16 runs, a score which was rather disappointing to their supporters, especially after the excellent play exhibited by the team in previous matches this season. (FN)

5 August 1905

Light Railway: scheme approved

The Light Railway Commissioners held an inquiry at Falkland on Monday regarding the proposed light railway from Falkland Road

20. Interior of Falkland Parish Church

Station to Falkland village. The Commissioners present were Colonel G. F. V. Boughey RE, CSI (Chairman), and Mr Henry Allan Steward, with Mr Alan D. Erskine as Secretary. There were also present Mr Arthur Dewar KC, who appeared for the promoters, and was instructed by Mr Thomas Dempster, of Messrs Robertson & Dempster, Perth, the agents for the promoters; Mr J. S. Pitman WS, for Lord Ninian Crichton-Stuart; Mr J. E. Grosset, Cupar, for Mr C. J. M. Makgill Crichton of Lathrisk; Mr Alexander Lawson of Annfield, Chairman of Cupar District Committee; and Mr William Meiklejohn, Glen Newton, and Mr Alexander Bonthrone, Newton of Falkland, appeared in their own behalf.

Mr Charles Jackson, Chairman of the firm of Charles Jackson & Co., Ltd., linen and floorcloth manufacturers, Falkland, and Chairman of the Committee promoting the railway, said his firm employed about 200 hands. He spoke of the necessity of the railway from a manufacturing and public point of view. He referred to the difficulty of visitors getting conveyances from the station to the village, and said the other Saturday about 40 people came off the train, while the 'bus only accommodated 16. Many people came to Falkland for a day, and wished to get a later train at night. Just now his firm had to cart about 5000 tons of material a year to and from Falkland Road Station, which was very expensive. The cost of the line was estimated at £18,500, including the cost of land and buildings. (FFP)

12 August 1905

Telephone

Dear Lord Ninian,

I have this morning received from the secretary to the Post Office the enclosed supplement agreement for your signature. It was thought best to fit up the telephone meantime in the billiard room, but in case of this kind it is almost essential to have an extension bell to ring somewhere near the servants' apartments, so as to ensure someone's attention being directed to the ringing of the instrument. Such an extension bell has accordingly been fitted up near the butler's pantry.

Your obedient servant, George Gavin. (FEP)

14 August 1905

Lunch invitation

Letter from Glasgow Archaeological Society, 79 West Regent St, Glasgow

Dear Mr Gavin,

I have been instructed by the council of this society to request the pleasure of your company at the luncheon to be held on 29th August at 1.30 p.m. in the Bruce Arms, Hotel, Falkland, on the occasion of this society's annual excursion.

Yours faithfully, A. H. Charteris. (FEP)

19 August 1905

Sewerage scheme

Work in connection with the new sewerage scheme for the burgh was commenced last week. (FN)

19 August 1905

Parish Church

The new heating apparatus in the Parish Church has been success-fully installed, and it is confidently expected that the system will

21. Ness's horse bus at Falkland, about 1905

prove a boon in many ways, not the least of which will be a marked decrease in the working expenses. (FN)

25 August 1905

Thunderstorm

At an early hour on Wednesday morning the inhabitants here were rudely awakened by terrific peals of thunder, which seemed to proceed from directly overhead. The storm commenced about 3 a.m., and with heavy and continuous rains lasted fully an hour. In some parts of the town flooding took place, and dwellers in the lower lying houses were put to considerable inconvenience. (FFP)

30 August 1905

Bruce Arms Hotel

Dear Sir,

In consultation with the tenant the following points may be kept in view in forming the staircase. He would like a broad flat midway if possible to take away the steepness. We have also thought that the space on landing on the end of bar next to lobby to the kitchen there should be a door with sliding glass opening for service to upstairs. The tenant thinks that bar pumps of a superior kind can be had second hand for the same price as ordinary ones, and accordingly it might be well to specify them meantime. There would be two of these under the bar counter. There will be the usual accommodation for bottles and glasses. And lead sink with fluted hardwood dripper for washing glasses. A new grate will be required for bar. I observe that the style of which I enclose a drawing is becoming commonplace for smoking rooms of hotels and bars. I think the present coal house and glass pantry in scullery should be removed, and a brick coal house built in corner near back door in close where urinal used to stand. This would give more room in scullery and avoid carrying coals through it to present receptacles for coals. In the scullery there will be two wash tubs with hot and cold water laid on, a sink there I fancy should be enamelled, but you can use your discretion. There will also be a sink in new pantry, with drip board. It would be well also to specify the new kitchen range and high pressure boiler and connection. The other work of covering the floor etc. of course I need not refer to as Mr Stewart will have notes as to this.

Yours faithfully, George Gavin. (FEP)

2 September 1905

Partial eclipse

The partial eclipse of the sun, an occurrence which has aroused considerable interest in many parts of the land, was distinctly seen from the village on Wednesday about one o'clock. Although the sky had been cloudy during the greater part of the forenoon, the sun broke forth in great brilliance just in the nick of time, and a good view of the phenomenon was obtained by many of the inhabitants. (FN)

2 September 1905

Sewage system

At a meeting of Cupar District Committee on Tuesday, Mr Bonthrone[1]

---

[1] Alexander Bonthrone, being from Newton of Falkland, hence outside the Royal Burgh, would have represented the "Landward" part of the parish, which included Balmblae.

referred to the fact that the Burgh of Falkland was at present carrying out an extensive sewage system, and he thought it desirable that Balmblae should be included. It was unanimously agreed to institute inquiries. (FN)

6 September 1905

Lighting the Chapel

Letter to Thomson Bros, Ironmongers, Kirkcaldy

Dear Sirs,

There is a matter connected with the introduction of light into the Palace Chapel here, regarding which I would like to see you. The proposal briefly is to light the place by means of candles set on standards, to be placed throughout the Chapel. If you could send one of your assistants here on Friday morning I could meet him and discuss the matter with him. I have now got the telephone in my office here and if anything occurs to you regarding this matter, or at any other time you can ring me up. Tele No XII.

Yours faithfully, George Gavin. (FEP)

6 September 1905

A problem priest

Dear Lord Ninian,

I regret to say that for sometime past we have had considerable trouble with Father De Stoop.[1] Both he and his housekeeper have conducted themselves by quarrelling. It has been so bothersome so I had to seek a personal intervention with Lady Bute in order to explain matters fully to her. The example to the public is calculated to bring us all into disrespect. He left on Sunday afternoon by train announcing that he would be away for a week, but I do not know where he has gone. Lady Bute called upon the archbishop in Edinburgh on Monday, but he was just leaving for a holiday, in fact we followed him to Princes' Street station where I spoke to him in a railway carriage. He could only agree to write cautioning him to moderate his actions until arrangements suspending him can be made. I do not care

---

[1] Father De Stoop seems to have been the only priest to have lived in the Palace

to write the details of what has been going on; but Lady Bute knows fully and will no doubt verbally explain them to Your Lordship. I enclose a copy of the last letter I received from Father De Stoop, which speaks for itself.

Your obedient servant, George Gavin (FEP)

Priest's Rooms.

The following accounts are for the furnishing of rooms in Palace for resident priest.

Brady & Sons, Perth, furniture. £34.2s.6d.

Thomson Bros, Kirkcaldy, ironmongery. £3.16s.

Duncan Bryce, Falkland, tablecloths, bedcover, blankets. £5.17s.5d.

Archibald Swan, Falkland, china and glassware. £1.18s.1d.

William Duncan, Falkland, carting furniture from Perth to Palace for priest's rooms. 17s.6d. (FEP)

---

6 September 1905

Prosecution for Cruelty to Horse

Henry Duncan, Dovecot House and Andrew Lawson, carter, Victoria Place were at Cupar Sheriff Court on Monday, before Sheriff Armour, charged with cruelly ill-treating a roan gelding belonging to Duncan and under the charge of Lawson, on 2nd August, by causing it to work when it was lame on the off fore leg.

The accused pleaded not guilty, and Inspector Walters of the S.P.C.A., said he was cycling through Newton of Falkland and overtook a bus driven by accused Lawson. He noticed that the horse yoked to the vehicle was lame on the off fore leg, and stiff on the other three legs. He examined the horse and found it suffering from a bony enlargement in the knee joint of the off fore leg. There was also a similar enlargement in the knee joint of the near fore leg, though not quite so serious. The animal was quite unfit for work. Constable Lumsden, Freuchie, said on that day in question Inspector Walters came to his house, and in consequence of the information received from the Officer, he waited till the horse came along. It was then under the charge of the accused Lawson, and was walking lame. Mr J. R. Baillie VS, Cupar, said he received a telegram from Mr Walters regarding the horse, and examined the animal near Falkland Road Station. He found the horse suffering from chronic inflammation of the off fore leg, and also in the other fore leg, though to a less extent. The horse was quite unfit for work of any kind. Henry Duncan, the owner of the horse said he had had the animal for sixteen years, and it was six years old when he got it.

The Sheriff: "Do you think this horse should be destroyed now?"

Accused: "I don't think so; I think it is fit for light work yet."

His Lordship said this was a case that required a more or less severe penalty. The horse was in the admission of its owner over twenty years old, and in addition to its age it was suffering from an ailment in one of its fore legs, which apparently gave it very considerable pain, especially when it was put to work. It was not that the accused had been working a horse with a sore that he did not know much about. He had deliberately worked a horse suffering from a serious disease in one of its legs, and not only that, but he apparently took the view that he might still work it notwithstanding the cruelty brought to his notice. His Lordship could not impose a less penalty in Duncan's case than £3 or twenty one days. He did not think the same blame attached to Lawson, who was merely a servant, and in his case the penalty would be 10s or four days. (FH)

12 September 1905

Letter to Father De Stoop

Dear Rev. Father,

I understand that you received the other day from Lady Bute a letter the purpose of which was that you should place your resignation as Lord Ninian's Chaplain in my hands. I asked you to call at my office today to explain this to you, but as you have indicated that you could not do so, it is necessary for me, to write you. I may say that I have Lord Ninian's distinct instructions to terminate your engagement, but you will quite see that for the sake of all parties concerned it will be better if you will carry out the suggestion of Lady Bute, and thus save me from having a disagreeable duty to perform.

Yours faithfully, George Gavin. (FEP)

18 October 1905

Candle stands

Letter to Thomson Bros, Ironmongers, Kirkcaldy

Dear Sirs,

I have to thank you for your estimates for range for the Bruce Arms, Hotel, which I shall consider and write you regarding by an early post. I have also specially to thank you for all the kind trouble you took in hurrying forward the Candle-stand Ariels.[1] They arrived all right on Saturday and were fixed up that evening. They are very satisfactory.

Yours faithfully, George Gavin. (FEP)

19 October 1905

Boiler

Letter to Thomson Bros, Ironmongers, Kirkcaldy

Dear Sirs,

I now accept your offer of £13. 3s.6d. to supply a Villa A1 Simplex Range,[2] as described by you, and with the accessories mentioned in your letter. There is included in the price a copper boiler and Simplex rising bottom, both of which I wish supplied along with the range. Kindly accordingly arrange for the range to be forwarded as soon as possible.

Yours faithfully, George Gavin. (FEP)

28 October 1905

Wanted

Wanted, at once, a few good navvies, apply Falkland Drainage Works. A. Gray & Co, contractors. (FFP)

3 November 1905

Bruce Arms Hotel

Dear Mr Gavin,

I have your letter of yesterday's date, and immediately after receiv-

---

[1] Not clear what is meant by "Ariels".

[2] The range was for the Bruce Arms, Inn.

ing it, went round to Frew & Co for the use of their telephone, and after waiting fully half an hour before getting on to the trunk only to find that I could get no reply, so I thought the better course would be just be to wire you. There is a very great difference between polished slate and enamelled, as the cost indicates, in our case it is only polished that is specified of which there is 32 feet at 2s.6d – £4.0.0., if black enamelled it would cost 3s.6d per foot – £5. 12s., and if white enamelled £6.8s., it was only because I thought that the cost for enamelled slate might be prohibitive, otherwise I would have specified it, because it is so nice and has such a fine surface, but it might be worth the plumber's while to get a quotation for enamelled slate before definitely fixing the matter and you could see what you think of it. I sent off a detail drawing to the Provost last night for the balasters and buffet.

Yours faithfully, D. Stewart, 8 High St. Perth. (FEP)

3 November 1905

Bruce Arms Hotel

Dear Sir,

We beg to advise you that kitchen range has been sent on to your address by Falkland Road Station. Seventeen parts and one box. You might kindly see that the parts are examined and if there should be anything wrong you might let us know and we shall see about the matter and instruct the railway company regarding same.

Yours faithfully, Thomson Bros. Kirkcaldy. (FEP)

11 November 1905

Municipal election

The bustle and excitement of a municipal election are again things of the past! Six candidates stood for four seats in the Town Council and the result of the poll, which was declared about 9.00 p.m. on Tuesday night, was as follows: J. W. Jackson, 91; A. Lister, 87; James Forsyth, 82; M. Reekie, 71; William Horne, 39; W. Strachan, 38. Of the four retiring Councillors, two sought re-election and were returned second and third. Of an electorate of 210, 70% recorded their votes. (FN)

2 December 1905

Football

Falkland Lomondvale continued their friendly engagements last Saturday, and again recorded a win at the expense of their neighbouring rivals, Stratheden Reserves. On account of illness amongst their regular League starters, the local players had to forego a League engagement, and a scratch team was only available for the field. The Strath Reserves were a plucky lot, and, although admitting defeat by four goals to nil, they offered at times a stubborn resistance to the attacks of their victorious opponents. Tomorrow (Saturday) the Vale meet Ladybank Violet in the first round of the Linton Cup, and a close game is anticipated. (FN)

2 December 1905

Falkland Light Railway

Messrs Robertson, Dempster & Coy., solicitors, Perth, agents for the promoters of this railway, have now received intimation that the Light Railway Commissioners have passed the order authorising the construction of the line as originally proposed by the promoters. The Commissioners have refused to accede to Mr Bonthrone's proposal that the railway as put forward by the promoters should be deviated so as to pass through his brewery. (FN)

14 December 1905

Bruce Hotel

Letter to Oliver Melville, Kirkcaldy

Dear Sir,

The new bar has now been practically completed at the Bruce Hotel. And I shall feel obliged if you will send a man here as soon as possible to permanently fix the indicator for the electric bells.

Yours faithfully, George Gavin. (FEP)

17 December 1905

Father De Stoop

Dear Mr Pitman

I am favoured with your letter of yesterday, from which I am glad to learn that you have managed to settle with Father De Stoop for so moderate a sum as £52. It is really more than he deserves, but it might have taken more. I was afraid to satisfy his demands. I shall put away carefully the papers I handed to you and which you have now returned to me including Father De Stoop's letter to Lady Bute of September 13th last tendering his resignation. The Archbishop's action in employing Father De Stoop is to say the least inexplicable. Proof of the latter's doings here is, I am sorry to say, only too abundant and I offered to supply him the names of people where integrity was not to be for a moment doubted and who could speak of actual facts; but he has chosen to discard the information which lay to hand. Personally I feel that his removal was of paramount importance for the sake of the reputation of the small body of respectable Catholics here.

Yours faithfully, George Gavin. (FEP)

18 December 1905
Christmas
Dear Lord Ninian,

I was keeping in view your Lordship's verbal instructions kindly given last year as to the Christmas tree and tea to the children being an annual event. I proposed holding it on a day of the week between Christmas and New Year. I gave the usual donation of £5 from your Lordship for coals for the poor the other day. I do not know (apart from old Sandy Dryburgh and the son of Mrs O'Conner, the teacher, who I am afraid is dying of consumption) of any particular cases where an extra gift should be given. I would suggest, however that it would be very greatly appreciated if out of the trapped rabbits which belong to your Lordship and are being consigned to a dealer, a pair of rabbits given not only to help the estate men but to some other poor people. Unless I hear to the contrary I shall arrange with Mr Kay regarding this.

Your obedient servant, George Gavin. (FEP)

Work at Bruce Arms

Payment to Thomas Ross, painter, for papering and painting part of the interior and exterior. £21. 0s.5d.+

Note: Work finished by another tradesman, J. C. Rolland & Sons, Markinch, papering and painting part of interior and exterior. £26.14s.7d.

Note: Completion of work taken out of the hands of Thomas Ross.

Payment to William Lawrie, Lawrie plumber work of alterations, consisting of new bath with hot and cold fittings and pipes; two enamelled wash basins with fittings; New gas brackets, and piping renewed for supply of gas; Beer pipes to cellar and general removal of plumber work. £36.10s.6d.

Payment to Oliver Melville, Kirkcaldy, fitting up electric bells. £3.10s.6d.

Payment to James Paterson, Newton of Falkland, account of masons work. £20.00.

Payment to Robert Miller, joiner, work of repairs to new tenant of upstairs portion of house, lathing and strapping whole rooms, new windows and floors where necessary, and wood work of new bathroom. £65.15s.3d.

Payment to William Lawrie, plumber, new lamp for outside door. £2.7s.6d.

Payment to Walter Peggie, plasterer, plaster repairs to upper portion of house including plastering on new lath in whole rooms, repairs to roofs. £18.14s.2d.

Payment to Thomson Bros, Kirkcaldy, new Kinnaird grate and tiles. £2.00.

Payment to Oliver Melville, Kirkcaldy, plates for numbering rooms and for fitting up front door bell. £1.15s.2d.

The following contractors for remainder of work, gutting out lower flat and constructing new bar, new staircase and enlargement of kitchen:

Payment to James Paterson, mason. £69.15s.4d.

Payment to David Smart, architect, Perth, for plans of new bar and internal constructional alterations to sight of licensing justices and chief constable of county. £21.11s.

Payment to Thomson Bros, Kirkcaldy, new kitchen range, parlour grate and wash-house boiler. £17.4s.6d.

Payment to William Lawrie, introducing water to stable. 18s.

Payment to William Mason, board for priest, three week-ends and also of Feast of Assumption [15 August]. £4.1s.

24 December 1905

Work at Bruce Arms

Letter from Mr D. A. Stewart, 6 Rosemount Place, Perth

Dear Mr Gavin,

I have your letter of yesterday's date and am glad to learn the work at the hotel is now pretty well advanced. I have given Westwood instructions about the brass rods and he has promised to have them sent off on Monday, addressed to the Provost. I have ordered six rods for the bar door, three for the outside and three for the inside. The hotel glass door would have three outside to correspond with the bar door. The first rod should be placed about six inches above the lock rail, or below the glass plate, and the others spaced about six or seven inches. The provost will manage to fix them alright. I hope every other thing is giving satisfaction. I intended going down some day soon, but I think perhaps I had better defer my visit until early in the New Year now, as I would like to get the different accounts.

Yours faithfully, D. Stewart. (FEP)

30 December 1905

United Free Church

The office-bearers have had under their consideration a proposal to erect a small hall to adjoin the church, and it has been resolved to proceed with the work as soon as the necessary funds are raised. The want of such an addition has been felt for some time, and it is hoped when the scheme is carried out that there will be a revival of interest in the work of the church, especially amongst the young. (FN)

1906

Shop break-in

Two youthful factory workers named James Robert Burt Mentiply and Alex. Robertson, residing at Falkland, admitted before Sheriff Armour at Cupar to-day, having broken into the shop occupied by Christopher Campbell Brunton, flesher, and stolen £2.

The Fiscal said they had got possession of a check key and opened the door to the shop. On the understanding that they would refund the money the accused were dismissed under the First Offenders Act. (DET)

27 January 1906
Lord Ninian Crichton-Stuart engaged

The engagement is announced of Lord Ninian Crichton Stuart, Scots Guards, and the Hon. Ismay Preston, only daughter of Viscount Gormanston, GCMG, and Viscountess Gormanston, of Gormanston Castle, Balbriggan, Ireland. Miss Preston has been a lifelong friend of the Marchioness of Bute. She was one of the bridesmaids at her wedding, and when Lord and Lady Bute visited Cardiff some months ago she accompanied her Ladyship on her daily visits to the poorer districts of the city. At the great garden party given to Lord and Lady Bute she made many friends in South Wales. (SAC)

27 January 1906

Holiday for engagement

In honour of the engagement of Lord Ninian Crichton-Stuart, of Falkland House to the Hon. Ismay Treston, [*sic*] of Gormanston Castle, Balbriggan, Ireland, the estate workmen here enjoyed a holiday on Thursday, besides an allowance of double wages for that day. (FFP)

6 February 1906

Tapestries for Chapel Royal

Dear Mr Schultz,[1]

I am favoured with your letter of 3rd inst. I am very pleased to hear that Lord Ninian has secured a fine set of tapestries for the Palace Chapel.[2] I think it was proposed when I had the pleasure of seeing you here, that the altar when created should run from the line of the highest of the three steps to the pulpit, that the steps would be wholly within the altar rail.

If the Royal Pew were moved 8 or 9 ft further east it would mean that it would, according to the above arrangement be so close to rail that the entrance door to pew (which you recollect is in the last end) would not have room to open. If however the altar rail were put in line with the lowest or first step it could easily be arranged to shift the Royal Pew 8 or 9 ft towards the altar end.

Yours faithfully George Gavin. (FEP)

8 February 1906

Tapestries for Chapel Royal

Dear Mr Gavin,

Many thanks for your letter, and I note what you say about the position of the pew. I think after what you have said as to the position, we had better not shift it. There is a join in the largest piece of tapestry, and I think we may be able to arrange them in another way so as not

---

[1] This was Robert Weir Schultz, architect. See the "Architects" section of the "Falkland's People" chapter below.

[2] The tapestries cost £1,537 18s.

22. The Chapel Royal in Falkland Palace
This shows the modern chapel, post 1950, and different tapestries; the 1906
tapestries were hung around the chapel and are now in the chapel gallery.

to interfere with the pew. It will probably be about a month before
they are repaired and ready to be sent off. I will give you due notice
of their dispatch. The tapestries are about 10ft 6ins to 11ft long. I
presume the wall under gallery to Chapel is high enough to get a
piece of tapestry in. Would you kindly get me the exact dimensions
of space taken up by little doorway leading to tower rooms, as I wish
to arrange the position of the tapestries before they are sent off.

Yours faithfully, R. W. Schultz. (FEP)

17 February 1906

Piped water
The water scheme is now making progress. Already the main pipes
have been laid in the streets, and the contractor, Mr Gray, has commenced to deal with connections. The tanks are also in an advanced
stage. (FFP)

8 March 1906

Telephone

Letter to Mr Hook, Post Office Dundee

Dear Sir,

I have hitherto refrained from troubling you regarding the instrument in my office here. It has from the first given us a very great deal of trouble, not only so but on many occasions. I have had to resort to the telegraph in order to get communication which ought to have been got by means of the telephone, interruption and breakdowns have occurred recently at least daily. The lines man has evidently done everything in his power to remedy the defects. Today for example after his visit it was ringing alright from Kingskettle at 12 o'clock and by 2 p.m. no communication could be got with the exchange. My patience has become entirely exhausted with the instrument and unless it be removed and an instrument which can be relied upon substituted I shall reluctantly have to take steps to cancel the lease. I regret to have to write so strongly but the matter of the nature of a farce.

Yours faithfully, George Gavin. (FEP)

14 March 1906

Poaching

Before Sheriff Armour at Cupar yesterday, William Stanner, labourer, residing at Well Brae, and Andrew Wallace, labourer, residing at High Street West, were each ordered to pay a fine of 5s with 20s of expenses, or ten days imprisonment for trespassing in pursuit of game on the Hardie Plantation, on the estate of Balbirnie. Mr R. O. Pagan WS prosecuted. (DC)

22 March 1906

House over Post Office

Letter to Mrs Garland, High Street.

Dear Madam,

After seeing the state of repair in which the dwelling house over the Post Office, I have come to the conclusion that is best to leave matters as they are at present. I have accordingly let the shop by itself to Mr Middleton, and there will for the present be no necessity for disturbing or altering the existing arrangement with you.

Yours faithfully, George Gavin. (FEP)

26 March 1906

Post Office

Dear Sir,

Yours of the 23rd inst to hand. Re The shop in High Street to be occupied by me as Post Office premises as at 15th May next. The terms of which I concur.[1]

Yours faithfully, William Middleton. (FEP)

3 April 1906

Tenancy of a house

Letter to John Affleck, China Merchant

Dear Sir,

I now confirm the arrangements verbally made with you on Saturday last, by which you are to become tenant of the house presently occupied by Mr Thomas Grant. Your entry will be as at 28th May next and the rent will be 35 shillings per annum payable half yearly in advance. The proprietor it is agreed will be under no obligation whatever to do any repairs upon the premises.

Yours faithfully, George Gavin. (FEP)

17 April 1906

Pipes for the burn

Letter to Charles Gulland

Dear Sir,

It is my intention to put 12 ins pipes into a small part of the burn where the present conduit in front of the brick outhouse of the Bruce Arms, Hotel (now used as a cycle shed) has fallen in. To do this will of course involve the turning off the water down the Back Wynd for a few days. Will you kindly say whether I may have the permission of the Town Council to temporarily direct the water.

Your faithfully, George Gavin. (FEP)

---

[1] William Middleton eventually rented the ground floor of the Town Hall.

19 April 1906

Quaint and rare old tapestries

A valuable set of 17th century tapestries recently acquired by Lord Ninian Crichton-Stuart has been hung on the walls of the Chapel Royal in Falkland Palace.[1] The complete room of tapestries came from an old house in Maarssen, Holland, which was built in 1400. The name of the house and estate is "Ter Keer" formally "Tuylenburg" and the tapestry has passed from family to family of those who owned the house. Sir Vincent Maximilian van Lakhorat, The Baron van Tuyll van Guylen, Die Marchie van Vanhuysen, Heer of Maarssen (Lord of the Manor), the Chevalier van Weede, Ambassador. The set of tapestries comprises six pieces, the largest of which measures fully 24 feet long by 9 feet high. Those strikingly quaint and rare old tapestries depict forest scenes with peacocks, swans, and other birds and beasts, huntsmen, shepherds among the foliage and in the foreground while here and there distant landscapes and castles peep through the trees. The texture is much finer than that of the ordinary verdure tapestry. (DC)

20 April 1906

Telephone bill

Letter to Controller and Accountant, General Post Office, London

Dear Sir,

You will recollect that sometime ago you wrote me reporting an account which you stated had been rendered to me previously, and asking payment of the account. I wrote in reply to say that the first statement of account never reached me. I have now received it herewith along with the cover which shows that it had been sent to the Falkland Islands. Apropos of this I may take the opportunity of mentioning that not a few letters addressed to Falkland find their way to the Falkland Islands. As an instance I may say that a dog's lead and collar was addressed by a saddler in London to me here. The articles evidently went missing at the time but arrived here a long time after having been sent to the Falkland Islands. The collar was destroyed,

---

[1] North British Railway Co., carriage and insurance of tapestries from London: £1 4s 10d.

evidently by the action of exposure to salt water. If you have an opportunity of mentioning this to the proper quarter it might obviate what happens with letters addressed to Falkland.

Yours faithfully, George Gavin. (FEP)

21 April 1906

New Post Office

The house at foot of Cross Wynd, opposite the Fountain, has again been secured for the Post Office, and the postal business has been transferred to it this week. (FFP))

27 April 1906

Bruce Arms Hotel

Letter to Oliver Melville, 310, High St. Kirkcaldy.

Dear Sir,

I observe that part (£1 15 2½d) of enclosed account was paid on 23rd February last. I observe also two gong bells and accessories charged. I ordered only one for front door but I believe for convenience to Mr Mason, the tenant, a second bell to ring in his bedroom.

Yours faithfully, George Gavin. (FEP)

5 May 1906

Local invention

The following is a description of a recent patent application sent us by Messrs Howard & Co, Agents, Chancery Lane, London.

Floorcloth. J. W. Jackson, Falkland Floorcloth Co. Floorcloth, wax cloth, oilcloth, linoleum and like goods have a pattern printed on both sides so as to be reversible. The side of the floorcloth not in use may be protected by laying it upon a covering of ordinary Jute Hessian over the floor. (FFP)

9 May 1906

Death

Dear Lord Ninian,

I regret to say that on my return home this morning I was told that

Mrs O'Conner's boy[1] died last night at 10 o'clock. I have seen her today and handed to her, as instructed by your Lordship, the certificate for the lair in the consecrated ground in the cemetery, and she asked me to express her sincere gratitude for this help which has been handed to her.

I am your obedient servant, George Gavin. (FEP)

10 May 1906

Marriage celebrations

Letter to Mr Pitman, Edinburgh

Dear Mr Pitman,

The tenantry, tradesmen and work people on the Estate had meetings about a fortnight ago regarding the presentation by them of gifts to Lord Ninian on the occasion of his marriage. Lord Ninian thinks that the rejoicings here should be carried out on somewhat similar lines as on his coming of age. As I don't know what the expense then amounted to perhaps will kindly give me some idea either as to the lump sum or rates per head, to help me in making arrangements for the marriage rejoicings.

Yours faithfully, George Gavin. (FEP)

11 May 1906

Festivities for wedding

Dear Mr Gavin.

I have your letter as to festivities in connection with Lord Ninian's marriage. I enclose some menus which will show you what the entertainments cost at the time of the coming of age. I note that Lord Ninian thinks that the rejoicing should on this occasion be carried out on somewhat similar lines. I can hardly think that his Lordship can want to spend so much money on such an elaborate scale. Surely an ordinary dinner to the tenants and trades people, a supper to the employees and smaller tenants and perhaps a school-children's tea would be sufficient. You will no doubt have to hire a marquee as there is no other suitable place in which to dine.

Yours faithfully, John Pitman, Edinburgh. (FEP)

---

[1] Mrs O'Conner was in charge of Brunton House School.

12 May 1906

The late Mr Alexander Bonthrone

A prominent figure has been removed from the Falkland district by the death of Mr Alexander Bonthrone, brewer and maltsman, Newton of Falkland.

Until a month or two ago Mr Bonthrone had been in his usual good health and was manifesting a lively interest in his own affairs and in the public business of the community. Illness overtaking him, he sought rest for a time; but his condition did not improve, and he passed away at his residence at Newton of Falkland on Monday morning (7th May) on his seventy-fourth birthday.

The representative of a family who have been long identified with Auchtermuchty and Falkland, Mr Bonthrone led an active energetic life. The brewing business of which he was the head, dated back to the times when Royalty lived in Falkland Palace. In later years Mr Bonthrone was assisted in his business by his youngest son, Mr David, who as is well known, patriotically volunteered for the front during the late South African war, and as a non-commissioned officer of the 20th Company, Fife & Forfar I.Y., made a narrow escape with his life at Nooitgedacht.

Mr Bonthrone took a keen interest in the public life of his parish and county. He had been a member of the School Board of Falkland since its formation and its Chairman for the past 22 years. He was a member of the Landward Parish Council, and as the representative of that body on the District Committee, of the County Council, he neglected no question bearing on the locality he sought to serve. In politics, he was a staunch Conservative who, when occasion offered fought valiantly for his party. Shrewdness and business ability were among his outstanding characteristic, and in his desire to be helpful in his day and generation was shown not only by his discharge of public office but by his readiness to oblige. The local Volunteers, for instance, were allowed the use of one of his parks for drill, and when the golf course was laid out, he placed two fields at the disposal of the Club.

He was predeceased by his wife several years ago, who was a daughter of the late Mr Barclay, Drums, a well-known Fife agriculturist up to his death fifteen or sixteen years ago. (FN)

19 May 1906

Wedding gifts

Letter from Hamilton & Inches, 47 George St, Edinburgh

Dear Mr Gavin,

Had the Provost and all his men and fixed them up with a very nice fruit service, and I can assure you that I did them well. I am sure that His Lordship will be most pleased with what they have taken, by the way what is the Provost's name and what does he do, let me know when next you write. I have sent by post the lot for your own and wife's approval and I hope you will be able to make selection.

Yours faithfully, William Hamilton.[1] (FEP)

20 May 1906

The dance

Letter from Fife & Forfar Imperial Yeomanry, Annsmuir Camp, Ladybank

Dear Sir,

I have fixed MC for your dance on Friday first. Our S.S. Major Montague can't get away so I am bringing S. S. Harry Cadic.[2] He is a steady gentleman and knows the business. Will you send the trap to the camp, that will be six of us, we would require to leave by 6.30 p.m. I trust that everything will go nicely and that you will have a happy night.

Yours faithfully, Brigadier D. G. Maule.

P.S. Would you have a little railed platform for the band, as the music will be heard to more advantage, and as good light as possible as I don't see so well. (FEP)

21 May 1906

Fruit service

Letter to Mr William Hamilton, 47 George St, Edinburgh

Dear Mr Hamilton,

---

[1] Hamilton & Inches, founded in 1866, are a leading firm of jewellers, still trading at George Street Edinburgh.

[2] S.S. Major and S.S presumably mean "Squadron Sergeant Major" and "Staff Sergeant" respectively.

I am glad to observe from your letter of 19th inst that you managed to arrange with the Provost and his colleagues for a fruit service. I feel sure it will be very pretty. The Provost's name is Robert Miller and he has a master joiner's business here. I received the salvers and other goods on approval quite safely. All of the men took up the view that they would prefer the larger salver and we have accordingly chosen it. Mrs Gavin and I have selected the pair of menu holders, and those we have retained. I have packed up and am returning to you today insured the articles sent on approval. I suppose you will now send me a draft of the inscription for the workmen's present. Personally I shall be delighted if you came over here with the articles.

Yours faithfully, George Gavin. (FEP)

25 May 1906

Women's Guild

By way of a variation, the closing evening of the session of the Falkland Women's Guild took the form of a surprise social when tea was kindly served to the members at the instance of Mrs Johnston of the Manse. (DET)

30 May 1906

Wedding gifts

Letter from William Hamilton

47, George St, Edinburgh.

Dear Sir,

As I said all being well on Friday I will come with the train leaving here 9.35 a.m. at Ladybank 10.52 and will bring the three presentations with me. Will you tell the provost, also Mr Tod, if you see him. Will you have the trap at Ladybank.

Yours faithfully, William Hamilton. (FEP)

6 June 1906

Marriage Celebrations

Letter to Mr Pitman, Edinburgh.

Dear Sir,

I waited for a considerable time for Lord Ninian's reply to my letter as to the exact sum to be spent, but not having heard from him arranged a very much reduced price per head for the dinners, and the purveying has been given, as instructed by Lord Ninian, to the tenant of Bruce Arms, who has had much experience of this kind of work. I am now issuing the invitations and enclose one for the principal dinner on Thursday the 21st curt. As I am going over to Ireland to his Lordship's wedding I am anxious to have the toast list completed within the next few days, and perhaps, accordingly you will kindly write me whether you will be present at the dinner, as I hope you will; and whether I maybe permitted to put your name upon the toast list for some appropriate toast.

Yours faithfully, George Gavin. (FEP)

7 June 1906
Car and driver needed
Letter to A. C. Penman, Motor Carriage Works, Dumfries
Dear Sir,

Lord Ninian Crichton-Stuart, a brother of the Marquis of Bute, is to be married in Ireland on Saturday 16th curt. He and his lady will arrive by the steamer "Princess Maud" from Larne on the evening of that day at 9.10 p.m., and is their intention to complete the journey by motor from Stranraer Harbour to Old Place of Mochrum, some miles from Kirkcowan Station. Can you undertake to send a good and reliable car with a thoroughly reliable driver, who knows the road to meet the steamer and take Lord and Lady Crichton-Stuart to Old Place of Mochrum. As his Lordship's man-servant will travel with them the car should have an extra seat beside the driver to accommodate him.

Yours faithfully, George Gavin, Falkland Estate, Factor. (FEP)

7 June 1906
Shipping the motor car
Letter to Traffic Manager, Larne & Stranraer Steamship Company, Belfast
Dear Sir,

I was much obliged to you for your reply to my telegram some days ago as to the shipping of the motor car. The arrangements as to the putting the car on board has for the present been abandoned. The couple on the 16th June are to travel by the "Princess Maud" from

Larne to Stranraer in the evening, His manservant will no doubt book
the passages at the time but as I making the arrangements for His
Lordship's journey from Ireland I write to ask if you will have the
kindness to reserve suitable accommodation for Lord Ninian and his
Lady on the steamer, as also for a man and maidservant. It maybe
well, I dare say, to reserve a private stateroom for them. (FEP)

7 June 1906

Lady's maid

Letter to Mr Maxwell, Galloway Arms, Newton Stewart

Dear Sir,

On the evening of Saturday 16th curt a lady's maid will arrive from
Stranraer by the Irish Express at Newton Stewart and she must be
driven at once to Old Place of Mochrum. It seems from the timetable
that the express arrives at Newton Stewart at 10.40 p.m., but you will
know exactly when the boat train arrives there.

It is the train by which the maid will arrive and I should like you,
as she reaches Old Place of Mochrum as quickly as possible; so have
awaiting her a light trap with a fast horse in order to take her there.

Yours faithfully George Gavin. (FEP)

8 June 1906

Complaint over Dance Cards

Dear Mr Gavin,

I am surprised at all the tenants getting cards for the dance and to
pass over ours. I would like to know the reason why I did not get one.
We gave our subscription as well as the rest of the tenants.

Yours faithfully, Miss Storrar. (FEP)

9 June 1906

Rail connections

Letter to Lady Bute

Dear Lady Bute,

As I do not know exactly Lord Ninian's manservant's address I
venture to ask your Ladyship if you will kindly see that he gets the
enclosed memo. There is only a space of twenty eight minutes in
which to effect the transference on the 16th inst from the Great

Northern Railway Terminus at Belfast to the Midland Company's, York Road Station, a distance of a little over a mile and to make certain that there will be no possibility of delay I have made certain arrangements which it is well that Brown should know.

Your obedient servant, George Gavin. (FEP)

9 June 1906

Car and driver

Letter to A. C. Penman, Motor Carriage Works, Dumfries

Dear Sir,

I am favoured with your letter of yesterday and I also received your telegram, for both I am much obliged. I note that you will send a 16 h.p. Albion to meet the steamer from Larne at Stranraer on the evening of 16th June, and I shall rely upon you having the motor there punctually.

Your proposal to send the man round by Old Place of Mochrum on his way to Stranraer is a good one and I feel sure that the journey will be accomplished with comfort. The only suggestion that I would make is that the car should have a hood or canopy in case of rain or dust.

Yours faithfully, George Gavin. (FEP)

9 June 1906

Marquee

Letter to Mr Scott, Marquee Co, Markinch

Dear Sir,

I am very much obliged to you for your telegram to the effect that the buffet will be arranged by the Provost and your man, from which I gather that you will be able to supply sufficient canvas and materials which, with the help of the joiner will rig up a sufficient buffet. This is very satisfactory and I shall be glad if, when your man is here on the 15th inst he will see Provost Miller and have a talk with him so that if anything has to be provided there may be no delay when the marquee comes on the Monday following.

Yours faithfully, George Gavin. (FEP)

9 June 1906

Dance invitations

Letter to Miss Storrar, West Port

Dear Madam,

I am in receipt of your letter of yesterday. The dance on this occasion having been organised principally for the farm tenants who did not participate in the one two years ago. I am unable to invite all the burgh tenants who, as you know were all invited on the former occasion, and I sent invitations accordingly only to those burgh tenants who were likely to dance, and there other burgh tenants who have not received invitations. However as you seem to wish to dance I send you a card. It is obvious that the marquee can only hold a certain number and that those who were invited on the last occasion cannot expect at this time to be invited to the exclusion of the farm tenantry and their wives and daughters.

Yours faithfully, George Gavin. (FEP)

9 June 1906

Dance invitations

Letter to Lady Margaret

Dear Lady Margaret,

I am favoured with your letter of the 7th inst. I shall have pleasure in inviting Maud and Janet Annan to the dance, although with Your Ladyship's approval, I shall not do so until about a couple of days before it takes place, because if it be known that they are invited others who think they ought to get cards will follow suit, and I shall not be able to go upon any principle in the matter. It is quite impossible of course, to invite all who think from some reason or other that they should be permitted to come to the dance, as I find that we should in that case have to entertain nearly the whole of the burgh, and I have accordingly had to proceed in issuing the invitations on a well defined principle. I know that a good deal of ill feeling will be directed against me personally and that jealously will exist amongst those who do not receive cards, but as I have said in a matter of this kind one can only go upon a principle and hold firm.

Yours obedient servant, George Gavin. (FEP)

11 June 1906
Toasts at the dinner
Letter to Mr J. Richardson, Schoolhouse
Dear Sir,

Unless I hear from you to the contrary by tomorrow morning I shall assume that I may put you down to reply to the toast of educational interests at the dinner on 21st curt.

Yours faithfully, George Gavin. (FEP)

11 June 1906
Toasts at the dinner
Letter to G. Somervil Carfrae Esq, 1 Erskine Place, Edinburgh[1]
Dear Sir,

I propose to put you down to propose the toast "The Town and Trade of Falkland" at the dinner on 21st curt, to which Mr Charles Jackson will reply. It is appropriate that this toast should be given by an outsider and I trust that as I have to get the toast list printed at once you will do me the favour of agreeing to it.

Yours faithfully, George Gavin. (FEP)

11 June 1906
Cost of festivities
Letter to Mr Pitman, Edinburgh
Dear Sir,

I have to thank you for sending me so full and complete details as to the cost of the coming of age festivities. I shall go carefully over these in detail; I need not say that before doing anything further I shall remind Lord Ninian as to the total cost of the coming of age functions, and ask his instructions as to what amount definitely he wishes to spend on the marriage rejoicings. There is no doubt a marquee will be required, but the flooring will not be available as it has been used up for estate purposes in connection with the Bruce Arms alterations.

---

[1] The firm of Bonnar and Carfrae were the ornamental painters for the Falkland Kirk in 1848. However Carfrae here probably refers to George Somervil Carfrae, an Edinburgh engineer.

Yours faithfully, George Gavin. (FEP)

12 June 1906
Marriage present
Letter to Mr J. Reid, 40 Princes St Perth
Dear Sir,

I am favoured with your letter of the 9th inst. It is certainly very kind of you to think of sending Lord Ninian a driving rug as a marriage present. The marriage presents are being sent to Gormanston Castle, Ireland, where he is to be married on Saturday first, and when the rug arrives here I shall see that it is carefully addressed to him there. I am going over to the wedding, leaving here on Thursday first.

Yours Faithfully, George Gavin. (FEP)

13 June 1906
Across Belfast as quickly as possible
Letter to Traffic Manager, Belfast
Dear Sir,

You are quite right in supposing that Lord Ninian and his bride will travel by rail from Dundalk, arriving at Belfast at 6.02 p.m. and will then drive across the city to the York Road Terminus to catch the 6.30 express in connection with your steamer. I was aware of the distance of over a mile between the termini of the respective railways with only 28 minutes in which to effect the transference and I asked the station master at the Great Northern Terminus to have a cab and vehicle for the luggage in waiting and he has kindly arranged for this, and also to have the luggage placed in the van so as to be easily removed on the arrival of the train. It is extremely kind of Mr James Cowie to arrange for a special saloon to be put on the 6.30 p.m. train and in the meantime will you kindly express to him my personal thanks.

Yours faithfully, George Gavin. (FEP)

12 June 1906
Reserved compartment
Letter to Mr Russell, Station Master, Belfast
Dear Sir,

I am much obliged to you for your letter of the 11th inst, and for your kindness in promising to reserve a compartment for Lord and Lady Crichton-Stuart.

Yours faithfully, George Gavin. (FEP)

13 June 1906
Programme of dances
Letter to Mr Maule, Provost Wynd, Cupar
Dear Sir,

Many thanks for sending to me the draft programme of dances for the 22nd inst. I have shown the programme to one or two and we think that in order to open the dance with some zest a reel should be substituted for the waltz. It has also been thought well to substitute a Highland Schottische for waltz 15, and you will observe that we have transposed Quadrille and Lancers at the beginning of the programme, otherwise it is an excellent one and we are much indebted to you for the trouble you have taken with it. I shall leave the matter of the MC in your hands and I feel sure you will bring someone suitable. Kindly let me know as to this by Tuesday next and also as to when you would like to be driven and where from.

Yours faithfully, George Gavin. (FEP)

13 June 1906
Repair to flask
Letter to W. Hamilton, 47, George St, Edinburgh
Dear Mr Hamilton,

Many thanks for your letter of yesterday and for so kindly sending on my flask. It is now as good as new and I had no idea that such a good job could be made of it. Mrs Gavin and I are going to the wedding tomorrow and shall endeavour to find out either from Lord Ninian or from his mother how the matter of the ink stand from the Mount Stuart servants stand, it is very unlikely that anything would happen to the present. He has acknowledged all the Falkland presents and so has Miss Preston.

Yours faithfully. George Gavin. (FEP) [1]

---

[1] Mr and Mrs Gavin stayed at Gresham Hotel, Sackville Street, Dublin.

16 June 16th 1906

Presentation to Thomas Myles

Mr Thomas Myles, clerk, has been presented by the staff and workers of the linen and floorcloth factories with a handsome Gladstone bag and purse of money on the occasion of his leaving for Canada.

At a regular Sunday morning meeting of the Young Men's Christian Association, the chairman, Mr Peggie handed a splendid Oxford Bible to Mr Myles as a present from the members on his going abroad. (FFP)

20 June 1906

Toast for the dinner

Letter from 10 Garscube Terrace, Murrayfield, Edinburgh

Dear Mr Gavin,

I am sorry to tell you that I am thoroughly chocked up with cold this evening and am very much afraid that I will require to keep my bed tomorrow and try and throw if off as quickly as possible. I was looking forward with pleasure to being with you tomorrow and I can assure you I am very much disappointed. To show you that I was prepared for my little duty I enclose in proposing the toast of "The Town and Trade of Falkland". I trust you will have no difficulty in getting someone to take my place. If the worst comes to the worst you can get someone to read it and never let on. I intend going in a hot bath and mustard poultice to see if that will give me any relief.

Yours faithfully, G. S. Carfrae. (FEP)

22 June 1906

Marriage rejoicings

The series of fetes arranged in honour of the marriage of Lord and Lady Crichton-Stuart were inaugurated yesterday within the historic grounds of Falkland Palace, when the tenantry on his Lordship's Falkland estate and the estate tradesmen were entertained to dinner. The function was held within a tastefully decorated and spacious marquee erected within the Palace Courtyard. Prior to sitting down to the well-appointed tables of Mr W. Mason, Bruce Arms Hotel, the company, numbering over one hundred, was photographed by Mr Milliken, Kirkcaldy.

23. Dinner for the tenants for Lord and Lady Ninian's marriage
The tenants assembled in the Palace courtyard

Mr George Gavin, factor on the estate, presided, and Bailie Jackson and Mr Alex Nicoll, Westfield, officiated as croupiers. The invited guests, most of whom were present, were, Mr George Dun, Woodmill; Mr John Lawson, Falkland Wood; Mr James Tod, Easter Cash; Mr John Morgan, Kilgour; Mr W. Duncan, Falkland; Mr George Burton, Shields; Mr James Galloway, Balmblae; Mr W. Ritchie, Plains; Mr R. Pringle, Nether Myres; Mr A. Ness, Cash Mill; Mr W. S. Henderson, Reedieleys; Mr James Bonthrone, Auchtermuchty; Mr A. Duncan, Dunshalt; ex-Provost Bonthrone, Auchtermuchty; Mr Wm. Malloch, Dunshalt; Mr W. Calder, Corston Mill; Mr J. M. Wilkie, West Mill; Mr T. Philip, Wester Cash; Major Cusin, Falkland; Mr C. Brunton, Falkland; Mr D. C. Bryce, Falkland; Mr Henry Duncan, Falkland; Provost Millar, Falkland; Bailies Sutherland and Jackson; Councillors Lister, Williamson, Peggie, Reekie, J. Angus, Jackson, Forsyth, Fraser, and Robertson; the Rev. J. H. Morrison, U.F. Church; Dr J. G. Jack; Mr John Richardson, Schoolhouse; Mr John Sheriff; Mr William Lawrence Reid; Mr McMillan, Newton of Falkland; Mr A. Anderson; Mr J. M. Wright; Mr George Robertson, jun; Mr John Methven, Edinburgh; Mr G. S. Carfrae, Edinburgh; Mr W. H. Massey, Edinburgh; Mr James Paterson, Newton of Falkland; Mr Joseph Thomson, Kirkcaldy; Mr D. Brown, Buckhaven; Mr J. H. Bonnar, Edinburgh; ex-Lord

Provost Love, Perth; Bailie Ferlie, Auchtermuchty; Mr Thomas Hutchison, Auchtermuchty; Mr R. Simpson, Auchtermuchty; Mr C. G. Simpson, Auchtermuchty; Mr J. R. Oliphant, Strathmiglo; Mr R. Suttie, Auchtermuchty; Mr J. Rafferty, Strathmiglo; Mr J. Peters, Auchtermuchty; Mr D. Galloway, Falkland; Mr David Thomson of Sang & sons, Kirkcaldy; Mr John Arnot, Sauchie; Mr Henry Suttie, Dunshalt; Mr Charles Jackson, Lomond Vale; Mr D. Inglis, Freuchie; Mr George Lumsden, Brunton House School; Mr Ross, Falkland.

A first class dinner having been served, the Chairman submitted the loyal toasts, remarking that Lord Ninian was the first member of the Bute family to don His Majesty's uniform, showing thereby loyalty to the King and to the Crown.

Major Lumsden, who responded for the toast of "The Imperial Forces" said that his business relations with Germany forced him to the conclusion that conscription absolutely helped industrial progress.

The Chairman announced that the following telegram was to be sent off to Lord and Lady Crichton-Stuart, who were at Old Place, Mochrum: "Tenantry and friends assembled at Falkland today send heartiest greetings and best wishes."

Mr James Tod, Easter Cash proposed the toast of "Lord and Lady Crichton-Stuart", and at the outset read a letter from Lord Ninian thanking the tenants and feuars for the handsome silver tea and coffee service they had sent him, and for their good wishes. Continuing, Mr Tod said they all hoped that Lord and Lady Crichton-Stuart would be long spared to each other, and that after his Lordship had won his spurs he would bring his lady to Falkland House, and there spend many happy days among them.

The Chairman, who acknowledged the toast, was sorry Lord Ninian was not present to hear the expression of goodwill to himself and his lady. He might mention that when he was over in Ireland the other day at his Lordship's wedding he was greatly impressed by the evidence on every side of the kindly feeling for and of the popularity of the bride's family. It was evidenced on the day of the wedding in a most marked degree, and he took that as a very happy augury of what would take place at Falkland when Lord and Lady Crichton-Stuart came to reside amongst them. They would all recollect the favourable impression Lord Ninian made upon them two years ago at the com-

Menu for the Dinner for the Tenantry

Soups
Julienne Kidney

—

Fish
Salmon Mayonnaise

—

Joints
Roast Beef Roast Lamb Mint Sauce
Roast Chicken and Ham

—

Vegetables
New Potatoes Peas

—

Sweets
Strawberries and Cream
Jellies Cream Trifles
Compote of Fruits

Supplied by William Mason Bruce Arms, Hotel.

ing of age rejoicings, and he felt sure, with the lapse of time, that that good impression would be increased.

Next in importance to the laird come the tenant said Mr Gavin, on rising to submit the toast of "The Tenantry on the Falkland Estate." Four years ago he came into Fife a complete stranger to the Kingdom and its people, and when he came his friends told him he would have to watch himself. Being an Aberdonian, he felt he was equipped with the necessary qualifications for residence in Fife, but he soon discovered that the Fifers were very much like other people and probably a little better, and he could say that much as regarded the tenantry on the Falkland estate, from whom he had received straightforward and honourable dealings. From personal knowledge, he could say that the relationship between Lord Ninian and his tenantry was of the best description. If they wanted to find out the capabilities of the Falkland tenants they had merely to take a look round the fields and peep into the steadings where they would find the most up-to-date methods of farming and of the handling and rearing of stock.

Mr John Lawson, Falkland Wood, in replying, said he had been under four different landlords and seven different factors, and he could say that every one of them had been the very best of gentlemen, and had shown consideration and kindness wherever it was necessary. Factors had an able method of dealing with the tenants, and one reason Mr Gavin got along so well with the tenants of Falkland was that he was always courteous and obliging. Lord Ninian ought to consider himself well off in having a gentleman such as Mr Gavin to manage his estate.

Major Cusin proposed "The Marchioness Dowager of Bute and other members of the Bute family", and said the Marchioness had shown a great desire to raise the fallen and to alleviate suffering. To her they were indebted for the district nurse, and if it was for nothing else, she was entitled to their grateful remembrance on that auspicious occasion. Lady Margaret was clever and accomplished, and able to take her position amongst the highest in the land. She has shown an original and venturesome disposition by becoming a master mariner. With regard to Lord Colum, who was on the threshold of manhood, with his career before him, they could assume that, with his father's example and his mother's careful training, he would maintain the highest standard of the name which he bore.

The Chairman acknowledged the toast.

Dr Jack gave "The Provost, Magistrates and Town Council of Falkland", and Provost Miller replied.

Replying to the toast of "Agricultural Interests", submitted by Councillor Jackson, Mr George Dun, Woodmill, said they were subjected to competition for the surplus production sound and unsound of the ends of the earth free of duty, while they could not even export a ton of potatoes without having to pay duty more than double their market value. No country would tolerate such treatment, and all the Scottish farmer wanted was fair play.

Mr John Methven, Edinburgh, gave "The Town and Trade," and Mr Charles Jackson, in reply said with regard to the proposed light railway, they were now adjusting the clauses for the passing of the

Order. He felt sure the railway would give a great impetus to the industry of that locality.

"Educational Interests" was proposed by the Rev. Lyon Johnston, and acknowledged by Mr McMillan, late of Clifton Bank School, St. Andrews.

Yesterday a dinner was given to the work people on the estate, and a children's treat, and a tenantry ball took place in the evening. The arrangements for the various functions were admirably carried out under the personal supervision of Mr Gavin. (DC)

23 June 1906

Lord Ninian's wedding

Lord Ninian Edward Crichton-Stuart, Lord Bute's younger brother, was married on Saturday at Gormanston Castle, County Meath, to the Honourable Ismay Lucretia Mary Preston, only daughter of Lord Gormanston, Premier Viscount of Ireland.

The village of Gormanston, situated almost on the borders of the counties of Meath and Dublin was *en fête* with triumphal arches and other decoration. The wedding took place in the quaint little chapel of Gormanston Castle, which had been specially overhauled and adapted for the accommodation of 50 guests. The Rev. W. Delaney, Dublin, assisted by the local Catholic clergy officiated, a special Dublin choir rendering the musical portion of the service. The bride was given away by her father, the bridegroom being attended by his brother Lord Colum Crichton-Stuart. There were six bridesmaids, three dressed in pale blue and three in yellow, in the early eighteenth century style, with hats to match. The bride's wedding gown was cream satin embroidered with silver shamrocks and oak leaves, her travelling dress being pink silk with a large picture hat and ruffle to match.

A rare collection of wedding presents included a set of four different coloured diamond bracelets, ermine coat, gold mounted dressing case, and Daimler motor car from the bridegroom to the bride. Lord and Lady Bute's present was a string of pearls. After the ceremony the distinguished guests breakfasted in the Castle, while Lord Gormanston's tenantry assembled in spacious marquees erected in the demesne. (FFP)

24. Lord and Lady Ninian's wedding photograph

23 June 1906

Falkland wedding presents

The presents were numerous and valuable, and included the following from Falkland:

Mr and Mrs Gulland, Millfield, pair of silver vases; Major Cusin, Chapelyard, silver cigarette case; Mr James Galloway, spinning reel of oak, grown on Falkland Estate; Mr and Mrs George Gavin, Falkland Palace, pair silver menu holders; Mrs Nicol, housekeeper at Falkland, two copper hot water cans with arms engraved; merchants and tradesmen of the Falkland Estate, five silver fruit dishes; farmers and feuars, Falkland Estate, silver hot water jug, teapot, coffeepot sugar bowl, milk jug, and salver; workmen on the Falkland Estate, two silver salvers. (FFP)

23 June 1906

Wedding rejoicings at Palace

The Lord and Lady Crichton-Stuart marriage rejoicings were concluded here yesterday. In the afternoon the children assembled in the Palace courtyard and engaged in games of various descriptions and partook of tea in the marquee. A dance attended by the tenantry and others took place at night in the marquee and was kept up with great vigour until early morning. Delightful music was provided by a band under the leadership of Mr David Maule, Cupar. The festivities have been greatly enjoyed by young and old, and everything passed off without a hitch, the excellent arrangements of Mr George Gavin being complete in every detail. (DC)

30 June 1906

Local festivities.

The festivities in connection with Lord Ninian Crichton-Stuart's wedding were continued on Friday.

The children of the Public School and also of the Marchioness Dowager of Bute's private school were feted in the afternoon in Scroggie Park. Races and other games were provided for the young people, who afterwards were marched down the private walk leading to the Palace, and were entertained to tea in the marquee. In the evening a dance for the tenantry and their friends concluded the series of entertainments. The company included Mr and Mrs Gavin, Falkland Palace; Mr Tod, Easter Cash; Mr and the Misses Lawson, Falkland Wood; Mr and Mrs and Miss Dun, Woodmill; Mr Jackson, Lomondvale; Bailie Jackson; Councillor Jackson and Mr James Jackson; Mrs Livingston; Mr Wright; Mr and Mrs Morgan; Mr Robert Miller jun and Miss Miller; Mr Nish, school teacher; Mr and Mrs Anderson; Miss Haxton; Dr and Mrs Jack; Rev. Johnston and Mrs Johnston; Mr and Mrs William Duncan; Miss Page; Miss Sharp; The Misses Williamson; Mr and Mrs Bryce and Mr McMillan.

Music supplied by Mr Maule's Quadrille Band, Cupar.

The evening was enlivened by numerous songs by members of the company. (FFP)

9 July 1906
Car for Wedding

Sir, your favour at hand. The charge for motor hire is at regular rates, 1s per mile, and I made no extra charge for the Sunday driving, although my mechanic gets double wages. 1s per running mile is the standard price for agreed car about 16 h.p. and I never let it out for less.

Yours faithfully, A. C. Penman. (FEP)

Some of the cost for the rejoicings

William Mason, Bruce Arms, Hotel, purveyor. £12. 3s.

Robert Miller, for flooring for Marquee. £25.19s.6d.

Markinch Marquee Co, Hire of Marquee. £9.5s.6d.

Herd & Robertson, Cupar, Hire of Chairs & Lamps £7.13s.

George Innes, Cupar, Printing Invitations & Toast Lists. £4.7s.5d.

Mr H. Diggle, Cupar, for Hire of Piano. £1.5s.

William Duncan, for carting back chairs to Cupar. 8s.

Mrs Ness, conveying band from and to Ladybank. 12s.

Chief Constable of Fife, wages for extra policeman. 19s.

Mr D. G. Maule, for Music. £7.10s. (FEP)

---

14 July 1906
Choir excursion

The members of the Established Church Choir, with the minister and elders, had their annual excursion on Saturday to Aberdour. The weather was somewhat cloudy, but it did not dull the enjoyment. The time honoured custom of singing an anthem before leaving in the morning and separating at night was duly observed. (FFP)

14 July 1906
B.O.A.F.G. meeting

The half yearly general meeting of the Lomond Oak Lodge was held in the Town Hall on Tuesday last. WM[1] Peter Robertson presiding. The balance sheet was submitted and showed an increase of funds of £31.1s.5d. Sick payment paid for half year was £9.9s.2d. Brother George Herd was appointed APM and Brother James Walker, OS. (FFP)

25 July 1906

Lord Ninian's Clothing

From St John's Lodge, Regents Park, London[2]

Dear Mr Gavin,

I am forwarding by passenger train today one trunk to Falkland Road Station till called for. Would you kindly send for same, the contents of which is Lord Ninian's kilts and all winter clothing, which His Lordship will not require for some considerable time. Would you have the same packed carefully away at Falkland House until such times they are required, and kindly return key and trunk to the above address as soon as possible.

Yours faithfully. A. Brown. (FEP)

11 August 1906

Opening of United Free Church Hall

It is only a few months since the office-bearers of the United Free Church decided upon building a hall adjacent to the church, and so well have their efforts been rewarded that they were able to declare the building open on Saturday.

A special flower service was held in the afternoon. The Rev. J. H. Morrison presided, and the Rev. Messrs Affleck and Morrison, Auchtermuchty, and Thomson, Kinghorn, assisted. In his opening remarks, the Chairman announced that the total cost of the hall was about £200, and the whole sum had been already practically collected, so that he was able to open the building free of debt. (Applause) Tea and cake were afterwards served. Games and other amusements were then entered into with great spirit by the young people on the green

---

[1] Worshipful Master – see Glossary for this and similar abbreviations.

[2] St John's Lodge was rented by the Bute family at this time. Andrew Brown was Lord Ninian's manservant.

outside the church. The collection of flowers was very handsome, and they were despatched to the Royal Infirmary, Edinburgh, by the afternoon train.

The various contractors engaged in erecting the hall were: Mr Henry Suttie, builder, Dunshalt; Mr Alex. Fraser, joiner, Falkland; Mr Walter Peggie, slater and plasterer, Falkland; and Mr Thomas Ross, painter, Falkland. (FN)

14 August 1906

Poaching

Heriot Bain Lawson, labourer, pleaded not guilty to a charge of trespassing in the pursuit of game on the Greenhill Park, on the farm of Westfield, on the estate of Lord Ninian Crichton-Stuart.

J. M. Mathieson, under-keeper, who was examined by Mr J. E. Grosset, Cupar, stated about seven o'clock on Friday night, 20th July, he saw accused putting a net on a gate, and subsequently chasing rabbits. That was on the Greenhill Park. He got a neighbour, and fifty yards distant they watched the accused, and saw him taking the net off the gate. When charged with poaching, the accused said his name was John Thomson, Newton of Falkland. He had a dead rabbit in a bag, and he saw him kill it. Patterson, another under-keeper, corroborated.

The accused in the witness-box stated that he was at Thornton games all day, having left in the morning at eight o'clock, and returned at nine o'clock at night.

The Sheriff found the charge proven, and passed sentence of a fine of £1, with 25s modified expenses, or twenty-one days imprisonment. (DET)

18 August 1906

Flower Show

The 15th annual exhibition and competition of the Falkland and District Horticultural Society took place on Saturday in the beautiful grounds of Scroggie Park, kindly granted for the occasion by Sir John Murray. Fears were entertained that the rain would spoil the day's enjoyment, but fortunately as the day advanced the sun shone out, and the Society were favoured with a good gate. (FFP)

1 September 1906

Continuation classes

The School Board have arranged for a course of evening continuation classes to be held during the winter months. The subjects to be taught are commercial arithmetic and English, and Mr Robertson the Head, is to take charge of the class. It is hoped that the young of the place will avail themselves of the opportunity offered for improvement. (FFP)

5 September 1906

Fire

Shortly after 10 o'clock on Saturday night a stack of hay was observed to be on fire at the Steading of Dovecot. By the exertions of many willing hands the flames were overcome before they spread to any other stacks. (FH)

14 September 1906

Local linen

Dear Mr Schultz,

Many thanks for your letter of the 13th inst. regarding Lady Margaret's Linen Industry. I agree with you that it is hopeless to think that much, if anything, can be done in the way of disposing of the linen through the medium of retail shops and that we should certainly have the same experience as we had with Messrs Maule & Sons. I feel sure that, in view of the debt which is being heaped up against the concern, the worst policy to adopt is to give up producing further supplies of linen and endeavour to part with the existing stock at as remunerative prices as possible and probably adopt one or other of your suggestions in carrying this out.

If Lady Margaret definitely decides to give up the industry and sell the looms I shall certainly take advantage of your kind offer to put me in communication with the Hazelmere Hand Weavers. Meantime I am communicating the contents of your letter to Lady Margaret.

Yours faithfully, George Gavin. (FEP)

16 September 1906

Golf Club

Dear Lord Ninian,

A deputation from the local golf club called upon me yesterday with reference to the matter of a site for the new club house, the fund of which they hope to raise by a bazaar held in December. The deputation explained that they would feel very grateful if your Lordship saw your way to granting them a site on a piece of ground forming part of the pendicle of Fiddlehall and abutting on the Common. I am this afternoon to meet the deputation on the ground and after examining it and preparing a sketch showing its position and extent I shall again write your Lordship fully regarding the proposal.

I am, My Lord, Your obedient servant, George Gavin. (FEP)

21 September 1906

Women Suffragists at Falkland

In pursuance of their attack upon East Fife, the suffragettes Miss Teresa Billington and Miss Kenney[1] addressed a largely-attended open air meeting last night at the Cross.

Miss Billington said they had been called many hard names during the last few months, but hard names had little effect on those who were trying to get reform. That was the way with people who were not content with being put off with promises. They were asking not for promises but for an Act of Parliament. There had been women's suffrage societies for the last forty years, so that they were not bringing a new doctrine before the electors. It was the old doctrine in a new form. They had waited too long, and wasted too many years in trying the old lady-like methods. Speaking on the necessity of women having a say in the Government of the country, she referred to the discussion in Parliament on the feeding of children, and said that possibly none of the men in the House of Commons who discussed that

---

[1] Annie Kenney was to become a leading figure in the Women's Social and Political Union, later imprisoned and force fed. Her name is on the plinth of the Millicent Fawcett Statue in Parliament Square. The attack on East Fife relates to the fact that Asquith was the local MP.

question could feed the children. If any of them tried to feed the children for a fortnight they would kill them. When men took upon themselves to decide upon the feeding of school children surely things had come down to an absolute absurdity.

Miss Kenney said they must go on fighting for all they were worth until they made it impossible for the Government to go on without giving them a vote. They wished to know what the supporters of Mr Asquith were going to do when he visited them on the 13th of next month. The women were trying to get a deputation to go to him, and one of his supporters had promised to do his best to persuade Mr Asquith to receive the deputation.

Questions having been invited, Mr George Robertson asked if they had ascertained Captain Gilmour's views on their agitation. Miss Billington said she knew absolutely nothing about Captain Gilmour, and their position was in no way connected with his candidature. The only position they took up was that they had been trying to force Mr Asquith to receive the deputation of women because as Chancellor of the Exchequer he took women's money. (DC)

28 September 1906
Nuisance in Cross Wynd
Dear Sir,

Complaints are being made that Maggie Page, Cross-Wynd, is notwithstanding repeated warnings by the sanitary inspector, continuing to empty dirty water and sewage on the street or into the street gratings. I instructed by Town Council to intimate that provision must at once be made for the disposal of the sewage.

Your faithfully, Charles Gulland, Town Clerk (FEP)

29 September 1906
Property in High Street
Letter to George Gavin from George Galloway[1],
Dear Sir,

---

[1] The writer was George Galloway (1862–1936), writing from Barochan Estate Office, near Houston, Renfrewshire, factor to Sir Charles Bine Renshaw, former carpet manufacturer and Unionist MP for West Renfrewshire.

You will excuse me taking the liberty of writing to you being a stranger to you, but it has occurred to me that you might be able to help me in a little private affair. I have connections with Falkland, as will be evident to you.

There is a house in ruin just opposite the Palace which has lain in a derelict condition in which it is at present for as long as I can remember, caused by the not uncommon disagreement in a family. Just recently through the good offices of Mr Gulland, writer, Falkland I have become part owner of this old house, and as you can well understand it is not a creditable possession to anyone in its present state, so my cousins and myself have decided now that we have the power to do so to try and dispose of the house and piece of ground, so that it may be put into a state of repair creditable to the Town of Falkland. It is first possible that to improve the amenity of the outlook from the Palace Lord Ninian Crichton-Stuart might be disposed to purchase the subject and if you can help to bring this about I would be very glad.

There is a small house adjoining, belonging to George Galloway,[1] who I think works in the Palace Gardens, which might be included in the sale. The two plots of ground put together would make a fair spread for building a new property on, which could be done by you, but which none of us I am afraid are in a position to attempt. Mr Gulland will give you all particulars, he has acted very friendly with the family throughout, and I am sure he will continue to do so until such times as we are able to get the property disposed off.

Yours faithfully, George Galloway. (FEP)

6 October 1906

New Teacher

The School Board have appointed Mr Edwin Justice, Addiewell, West Calder to the post of assistant male teacher, vacated by Mr Nish. Arrangements have been made to give a course of tuition in cookery to the advanced girls attending the Public School. The class is to be conducted by Miss Mitchell, teacher of cookery, and will be held in the Town Hall each Wednesday afternoon. (FFP)

---

[1] In a second letter the writer refers to this George Galloway as his cousin.

SATURDAY, 10TH NOVEMBER 1906:
EXTENSIVE SALE OF HOUSEHOLD FURNITURE
at WESTFIELD, FALKLAND

The Subscribers, favoured with instructions from Messrs Nicoll & Findlay, will sell by auction on the above date, the following:

DRAWING-ROOM. Walnut Cottage Pianoforte; Walnut Suite in Blue Repp, consisting of Settee, 2 Easy Chairs, and 6 Small Chairs; Roll-top Writing Desk, 3 Small Tables, Gilt Mantel Mirror, Brussels Carpet, Axminster Hearth Rug, Skin Mats, Kerb Fender, and Brass Fire-Irons, Mahogany Curtain Pole and Curtains, Whatnot, Pictures and Ornaments.

DINING-ROOM. Mahogany Suit in Leather, consisting of Couch, Lady's and Gent's Easy Chairs and 6 Small Chairs; Walnut Suite in Leather, Ditto; Mahogany Sideboard, Mahogany Telescope Table (3 leaves), Gilt Mantel Mirror, Coal Vase, Mahogany Curtain Pole and Curtains, Brussels Carpet and Hearth Rug, Kerb Fender and Brass Fire-Irons, Skin Mats, Pictures, Ornaments and Sundries.

PARLOUR. Mahogany Oval Table, Sofa in Hair Cloth, Easy Chair, Small Arm Chair, 4 Hair Cloth Chairs, Carpet, Waxcloth, Mats, Fender and Fire-Irons.

BEDROOMS. Walnut Bedroom Suite consisting of Wardrobe, Dressing Chest with Mirror Attached, Marble Basin Stand, Commode, and 2 Chairs; Brass Railed bedstead, 6ft 6in by 4ft 6in; 2 Mahogany Half-Tester Upholstered Bedsteads, Mahogany Chest of Drawers with Large Swing Glass Attached, 2 Mahogany Basin Stands (Marble Tops), 3 Iron Bedsteads, Wicker Chair, Easy Chair, 6 Small Chairs, Mahogany Chest of Drawers, Bedroom Ware, Carpets, Rugs, Fenders, Fire-Irons, Coal Vases, Curtain Poles and Curtains, Trinkets, and the Whole Bed and Table Napery.

KITCHEN. Dresser, Table, 4 Chairs, Iron Bedstead, Stools, Wag-at-the-Wall Clock, Delft, Pots and Pans.

LOBBY. Umbrella Stand, Wax cloth, Set of Croquet, Lobby and Stair Carpet and Rods.

Also Garden Seat and the whole Dairy Utensils.

Sale to Commence at 12 noon
Terms Cash.

THE FIFESHIRE AUCTION CO. LTD. LADYBANK.

10 October 1906

Poaching

William James Reid, labourer, High Street East, was convicted on evidence at Cupar yesterday on a charge of poaching on the east side of the Plantation known as the Blue Brae, on the estate of Lord Ninian Crichton-Stuart. Mr J. E. Grosset, Cupar, prosecuted. Sentence of a fine of 5s, with 30s of expenses, was imposed. (DC)

25 October 1906

Theft

John Lawson, labourer, Cross Wynd was charged at Cupar Sheriff Court yesterday with the theft of 269 lbs of lead piping from the Briggs Plantation Falkland Estate on 17th July. He denied stealing the piping, but admitted having reset it. The Fiscal accepted the plea and Sheriff Thomson passed sentence of 10 days imprisonment. (DC)

1 December 1906

Golf Club President

Letter to Mr James Peggie, Secretary of Golf Club

Dear Sir,

While I think that someone more actively associated and better acquainted with the pastime than I am might easily have been got to fill the office of President, I am willing to accept the honour confirmed upon me by the members of the club, if they think I can be of any assistance to them.

Yours faithfully, George Gavin. (FEP)

24 December 1906

Sale of Work

By a Female Correspondent.

Very pretty and seasonable were the decorations in the Public School on Saturday, when a bazaar was held in order to raise funds for the improvement of the golf course and to erect a pavilion or clubhouse. The four stalls, two laden with useful and fancy goods, one with cakes, sweets and toys, and another with game and produce, were arranged in the largest classroom, while two other rooms were utilised for refreshments and amusements.

At Stall 1, with its tasteful draperies of purple, lavender, and white, and badges of violets, Mrs Gavin, Falkland Palace, was daintily gowned in helio colienne, white silk blouse and white fur toque, with lavender. She had as assistants tiny Miss Margaret Gavin in white, Mrs Dun, Woodmill, in stylish black costume, the coatee opening over a cream blouse threaded with helio velvet ribbon, and purple velvet toque adorned with high loopings of violet and green ribbon; Miss Madge Dun in grey and blue tweed, and mole-coloured velvet hat; Miss Harriet Dun in a prettily braided costume of pale green serge, and hat to match. Miss McGregor, Cupar, was also in green, with stone marten fur necklet; Miss McDonald, Perth, in floral crepe de chine, shoulder frill, and belt of helio silk and dainty white fur toque; Miss Venters in black, Miss Matthew, who acted as palmist, in grey green tweed, and Miss Ada Bain, Burnside, Boarhills, in smart purple cloth costume, white fox fur, and white beaver felt hat. Also at this stall were the Misses Lawson, three, Falkland Wood.

Stall 2. The colours of which were crimson and green, was superintended by Mrs Johnston, The Manse, attired in cinnamon brown face cloth, and brown hat trimmed with ruches of cerise satin ribbon. She had the help of Miss Gulland, Millfield, who wore a black hat with her cream serge toilette; Miss Murray, House of Falkland, and her sister Miss Rhoda in navy and scarlet, while little Miss Winifred Murray was all in crimson; Miss Miller in brown and Miss Sharp, Cupar, in black, white silk blouse, and violet velvet hat.

The ladies at the Cake, Sweets and Toy Stall were Miss Bonthrone, Newton of Falkland, in smart black toilette, with sable furs; Miss Jack, also in black, with caracul[1] coat and white felt toque with purple flowers; and Mrs Livingstone, Lomondvale in black and white. They had as assistants Mrs Bonthrone, Kinsleith, Cupar; Mrs Webster, Nisbetfield, in petunia velvet and grebe toque; Miss Bryce, Falkland, in navy blue, with beaver fur toque; Miss Horn and Miss A. Laing, while Masters John and Tom Murray (the latter in Highland Dress) assisted by Master J. M. Chrystal, were energetic vendors of confectionery. The refreshments were in charge of Mrs Peggie, assisted by

---

[1] Caracul coat is made from pelts of very young caracul lambs.

the Misses Anderson, Hardie, Page and Flo Richardson,[1] who all wore white caps and aprons.

The Visitors

Amongst the visitors were Lady Murray, House of Falkland, who was wearing sable furs, with a black costume and velvet toque with white plumage; Mrs Tarbolton, Edinburgh,[2] also in black, with seal coat and crimson velvet toque with cherries; Mrs Makgill Crichton of Lathrisk; Miss Lumsden, in navy, with seal coat and fur toque with wings; Mrs Morrison in claret coloured cloth costume, sable furs and velvet hat; and Mrs Shearer, Auchtermuchty, in black, was accompanied by Miss Shearer. Mrs Jackson, Lomondvale, wore a stylish terra hat with shaded plumes, and caracul coat over black. Miss Martin of Priestfield was present; Mrs Ogilvy, Westfield, in black with sealskin coat and grebe toque; Mrs Richardson, Schoolhouse, in black and white; Mrs Michie in black and caracul coat; Miss Robertson, Edinburgh, in lavender tweed and pale pink felt hat; and Miss Davidson, Abernethy, in dark green. Miss Morgan, Nochnary, was in dark blue and hat to harmonise with sable tails.

Delightful concerts were given at intervals, the performers at which included the Misses Madge Dun, Bain, Davidson, Bryce, Matthew, McLeod and Melville; and Messrs D. McGregor, Edinburgh (cello), Stewart Innes, Cupar, and Joe Hunter, Perth. Mr Anderson proved an energetic secretary, and Mr C. Jackson, jnr, acted efficiently as convener of the amusements Committee. (DC)

---

[1] Flo is probably Flora Richardson, daughter of John Richardson the head teacher at Falkland. Her sister Janet married Robert Miller Jnr.

[2] Beatrice Tarbolton was the daughter of Charles Gulland, the Town Clerk, and the wife of Harold Ogle Tarbolton, architect who did work at the House of Falkland and designed the Falkland Town Clerk's Office.

1907

10 January 1907

Use of the approach

Letter to George Gavin

Dear Sir,

I received your note today about going through the Lodge Gate. For myself I never go except going with the trap for Mr Ogilvie,[1] for my children I told them not to go and I will see that they don't go for the ploughmen.

I told them after I saw you that they were not allowed through the gate but the young men says they won't stop. I can't do no more and if I hear much more about it I will leave the place altogether.

Your faithfully, James Martin,[2] Westfield Farm. (FEP)

13 January 1907

Slaughterhouse

An offer by Mr Christopher Brunton, butcher, to rent a slaughterhouse if provided for by the Burgh, or alternatively to pay so much for each animal killed, was submitted but it was considered inadvisable for the Council to undertake the building of a slaughterhouse, and if Mr Brunton were to erect premises for himself suitable as a public slaughterhouse the Council might be prepared to consider

---

[1] Mr Ogilvie was the tenant farmer at Westfield.

[2] James Martin was the grieve at Westfield.

favourably the taking of them over at mutual valuation when the occasion arises but without any definite obligation whatever to that effect on the part of the Council. (FTCM)

19 January 1907

Concert

A recital of the sacred cantata, *The Messiah's Coming.* was given by a select choir in the United Free Church on Saturday evening. The various choruses, solos, were rendered exceedingly well. The part singers were Misses I. Hill, A. Peggie, A. Jobson, J. Couper, and Messrs Wotherspoon. T. Grant, A. Grieve, D. Peggie, J. Balfour. Miss Bryce played the accompaniments, and Mr Burgon was conductor. (FFP)

19 January 1907

Sale of Work

The committee of the recent Sale of Work held by the Golf Club met in the Town Hall on Monday evening. Mr McMillan, president, occupied the chair. The financial statement of the Sale of Work was submitted, showing the drawings to have been as follows:

Subscriptions by members of club and donations, £22 16s; tickets for grand prize drawing, £49 19s; Work Stall: Mrs Gavin, £57 2s 3d; Mrs Johnston, £6 15s 8d; Cake and Toy Stall: Mrs Bonthrone, Mrs Jack and Mrs Livingstone, £25 17s 8d; Games and Produce Stall: Messrs Bonthrone and Gavin, £12 4s 7d; Refreshment Stall: Mrs Peggie, £10 7s 6d; Entertainments, £5 4s 3d; Admission to Sale, £4 12s; Miscellaneous, £1 4s 6d; total: £251 8s 8d. ; total expenditure: £31 5s 6d; total £220 3s 2d. The Rev. Lyon Johnston proposed vote of thanks to the convener, secretary and stallholders. (FFP)

19 January 1907

Recital

A humorous and dramatic recital of outstanding merit was delivered by Mr J. Augustus Beddie, Edinburgh, in the Drill Hall on Friday last. Mr J. Richardson presided over a large audience, who, by their unstinted applause, put the seal of approval upon the evening's entertainment. Mr Beddie's programme, including as it did such well known recitations as "A Fight with Death" (from Ian McLaren's "Beside the Bonnie Briar Bush"); "The Twa Courtin's"; "The Spoken Word" (an American story); "Sandy McGlashan's Courtship" and "Waterloo" (Conan Doyle), gave him ample scope for elocutionary powers of which he is no mean master. At the close of the recital, which lasted an hour and a half, the lecturer and the Chairman received the customary votes of thanks. (FN)

22 January 1907
Handloom weaving
The Handloom Weaving Industry carried on by Lady Margaret Crichton-Stuart has now been given up. This concern was started some years ago by her Ladyship in order to revive a dying industry, but the experiment has proved most unprofitable and has had to be abandoned. (FEP)

23 January 1907
Garden produce
Letter to Mrs Wilson, Housekeeper, Ovington House, London
Dear Madam,
   I am sending today addressed to Lord Ninian Crichton-Stuart a box containing garden produce from the Palace gardens. The box will continue to be sent weekly thereafter. I enclose a label addressed to the gardener which you might attach to the box when returning it. In future the gardener's address will be written on the back of the label sent with the box, and it will accordingly be necessary merely to turn the label when returning the box.[1] It will be a favour if you will see that the boxes are regularly returned.
   Yours truly, George Gavin. (FEP)

8 February 1907
Palace telephone
Dear Sir,
   You must doubtless be aware of the trouble which I have had ever

---

[1] The padlocks on the boxes were found to be destroyed when they were returned to the gardener.

since the telephone was put into my office here. Recently the linesman has been in almost daily attendance, but immediately on his departure I have been unable to call the exchange. Scarcely a day passes without my having to go to Falkland Post Office to ask them to telephone the exchange, as I am unable to do so. I wish you to verify this statement from the Postmaster in Falkland and also from the officials in the exchange at Kingskettle.

I have borne with the matter until I am now unable to do so any longer. I have had to expend much money on telegrams owing to the instrument not being available, and the aggravation is now such that as I say I can tolerate it no longer. Your officials seem entirely unable to discover the fault and have come and gone almost daily without any result. I have to intimate to you that I shall cease to use the telephone in my office as from this date, and shall refuse to pay the proportion of the rent as from now. Apart from the fact that the Post Office have committed a breach of contract and there is further to be considered, the annoyance not only to myself but to Sir John Murray, tenant of Falkland House, who has been put very frequently to great inconvenience.

Yours faithfully, George Gavin. (FEP)

9 February 1907

B.O.A.F.G. social

The members of the Lomond Oak Lodge held their annual social and ball on Friday evening, Provost Miller presided. After tea a splendid and varied programme was sustained by Mrs Davis, Uddingston; Miss A. Melville, Newburgh; Miss Margaret Murray, Falkland and Mr James Craw, Kirkcaldy. Dance music was supplied by a quadrille band from Kettle. Messrs R. Miller and P. Robertson acted as MCs. (FFP)

11 February 1907

Golf Club pavilion

Letter to Mr Pitman, Edinburgh

Dear Sir,

You may recollect that some considerable time ago I mentioned to you that I had been asked by the local golf club to approach Lord

Ninian with the view of getting his Lordship to give the club a site for the erection of a pavilion or club house. The course is over the Myre or Falkland Common, and while the present magistrates and councillors of Falkland were willing to grant a site, the club considered that, as this grant might be withdrawn by any future body of magistrates and town councillors there would be no security of tenures, and there being a corner of land on Fiddlehall belonging to Lord Ninian, immediately adjoining the common which in their view would be eminently suitable for the purpose. The officials of the club resolved to ask his Lordship if he would give this small piece of ground on which to erect a club house, funds for which were raised at a bazaar or Sale of Work. The ground extends to twenty six yards and is part of the land presently let to the tenant of Fiddlehall, who is quite willing that the small corner should be given off, as it will straighten field.

Yours faithfully, George Gavin. (FEP)

14 February 14th 1907

Golf Club pavilion

Dear Mr Gavin,

I duly received your letter of 11th and the parcel containing an Ordnance Survey Sheet. You suggest that Lord Ninian shall give a lease of ground for a pavilion and be used by the Golf Club at a nominal rent, and you ask the longest period for which Lord Ninian could legally give such a lease. In view of the peculiar terms under which Lord Ninian holds the property he cannot grant a lease for such a purpose for a longer period than his own life. In fact he cannot give any security of tenure, as the lease would come to an end at his death. The Magistrates of Falkland are willing to grant a site on the Common, but the Club considered that this grant might be withdrawn by any future body of Magistrates, and therefore there would be no security of tenure. Now it appears to me that the right of playing golf over the Common may just as well be withdrawn by any future body of Magistrates, and if this were done, any pavilion erected on Lord Ninian's property would become useless. Surely the right to play the game and the right to a site for the pavilion should come from the same source? On the grounds I am certainly of opinion that the site shall be on the Common and not on Falkland Estate. I retain the plan in the meantime is case you wish to communicate further on the subject.

Yours truly, J. Pitman 48, Castle St. Edinburgh. (FEP)

15 February 1907

Palace telephone

Dear Sir,

With reference to my letter to you of the 8th inst. I now write since almost a week has elapsed since you stated that you were "having special attention given to the matter". I do not know to what you refer when you mention "special attention". It is the case, however, that a week has elapsed during which no attention of any kind has been paid to the matter. No one has come here at your insistence. I have, however, to explain to you that if the "special attention" which you intend to give to the matter consist of sending a linesman or engineer here you need not take the trouble to do so, as from the prolonged experience I have had of this attention I feel quite certain that no result will follow, and that, immediately on their departure, I shall be unable, as has hitherto been the case, to call the exchange.

I write specially to make my position perfectly clear to you. I do not care whether I have a telephone or not, it was put on here as an appendage to the one in the House of Falkland and would not have been such a source of aggravation to me since its installation that it has been worse than useless, as I mentioned in my previous letter. I refuse to pay any further rent. I have not used it since I wrote you and do not intend to do so. Having thus explained my position in the matter you can remove the telephone if you think fit. I have no further responsibility with regard to the matter.

Yours faithfully, George Gavin. (FEP)

15 February 1907

Lodge Gates

Letter to Mr Ogilvy (or Ogilvie) Westfield Farm

Dear Mr Ogilvy,

The lodge keeper has complained to me that the foreman's wife came to the Lodge Gates again, the worse of liquor, and insisted on going up the approach. Will you kindly again speak to this woman

25. Brunton House

Photographed in 2018 – a view that would have been impossible before the
demolition of houses opposite to form Brunton Green.

and her husband and impress upon them that conduct of this nature
at the policy gates is reprehensible.

  Yours faithfully, George Gavin. (FEP)

18 February 1907

Weaving

Letter to Melville & Lindsay, Edinburgh

Dear Sir,

  A letter over a year ago when Miss Lane Fox resigned the secretarial duties in connection with Lady Margaret Stuart's home loom
weaving here. It was arranged that I should take over the work. At
that time there was a balance of about £250 of an overdraft due to the
bank, and since then owing to the lack of sales the debt to the bank
has gradually increased. Some time ago Lady Margaret definitely
resolved that the industry would have to be given up. No yarn has,

accordingly, been purchased since her Ladyship's resolution was taken, and in the meantime there are only two old men employed to weave up the yarn which was in hand. On this being accomplished actual work will cease, and the manageress Mrs O'Conner, Brunton House School, will as opportunity offers, sell off the stock in hand which is of as much value as will, when completely realised, repay Lady Margaret Stuart the sum due to the bank. It will now accordingly be necessary to give up the rented loom shops. As you know they are as follows: two in Balmblae, proprietor Miss Agnes Birrell; one in West Port, proprietor Mr Robb London; one in High Street West, proprietor Mrs Harvey;

As you have paid the rents of these shops I have no doubt you will have the names and addresses of the proprietors in full. Kindly therefore on Lady Margaret's behalf send them the usual notice, forty days, before Whitsunday.

Yours faithfully, George Gavin. (FEP)

2 March 1907

Telephone

Letter to Superintendent Engineer, PO Telegraph, Edinburgh

Dear Sir,

I am very much surprised to hear for the first time that the switch in my office has not been manipulated in accordance with the card of instructions. Let me at once say that this is not the case, and that, while the linesman explained the use of this switch to me when the instrument was fitted up, he has never since on any of his numerous visits here, again referred to the matter of the switch. My assistant is able to speak to this, as also to the fact that the switch has always been used correctly and left in its proper position. I cannot, accordingly, allow you to make such a statement, and if you have occasion again to write me regarding this matter it would be well that you should take care before doing so to verify the statements of your officials. If this switch had not been properly used in my office there were bound to have been complaints.

Yours faithfully, George Gavin. (FEP)

6 March 1907

New gamekeeper

Dear Sir,

I shall have your furniture carted to Chancefield on its arrival on Wednesday. [1] I shall send your own men over to the station to assist in the unloading and they can return with the carts. I shall send a conveyance to take your family to Chancefield and you might send me a note as to when you will reach Falkland Road Station. There is a train at 9 a.m. from Dundee reaching Falkland Road at 10 a.m., and which seems to be just suitable if not too early. The next train does not reach here till 2.15 p.m.

I am having the chimneys swept, the ceiling whitewashed and the house washed out.

Yours truly George Gavin. (FEP)

11 March 1907

Orphan boys

Dear Father Vignoles,

Two boys in St Andrew's Home here, Walter Wilson and James Davis have now attained the age of fourteen and are, accordingly, ready to be sent to Craigeach School. The boys have been specially well trained by the matron, Mrs Quilter. They are well mannered, obedient and in every way good boys and I should think will turn out to be a credit to themselves. I can send them to you anytime after the 25th inst., and I shall be glad to know if it will be convenient for you to receive them.

I forgot if I mentioned to you that Robert Grubb has obtained a very good situation as a gardener in Kirkcaldy, about ten miles from here, and is doing very well

With kind regards, George Gavin. (FEP)

25 March 1907

Midden

Letter to William Duncan, Lomond Cottage

---

[1] Gordon Sturrock moved from Barramore Cottages, by Rothesay.

Dear Sir,

I was very much disappointed the other day to find that you are still continuing to have a midden in the Crackland Hillpark. There are scattered over the park a number of tin cans and the hedge side is littered with these and old boots, a part of the Loan's refuse evidently. Be good enough at once to remove the midden stance and carefully clean up the hedge sides. I trust that you have taken away the rubbish laid in the Orchard Park. I observe that you have not cleaned up the paper lying at the side of the Strathmiglo road. As I have frequently mentioned to you the disappointment I feel that you will persist in dumping unsightly refuse upon lands let to you, I have now to say that the terms of your lease prohibiting the laying down of the town's refuse will be strictly enforced, and in future all the town's refuse carried by you must be laid up in the town's common and not any part of Lord Ninian's lands. I cannot allow the lands let by you to be used as a dumping ground for unsightly refuse.

Yours faithfully, George Gavin. (FEP)

1 April 1907

Birth of son and heir

Early this morning a telegram was received at Falkland announcing that a son and heir had been born to Lord Ninian Crichton-Stuart.[1] The announcement was soon converse throughout the town by the ringing of the town and church bells, and flags were hung from the battlements of the palace and from the windows of the Town Hall. A congratulatory telegram was sent to his Lordship conveying good wishes from the Provost, magistrates, and burghers of Falkland. Preparations are being made for a huge bonfire on a prominent part of the Lomond Hill, overlooking Falkland House in the evening. (DET)

6 April 1907

Treat to school children

Sir John and Lady Murray entertained the school children of Falkland

---

[1] Young Ninian Patrick was born on Easter Day (31 March) at his parents' residence, Ovington House, Ovington Square, London. He was known in the family as Ringan.

(numbering about 200), under the direction of Mr Richardson, headmaster, Public School, and Mrs O'Connor,[1] Brunton House Catholic School, on Tuesday afternoon, on the lawn at House of Falkland. The treat commenced with a varied programme of races on a course marked off with flags, under the able direction of Mr D. McMillan, Newton of Falkland. After frolicking for two hours, the children sat down to a sumptuous tea, set out on tables in the quadrangle behind the house. The tea was done full justice to, and at the close Master Jack Murray, in a capital speech to the children, said he hoped they had enjoyed themselves and wished them long life and prosperity. Three rousing cheers were given for Sir John and family. Thereafter prizes were distributed by Lady Murray and the little guests each received a bag of sweets and an orange. During the afternoon a piper enlivened the company with selections.

The following ladies and gentlemen were also present: The Rev. A. Lyon Johnston and Mrs Johnston; Mr and Mrs Gavin and Miss Macdonald; Miss Fairlie, Myres Castle; Miss Gulland, Falkland; Dr and Mrs Howell, London; Dr Jack, Falkland; Mr and Mrs Archibald Walker, Auchtermuchty. Tea was tastefully laid for these in the house. (FN)

3 April 1907

Post Office

Dear Sir,

I hereby give notice that I shall cease to occupy the Post Office premises tenanted by me after 28th May next.

Yours truly, William Middleton. (FEP)

15 April 1907

Old Mrs Ramsay

Letter to Lady Margaret Crichton-Stuart, St John's Lodge, Regents Park, London

Dear Lady Margaret,

Some considerable time ago I mentioned in one or more of my letters that old Mrs Ramsay had ceased to be able to work. She has

---

[1] Sometimes spelt O'Conner.

been in a very poor state of health for several months and is now evidently in reduced circumstances.

Nurse Fraser[1] called upon me the other day to say that Mrs Ramsay was very anxious that her case should be brought under your Ladyship's notice and asking if I would write you regarding it. While it is the case, I am satisfied that she has now no means it must be said that if she has taken care of what was left her at her husband's death she ought not to be in the position in which she is now. Still, she is very necessitous and I have no doubt she thinks that, having been employed by your Ladyship at the weaving, she has some claim for assistance in her present straits. There is, of course, really no claim upon your Ladyship, but as she is a poor creature and in very delicate health no doubt she is in want of assistance.[2]

Yours faithfully, George Gavin. (FEP)

17 April 1907

Too many licences

An application was received from John Kennoway, miner, East Wemyss, for transfer of certificate for the Lomond Tavern. The clerk read a petition signed by a number of influential residents in Falkland objecting to the granting of the licence.

To do so the petition said, would be to make the number of licences in the town excessive, there being at present a licence for every 116 inhabitants. The Rev. Morrison said that an excessive number of licences in any one place was in itself a sound and sufficient reason for reduction. (FH)

17 April 1907

Use of the Approach

Letter to John Ogilvy, Westfield Farm

Dear Sir,

---

[1] There was of course no National Health Service at this time – district nurses were funded by charity.

[2] Payment to Mr Brunton, butcher, supplied to sick/poor per Nurse Fraser. 9s. Payment to Mr Brunton, butcher, chicken etc supplied to sick/poor per Mrs Gavin. 5s.8d.

I regret to say that young Martin again came down the approach to the Lodge Gates on the evening of Monday, between 8 and 9 p.m. and was challenged by the Lodge-keeper. It seems perfectly clear that this lad does not intend to keep his promise to you and that it is his intention to set the instructions given him at defiance.

Yours faithfully, George Gavin. (FEP)

7 May 1907

Old curling pond

The Town Council had to deal with the question as to the maintenance or abolition of the site of the old curling pond and curling house in the Myre. Mr Gulland submitted a letter from the secretary of Falkland Golf Club relative to the subject, and after reference was made to the terms of the grants to the respective clubs and discussion the Council agreed that the Curling Club should retain the old site and curling house, have the house cleared out, locked up and kept in a sanitary condition and further it was recommended by Mr Charles Jackson that the Clerk should write to the secretary of the Golf Club drawing their attention to the conditions of the grant and suggesting that in the event of any further facility being required the Council should be consulted. (FTCM)

7 May 1907

Football Club

An application was submitted to the Town Council from the secretary of the Football Club for permission to form a pitch in the Myre. Mr Forsyth moved and Mr Lister seconded that this should be granted and that a committee of the Council be appointed to meet the Football Club on the ground with a view to fixing a suitable pitch and to report to the next meeting. (FTCM)

1 June 1907

Death – Jackson

At Lomondvale, Falkland, on the 25th ult., Euphemia Walker, wife of Charles Jackson, manufacturer. (FN)

June 8th 1907

House sale

To be sold by public roup, within the Bruce Arms, Hotel, on Wednesday 26th June 1907, at 3 p.m.

That dwelling house, situated at High Street (East), at present occupied by George William Galloway.

Upset Price, £45. Rental, £3

No Feu Duty.

Further information will be given by the subscribers, who have the titles and articles of roup.

T. & T. Johnston, solicitors, 180 High St. Kirkcaldy. (FFP)

15 June 1907

Post Office

Preparations are being made for the removal of the Post Office to the shop in High Street, recently re-modelled next door to the present office. (FN)

15 June 1907

Photographing the Palace

Letter to George Gavin

Dear Sir,

Re. your letter of the 11th inst. I called on Wednesday the 12th inst to give you a personal explanation but you were from home. The facts of the case are as follows. We called at the Palace about 12 o'clock and asked the official in charge if we could have permission to photograph the courtyard for the purpose of reproducing it as a picture post card. He replied that we could but that we had to pay for admission, we duly did so as your visitors book will testify. The camera was put up and the children were playing about, evidently wishing to be photographed.[1]

The light was unsuitable for our purpose so we had to go back again in the afternoon. The children were there again so we had either to photograph them or ask them to run away, and as we concluded those in charge knew they were to be photographed, we did so. We were entirely unaware of the identity of the children until we received your letter.

We have to express our great regret at your evident displeasure, and to assure you that it was done inadvertently and with no intent of making capital out of the children. We trust this explanation will satisfy you.

Yours truly, John Gilmour, 94, Bonnygate, Cupar. (FEP)

19 July 1907
Paper for the nursery
Letter from Strum & Knight, 67, South Audley St., London.
Dear Mr Gavin,

We are requested by Lord Ninian Crichton-Stuart to inform you we are sending 16 pieces of Moire paper, 12 yards long by 21 ins wide, for the Nursery. Will you kindly have the room measured and see if it requires more, his Lordship thinks it will. Will you please send us at once the quantity of frieze for the top requires, it is 19½ ins, deep and a hunting frieze, made in panels 5 ft. long, so that if you could give us the different lengths all round the room we could help you with it and have it right. Thanking you in anticipation,

Yours faithfully, Strum & Knight. (FEP)

---

[1] These were presumably the Gavin children, who lived at the Palace with their parents.

19 July 1907

Lord Ninian moving to Falkland

Dear Provost Millar,

I have been asked by Lord Ninian Crichton-Stuart to acquaint the Magistrates and Town Council that he is coming early in September, along with Lady Ninian and their son, to take up residence permanently at House of Falkland.[1] Will you kindly accordingly inform the Town Council at their first meeting.

Yours faithfully, George Gavin. (FEP)

23 July 1907

Milk for House of Falkland

Letter to Lord Ninian

Your Lordship,

I have seen Mr Ogilvie of Westfield, who will be ready to set aside a special cow and to supply the very best milk. I have impressed upon him the importance of this, but as both Mr Ogilvie and his wife are very superior people your Lordship may thoroughly rely upon their taking the utmost care with the milk supply. I propose to have the pails or vessels in which your son's milk will be conveyed from the farm to House of Falkland constructed with a small padlock and key so that the risk of interference will not happen. If it were possible it would help Mr Ogilvie if I could be told what quantity of milk will be required for the establishment daily, he will also be prepared to supply butter and fowls.

Your obedient servant, George Gavin. (FEP)

27 July 1907

Lord and Lady Ninian Crichton-Stuart

We understand that Lord and Lady Ninian Crichton-Stuart with their son are expected home to House of Falkland in the first week of September, and that they will thereafter make it their permanent residence. A public welcome is likely to be offered them by the Provost, Magistrates and others. (FN)

---

[1] Sir John Murray had moved out at the end of the four-year lease.

30 July 1907

Perth race meeting

Letter to Henry Jamison, Esq., Perth

Dear Sir,

Many thanks for your reply to my telegram of this afternoon as to the dates of Perth Meeting. The information was required for Lord Ninian Crichton-Stuart, who is presently in Ireland, but who along with Lady Ninian is coming to take up residence permanently at House of Falkland early in September.

Yours faithfully, George Gavin. (FEP)

30 July 1907

Race meeting dates

Dear Lord Ninian,

On receiving your telegram of this afternoon I wired to Mr Harry Jamison, secretary of the Perth meeting for the dates and reply to your Lordship as follows "Perth Balls 25th and 27th, races 26th and 27th September.

Your obedient servant, George Gavin. (FEP)

30 July 1907

Furniture arriving

Letter from Henry Burgess, Brompton Road, London

Dear Sir,

We beg to inform you that we have dispatched to Ladybank Station today a pantechnicon van containing goods from Square.[1] We are informed that the van will be at Ladybank on Friday morning. Will you kindly arrange for three horses and cart from the station. We have also sent a railways trunk load of furniture consigned to Falkland Road Station. I am sending a man down Thursday night to unload the van on Friday morning and it is then proposed that the van after being unloaded at Falkland House should go to Falkland Road Station and pick up the furniture from the railway trunk. It is better for the man who packs the trunk here to unpack it on arrival. I hope

---

[1] i.e. Ovington Square.

26. Falkland Road Station

The station was about a mile south of Freuchie and three miles east of
Falkland. It opened in 1847 and closed in 1958. There is no trace of it today.

all these arrangements will meet with your approval. The carriage
will be paid this end.

Yours Faithfully, Henry Burgess. (FEP)

31 July 1907

Furniture delivery

Letter to Mr Henry Burgess, c/o Messrs W. D. Hodge and Co Ltd, London
Dear Sir,

I am favoured with your letter of yesterday. I shall send three good
horses to Ladybank Station on Friday morning to bring the pantechnicon over to House of Falkland. I shall also have men in attendance
at the house to assist your man to unload. I note that the horses will
be required to go to Falkland Road Station to bring here the contents
of an ordinary van. A number of servants from Ovington House are
coming on Thursday by the 8.45 p.m. train from Kings Cross, arriving
at Falkland Road Station at 7.45 a.m. on Friday. A conveyance will be
meeting that train and if your man would travel by the same train he
would be driven from the station along with the servants.

Yours Faithfully, George Gavin. (FEP)

1 August 1907

Local wedding

A large gathering of interested spectators filled the Parish Church of Falkland yesterday on the occasion of the wedding of Miss Helen Lawson, daughter of Mr John Lawson, the respected tenant of Falkland Wood Farm, to the Rev. Andrew Robertson, parish minister of Mochrum, Wigtonshire. The ceremony was performed by the Rev. Johnston, Falkland, assisted by the Rev. W. W. Clark, one of the chaplains to the Edinburgh garrison. The bride was handsomely attired in cream satin mousseline, the train adorned with lovers' knots in silk puffings, and the bodice richly trimmed with lace. The pretty yoke of cream and gold embroidery was caught with clusters of white heather and orange blooms. She also wore a long tulle veil and wreath of orange blossoms. Her present from the bridegroom was a lovely amethyst and pearl pendant.

Misses Isa and Cathie Lawson, the bride's sisters, attended as bridesmaids, and wore dainty frocks of turquoise blue colienne, trimmed with lace and ruches of ribbon. White crinoline hats draped with tulle and hydrangeas completed their pretty toilettes. Their presents from the bridegroom were pearl pendants. The bride's mother was gowned in black with heliotrope flowers in her crinoline straw bonnet. The groomsman was the Rev. John Dale, Rothesay.

A reception was held after the wedding at Falkland Wood, when Mr and Mrs Lawson entertained a large number of guests. Numerous and handsome gifts were received by the young couple, who left soon after on their honeymoon tour. Mrs Robertson's travelling gown being champagne voile, worn with a becoming hat wreathed with blue flowers. (DC)

2 August 1907

Flower show

Dear Mr Gavin,

As Treasurer of the Horticultural Society here, I will be pleased to have Lord Ninian Crichton-Stuart's annual donation to our fund.

Our annual show and sports is to be held on Saturday 17th inst.,

and we shall be pleased to see you over as representing his Lordship
on that occasion. To try and have a larger interest taken in the society
we have this year introduced a few sports to take place during the
afternoon of the show, and as they take a considerable amount to
provide prizes for same we hope the attendance may be much larger
and the drawings better than in past years.

   Yours faithfully, A. Reekie. (FEP)

3 August 1907
Sudden death

Mrs Edmiston, wife of a factory employee at the linen works of
Messrs Jackson died suddenly on Wednesday morning. She was
going about as usual, and had just returned from shopping in time
for breakfast when she dropped down, death ensuing before medical
aid could be procured. Much sympathy is felt for Mr Edmiston and
his little girl and the other relatives in their sad loss. (FFP)

3 August 1907
Stable block

In connection with the prospective homecoming to Falkland House
of Lord and Lady Crichton-Stuart, considerable alterations and exten-
sions are being made to the stables. The work has already commenced. The contractors are: Mr James Forsyth, Falkland, building
and mason work; Mr Alex Fraser, Falkland, joiner work; Mr W.
Peggie, Falkland, slate and plaster work; Mr W. Stewart, Cupar,
plumber work. (FFP)

10 August 1907
Coachman needed

Letter to Mr Charles Pollock
Dear Sir,

   Lord Ninian wishes to engage for Falkland a single man as head
coachman. He handed to me the other day when I saw him at
Gormanston Castle a letter from George Levenston, who was under
you at one time and his Lordship asked me to enquire as to him. I
hear however that he is now married and consequently need not be
further considered. Could you recommend a single man. He would

live in the Mess Room as your late house[1] is now to be occupied by the butler. As his Lordship and Lady Ninian come here on the 31st inst. a coachman would be required to be here before them, so there is very little time. I shall accordingly be very much obliged if you would write me by return saying whether you know of any suitable man.

Yours faithfully, George Gavin. (FEP)

12 August 1907

Advertisement for coachman

Coachman wanted for nobleman's establishment in Scotland; must be unmarried and able to commence duties fortnight hence. None need apply who have not first class experience and references. Reply stating age and qualifications to *Scotsman* Office. (FEP)

12 August 1907

Wine bins

Dear Mr Gavin,

We thank you for your letter of 9th inst., and we have ordered the racks for the bins in the dispense room. Could you get the joiner to supply for each bin in the Main Wine Cellar a rough wooden batten two inches square and whatever is the width of the bins (say 3ft.) in length? This is for the necks of the first row of bottles to rest upon and it saves using laths of which several thicknesses are required. 44 dozens of wine are to be sent off from our London cellars to Falkland Road Station on Wednesday 14th inst., but we have not yet heard of the despatch of the Oxford wines. We shall be able to get the Oxford and London wines into 15 or 16 bins. How would it do to subdivide say 5 of the bins on the left-hand side of the cellar by wooden partitions into 4. In these we could stow the oddments which we have packed up at Falkland? They would thus be kept separate and would be easily got at.

Yours faithfully, Page & Sandeman, Buchanan St. Glasgow. (FEP)

---

[1] The East Lodge.

17 August 1907

Lord and Lady Ninian Crichton-Stuart

Lord and Lady Ninian Crichton-Stuart, with their infant son, are to take up their residence in Falkland House on Saturday 31st inst. To give them a fitting welcome, the Town Council have resolved to meet them at the Fountain at Falkland Cross and present them with an address. The Cross will be surmounted by a festive arch. (FN)

19 August 1907

Chauffeur's furniture

Letter from Hodges & Co Brompton Road, London

Dear Mr Gavin,

I am sending tomorrow the chauffeur's furniture, it will be packed loose in a railway company trunk, which leaves London tomorrow and will be consigned to Falkland Road Station. Will you kindly arrange for a cart to collect same from the station about Friday next. It is not worth while sending a man down to unpack same. We will pay carriage this end.

Yours faithfully, Henry Burgess. (FEP)

21 August 1907

Coachman

Dear Lord Ninian,

Having endeavoured to trace a man who was second coachman to Sir Robert Moncreiffe six years ago, and who was an excellent whip and always turned out smart, but was unsuccessful in finding him. I inserted an advertisement and got various applications of sorts. I selected three to meet me in Edinburgh whose application looks all right on paper, but I did not consider any of them suitable when I saw them. Meantime I had written Pullen for the address of your Lordship's London saddlers. Pullen wrote him direct asking him to send me particulars. As time was pressing I wired your Lordship the report of Venables letter and received your reply to send the man to the Bachelors Club at 12 a.m. on Thursday. I wired Venables to arrange this and have his reply that the man will be there.

Yours obediently, George Gavin. (FEP)

23 August 1907

Lord Ninian's homecoming

Dear Lord Ninian,

It has been arranged that on the afternoon of Saturday 31st, on arrival of yourself and Lady Ninian the carriage will be stopped for a few minutes in front of the Town Hall, or rather on the old market cross, when the Town Council, by the hands of the Provost, will present an address of welcome. The tenantry and workmen will greet the carriage at the Lodge Gate and escort it to the front door of House of Falkland. One of the oldest tenants, Mr Tod, Easter Cash, will on behalf of the tenantry welcome your Lordship and Lady Ninian. There is a Saturday train from Waverly at 2.15 p.m. reaching Falkland Road Station at 3.56 p.m. also an ordinary train from Waverly at 2.25 p.m. due at Falkland Road Station at 4.22 p.m.

I have written to the Roxburgh Hotel, Edinburgh and the rooms are reserved for the night of Friday 30th inst. A reserved compartment will be kept on the train from Ardrossan to Central Station, Glasgow, and on the connecting train from Glasgow to Edinburgh.

Your obedient servant, George Gavin. (FEP)

25 August 1907

Hotel Room for Lord and Lady Ninian

Letter to Manager, Roxburgh Hotel, Edinburgh

Dear Sir,

I have been requested by Lord Ninian Crichton-Stuart to ask you to reserve for himself and Lady Ninian a bedroom for the night of Friday 30th August.

A bedroom will also be required for their infant son and his maid on the same night.[1] This room should be a large one. They would only be required for one night. His Lordship along with her Ladyship, their son and the nurse will reach Edinburgh by the train from Glasgow arriving at 11.10. p.m.

Yours faithfully, George Gavin. (FEP)

---

[1] Roxburgh Hotel is in Charlotte Square. Mr Nichol, Station Master at Falkland Road Station, would meet them when they arrived.

26 August 1907

Horses and carriages

Dear Lord Ninian

I have received your telegram of this afternoon. I am sending Birrell to London tonight to bring down the horses and carriages. [1] I have wired Webb asking him if he can meet him. I have advised in the wire that your Lordship wishes old livery sent. I shall instruct Birrell fully (three horses, one carriage) and can easily get a reliable temporary man to drive your Lordship and Lady Ninian from Falkland Road Station on arrival at 3.56 p.m.

Your obedient servant, George Gavin. (FEP)

26 August 1907

Arrival of Lord and Lady Ninian

Letter to Provost Miller

Dear Provost,

I have just received a telegraph from Lord Ninian, in which he says that he will arrive along with Lady Ninian at Falkland Road Station at 3.56 p.m. on Saturday. I am notifying the Town Clerk to this effect so that he may inform the Magistrates and Town Council.

Yours faithfully, George Gavin. (FEP)

26 August 1907

Photography at homecoming

Letter from The County Studio, Cupar

Dear Sir,

We, if weather favourable, coming to Falkland on Saturday 1st to photograph the ceremony at Falkland Cross (presentation of address by Town Council) for press purposes. We should esteem it a favour if you will be kind enough to inform us at what hour the ceremony has

---

[1] Only two horses in London to come here, other at Aldershot. Birrell arrived home from London early August 29th. Barnstaple will be at station at 3.56 p.m. with carriage. Barnstaple appointed coachman September 1907. Great Northern Railway Co. account for conveyance from London to Falkland of carriages, horses, motor car and dog; also for two third class tickets for chauffeur and wife. £36 17s 5d.

been arranged for.

Yours respectively D. Gordon & Son, Cupar. (FEP)

29 August 1907

Piper for homecoming

Dear Sir,

With reference to our conversation re. Piper. I have arranged with Donald MacDonald, presently with us in the nurseries to be with you on Saturday. He will leave here by 10.59 a.m. train, and will report himself to you when he reaches Falkland. I trust you will have good weather to welcome His Lordship home and that the ceremony will be pleasant to all. I am afraid I will not be able to be present myself. I trust MacDonald will give satisfaction, as I am sure he will do.

With kind regards and best wishes. I remain yours faithfully, D. Thomson, Edward Sang & Sons, Kirkcaldy. (FEP)

2 September 1907

Football Club

Dear Mr Gavin,

Referring to our meeting in Mr Gulland's office. Seeing that the Golf Club are already established on the Myre, our Football Club have decided that it would be very undesirable and indeed incorrect to press our claim for a pitch thereon. We however, would be greatly pleased if you would approach Lord Ninian Crichton-Stuart on our behalf, to ask him if he would kindly allow us a pitch on his Lordship's estate, whereon we could practice and play our matches.

Solicitous as to his Lordship's favourable reply, and as the season is now upon us, we shall be gratified by your answer at an early date.

For the Lomondside Football Club

I am, Sir, your obedient servant. William Lamb, Horsemarket (secretary). (FEP)

3 September 1907

Town Council entertained at the Palace

Letter from George Innes, Fife Herald & Journal, Cupar

Dear Mr Gavin,

If you have time to ring me up on the phone tomorrow. I would be glad to get 3 or 4 lines from you of the entertainment to the Town Council at the Palace on Saturday night. Were you in the chair? John Lawson was telling me today that Lord Ninian joined the company there also. He evidently enjoyed himself on Saturday and seemed greatly pleased with the reception given him. What is the proper title to give the son and heir when speaking of him?

I have to thank you very much for so kindly introducing me to Lord Ninian, I was quite charmed by his courtesy and most agreeably surprised that he should have remembered about the photo. [1] I hope you will have great pleasure in all your intercourse with him and his Lady.

Believe me,

Yours very sincerely, George Innes. (FEP)

5 September 1907

Coachman appointed

Letter to Mr Barnstaple, Head Coachman

Dear Sir,

I think it well to put in writing the terms of your engagement by Lord Ninian Crichton-Stuart as his coachman. Your duties will be those of head coachman, and you will be provided with such help as his Lordship may consider necessary. Your wages will be at the rate of £70 per annum, and you will be provided with stable clothes and livery. You will be provided with accommodation in the mess-rooms at the stables, and the services of a woman to clean the rooms will be supplied. The engagement will be terminable on one month's notice from either party, which notice will apply also to the occupation of the rooms at the stable.

Yours faithfully, George Gavin. (FEP)

7 September 1907

Homecoming

There were unwonted signs of rejoicing in front of the royal and ancient Palace of Falkland on Saturday afternoon, when the town was

---

[1] George Innes asked for a photo of Lord and Lady Ninian and their baby for the *Fife Herald*.

27. Lord and Lady Ninian being welcomed to Falkland
The scene at the arch by the fountain.

gaily decorated. The occasion was the arrival from Ireland of Lord
and Lady Ninian Crichton-Stuart and their infant son, to take up
residence at the House of Falkland.

On arrival of Lord Ninian, his wife, and son, the carriage was
drawn up under the arch at the fountain, and the Provost, magistrates
and Councillors, presented an illuminated address. Lord Ninian in
reply, said it gave him great pleasure to be once more with them. He
and his wife had been looking forward to coming to Falkland. On
reaching the lodge gate the horses were unyoked and the carriage was
drawn by young men up the avenue. Another address was presented
in the name of the tenantry on the estate. Lord Ninian suitably
replied, remarking that he could not thank them sufficiently for their
extraordinary welcome. The company later proceeded to a large
marquee in the grounds, where a cake and wine banquet took place.
Later in the evening Falkland Town Council and the leading residents
in the town were entertained to another banquet in the Palace, over
which Mr Gavin presided. A similar toast list was gone through, and
the whole proceedings were marked by cordial good feeling.

Although a good deal of rain fell throughout the evening, fair weather prevailed during the open air ceremonies, and when the heaviest showers came on the company were sheltered in the marquee.[1] (FFP)

7 September 1907

Bicycle accident

The groans of a working man lying beside his bicycle at the side of the public road half-a-mile south of New Inn attracted the attention of a picnic party driving to Falkland on Saturday afternoon. A halt was at once called, and several of the male members went to the unfortunate man's assistance. His head and face were terribly cut and bruised. It was learned that his name was David Bonthrone, that he was a drystone dyker, and that he lived with his mother at Muirhead. He was thereupon taken home by his rescuers. Medical aid was summoned, and his wounds dressed. (FN)

7 September 1907

Band excursion

The members of the Barry, Ostlere & Shepherd Band[2] drove from Kirkcaldy to Falkland on Saturday afternoon. The weather at the start was threatening, and except for a heavy shower experienced on the road, it kept up well during the afternoon. The destination was

---

1 Payment to James Carmichael, Cupar, for Stuart Tartan ribbon for decorations at homecoming. 2s 6d. Payment to Galloway's Emporium, for flags for homecoming. £1 10s 8d. Payment to William Mason, Bruce Arms, Hotel, purveying cake and wine banquet to tenantry on occasion of homecoming and hire of Marquee, also banquet to Magistrates and Town Council. £41 3s 6d. Payment to Foresters men for assisting at decorations for homecoming. £3 6s 6d. Payment to Thomas Williamson, saddler, for rope and twine for decorations for homecoming. 4s 5d. Payment to Robert Miller, joiner work of arches at homecoming. £7 17s 1d.

2 Barry, Ostlere & Shepherd were a floorcloth manufacturing company in Kirkcaldy.

reached in good time, and after partaking of an excellent tea in Ness's Temperance Hotel, the company broke up to explore the historic old town. All the houses were decorated in honour of the homecoming of Lord Ninian Crichton-Stuart, and the visitors had an opportunity of witnessing the welcome given. A thoroughly enjoyable time was spent, and when the brake arrived home at Kirkcaldy at 10.30 all expressed themselves delighted. (FN)

10 September 1907
Use of the Lodge Gate approach
Letter to John Morgan[1], Kilgour
Dear Sir,

Now that Lord Ninian has taken up permanent residence at House of Falkland it will be necessary that the privilege which you have hitherto exercised, of using the Approach to House of Falkland in going to and from the Church on Sundays, should cease. I feel sure that you will quite understand that the approach to the House should not, in the altered circumstances, now be made use of.

Yours faithfully, George Gavin. (FEP)

14 September 1907
Lord Ninian Crichton-Stuart
At a meeting of Cardiff Conservative Association on Monday night, Lord Ninian Crichton-Stuart of Falkland, who has resigned his position in the Guards to enter political life, was virtually adopted as Conservative candidate for Cardiff at the next election. His Lordship, who had a most enthusiastic reception, said he stood before them as a loyal supporter of Mr Balfour, whose policy in placing tariff reform as the first constructive plank in the Conservative policy he heartily endorsed. If returned, he would, in season and out of season, further the policy of uniting by close commercial bonds, the mother country and the colonies. (FN)

---

[1] John Morgan was the tenant farmer at Kilgour.

28. Ness's Temperance Hotel and Stabling, Liquorstane
The Nesses made several unsuccessful applications for a liquor licence.
The building subsequently became a masonic lodge and in 2020
is to be converted to a pharmacy.

14 September 1907

Paintings

Dear Mr Gavin,

I thought you might be interested in seeing three small Falkland paintings, which I am exhibiting at Galloway's Emporium. I am also producing others, all from recent sketches.

Your faithfully, William Wood, Coburg Ave. Stirling. (FEP)

19 September 1907

Car Hire

Letter to Messrs Descamps[1]
Dear Sir,

---

[1] Descamps was a motor specialists at Wemyss Buildings, West End of High Street, Kirkcaldy.

I am instructed by Lord Ninian Crichton-Stuart to enquire if His Lordship can have the hire of the car, which he had recently at Falkland, on the nights of Wednesday and Friday next week. His Lordship is to have a house party, and the car is required to take some of the party to the Perth Race balls on three nights. The car would accordingly be required all night in order to take the party home again in the morning. Lord Ninian's own car will also be going. Kindly write me on receipt whether you will be able to send the car and I shall let you know the exact hour when the car should reach House of Falkland.

Yours faithfully, George Gavin. (FEP)

20 September 1907

Golf clubhouse opening

Letter to Hon. Thomas Cochrane MP, Crawford Priory, Springfield

Dear Sir,

As a member of the building committee of Falkland Golf Club if you could kindly see your way to introduce in a few words Lady Ninian Crichton-Stuart tomorrow when she has consented to open the new pavilion. I have to thank you for your reply in the affirmative, and to express the thanks of the committee for your kindness in having agreed to this duty. The committee are deeply grateful to you. I may explain that it had been arranged that Mr Fairlie of Myres Castle should undertake this part of the ceremony but Mr Fairlie has been rather ill and has been confirmed to bed, and he has written that he is not able to be present on Saturday on account of this illness. I enclose a cutting from the *Fife News* of today, which will briefly give you particulars regarding the Club House. It is situated quite near the Palace, and if you could come here or to the Golf House a few minutes prior to the opening ceremony I shall give you any further particulars which may be necessary. I may add that reference to the granting of the site by Lord Ninian Crichton-Stuart is to be made by a member of the Golf Club, (probably the Parish Minister, The Rev. A. Lyon Johnston) in a speech thanking her Ladyship for opening the Golf House.

00Yours faithfully, George Gavin. (FEP)

29. The opening of the Golf Clubhouse

23 September 1907

Golf Clubhouse

The handsome and convenient clubhouse which the Falkland Golf Club have erected from the proceeds of their recent Sale of Work was formally opened on Saturday afternoon by Lady Ninian Crichton-Stuart in [the] presence of a large gathering, including: Lord Ninian Crichton-Stuart of Falkland; the Hon. Thomas Cochrane MP and Lady Gertrude Cochrane of Crawford Priory; The Hon. F. Hanbury-Tracy; Mr Rae Arnot of Lochiehead and party; Mrs and Miss Gulland and Mrs Howell of Millfield; Major Cusin; the Rev. Lyon Johnston and Mrs Johnston; the Rev. J. Morrison and Mrs Morrison; the Rev. Charles Fraser and Mrs Fraser, Freuchie; Mr George Gavin (Falkland Palace) and Mrs Gavin; the Rev. Mr Thomson, Allan Park; Provost and Mrs Millar; Provost and Mrs Ferlie, Auchtermuchty; Dr and Mrs Jack; Dr Shearer, Auchtermuchy, Mr David Bonthrone and Mrs Bonthrone, Newton of Falkland; …

The Hon. Thomas Cochrane said he had been asked to undertake t0he simple task of introducing Lady Ninian Crichton-Stuart, whom they were extremely glad to see there that day. Her kindliness and popular manners would soon make her the most popular and well-liked personage in the whole district. (Applause) It was very appropriate that Lady Stuart should take an interest in sport. She was Irish, and Irish people were fond of sport, and besides, she had married into a good Scottish sporting family. (Applause) In taking an interest in the great national game of golf, her Ladyship was carrying on the work that was begun by the Royal House of Stuart. Bonnie Prince Charlie's first invasion into England was to teach the benighted people there how to play golf, (Laughter) and that invasion of their Scottish game of golf was fairly putting cricket utterly to rout. He trusted there would be reared up at Falkland a class of excellent golfers, who would well maintain the character of Scottish golf, and help to keep and maintain the national trophy of golf where it always ought to be, at home. (Applause) In presenting Lady Ninian Crichton-Stuart with a silver key for the pavilion, all he could say was he felt certain no key was necessary to enable her Ladyship to enter into any house in any part of that district.

Lady Ninian Crichton-Stuart said she was afraid she was not much of a golfer, as she had not hitherto lived near any golf centre. Curiously enough, the first place ever she saw golf played was in the Antipodes ten years ago, when her father was Governor of Tasmania. Some enterprising ladies and gentlemen, they were all Scottish people, started the game there, and they asked her to join. She was afraid she was rather a wild child, but her father said she had better join, and she did. She went up to the links, and was taught more or less how to play, but she was afraid she broke many clubs and lost lots of balls, and never succeeded in doing a hole under ninety. (Laughter) On one occasion, too, she remembered, in a foursome being caught surreptitiously pushing her ball through a fence with her cleek where she was badly trapped. (Laughter). Golf was an excellent game, and gave splendid open-air exercise. (Applause)

She hoped the Falkland Club would be successful and the game popularised in the district. Her Ladyship then gracefully opened the door of the clubhouse amid cheers.

On the motion of the Rev. Lyon Johnston, a hearty vote of thanks was passed to Lady Ninian, and a similar compliment was awarded to the Hon. Thomas Cochrane, on the call of Mr George Gavin.

The Ladies Committee of the club then dispensed tea to the visitors.

After tea a sweepstake competition took place over the Links, which were in capital order, and gave a good game. (DC)

2 October 1907

Chapel chairs

Dear Mr Gavin,

We beg to acknowledge receipts of your esteemed favour of the first inst, and have put in hand twenty four chairs similar to those supplied by us in July 1905. The tops and backs will be made as desired.

We have written to the manufacturers to give prompt delivery, and to exercise care in packing so as to avoid breakage in transit. We are obtaining illustrations to be sent you tomorrow.

Yours faithfully, The Bennet Furnishing Co. Ltd. (FEP)

27 October 1907

Town Council

At a meeting of the Town Council on Monday evening, a heated discussion arose over a motion by Bailie Sutherland that the factories should be assessed for water at domestic rates and upon full rental. The motion was rejected, and the assessment fixed at a quarter of the rental, as usual according to the terms of the Burgh Police Act. A letter was read from Mr George Baxter tendering his resignation as Town Officer. (FN)

28 October 1907

Use of the Approach

Letter to Mr Ogilvie, Westfield

Dear Sir,

Martin, the grieve, and two men were again discovered using the approach to House of Falkland on Saturday night, and were caught by the police constable. One of the men committed a breach of the peace not far from the Lodge Gates, and there is no doubt that, had these men not been caught by the constable on Saturday night, unseemly conduct would have taken place on the Approach. I have written Martin regarding the matter.

Yours Faithfully, George Gavin. (FEP)

28 October 1907
Use of the Approach
Letter to Mr Martin, Westfield

Dear Sir,

It has been reported to me that you, as well as other two men at Westfield, again made use or attempted to make use of the Approach to Falkland House in going to Westfield on Saturday evening, and that the police constable, who has my instructions shocked you. I cannot understand why, in view of the promises you have repeatedly made to me that you would cease to give me further trouble with reference to his matter, you still persist in doing what you know you have no right to do. I have given the police constable full instructions in regard to your case, and should you attempt to use the Approach again, I shall have you dealt with. I may add that the conduct of one of your men was most unseemly not very far from the Lodge gates, but this matter which simply aggravates the conduct of you and the men in this persisting in using the Approach, will be dealt with by the proper authorities.

Yours faithfully, George Gavin. (FEP)

20 November 1907
Train to make extra stop at Falkland Road
Letter to Mr David Deuchars, Line Superintendent, Waverley Station

Dear Sir,

My constituent Lord Ninian Crichton-Stuart has instructed me to ask if you will kindly cause the express train which passes Falkland Road Station about 10 o'clock in the evening to be stopped there on the night of Wednesday 27th inst, in order to pick up his Lordship and the Hon. F. Hanbury-Tracy who are travelling to London. Lord Ninian will send his servant to Edinburgh by the ordinary slow train with the luggage, so that there will be no servants or luggage to cause any delay to the train.

Yours faithfully, George Gavin. (FEP)

21 November 1907

Gardener and Lodge Keeper wanted

To the Publisher, The Aberdeen Catholic Herald

Dear Sirs,

Kindly insert the annexed advertisement in your next issue.

Yours faithfully, George Gavin. (FEP) [1]

Married Couple. (Roman Catholics), without family, wanted to enter upon duties immediately. The man must be capable gardener, and able to take charge of lawns and flower beds; wife to take charge of Lodge. Good wages with free house, coals and light will be given to suitable parties. Apply with references to George Gavin, Estate Office, Falkland Palace, Falkland, Fife.

---

23 November 1907

Elocutionary recital

Mr Charles Garvice, novelist and elocutionist, appeared in the Drill Hall on Friday evening in connection with the course of public lectures. The chair was taken by the Rev. A. L. Johnston, the President, in the absence of Lord Ninian Crichton-Stuart. The subject was entitled "Some Humorists, Grave and Gay."

Mr Garvice, at the opening, explained that his object would be to ask his audience to accompany him, in fancy, round a well-stocked library, from which he would select a book here and there, and recite something from it. He opened with

30. Charles Garvice (1850–1920)

A prolific British writer of romance novels. He also used the pseudonym Caroline Hart.

---

[1] Also put in the *Edinburgh Catholic Herald,* the *Glasgow Observer* and the *Catholic Times* and *Tablet* London.

Burns' "A man's a man for a' that". This was followed by "The Italian Guide", by Mark Twain, and "The Enchanted Shirt", by Colonel John Hay. The audience were delighted by the power of mimicry displayed in the rehearsal of these American sketches; and it was then a treat to hear Hood's "Song of the Shirt" vividly portrayed. "How I Edited an Agricultural Newspaper" afforded further scope for that ability to personify and power to convey the subtle under-currents of humour possessed by the lecturer. "A glimpse at England's greatest actor, David Garrick", was much appreciated. The closing item was "The Mustard Plaster", one of Mr Garvice's own writings, and which he described as pure nonsense, but which brought forth much laughter from the audience. (FN)

28 November 1907
Telephone
Letter to the Secretary, Post Office, Telegraphs, Edinburgh
Dear Sir,

I write to complain very strongly as to the service which I am getting in connection with the telephone in my office. I have verbally complained frequently of the delay to the exchange at Kingskettle, and to Mr Scott, post master, Ladybank. This forenoon I put a call on to Edinburgh and did not get connected for three quarters of an hour at least after putting on the call. It is perfectly correct for me to wait on an Edinburgh call for at least half an hour, so much as that on several occasions I have forgotten that a call was put on and gone out on business.

Calls to Kirkcaldy are never got under twenty minutes, and I have waited on a Kirkcaldy call half an hour on various occasions. It is quite apparent that with such a rental as I pay the service I am getting is perfectly inadequate and troublesome. The nature of the service in this district is giving rise to a great annoyance. The cause I presume is the insufficiency of wire, and I cannot see that the department can fairly draw the very heavy rent which I pay and not provide facilities for having the use of the telephone.

Yours faithfully, George Gavin, Estate Factor. (FEP)

29 November 1907
Under gardener
Letter from Benjamin Reid & Co, Aberdeen.
Dear Sir,

With reference to your conversation with our Mr Duthie, we are advertising, both in the daily papers and *People's Journal*, for an under gardener, wife to keep lodge, Catholic preferred, all at the terms mentioned to him. No applications have come in as yet, but we hope to have the names of suitable men to lay before you in a post or two. We have the names of quite a number of men on our books but all are Protestants.

Yours faithfully, B. Reid. (FEP)

30 November 1907
Music
Wanted for Falkland Cricket Club Dance, 20th December. Violin and Piano. Lowest offers to Michie, Newton of Falkland. (FFP)

5 December 1907
Chapel heating
Dear Mr Gavin,

Lord Ninian asked me to write Re. Heating of the Chapel. He thinks it very expensive, but it is necessary the work must start at once, but he thinks it unnecessary to heat the corridor (£15) and the room over the Priest's Room (£5 5s). He leaves it to you to decide whether it is necessary to heat the Priest's Room or not.

Hope you and Mrs Gavin are well.

Yours sincerely, Felix Hanbury-Tracy. (FEP)

6 December 1907
Telegraph poles
Letter to Secretary Post Office London
Dear Sir,

I have to thank you for your letter of the 5th inst, intimating that your department is willing to erect the proposed attachments to the telegraph poles between to House of Falkland and the stables on payment by me of the expense of £1 12s. I shall have pleasure in paying this amount, and trust that the work will be carried out without delay.

Yours faithfully, George Gavin. (FEP)

11 December 1907

Chapel altar rail and heating

Dear Mr Gavin,

I have received your letter and in accordance with Lord Ninian's instructions I have accepted Messrs Keith & Blackman's estimates for heating the Chapel and the Sacristy. I note that Lord Ninian does not wish the corridor or the room over the Sacristy heated at present.

Messrs Keith & Blackman give an estimate for painting the whole work, but I think perhaps you could do this more economically with your own painter, so that I have given them no instructions on this head. [1]

Proposed Temporary Altar Rail. I send herewith a drawing of proposed temporary rail which I shall be glad if you will submit to Lord Ninian for his approval and would you at the same time state to Lord Ninian that I think the simplest and most convenient form is the one that is drawn, viz, to combine the rail with the kneeling board. I have shown the rail as simple as possible, but if his Lordship would like it a little more ornamental, I can substitute turned balusters for the plain diagonal uprights. The brackets shown on the altar side of the rail are necessary to resist any pressure put on the rail by people leaning on it. If his Lordship does not like the idea of the hook and cord for the central opening, double gates similar to the rest of the rail can be made to slot in its place. My idea is that when the completion of the Chapel is taken in hand and the permanent oak altar rail is fixed in position, this temporary rail can be used to put across the Chapel further back to keep visitors from coming too far forward. This is simply an idea that occurred to me. I propose to make the rail in ordinary yellow pine and to stain it down to some colour such as green or red, or paint it as his Lordship prefers. I daresay I shall be at

---

[1] Thomas Ross was probably the painter as he was the only painter in Falkland at that time.

Falkland again by the time this is ready and we can settle this matter then. If his Lordship approves of this design and you will return the drawing, I will send Miller further details and instructions.

Yours faithfully, Robert Weir Schultz. (FEP)

14 December 1907

Chapel heating

Letter from James Keith & Blackman Co., High St. Arbroath

Dear Mr Gavin,

We have received instructions from our Head Office to proceed with the work in connection with the extension of the warming of the Palace, and we shall be sending the material on Monday next. We understand you wish the work proceeded with at once, and that being so, our men will be at Falkland on Wednesday next to make a start, we trust this will be convenient to you, otherwise will you kindly let us know.

Yours truly, James Keith & Blackman. (FEP)

17 December 1907

Chapel heating

Letter from James Keith & Blackman Co., High St. Arbroath

Dear Sir,

We thank you for your favour of yesterday. We have sent part of the material away yesterday, but we are afraid that the other material, which we have ordered forward will not be delivered at Falkland before Thursday or Friday, so we think in the circumstances it will be better not to send our men until Thursday morning. We note that you will arrange for a mason and joiner to do the cutting away etc., so if they are available on the Friday, it will be soon enough, because our men will have to take down the boiler and re-erect same with the new sections, and it will be Friday before they would know exactly what cutting away would be necessary. We mention this, with a view to saving the expense of your men standing about.

Yours truly, James Keith & Blackman. (FEP)

17 December 1907

Chapel heating

Dear Mr Gavin,

On my return to town I have just received your letter of the 13th inst., which was received here yesterday morning. I note what you say about the Altar Rail and am sending full particulars on to Miller by tonight's post.

I think the kneeling board across the opening ought to be made moveable so that it can be either hinged over the other or completely taken away. I will however send Miller particulars and leave it for him to arrange what is best and what Lord Ninian would approve of.

Miller makes a suggestion with regard to the heating pipes of the Chapel which I think might be considered. It is that instead of taking the pipes round the front of the private pew, to take them through the wall into the Corridor and back again into the Chapel at the other end of the private pew. This would give a little heat to the Corridor, and if necessary a radiator could be fixed outside at some future time. I am afraid if the pipes are taken round the front of the pew they will assert themselves very much. You might perhaps get Lord Ninian to look at the suggestion and if he approves of it, the man could be told to take the pipes round that way. [1]

Yours faithfully, Robert Weir Schultz, 14 Gray's Inn Square, London. (FEP)

27 December 1907

Typewriter for estate office

Dear Sir,

I am in receipt of your favour of 24th inst., confirming the order for No 4 Typewriter which I am very pleased indeed to have. The machine was sent you on 24th inst., and I trust it has arrived safely. If you have any special difficulty in its manipulation please let us know, and we shall arrange to send someone to give you instructions. I shall be pleased to hear from you whether Lord Ninian has done anything

---

[1] Robert Miller's account for work in connection with erecting temporary altar rail, covering stairs with wood and attending on heating engineers, £26 4s 3d.

about the matter of a machine for his own use. Our typewriter fitted with "elite" type does very pretty work, and if he has not yet decided anything definite, we shall be pleased to send him one of the machines on approval.

Thanking you for your esteemed order.

Your faithfully, W. Webster, The Smith Premier Typewriter Co. (FEP)

1908

New Year

Quietness characterised both the advent of the New Year and the condition of the town. The closing of the licensed houses had a most beneficial effect in this respect. The linen and floorcloth factories have the whole week as holidays. (FFP)

8 January 1908

Orphan boys' school hours

Letter to George Gavin

Dear Sir,

I am sorry to trouble you but will you give me permission to send my boys to school during the winter months at 9.30 instead of 9, the first winter they were here it was 9.30, but since it has been 9, while others go at 9.50. With the few boys I have I find it impossible to get the work done at 9, some is left over and instead of play at 12 they have to work. We have been getting up at 6 o'clock but this week we have started at 6.30. And then even it is too early for these cold dark mornings, they cannot get the work done, although they all do their best.[1] Failing this favour, may I keep a boy as I asked to keep the post boy till 9.45 to finish up, but I would rather have them all till 9.50, then they could get some play at 12 o'clock. I have no objection to

---

[1] British Summer Time was introduced in 1916,

them making up the time in the afternoon, leaving at 4.50 instead of 4. If I send a boy this evening will you give him your answer.

Yours truly, Mrs G. Quilter. (FEP)

23 January 1908
Orphan children
Letter to J. & F. Anderson, 48 Castle St, Edinburgh
Dear Sirs,

I am favoured with your letter of yesterday's date, returning to me the two letters relative to the boy Charles Dady. I shall arrange that this boy shall be handed over to his relatives. It is the case that no new boys are being sent to St. Andrew's Home, and that the number is gradually working down as they leave. There were originally 13 boys in the home. There are only 9 now, and when the boy Dady referred to leaves on first February the number will be reduced to 8. Two others attain the age of 14 years a few months hence, which will further reduce the number. When the Marchioness Dowager of Bute was at Falkland at Christmas I had an opportunity of speaking to her Ladyship regarding the future of the Home and the remaining orphan children. I pointed out that, as in a very short time there would be only 6 boys left in the Home, it was not economy to keep up a house here and pay a matron to look after these few children. Her ladyship quite agreed, and it was arranged that the month of May, by which time the numbers will be reduced to 6, Lady Bute would arrange to have the remaining children sent to a larger institution, and the Home here closed.

Yours faithfully, George Gavin. (FEP)

6 February 1908
Train to make extra stop at Falkland Road
Letter from North British Railway Company
Dear Mr Gavin,

I am in receipt of your letter of the 4th inst, and in reply have to say that the 7.45 p.m. express from Aberdeen has already been ordered to call at Laurencekirk on Monday 10th curt, and as the train is not keeping good time at present, I am sorry the arrangements do not admit of its being stopped at Falkland Road Station, also I would, however, be glad to give orders for the 5.35 p.m. express from Aberdeen to call to take up Lord Ninian Crichton-Stuart. if this would be suitable, and shall be pleased to hear from you early as to this.

Yours faithfully, Deuchars. (FEP)

6 February 1908

Problems with servants

Dear Lord Ninian,

I duly received your letter of the 1st inst from Valescure. It was only a couple of days before receiving your letter that I incidentally heard that Charles, the second footman had given notice to leaving on 1st March. While it is annoying that he should have taken this inopportune time to give notice, it is a good thing that he has done so. I hear that he is a relative of Ainslie, and if this be the case, there is always the chance that he might not be loyal to any butler who succeeds Ainslie.

I regret to say, however, that matters at House of Falkland have recently come to a crisis. On two occasions last week, I am sorry to say, Mrs Mullins was intoxicated, and created such disturbances with the servants as led them to come to me about her conduct. I have made minute enquiries, and find that it is only too true that on both the occasions mentioned, at least, she had taken liquor to excess. On Friday evening of last week she went to the laundry at 2 o'clock in the afternoon and used language to the head laundry maid which she ought not to have done. By 6 o'clock in the evening she was considerably under the influence of liquor, and her language was so shocking as not to be able to be repeated. As I say, there is no exaggeration in the statements made as I have taken great care to find out exactly what took place. The laundry maid, who is a most capable woman, I think, stated to me that she also would leave if Mrs Mullins's services were to be retained as housekeeper. Mary Ryan, the Stillroom maid, who came down to her parents' house on Friday evening in a state of intense agitation owing to the language used to her, has handed in her notice. I sent for Charles, and find that his giving notice is due to the fact that he is unable to live in the house.

I find now that all the servants had suspected that Mrs Mullins took liquor, but no one ever suggested such a thing to me, and until matters were brought before me in the way indicated, I had no idea of any such thing. The matter has caused me considerable anxiety, and I may add that from the enquiry I have now made it seems quite clear that, apart from the fact of her taking liquor, which in itself would incapacitate her for the duties of housekeeper at House of Falkland, she is not really capable of carrying out such duties satisfactory or with the knowledge which she ought to have. It is a great pity that this did not emerge sooner, as it seems perfectly plain that she must now be asked to leave.

Your obedient servant, George Gavin. (FEP)

10 February 1908

Laundry maid

Memo to Mary Dickson

I am instructed by Lady Ninian Crichton-Stuart to say that she will not require your services as laundry maid after this date. As her Ladyship wishes you to go at once I shall pay you a month's wages and board wages as from this date. Her Ladyship will give you an excellent character as a good laundry maid. Kindly make arrangements to leave House of Falkland not later than the morning of Thursday first.

George Gavin. (FEP)

11 February 1908

Servants leaving

Memo to Mrs Mullins

According to instructions from Lady Ninian I have to ask the two laundry maids to leave on Thursday morning, and I will pay them a months wages and board wages. Charles leaves for Castell Coch today and the scullery maid has also to go there. Will you accordingly ask him to come here tonight at 6 o'clock, and you might also send down at the same time Maud Davis as I want to see her.

George Gavin. (FEP)

11 February 1908

Bird show

A visit to the Falkland Ornithological Society's forty-third show, which was held in the Drill Hall yesterday, could not be conscientiously set down as being fraught with pleasure, for the space was so limited that one was jostled about in a most disagreeable manner, and unless on bended knees, when there was every chance of being trampled upon, and applying artificial light, the birds caged on the floor could not be seen.

The entries numbered about 350, and we were informed by a not too obliging secretary that that was about one hundred more than last year. Taken all over the quality was fairly good, some very fine birds being forward. The judging did not give unqualified satisfaction, and complaints were forthcoming that birds which at larger and more important shows stood well at the front were relegated to the consolation tickets. David Robertson, Falkland, with his well-known Dorking cock, carried off the members cup for the best male bird in show, and the cup for hens was awarded to William Lawson, Kirkcaldy, for his stylish black red bantam pullet. (DC)

13 February 1908

New house opposite Palace

Dear Lord Ninian,

With reference to the conversation which we had regarding the above matter when you were here, I had a call from Mr Galloway, who is building the new house, and the mason contractor for the work on Tuesday morning. I find that the cost of the mutual gable may amount to from £50 to £55, and your Lordship may, accordingly, have to pay a sum of about £25 in respect of your share. This is rather more than I anticipated, but there is no doubt, looking to the fact that it is your Lordship's intention to build a house on the vacant piece of ground, that it is to your advantage to have a mutual gable erected. The half of the cost of a mutual gable is much less than the cost of a single would be, and there is this further advantage, that the single gable would be wholly on your property, while the mutual gable will be halfway upon it and halfway upon Mr Galloway's property. As the site is, in this instance, in any case, rather cramped, the advantage is thus even greater than in some cases. The mutual gable will, of course, contain recesses for the fireplaces and wall presses of the new building, and it will also contain the vents and vent linings in the chimneys, so that the cost of all these will be saved ultimately. I propose, accordingly, unless I hear from your Lordship to the contrary, to say to Mr Galloway that you will bear half the cost of the mutual gable.

I am My Lord, your obedient servant. George Gavin. (FEP)

15 February 1908

Lord Ninian at Castell Coch

During the next two months Lord Ninian Crichton-Stuart is to be residing at Castell Coch, Ton-Gwyn-Las, Wales. (SAC)

15 February 1908

Newton of Falkland

There is a prospect of a big road improvement being effected in the village of Newton of Falkland, by the demolition of the old licensed property. A sub-Committee of the District Committee visited the property on Monday. The house is a very old one, being erected in 1744, and it is understood the proprietor, Mr David Bonthrone, is favourable to the proposal of the promoters of the improvement. Lord Ninian Crichton-Stuart; Mr Alexander Lawson of Annfield; Mr W. D. Patrick, the county clerk; Mr Thomas Aitken MICE, road surveyor, were among those who inspected the property. (FN)

15 February 1908

Properties in Parish of Falkland for sale

To be exposed to sale, by Public Roup, within the Royal Hotel, Cupar, Fife, on Tuesday, 24th March 1908, at twelve o'clock noon (in virtue of the powers contained in a Bond and Disposition in Security):
The following subjects which belonged to the late James Arthur:

1. Land adjoining and lying to the south of Floorcloth Factory, Falkland, extending to 2½ acres or thereby, and presently occupied by Alexander Douglas.
2. Land adjoining and lying to the east of Lot 1, extending to ½ acre or thereby, at present occupied by the said Alexander Douglas.
3. Land lying to the west of Templelands, extending to 2.115 acres, and occupied by the said Alexander Douglas.
4. House, garden, and byre in Cross Wynd, Falkland, tenanted by Jane Hamilton.

Rental or Annual value: Land, Lots 1, 2,and 3, £11 10s; House etc., £5. The Feu-duties payable from Lots 1 and 2 are 4s 7¾d. Upset Prices: Lot 1, £170; Lot 2, £15; Lot 3, £70; Lot 4, £35. For further particulars, apply to Charles Gulland, Writer, Falkland, who has the Title-Deeds and Articles of Roup. Falkland, 5th February 1908. (FN)

15 February 1908

Breach of the peace – constable attacked

On Sunday, an exciting scene was witnessed while the church bells announced the hour of evening service. A party of seven young men from Leslie visited the bar in the afternoon and, having had some liquor refreshment, proceeded to the ice-cream shop occupied by George Garland, for food. Trouble arose, and Police-Constable Calder was summoned. David Clement struck the constable, whereupon the latter took hold of him and asked him to come to the police office. He refused. The constable dragged Clement to the door, and then the others of the company endeavoured to obstruct the officer. The constable and his charge practically rolled down the Cross Wynd, the former being badly mauled on the way. By the time the foot of the Wynd was reached, the constable's coat was torn from his back, and his shirt sleeves were also torn. Mr John Angus, of the Commercial Hotel, on being appraised of the policeman's plight, rushed to his assistance, but he was knocked down and kicked behind the ear and on the knee. He soon regained his feet and held on to the prisoner, the constable by this time being well-nigh exhausted. At length the police office was reached, but it was with difficulty that the prisoner was got inside. Here while being searched, Clement struck the constable a dastardly blow on the eye. On Monday morning Clement, who was described as a labourer from Leslie, was brought before the Police Court at Falkland. He pleaded guilty, and the Fiscal (Mr Reekie) detailed the circumstances. Provost Millar said it was a most cowardly assault. He had to compliment Mr Angus on the timely assistance he had rendered to the constable. Sentence upon Clement was passed of a fine of 50 shillings, or thirty days' imprisonment. (FN)

18 February 1908

Mrs Mullins

Dear Lady Ninian,

In reply to your letter of the 16th inst handed to me today by Mr Hanbury-Tracy, I have thought it well to take written statements from those who previously made verbal ones to me regarding Mrs Mullins. I have put these statements as far a possible in the actual words of the parties who made them, and I now enclose them herewith, they are signed by the parties and attested as being the truth.

One would scarcely conceive what interest Ryan and his wife would have in trumping up stories about the housekeeper. I am afraid, indeed I am certain, from what I have now learned for the first time, that Mary Ryan, has been a troublesome girl, and has no doubt aggravated Mrs Mullins considerably. Unfortunately, the laundry maids, whose statements were very strong as to the fact of Mrs Mullins being intoxicated on the Friday referred to, have gone, and I cannot, accordingly, get their statements in writing, but I may say that the head laundry maid distinctly stated that by 6 o'clock on the Friday evening particularly referred to Mrs Mullins was staggering. On the whole I am inclined to think that the truth will be found to lie midway between the parties statements, that is to say, while Mary Ryan and William Smith may have exaggerated to some extent, there is sufficient corroboration of their statements to show up Mrs Mullins in a bad light, the language which she uses more or less frequently is not such as to command the respect of any servant, apart from the fact that it is not what is expected from one in her position.

Your obedient servant, George Gavin. (FEP)

19 February 1908

Housekeeper dismissed

Memo for Mrs Mullins

I have now heard from Lady Ninian Crichton-Stuart with definite information as to when she wishes you to leave House of Falkland. Her Ladyship desires you to leave on Monday, the 2nd March. George Gavin. (FEP)

19 February 1908

Lord and Lady Ninian in Cardiff

Lord and Lady Ninian Crichton-Stuart have taken up residence at Castell Coch, a picturesque mediæval castle near Cardiff, the property of the Marquis of Bute. (DET)

25 February 1908

Housekeeper dismissed

Dear Lady Ninian,

Mrs Mullins has sent me word that she is coming here at 11.30 today. I gather that she wants to talk about the statements recently taken, but if so, I shall, of course, say that this matter is past and done with, and that I have nothing whatever to say to her. I shall complete this letter after I have seen her, in case there should be anything material which your Ladyship should know.

P.S. As I anticipated Mrs Mullins entered into a long story in vindication of herself. I listened to her without remark and when she had finished said that anything she now said could not alter matters and she need not prolong her explanation. She is to hand over to me the house keys on Saturday forenoon and leaves early on Monday morning.

Your obedient servant, George Gavin. (FEP)

3 March 1908

New Houses in High Street

Letter to Mr James Galloway, Balmblae

Dear Sir,

With reference to our recent conversation and meeting which we have had at the site of the property which you propose to erect in the High Street situated immediately to the east of the site belonging to Lord Ninian Crichton-Stuart.

I now write to say that, on behalf of his Lordship, I agree to pay one-half of the cost of a mutual gable between your property and that of my constituent, the usual provisions being made for grate and press recesses, and vent linings being carried up for the chimneys.

I also agree to the curtailment of the mutual passage on the east side of your property to a breadth of 3½ feet in respect to your having agreed to the broadening of the continuation of that passage to Lord Ninian Crichton-Stuart's ground on the south side of your property to 4 feet in width.

You will also, as arranged, erect suitable steps at the end of this passage to suit the altered level of the ground.

The boundaries of your proposed building have been arranged and fixed by us on the ground, and I approve of them and agree to them as arranged by us. Kindly acknowledge receipt of this letter.

Yours faithfully, George Gavin. (FEP)

8 March 1908

Kilts for gamekeepers

Letter from R. W. Forsyth, Edinburgh[1]

Dear Sir,

Kilts for Gamekeepers. Kilt jacket and vest, Ancient Stuart, Cheviot Kilt, Skean Dhu and Hog-skin Sporran for four Gamekeepers. Estimate for each is £8 13s.

The estimate however did not include stockings.

Your faithfully, R. W. Forsyth. (FEP)

11 March 1908

The Falkland Estates

Large and Small Holdings – A Worthy Factor

The fine and charmingly situated estate of Falkland was purchased by the late Marquis of Bute from Mr Andrew Hamilton Tyndall Bruce in 1887, the year of the late Queen Victoria's jubilee. Lord Ninian Crichton-Stuart, the second son of the Marquis, succeeded to the property when he came of age in 1904, his father having died four years previously. In addition to the Falkland estates Lord Ninian also inherited the Priory at St Andrews, where the Marquis carried out at great cost important and valuable restoration work. The ancient palace of Falkland, of which the late Marquis was the hereditary keeper, a position now held by Lord Ninian, was also restored by the munificence of Lord Bute, and a good idea can now be obtained of the

---

[1] R. W. Forsyth was a very well-known outfitters in Edinburgh's Princes St until 2012.

grandeur of the palace as it existed in the days when Scotland's kings lived and ruled within its walls.

High-Class Farming

The Falkland estate, which is bounded on the south by the Lomond Hills – "the pride and ornament of Fife" – stretches along the fertile plain known as the Howe of Fife, and extends over six thousand acres. There are fifteen large farms all let to excellent tenants. The more extensive of the holdings are Woodmill (Mr Geo. Dun's), Falkland Wood (Mr Alex. Shanks', a pupil of Mr Henry Thomson Percival, who recently succeeded Mr John Lawson), Easter Cash (Mr Jas. Tod's), Westfield (Mr Barry Ogilvie's), Wester Cash (Mr Thos. Philp's), Plains (Mr Wm. Ritchie's), &c. These lands are all very highly farmed, and the equipment is the highest standard of excellence. The hand of a generous landlord is evidenced in the up-to-date steadings and the general air of substantiality and comfort that obtains throughout the farms.

Small Holdings

These remarks apply with equal force to the smaller holdings on the estate. It is interesting, in view of the small-holding agitation, to note that his Lordship has on his estate a score of small holders whose lands extend from four to fifty acres, and let at rentals varying from £6 to £50. These holdings lie principally in the immediate vicinity of Falkland, Auchtermuchty, and the hamlet of Dunshalt. There is no rack-renting. The land is first-rate quality, and the highest rents charged are per acre in the neighbourhood of the Royal burgh of Falkland. Industrious, hardworking people man these holdings, and they live happy and contented lives. Lord Ninian also owns about one-third of the house property in Falkland, and he is also proprietor and supervisor of the old-world hamlet of Dunshalt, with a small exception. The brick and tile works on the estate at Dunshalt, which for more than half a century have given employment during the working season to about thirty men, are, it is understood, about to carried on by the proprietor mainly for the purpose of maintaining the industry and keeping the workmen in employment. The Dunshalt roofing tiles are famed far and near.

Forestry Experiments

One of the features of the estate are the beautiful woods that dot the hillsides, and afford shelter in the vales. They extend to about 1300 acres, and the principal crops are coniferous trees, consisting mainly of larch and Scotch pine, and the new and much-boomed Douglasii[1] is also being extensively planted. An interesting experiment is being carried out on a slope of the East Lomond to test the relative merits of European and Japanese larch. The two varieties are planted in juxtaposition, and careful notes are being kept of their growth and their condition as regards disease A working plan of the woods has been prepared, and the treatment of the woods is all fixed and arranged for many years to come.

31. George Gavin, Factor
in the Palace courtyard

The Factor

The factor on the estates is Mr Geo. Gavin, a gentleman whose sterling worth and fair and open mindedness and straight dealing have won the confidence and esteem of all the tenants, big and small. He has held the office for six years, since May, 1902, and he succeeded the late Major Wood, who factored the property for the long period of thirty-two years.

At the end of a year's faithful work at Moncreiffe. Mr Gavin received the important appointment he now holds, and removed to Falkland, where he has, as in his other spheres, gained the entire confidence of his Lordship and of all having business relations with the

---

[1] The Douglas Fir (really a pine, *Pinus douglasii*) is extensively used for softwood timber. It now has a new botanical nam,e *Pseudotsuga menziesii*.

estate. The fetes connected with the coming-of-age of Lord Ninian, his Lordship's marriage, the birth of a son and heir, and the homecoming of Lord and Lady Ninian and their young son in September last year were all admirably carried out under the direction of Mr Gavin. and reflected great credit his organising skill and ability. To every good cause Mr Gavin is ever ready and willing to lend his aid, and to approach his Lordship for support in the public interest. The Golf Club of Falkland got a fine site for their clubhouse from Lord Ninian. and Mr Gavin had not a little to do with that and other concessions. Mr Gavin is a member of Falkland Parish Council, a member of the Executive Committee of the County Council, and a Director of the Fife Agricultural Society. (DC)

13 March 1908
Lathrisk House rented out
The Hon. Felix Hanbury-Tracy has, it is understood, taken a five years' lease of Lathrisk mansion-house. Mr C. J. Maitland Makgill Crichton of Lathrisk is take up his residence on his return from France at Monzie Castle,[1] Perthshire. (DC)

14 March 1908
Light railway
It is announced that an arrangement has been come to between the promoters of the light railway between Falkland Road Station and Falkland, and the North British Railway Company, whereby the latter are to work the line. The working terms have been provisionally fixed, and it is expected that an effort will be made to get the undertaking under way as soon as possible. (FN)

16 March 1908
Unionist candidate for East Fife
From East Fife Unionist Organisation Conservative Club Cupar
Dear Mr Gavin,
    You are requested to attend a meeting of the Unionist Committee for the Parish of Falkland, to be held in the Commercial Hotel, Falk-

---

[1] The interior of Monzie Castle was destroyed by fire in April 1908.

land, on Thursday 19th curt at 8 p.m. The meeting is called for the purpose of meeting Col. Sprot, prospective Unionist candidate for this division. Also to revise the list of the parish committee and to go over the roll of voters and make polices and removals, and to transact any other business which the chairman may consider.

Yours faithfully, Andrew Smith, organising secretary. (FEP)

16 March 1908

New servants

Letter from Captain Slacke

Dear Mr Gavin,

Probably Lord Ninian has told you that I am going to him as private secretary. I have engaged for him a butler and footman, and am also looking out for an odd man, all of whom will be going up to Falkland on Tuesday next. Will you kindly send me the money for their journey. I suppose about two guineas each is what he allows, as the ticket to Edinburgh is about 33 shillings and I suppose about 4 shillings over, at any rate you will know.

Yours faithfully, Capt. Slacke. (FEP)

32. Captain Slacke
Lady Ninian's cousin and Lord Ninian's secretary

24 March 1908

New servants

Letter from Captain Slacke

Dear Mr Gavin,

I sent you a wire from London today saying that I was sending three man servants viz, Butler, Footman and oddman, by the night train tonight to Edinburgh, arriving Falkland Road Station at 9.10

tomorrow. [1] Lord Ninian told me the footman has not to get his livery in London, and if I let you know that you would arrange that he had a suit of livery made by the tailor who made the black livery, would you kindly see to this, and then when I get up to Falkland I shall make a contract with him for the supplying of the livery, as is usually done. I shall arrive at Falkland Road on the 1st.

I shall write and let you know the train if you would be kind enough to order some conveyance to meet me.

Yours Faithfully, Capt. Slacke. (FEP)

24 March 1908

Falkland House servants

Dear Lady Ninian,

I duly received your letter and note that there will be relays of servants arriving all this week. I shall see that Birrell meets them at the station with the luggage cart. I had a telegram from Edinburgh this morning from Vassal to the effect that he and the French cook are arriving here this forenoon. I shall take to House of Falkland with me the keys of the plate-room, and give out to Vassal the candlesticks, silver ornaments and writing table things, leaving the remainder of the silver plate locked up, and to be handed over to the butler when he arrives.

I also note that your Ladyship will reach Falkland on Saturday first in the morning, and I trust when you come you will find everything in order.

I am, My Lady, Your obedient servant, George Gavin. (FEP)

27 March 1908

Women's Unionist Association

At a largely attended meeting of ladies in the district, convened by Mrs Sprot of Stravithie, it was agreed to form a branch of the Women's Unionist Association. Mrs Sprot presided, and delivered an interesting address. Lady Ninian Crichton-Stuart was appointed president of the branch; Mrs Gulland, Millfield; Mrs Dun, Woodmill;

---

[1] A single fare from London was £1 12s 8d and 2s 1d from Edinburgh to Falkland Road Station.

Mrs Gavin, Falkland Palace; and Mrs Livingstone, Lomondvale, vice-presidents; and Miss Madge Dun, Woodmill, Hon. Secretary. Arrangements were made for having an address from Miss Collum, London, on an early date. (DC)

6 April 1908

Scroggie Park

Letter to Mr Ogilvie, Westfield

Dear Sir,

You were good enough to say some time ago that you would have all the tracks in Scroggie Park[1] harrowed and sown with grass seeds. I am reminded of this by the fact that the first match of the season takes place today, and the field will, accordingly, be now constantly in use. Would you kindly, accordingly, have the work done as soon as you possibly can.

Yours faithfully, George Gavin. (FEP)

8 April 1908

Not genuine sweet milk

John Swinton, dairyman, Victoria Place, was charged at Cupar yesterday with a contravention of the Food and Drug Act in respect that by the hand of his wife he sold one penny worth of milk which contained not more than 2.53 per cent of milk fat. He pleaded guilty and explained that the only reason he could give for the deficiency was that the cows had been feeding on yellow turnips of an inferior quality. He was fined 20s. (DC)

8 April 1908

Gamekeepers' suits

Letter to R. W. Forsyth, Edinburgh

Dear Sirs,

I am favoured with your packet containing a selection of patterns for game-keepers' suits. I have had an opportunity this forenoon of submitting the patterns to Lord Ninian Crichton-Stuart, who has cho-

---

[1] Scroggie Park was and is the Falkland cricket ground.

sen the enclosed, No 212W, for the whole of the four suits, and who now wishes you to proceed with the making of the suits, kilt, jacket and vest. You will recollect it was arranged that an assistant should come over here to measure the three under-keepers, and on your letting me know what day it would be convenient for you to do so I shall have the three men at the kennels. His Lordship wishes the buttons on the jackets and vests to be of platted leather. He showed me today the button referred to on one of his own kilt suits. It resembles brown leather laces platted closely together, and no doubt you will be acquainted with the button. In order to avoid any mistakes, however, your assistant who comes here might bring one with him, and I shall tell him if it is the correct thing. If not, I shall show him the buttons on one of Lord Ninian's suits. I shall give your assistant particulars also as to the crest for the bonnets, and as long safety pins for the kilts. I return per separate packet the patterns sent to me.

Yours faithfully, George Gavin. (FEP)

9 April 1908
Gamekeepers' suits
Letter from R. W. Forsyth, Edinburgh
Dear Sir,

We beg to acknowledge receipt of your favour of the 8th inst enclosing pattern of tweed selected for jackets and vests. We shall send our cutter to measure the men on Tuesday next, 14th inst. He will leave Edinburgh by the 10.15 train arriving at 12. 05. He will bring with him a sample leather button, for your approval.

Your faithfully, R. W. Forsyth. (FEP)

10 April 1908
Wanted
Boy (stout) wanted for ice cream shop. 4 shillings weekly, with board. Apply George Garland. Falkland Fife. (DC)

11 April 1908
Lord and Lady Ninian Crichton-Stuart
Lord and Lady Ninian Crichton-Stuart have concluded their extended visit to Cardiff and returned to their home at Falkland

House. Lord Ninian has spent over two months in the city as prospective Unionist candidate for the constituency, and has greatly advanced his claims. His Lordship has addressed meetings in every ward in the city, together with more gatherings in the largest halls. He has been received with the unfailing enthusiasm of his party, the leaders and rank and file having rallied to his support in every quarter of the Parliamentary division. Lord and Lady Ninian have also taken part in a large number of social and civic functions and have made friends among all classes. During their stay in the city, they have resided at Castell Coch, a medieval house with extensive grounds, the property of the Marquis of Bute. (FN)

11 April 1908

Enthusiastic Tariff Reform meeting

A public meeting under the auspices of the newly-formed Women's Unionist Association was held in the Town Hall here on Tuesday night, when an address was delivered by Miss Collum on Tariff Reform[1]. The hall was filled to overflowing, one of the ante-rooms being required to hold part of the audience. Lady Ninian Crichton-Stuart presided, and the proceedings were opened with the singing of the Union song, after which other songs were sung by Miss Sprot, Stravithie, and Miss Dun, Woodmill. Miss Collum spoke at great length and with great eloquence on the subject of women's influence and on Tariff Reform. At the close, Mrs Dun, Woodmill, proposed, and Mr Gavin, Falkland Palace, seconded a vote of thanks to the lecturer. Lord Ninian Crichton-Stuart moved a vote of thanks to Colonel and Mrs Sprot, who were present, for bringing the lecturer to Falkland and for their exertions in the Unionist cause. Lady Ninian Crichton-Stuart was cordially thanked on the call of Colonel Sprot for presiding. The meeting was the most enthusiastic that has been held in Falkland for years. (FN)

---

[1] Tariff Reform was a key Conservative policy at this time: the aim was to transform the British Empire into a single trading bloc, with tariffs on imports from foreign countries.

14 April 1908

Burglary insurance

Dear Sir,

I am favoured with your letter of yesterday's date, and regret to say that I have no record of the above policy. The full name of the insured is William Middleton who is sub-postmaster here, and the insurance covered is the stock of postal orders etc, and also I think to some extent his stock as a tobacconist etc. He kept premises in High Street, but removed a year ago to a shop two door further west. The risk is practically the same, and I do not think any special endorsement is necessary regarding the change of premises. The address is the same, and, as I say, the conditions are unaltered.

Yours faithfully, George Gavin. (FEP)

14 April 1908

Chapel tapestries

Dear Lord Ninian,

With regard to the Chapel at the Palace. In order to enable us to arrange the finishing of the sanctuary, which your mother is going to do, it will be necessary to make drawings showing how the tapestries will be permanently arranged in oak panels.

Yours faithfully, Schultz.[1] (FEP)

15 April 1908

Orphan boys

Dear Lady Bute,[2]

Mrs Quilter asked me about a week ago if Andrew Brunton, one of the boys in the Home, who had attained the age of fourteen, might be sent to his grandmother in Muirkirk, Ayrshire, at once, as his language had become very bad and his conduct otherwise was such as to be bad for the other boys. I asked her to write to his grandmother, and ascertain if she would be willing to receive him. She called today to show me a letter from the grandmother to the effect

---

[1] Robert Weir Schulz was the architect in charge of the work at the chapel.

[2] The Dowager Marchioness of Bute (Lord Ninian's mother).

that the lad could be sent to her. I am, accordingly, arranging to send Mrs Quilter as far as Glasgow with him on Saturday, and to have him put on the G.&S.W. train in charge of the guard for Muirkirk.

Your obedient servant, George Gavin. (FEP)

15 April 1908

Orphan boys

Letter to Messrs Anderson, Edinburgh.

Dear Sirs,

It is, of course, as you know, intended to close this Home in the month of May. I wrote Lady Bute some time ago with reference to instructions being given as to the date of closing of the Home and giving the Matron, Mrs Quilter, written notice, but I have no reply from her Ladyship. Mrs Quilter was, of course, told by me in the month of February, as arranged with Lady Bute at Christmas time that the Home would be closed in May and the remaining boys transferred elsewhere. She had been several times complaining loudly as to being ill-treated. As I have mentioned on previous occasions she is a most troublesome woman, and if the Home is to be closed in May, the matter should be definitely arranged in writing so that she will know exactly where she stands.

Yours faithfully, George Gavin. (FEP)

20 April 1908

Telephone

Letter to J. H. Haynes, Sectional Engineer's Office Dundee

Dear Sir,

I regret that you have not sent a man here to do the work necessary to the telephones regarding which I wrote some time ago. Kindly do so at once, as the matter is causing considerable inconvenience, and only today, I may mention, Lord Ninian Crichton-Stuart rang me up on the telephone. I happened to be out and my assistant answered the message. On coming in a few minutes later I rang for a considerable time to House of Falkland without any result. As a consequence I had to walk to House of Falkland to see his Lordship, only to find that he had left a few minutes prior to my reaching the house. The telephone is, of course, of little or no use as it is at present, and I thought you would have gathered from my previous letter that the matter required to be attended to immediately.

Yours faithfully, George Gavin. (FEP)

21 April 1908

Orphan boys

Letter to J. & F. Anderson, Castle St. Edinburgh

Dear Sirs,

I have a letter from the Dowager Lady Bute this morning in which she says that before any of the boys are moved it will be well at once if I ascertained whether any of the remaining boys had relatives who could take them. Her Ladyship suggested that I should write to Sr Ethelburga, Durranhill House, Carlisle, for information regarding the parents or relatives of the boys still remaining in the Home.

Lady Bute in her letter again refers to Nazareth House Aberdeen, as the best place to which the boys could be sent, and asks me to write the Rev. Mother to find out if she could take them.

I enclose a statement a copy of which I am sending to Lady Bute, containing particulars as to the boys in the Home so far as I can gather them here. I have also sent a copy of the statement to Sr Ethelburga, asking her to send me, if she can do so, information as to the boys whose parents are not known. I shall keep you informed as to what further is done regarding these children.

Yours faithfully, George Gavin.

P.S. There was another scene with the Matron today, when she again complained as to being ill-treated, being turned out, etc. etc. (FEP)

21 April 1908

Orphan boys

Dear Sister Ethelburga,

As you may be aware, the Home here has now been reduced by the boys attaining fourteen years of age, to such an extent as to make it inadvisable to continue it any longer. At present there are seven boys in the Home, and from the enclosed statement you will observe that in a couple of months time another two boys attain the age of fourteen years, and will, accordingly, leave the Home. The consequence will be that only five boys will be left. It is proposed to send the remainder to Nazareth House, Aberdeen.

In a letter which I have from Lady Bute today she suggests that I might write to you asking if you knew anything about the relatives of any of the boys, in case they might be sent to their relatives. If you can give me any information as to the relatives of the boys, Duffy, Scott, McCoy, and McGowan, I need not say that I shall be very pleased to have it.

Yours faithfully, George Gavin. (FEP)

24 April 1908

Gamekeepers' suits

Letter from R. W. Forsyth, Edinburgh

Dear Sir,

Replying to yours received yesterday a.m. We much regret to have your complaint regarding the keepers' kilts. In accordance with your desire, we intend sending our kilt cutter on Saturday by the 2.15 p.m. train, due at Falkland Road 4 o'clock, on which day and hour, we trust it will be suitable for you to get keepers together. Our cutter will give the matter his most careful and prompt attention, and we assure you at the outset that the kilts and everything else will be turned out thoroughly satisfactory. Two points you can also instruct our cutter on, namely, that the cap crests, and that of the Skean Dhus. Owing to the long distance between the station and the estate, would it be possible for you to arrange a conveyance to meet the train. A favour usually conceded to us by customers under similar circumstances.

Your faithfully, R. W. Forsyth. (FEP)

12 May 1908

Orphan children

Dear Mr Gavin,

We are favoured with your letter of yesterday's date with reference to the arrangements proposed for the three boys, who are to be sent to the Catholic Working Boys Home in Lauriston Place. If the Dowager Lady Bute approves of these proposals, you may take it that we shall be ready to concur on behalf of Lord Bute.

Yours faithfully, J. & F. Anderson. (FEP)

16 May 1908

A hot water dispute

Motion ruled Incompetent

The Town Council met on Monday night – Provost Miller presiding. Bailie Sutherland had given notice of a motion that, as Messrs Jackson had refused to abide by the table of water charges approved by the Council, the water be cut off from their works and garden. Mr J. W. Jackson asked if the motion was in order. Mr Anderson, the acting Town Clerk, stated that Mr Gulland, the Town Clerk, who was not able to attend the meeting, did not think the motion as it stood was competent.

Bailie Sutherland – "What is incompetent about it? The fact remains that there are three supplies of water for the domestic supply granted to the factory for which nothing is paid. My motion is plain English. You know what I mean."

Mr Lister – "In his motion Bailie Sutherland says that Messrs Jackson have not complied with the arrangements of 1905. These arrangements of the water rates only existed for a year. They were not workable."

Mr Jackson – "The Council abandoned them."

Bailie Sutherland – "All that was abandoned was the reference to the stables and byres. I stand by my motion, and I shall appeal to a higher authority. The Council last year assessed the Co-operative Store on the whole rental."

Mr Jackson – "If the Co-operative store pay a tax they should not pay, that is their fault."

Bailie Sutherland – "You pay the public rate, which gives you no right to water. You have three supplies you have no right to. I don't see why you should throw dust in people's eyes."

Mr Jackson – "I have no intention of throwing dust in people's eyes, and I shall not be talked to like that by you."

Mr Anderson read the various minutes on the matter, beginning in 1871, when Mr Jackson was granted a supply for his factory from the overflow. Provost Miller said the water was first granted from the overflow, but since then they had had an expensive scheme, and it should be made clear that they had no right to give away the rate-payers' water for nothing.

Mr Lister – "Are we giving it for nothing?"

The Provost – "Yes."

Mr Lister – "They pay on a quarter of the valuation."

The Provost – "Suppose they got no water from us at all, they would have to pay that."

Mr Jackson – "That is true, but you can get a water supply for drinking purposes and still continue to pay on a fourth of the valuation. The supply that comes from the overflow is surplus water."

Bailie Sutherland – "You were offered it from the main."

Mr Jackson – "We have never been offered it from the main. You are the only one that offered it. You are not the Council, though you try to be. If we require to take water from the main we shall be willing to pay for it. I want to make it perfectly clear that I don't want to be bullied."

Mr Lister – "I think it is a piece of animosity and ill-will."

The Provost – "Order."

Bailie Sutherland – "I have no cause for animosity."

The Provost ruled that the motion was incompetent, and it was agreed to take the advice of the Convention of Burghs on the whole matter. (FN)

23 May 1908

Birth – Bonthrone

At Newton House, Newton of Falkland, on the 15th inst., the wife of David Bonthrone, of a son. (FN)

23 May 1908

Wanted

Wanted smart honest girl, to look after Fruiterer's Shop and Billiard Table in Falkland. Apply Gallon, Cross Wynd, Falkland. (DC)

30 May 1908

Flagstaff presented

An interesting function was performed in the playground of the Public School on Friday. Mr J. L. Lumsden, Chairman of the School Board, has presented a flagstaff and Union Jack to the school, and the

33. The Billiard Room fireplace, House of Falkland

The shield combines the arms of the Crichton-Stuart (left) and Preston (right)
families, with *Nobilis est ira leonis* ("Noble is the lion's wrath" – the motto of
Clan Stuart of Bute) and the date 1909, Above are the initials of Lord and
Lady Ninian (NECS and ILMCS).

ceremony of unfurling the flag was performed with due honour. (FN)

3 June 1908

House of Falkland telephones

Letter to Mr Haynes, Post Office, Dundee.

Dear Sir,

The linesman came some time ago and disconnected and took
down the telephone in the Billiard Room, as also the private telephone to Stables in the Service Room, which room is now being
thrown into the Billiard Room, as part of the alterations now going on
in the House. It was explained to your assistant Mr Brown when here
that in lieu of the fixed telephone for private service to the Stables a
table instrument could be substituted. He, of course, explained that
the Post Office could not supply this instrument, but that, if instructions were received to do so, the department would attach it to the

wires when they were shifting the wires to suit the removal of the post office telephone from the Billiard Room to the Gull Room.[1] I have now received this table instrument, and shall be glad to know when you can send your man to fit up the department's telephone in the Gull Room, and when you will instruct them at the same time to do the work necessary in connection with the private telephone, the wires for which will now be carried wholly on the post office poles, we paying an additional 1s per pole of rental for each pole so used. Mr Brown would, of course, report to you that Lord Ninian Stuart was desirous to have a table instrument for the post office telephone in place of the fixed one hitherto in use.

Yours faithfully, George Gavin. (FEP)

3 June 1908

St Andrew's Home

Letter to J. & F. Anderson, Edinburgh

Dear Sir,

I have today settled with Mrs Quilter, paying her £25 as a final payment from the Marchioness Dowager of Bute, along with her wages and board wages to the 1st inst. In the end I had to give her the full sum of £25, as, while I originally arranged to give her £20 and her railway fares, it turned out that the railway fares of herself and her son and carriage of his invalid chair and excess luggage on their personal belongings to Chelmsford somewhat exceeded £5. Mrs Quilter has made all arrangements to leave tomorrow. (FEP)

9 June 1908

Masonic church parade

A Masonic church parade under the auspices of Lodge St John Falkland took place on Sabbath afternoon. In response to the invitation issued by St John, brethren responded from Cupar, Kirkcaldy, Newburgh, Auchtermuchty, Ladybank and Thornton. Assembling at the Drill Hall, the brethren marched in processional order to the Parish

---

[1] The "Gull Room" was originally Lady Margaret Crichton-Stuart's sitting room, which (perhaps reflecting her nautical interests) features a flock of three-dimensional seagulls round the walls.

Church, where the Rev. Gordon, Kettle preached an able sermon on brotherly love. The lessons were read by the minister of the parish, Brother Lyon Johnston. (DC)

20 June 1908

Marriage of The Hon. F. Hanbury-Tracy

The Hon. Felix Hanbury-Tracy, late Scots Guards, third son of Lord and Lady Sudeley,was married on Thursday last week, at Lacock

34. Hon. Felix Hanbury-Tracy

Church, Wilts. to Miss Madeline Llewellan Palmer, only daughter of Mr and Mrs George Llewellan Palmer of Lackham, Lacock, Wilts. [1]

The church was beautifully decorated with white roses, and the Rev. the Hon. Alfred Hanbury-Tracy, with the Rev. T. S. Wood officiated. There were two small pages and four bridesmaids in attendance upon the bride, who was led up the aisle by her father, and wore a dress of ivory satin charmeuse, arranged with Limerick lace, and a veil of the same lace. The pages wore white satin Court suits with capes slung from the shoulder and lined with silver cloth, while the bridesmaids were attired in dresses of white tulle over silk, the skirts finished with deep hems of cloth of silver, and they also wore Louis XV hats in white tulle with crowns of white roses and streamers of silver ribbon. Viscount Northland was best man, but owing to mourning in the bride's family, because of the sad death of a brother, there was no formal reception at Lackham after the ceremony.

The marriage, it need hardly be said, has awakened much interest

---

[1] Felix was to be killed on the Western Front in December 1914. His father, the 4th Baron Sudeley had been a Government whip under Gladstone.

in Falkland and district, where the bridegroom through his connection with Lord Ninian Crichton-Stuart, and the active part he has taken in local cricket and other sports, to say nothing of his own agreeable manners, has made himself highly popular. He is to reside at Lathrisk House, and is expected there with his young wife this week. He is a brother of Mrs H. T. Anstruther, whose charming disposition endeared her to all she met when her husband was MP for the St Andrews Burghs. (FN)

25 June 1908

Inspection of drainage system
Letter from J. Anderson, 48 Castle Street, Edinburgh
Dear Sir,

The Sanitary Protection Association have fixed Wednesday next, the 27th inst for their inspection of the drainage system of Falkland. We shall be obliged if you will send a trap to meet the early train from Edinburgh, to carry Mr Welsh, the inspector and his testing apparatus to Falkland House. Please also have a plumber to be present as the inspector will require his assistance.

Yours faithfully J. & F. Anderson. (FEP)

4 July 1908

Sale of Work
Dear Lord Ninian,

I have an application from Mrs Dun, Woodmill, for a small donation of rabbits for her stall at the sale of work in connection with the Parish Church, to be held on Saturday first, and which Sale of Work is to opened by Mrs Hanbury-Tracy. On two previous occasions Mrs Dun has been given rabbits for her stall, twenty couples, I think, on each occasion. Will your Lordship kindly write me or wire me whether I shall again give her the rabbits. The proceeds of the Sale of Work on this occasion are to be set aside as the nucleus of the fund which it is proposed to raise for the building of a hall in connection with the Church, which is also to be used as a Town Hall. As your Lordship knows, there is a strong opinion by many of the people of the town that the arrangements proposed is not a very practicable one, and ought not to be entered into. However, the rabbits were given to this Sale of Work, which, on former occasions, was held for the purpose of raising money for foreign missions, I believe, your Lordship may, apart from any consideration connected with the project as to the hall, agree to give the rabbits. If the rabbits are to be given, I shall have to instruct Sturrock to get them, perhaps your Lordship will kindly write me by an early post.

I am My Lord, your obedient servant. George Gavin. (FEP)

10 July 1908

St Andrew's House

Dear Mr Gavin,

We have now received from Lady Margaret Crichton-Stuart in regard to this house. Taking into consideration the original cost and what has been spent on the building, Her Ladyship thinks that the rent should be £14 per annum, and that the repairs now necessary, amounting, as per the estimates you sent us, and which we now return, as noted hereon, should be executed one half by her Ladyship and the other by Lord Ninian Crichton-Stuart, that is to say, she is willing to spend £3 10s, if Lord Ninian is willing to spend the same amount. It will be a condition of the let that the articles belonging to the Dowager Marchioness will be stored in one of the rooms, which you will keep locked. Her Ladyship does not say anything about the period of endurance of the let, but we think it had better run from Whitsunday to Whitsunday and of course the rent will be payable half yearly. If, on behalf of Lord Ninian, you agree to these terms please write us and we shall hold the matter settled. The rent will be payable half yearly at Whitsunday and Martinmas. The first half year being subject to a proportionate abatement from Whitsunday to the date of entry, which can be the 12th curt.

Yours faithfully, Melville & Lindsay, Edinburgh. (FEP)

11 July 1908

St Andrew's House

Dear Lord Ninian,

I am anxious, now that this house is vacant, to have the gardeners transferred to it as soon as possible, and have been in communication with Lady Margaret's agents with regard to the rent to be paid for the house and the trifling repairs which are necessary before it can be inhabited. Finding from the Valuation Roll of the Burgh that the rent returned for the house was £15, I pointed out to the Burgh Assessor that this sum was very much in excess of any rents which could be obtained for it in its present condition. I wrote to Messrs Melville & Lindsay suggesting that if your Lordship paid a rent of £10 it would surely meet the case. Your Lordship will observe from their reply that Lady Margaret thinks the rent should be £14. I have today written Messrs Melville & Lindsay to say that I cannot advise your Lordship to give a rent of £14 for the reason that, apart from its present condition, the house would not, if an attempt were made to let it, bring more that £10 of annual rent, but that I was taking your instructions. I think, however, if Lady Margaret agrees to accept a rent of £10 that your Lordship might pay one half of the cost of the repairs.

Your servant, George Gavin. (FEP)

11 July 1908

Shooting competition

The second competition for the handsome trophies presented to Freuchie and District Rifle Club by Major G. J. Lumsden, late 6th (Fifeshire) Royal Highlanders, took place on Purin Range, Falkland, on Saturday. Principal results:

A Class – 1 Ex-Corporal James W. Leishman, Freuchie, 93; 2 ex-Corporal J. Robertson, Freuchie, 85; 3 ex-Private George Lindsay, Kettle, 83.

B Class – 1 R. Boucher, Ladybank, 78; 2 A. Mitchell, Kettlehills, 68; 3 James Maxwell, Kettle, 64.

Ranges – A Class – 200 yards, J. W. Leishman, 33; 500 yards, R. Lindsay and A. Wilson, 31 each; 600 yards, J. W. Leishman, 30

B Class – 200 yards, T. Donaldson, 27; 500 yards, J. Maxwell, 30; 600 yards, R. Boucher, 30. (FN)

18 July 1908

Parish Church Sale of Work.

A very successful Sale of Work was held under the auspices of the Women's Guild on Saturday. The sale was opened at two o'clock in the presence of a large audience by the Hon. Mrs F. Hanbury-Tracy,

Lathrisk. She expressed the great pleasure it gave her to be present and thus to show her interest in the community. She hoped the sale would be most successful. Dr Jack moved a vote of thanks to Mrs Hanbury-Tracy. The stalls were well filled with many beautiful and useful articles. The stall-holders were as follows: Guild Stall – Mrs Johnston, Mrs Miller, Sutherland and Myles; Misses Crombie and Allan. Work and Produce Stall – Mrs and Misses Dun, Mrs Morgan, Mrs Shanks and Miss Morgan. Sweet Stall – Miss Gulland, Miss Lyell and Miss McInnes. Tea Stall – Miss Sharp, Mrs Henderson, Miss E. Williamson, Miss Sutherland and Mrs Robertson.

A missionary alphabet demonstration was given during the afternoon and evening. In this the children were dressed in native costumes representing the different mission stations under the Church of Scotland. These demonstrations were greatly appreciated. At the close, the Rev. A. L. Johnston announced that the sale realised £124 0s 7d. (FN)

1 August 1908
Golf
Falkland Club: In the annual competition for the Morrison Medal (scratch), the winner was Mr Walter Peggie with a score of 85.

Falkland Ladies Club: The first competition for the rose bowl presented to the Club by Miss Gulland, the captain, was won by Miss Brunton with a score of 57. (FN)

14 August 1908
Falkland Police Station
Dear Mr Gavin,

When visiting Falkland the other day, I found that the fence in front of the station requires repairing and painting otherwise the wood will soon perish. Some of the windows also require to be puttied to keep the rain out. I shall be obliged if you will have this matter attended to at your convenience.

Yours faithfully, J. Gordon. Chief Constable[1]. (FEP)

---

[1] James Tennant Gordon was Chief Constable of Fife (originally including Kinross) from 1904 (succeeding his father-in-law Captain J. Bremner) until

15 August 1908

A unique political entertainment

On Thursday evening last week, an excellent entertainment was given in the Drill Hall under the auspices of the Women's Unionist Association. An enthusiastic and highly appreciative audience was ably presided over by Lady Ninian Crichton-Stuart, the president. The musical programme was sustained by the President, Mr Slacke, Miss Dun, and Mrs Pierson, whose song, "Tariff Reform" proved very popular.

An instructive address on "Tariff Reform as a working man's question", was then given by Mrs Pierson, who told of her personal experiences and urged the need of a change in our present fiscal policy. Numerous instances were given of declining industries in various parts of our country, and the consequent distress among our industrial population. Mrs Pierson begged her audience to put aside party bias, and look at this matter as a national question, and above all as a working man's question to which our working classes must give attention and consideration for a policy which compels our men to stand idle for want of work, while we pay workmen of other countries for doing it, cannot be a policy for sensible working men to support.

A little sketch was then admirably represented, entitled "John Bull at Market". Where all acquitted themselves so well, it is difficult to give individual praise, but certainly Miss Sprot, as "Tariff Reform", was excellent, also Mr Bell as "John Bull", Miss Dun as "Free Trade", and Miss Huntingdon as "France". "John Bull" was discovered at market, with his hands tied, and accompanied by "Free Trade". After some discussion on the blessings or otherwise enjoyed while "Free Trade" has managed "John Bull's" estate, "Free Trade" sits beside "John Bull", as "America" enters to trade with him, followed by "Germany", "France", "Russia", "Italy" and "Switzerland", who trade with each other, and then with "John Bull". "Germany", too, dumps down his goods at "John Bull's" feet, whether they are required or not; the others follow suit, and all bully "John Bull" who is unable to defend himself because his hands are tied. "Free Trade" takes no

his death in 1934. *Leven Advertiser & Wemyss Gazette*, 27 November 1934.

notice of his cries or struggles, while he is so unfairly treated. In response to "John Bull's" cry for help, however, "Tariff Reform" enters, followed by "Prosperity", "Employment", and "Happiness", and severs the bonds which have held "John Bull" so long. He is then enabled to clasp hands with his children, the colonies, who group around him, (with "Tariff Reform" and the representatives of the Women's Association), each carrying the British Flag, and with the foreign countries in the background, form a final tableau singing "Rule Brittania".

Lady Ninian Crichton-Stuart, from the chair, in a charming little speech, proposed a vote of thanks to Mrs Pierson for her excellent address, also to those who had contributed to the success of that evening's entertainment. This was heartily accorded by every one present, and Mrs Pierson suitably responded, saying that she knew that everyone who had taken part in arranging and carrying out the programme was only too happy to do what had to be done. Colonel Sprot, who was present with Mrs and the Misses Sprot, proposed a vote of thanks to Lady Ninian Crichton-Stuart for so kindly presiding, and in a few well-chosen words, showed how much the Association owed Lady Ninian for her kind assistance, not only in presiding, but in singing her beautiful songs. Mr Gavin, the factor, then suggested that thanks should be given to Colonel Sprot and Mrs Sprot for their attendance that evening, and hoped that Colonel Sprot would be in the future even more closely identified with Falkland and its interests, which evoked hearty applause, to which Colonel Sprot briefly responded. After singing the National Anthem, the company dispersed, highly delighted with one of the most successful gatherings ever seen in Falkland.

The characters in the sketch were represented by the following: "John Bull", Mr F. Bell; "Free Trade", Miss Dun; "Tariff Reform", Miss Sprot; "America", Mrs Pierson; "Germany", Mr G. Dun; "France", Miss D. Huntingdon; "Italy", Miss Amos; "Russia", Dr Jack; "Switzerland", Miss Isobel Dun; "Canada", Miss R. Sprot; "India", Miss Lyell; "Africa", Mr Morgan; "Australia", Miss Chisholm; "Prosperity", Miss M. Chisholm; "Employment", Master A. Gavin; "Happiness", Miss D. Dun; "Representative of the Women's Association", Miss Dun. (FN)

15 August 1908

Flower show

The Falkland and District Horticultural Society held their annual competition and exhibition of fruit, flowers, vegetables, &c., in Falkland House Park on Saturday, kindly granted for the occasion by Lord Ninian Crichton-Stuart. The show was not a large one, but the quality of the exhibits was good, more especially in vegetables and cut flowers. The judges were, Vegetables: Messrs Utterson, Pitlour, and Wallace, Fettykil. Flowers: Messrs Henderson, Balbirnie and Coventry, Myres Castle. Industrial: Lady Ninian Crichton-Stuart, Falkland House; Mrs M. Robertson, West Port; and Mrs Gavin, Falkland Palace.

The principal prize winners were: For vegetables: Messrs Andrew Lister; Alex. Bisset; Thomas Page; R. Strachan; A. Taylor; D. Inglis; and J. Fleming.

For fruit: Messrs Thomas Page; J. Craig; M. A. Page; Andrew Lawson; and Peter Dick.

For cut flowers: Messrs J Matheson; W. Falconer; Thomas Page; J. M'Coll; J. Allan; and G. Baxter.

In cottagers' competition Messrs J. Craig; J. Steedman; and A. Fernie.

For pot plants: Messrs Tom Page; J. McColl; and J. Christie.

For bee produce: Messrs Tom Page; A. Fernie; and Peter Dick.

In industrial department: Mrs A. Thomson; Mrs Sturrock; William Duncan; Mrs Fordyce; and Mrs Galloway.

For flower wreaths the first prize was awarded to Mr J. Methven.

In the competition for bunches of wild flowers the chief prizes went to Messrs James Gray; John Morgan; Miss Annie Morgan; and Mr Tom Dryburgh.

For basket of flowers (confined to ladies) the prize was won by Miss M. A. Page.

This is the fourth year of the Angus Cup and the section for competition was the "cottagers". Mr John Craig won it.

As usual a table of plants was exhibited by the gardener of the Palace gardens. It was a very nice collection. Auchtermuchty Brass Band was in attendance, and discoursed choice music in the afternoon. A troupe of step dancers was also in attendance. (DC)

22 August 1908

Presentation

Deputations from the employees at Pleasance and St. John's Works waited upon Mr John Walker Jackson, Lomondvale, and presented him with a handsome hall clock and silver lamp on the occasion of his marriage. Both presents bore suitable inscriptions. (FN) [1]

24 August 1908

Butter making classes

Dear Mr Gavin,

On the 18th curt I called at Falkland Palace to see you with reference to the formation of a class in Dairying, but was informed you had gone for a short holiday.

Under the auspices of the Fife-shire County Committee the Edinburgh College of Agriculture have lately been conducting a number of classes, of three weeks duration each, throughout the county. As you are probably aware, pupils are enrolled and instructed in Butter making, a fee of 2s 6d each, being charged for the course. We should be glad to know whether you think a class could be successfully formed at Falkland, to open, say, on September 8th, or on a later date. Your assistance in this matter would be greatly appreciated. I have written to Mr Dun, Woodmill, also on the same subject.

Yours faithfully, J. G. Stewart. (FEP)

28 August 1908

Butter making classes

Dear Mr Stewart,

I regret that I was from home when you called on the 18th inst. I have been in Belgium for a fortnight, and only returned last night. I need not say that it will give me pleasure to be of any assistance I can in the formation of a class in butter making to be held here. I am glad you called upon Mr Dun, Woodmill, as he would be able to give you a good deal of local information, and, if you will kindly let me know

---

[1] September 27th 1908 at the Caledonian Hotel Edinburgh by the Rev. Walter F. Lee, East Parish Perth, assisted by the Rev. Lyon Johnston, Falkland.

in what particular way I can be of any use I need not repeat that I shall be very pleased to do what I can.

Yours faithfully, George Gavin. (FEP)

29 August 1908

Rifle Club

A Rifle Club shoot was held on Lomond Hill Range, near Newton of Falkland, on Saturday. Principal results:

A Class – Ex-Corporal Harry Dick, 62; ex-Corporal J. W. Leishman, 57; Wm. Fairbairn, 56; ex-Drummer Archie Henderson, 56; ex-Sergeant J. Duncan, 56; ex-Sergeant A. Wallace, 53; ex-Corporal J. Robertson, 52; J. Milne, 47.

B Class – Thos. Donaldson, 40; J. Maxwell, 39; J. Donaldson, 33.

200 Yards – Ex-Sergeant J. Duncan, 32; ex-Corporal H. Dick, 32.

500 Yards – Ex-Corporal H. Dick, 30; W. Fairbairn, 30. (FN)

9 September 1908

Shop and house in High Street

Letter to Thomas Ross, Painter

Dear Sir,

I now write to confirm the arrangements verbally made between us whereby Lord Ninian Crichton-Stuart lets to you the shop and dwelling house in High Street, presently unoccupied on the following conditions.

The rent will be at the rate of £12 per annum, payable half yearly at the terms of Whitsunday and Martinmas. Your entry to the premises will be from Martinmas 1908, although you may have occupation of the house earlier without payment of rent if you wish to have it. The proprietor will build in for you in the back kitchen a boiler for washing, it being understood that you yourself will do any papering and painting necessary for the house, and that the proprietor will not be under obligation to incur any other expense whatever in connection with the house. Kindly write me that you are agreeable to the above terms.

Yours faithfully, George Gavin. (FEP)

35. The East Lodge and pond

12 September 1908

Glasgow publican mysteriously drowned

The dead body of a man was found about five o'clock, in the pond at the rear of the entrance lodge to Falkland House, on Thursday evening last week. The discovery was made by some masons who were going home from work. The body was identified as that of John Drake, 62 years of age, a publican, residing at Hill Street, Garnet Hill, Glasgow. Drake, who had just arrived at Falkland from Glasgow on the Thursday morning for the purpose of taking home his wife, an invalid, who had been living in Falkland for the past month, was last seen about three o'clock in the vicinity of the pond. (FN)

21 September 1908

Butter making class

Dear Sir,

The Butter Making Class has made a fair start, and while the number of members is not large as might have been, I hope that more may come by another week. Miss Barbour endeavoured to arrange that the schoolmaster should allow some of the larger girls to attend the class, but he explained that as they are already being allowed to attend a cookery class held in the Town Hall, under the auspices of the County Council it would be impossible to permit of there being spared more to attend the butter making class. I hope to see you as you indicated when the examination takes place.

Yours faithfully, George Gavin. (FEP)

27 September 1908

Testimonial for Mrs Quilter

Dear Mr Gavin,

I received your testimonial and thank you very much for it. I am thinking now nothing will do much good. I have posted off my 82nd letter in answer to advertisements, have spent a lot of money in advertising and going to see people, and a lot of hope in the promises of people to help me to work, which they never mean to do, old people are not wanted in the world, they are not supposed to live.

James Wright paid us a visit last week, he came through Chelmsford on his motor cycle for his holiday, he came on Monday and stayed one night with us and left on Tuesday for London. We did enjoy his visit so, George in particular, as he has a strong affection for Mr Wright. Which is returned. George took his photo in the garden, as before he had no photo of his friend. I was sorry to hear about Pat Duffy, and blame myself for not writing to him, but my heart ached so for all of them. I tried to forget them. Again thank you for the testimonial.

Yours truly, Gertrude Quilter. (FEP)

2 October 1908

Speeding

Dear Mr Gulland,

I submitted your letter containing the resolution of the Town Council with reference to the speed of motor cars passing through the streets of the town, to Lord Ninian Crichton-Stuart. His Lordship has given such instruction to his chauffeur as well. I trust, that there will be no danger to the public while driving the car through the narrow streets of the town.

Yours faithfully, George Gavin. (FEP)

3 October 1908

The Falkland Light Railway Company

Advertisement Column Notice

NOTICE IS HEREBY GIVEN, that a SPECIAL MEETING of the FALKLAND LIGHT RAILWAY COMPANY will be held in the OFFICE of the COMPANY at FALKLAND on SATURDAY, the 17th day of October 1908, at Three o'clock Afternoon, for the purpose of considering and, if thought fit, approving of the following Provisional Order, for which application has been made to the Secretary for Scotland under "The Private Legislation Procedure (Scotland) Act, 1899", which Provisional Order will be submitted to the Proprietors of the Company at such Meeting, namely:

"A Provisional Order to confer further powers upon the North British Railway Company in relation to their undertaking; to provide for the amalgamation of the West Highland Railway Company with the North British Railway Company; to confirm and give effect to agreements between the North British Railway Company and the Invergarry and Fort Augustus Railway Company and the Falkland Light Railway Company respectively; to empower the Forth Bridge Railway Company to raise further money for the purposes of their undertaking; to raise additional Capital; and for other purposes."

CHAS JACKSON. Chairman.

GEORGE ROBERTSON, Secretary. (FN)

10 October 1908

Water

The water assessment has been fixed at 8d – 2d of an increase as compared with last year. (FN)

24 October 1908

Town Council assessments

The burgh assessments for the current year are as follows:

Lunacy, etc. – owners 1d, occupiers 1d (being same as last year);
roads and bridges – owners 5d, occupiers 5d (2d up);
public health – owners 1d, occupiers 1d (½d up);
water – owners 2d, occupiers 2d (1d down);
sewerage – owners 7d, occupiers 7d (1d down);

burgh general – occupiers only 1s 1d (1d up);
Total – owners 1s 4d, occupiers 2s 5d (being ½d up over all for owners and 1½d for occupiers compared with last year). (FN)

31 October 1908

Town Council contest

Nine nominations have been made for the five vacancies on the Town Council, viz., Messrs Michael Reekie, William Horne, John W. Jackson, David Chisholm, Andrew Lister, Christopher C. Brunton, Robert Strachan, William A. Mason, and James Peggie. The first five are the retiring members. (FN)

7 November 1908

Town Council election

Nine candidates for five vacancies:
Mr Brunton, 101; Mr Jackson, 86; Mr Mason, 86; Mr Lister, 84; Mr Reekie, 73. Unsuccessful – Mr Horne, 71; Mr Chisholm, 71; Mr Peggie, 44; Mr Strachan, 29. (FN)

5 December 1908

Lecture

An interesting lecture on "The Fungus Pests of the Farm and Garden" was delivered in the Drill Hall on Friday evening by Dr John H. Wilson, Lecturer in Agriculture in St Andrews University. Mr Richardson, the Schoolhouse, presided. (FN)

19 December 1908

Birth – Bryce

At Royal Terrace, Falkland, on 12th inst., the wife of R. B. Bryce, of a daughter. (FN)

1909

2 January 1909

Snow

The square of Falkland was completely blocked. The snow was above the window sills and the inmates of the Commercial Hotel had to dig themselves out. At the Newton of Falkland the drift was eight feet deep and a passage was only cleared on Wednesday afternoon. To get communication with Falkland Road Station, the only possible road was up the hill and round by the New Inn. The local post office issued orders to their runners to spare no expense in getting their deliveries carried out and to hire a horse, if required. (SAC)

7 January 1909

Jessie Annan

My Lord,

I went to the Deaconess Hospital[1] and saw poor Jessie Annan. She has been operated upon for abscess on the liver and is looking very thin. She was delighted to see me, and more so that your Lordship had remembered about her. She was particularly anxious to know if Lady Margaret had heard of her illness. Jessie returns home to Falkland on Monday, and as she has to get a close conveyance to take

---

[1] The Deaconess Hospital in Edinburgh was founded in 1894 to provide nursing training for Church of Scotland Deaconesses. It is now student accommodation.

her up, I have asked Lady Gormanston[1] this forenoon to speak to Lady Ninian about sending the yellow motor car for her to Falkland Road Station.

Your obedient servant, George Gavin. (FEP)

7 January 1909
Children's magic lantern show
My Lord,

This has been arranged for the afternoon of Monday at 5.30. I have arranged that Feathers, Dundee, will give the entertainments, his charge being two guineas and railway expenses.

Your obedient servant, George Gavin. (FEP)

8 January 1909
Major Cusin
My Lord,

It was only last night in conversation with Dr Jack that I learned that Major Cusin, Chapelyard, is seriously ill. I gathered from Dr Jack that Mr Cusin is suffering from diabetes, and at his age the matter is serious. I am to call at Chapelyard this afternoon.

Your obedient servant, George Gavin. (FEP)

9 January 1909
Seasonable generosity
By the generosity of Lord Ninian Crichton-Stuart and Mr C. J. M. Makgill-Crichton of Lathrisk, the annual distribution of coals to about forty poor people in Falkland and Newton of Falkland was made the other day. The distribution was undertaken through the medium of the Kirk Session.

On Saturday afternoon, the children attending Brunton House School and the children of the employees, to the number of fifty, were entertained at tea at House of Falkland by Lord and Lady Ninian Crichton-Stuart. After a sumptuous tea, partaken of in the hall, the children were conducted to the dining room where a large Christmas tree had been erected, laden with toys which Lady Ninian afterwards

---

[1] Lady Ninian's mother.

distributed to the children. (FN)

9 January 1909
Children's treat
Through the kindness of Miss Gulland, Millfield, the children of Falkland were entertained at an excellent treat in the Drill Hall on Wednesday night last week. Notwithstanding the stormy weather, the children turned out full muster. The tea tables were beautifully decorated and laden with good things. During the serving of tea, bagpipes were played, and selections given from a gramophone. Thereafter action songs were sung by a number of the children. Captain Slacke also contributed a few amusing songs, and was accompanied on the piano by Miss Gulland. A magic lantern entertainment was among the good things provided. Before the children dispersed, after a very pleasant evening, the Rev. A. L. Johnston proposed a hearty vote of thanks to Miss Gulland for her kindness, which was heartily responded to. (FN)

16 January 1909
Sudden death
The death of the widow of Mr Walter Lumsden took place under very pathetic circumstances on Wednesday. Her friends, who had been at the funeral of her sister, were parting with her in the afternoon, when she suddenly expired. Deceased was fully 80 years of age, and had been in failing health for some years. (FFP)

22 January 1909
Rent for dairy classes
Letter to Mr Stewart, College of Agriculture
Dear Sir,
  The treasurer for the Drill Hall has asked me for the rent of the Hall during the time as occupied by the Dairy Class. The amount is 15s, and perhaps you will kindly remit it direct to himself "Mr Andrew Lister, Baker, Falkland", or to me, and I can hand it to him.
  With kind regards, I am yours faithfully, George Gavin. (FEP)

23 January 1909

Unionist meeting in Drill Hall

On Tuesday evening, a largely attended and enthusiastic meeting was held in the Drill Hall, Falkland, presided over by Lord Ninian Crichton-Stuart. The principal speakers were: Colonel Sprot and Mr R. E. Noble, barrister, London. The latter, who had to leave for London by the night mail, spoke first, and dealt principally with the legislative failures of the present Government, referring specially to the various Education Bills and the Licensing Bill. Colonel Sprot confined his remarks to Tariff Reform, which he handled in a most interesting and lucid manner. The meeting closed with a vote of thanks to Colonel Sprot, proposed by Captain Slacke, and with a similar compliment to the Chairman by Colonel Sprot. (FN)

6 February 1909

Balmblae dyke

Dear Mr Gavin,

I beg to draw your attention to the dyke in Balmblae at the garden ground belonging to Lord Ninian Crichton-Stuart and tenanted by Peter Robertson, which has fallen down. This dyke is at the back of my property and is causing great inconvenience to my tenant. I trust you will give this your earliest attention.

Yours truly, Michael Reekie, South Street. (FEP)

25 February 1909

Correspondence and an accident

Dear Captain Slacke,

I met Lord Ninian as arranged on Tuesday morning at Ladybank, taking with me all the letters I got from Clifford. His Lordship retained certain of them, and handed over to me those which accompany this letter in order that I might forward them to you. He gave me no instructions with regard to them, except in the case of the letter asking for a loan of a motor car for the Forfarshire election. He did not care to send the yellow car, and, accordingly, said that the reply would be that he regretted he was unable to send a car at present. His Lordship only stayed in House of Falkland for about half an hour,

36. Lord and Lady Ninian in their motor car
at House of Falkland

The car is probably the Daimler which formed part of Lord Ninian's
wedding present to his bride, also referred to as 'the yellow motor car'.
The chauffeur sits in the back of the car, ready to take over the driving
when called upon.

devoting the remainder of his time to visiting the gardens, tile-works,
and other places on the Estate. If you saw him before he left for
Egypt,[1] he would tell you that Descamps' car never reached Cupar,
having broken down at Markinch, and he hired a car from Outhwaite
in Cupar.

Yours faithfully, George Gavin.

P.S. – Since dictating the above, Duggan, the house carpenter, has
come in with his arm in a sling. The gas engines had gone wrong
again late last night. He had to refill the petrol tank at the House, and
when doing so the petrol took fire and exploded, and burned his
hand. He had to go to Dr Jack to have it dressed, and I am afraid he
will not be able to work for some time. This matter suggests to me
that you may have not added Duggan to the list of servants who are

---

[1] Lord and Lady Ninian were staying at the Hotel d'Angleterre, Cairo.

insured. No doubt, you will now have him included.(FEP)

6 March 1909

Successful dance

The employees in the linen and floor cloth factories were treated to a dance by Messrs Charles Jackson and Sons Ltd, on Wednesday, in the Drill Hall. The entertainment, which had been postponed, was given to celebrate the marriage of Mr John W. Jackson, which occurred some months ago. Music was supplied by Mr Adamson's quadrille band, Kingskettle; and Messrs J. Drysdale, D. Munro, and A. Grieve acted as MCs. (FFP)

7 March 1909

Lord and Lady Ninian travelling

Letter to Hamilton & Inches, 47, George St, Edinburgh

Dear Mr Hamilton,

I am favoured with your letter of 6th inst, and am glad to hear from you, and to see from it, as you say, that you are still "above ground". I shall look in and see you when next in Edinburgh. The reason I have not looked in to see you is really that when I go to Edinburgh I am always more or less rushed, and as none of my friends have been married recently (Thank goodness, but, of course, you will not agree with me in this) I have not personally required any small articles in your line. Lord Ninian is off to Egypt with her Ladyship, who has had influenza. They go on afterwards to Ceylon, and do not return here till the month of May. They are happy people who can so escape splashing, as we are doing now, knee-deep in slush.

Yours faithfully, George Gavin. (FEP)

25 March 1909

Cricket Club

Memo to Lodge-keeper

The annual meeting of the Cricket Club took place last night when it was decided that practice should begin on Saturday 10th April. The arrangements will be exactly the same as last season, and you will see that you are supplied with a list of the members so that no others will be admitted except when matches are played on Saturdays. If, prior to the 10th April one or two of the members wish to visit the pitch, they can be allowed to do so.

George Gavin. (FEP)

27 March 1909
Mr Francis Henderson

Mr Francis Henderson,[1] of the British Linen Bank, has received the appointment of teller in the Bank at Carluke. (FN)

27 March 1909
School Board

At a meeting of ratepayers on Monday evening, Provost Miller presiding, the following four names were put forward: Robert Miller, joiner; Charles Jackson, manufacturer; David Bonthrone, maltster; and Rev. A. L. Johnston, E.C. minister. The first three are members of the old Board. (FN)

3 April 1909
Hawking beer

George Knox, van driver, Newton of Falkland, was fined two guineas by a JP Court at Kirkcaldy on Friday. Knox admitted having hawked six pints of excisable liquor on the highway near Markinch on 27th February. The police suspected that such a practice was frequently carried on by Knox, and they set a watch. The officers were in plain clothes, and, unobserved by Knox, went into the field, and saw him sell the liquor to three men. In his defence the accused

37. Robert Miller
Wearing the provost's
chain of office.

---

[1] Frank Henderson was the son of Margaret Allan Reid of Viewhill. He later went to work for a bank in South America, came back to serve in WWI and was killed in 1916.

said one of the men had ordered the drink. Whitecross, coachman, Rothes; Henry Laird, labourer, Balgonie, and Henry Hood, Balgonie, were charged with inducing Knox to sell them two pints of beer each. They admitted the offence, and were fined 10s 6d, or three days' imprisonment. (FN)

3 April 1909

A son and heir

Much satisfaction has been expressed here with the news that a son and heir was born to the Hon. F. Hanbury-Tracy, Lathrisk House, in Edinburgh on Monday. Mr and Mrs Tracy have received many hearty congratulations. (FN)

10 April 1909

Presentations

On Wednesday evening, 31st March, Mr Francis Henderson, British Linen Bank, was met by a few of his friends and well-wishers in Mrs Ness' Temperance Hotel, and presented with a handsome gold watch and chain, the occasion being his promotion to be teller in the Bank's branch at Carluke.

Mr Charles Jackson, Lomondvale, in a few well-chosen and appropriate sentences, made the presentation, and Mr Henderson suitably replied. The Rev. Mr Johnston and Mr Richardson also expressed their good wishes for Mr Henderson's future welfare and prosperity, and, after some songs were contributed, the evening came to a close by the singing of "Auld Lang Syne". Mr H. Adamson, jeweller, Cupar, supplied the watch and chain, which were suitably inscribed.

On Tuesday evening Mr Henderson was the recipient of an Oxford Teacher's Bible as a parting gift from his fellow members of the Y.M.C.A. (FN)

12 April 1909

Shop on corner

Letter to James Page, The Terrace.
Dear Sir,

On behalf of Lord Ninian Crichton-Stuart I now write to say that I am prepared to let you from year to year as from Whitsunday first, the shop situated at the corner of High Street and Cross Wynd, at an early rent of £5. As verbally mentioned to you the shop is let on condition that the proprietor is to be at no expense whatsoever in connection with repairs, and any repairs required will be executed by yourself.

Yours faithfully, George Gavin. (FEP)

12 April 1909

House in Bruce Buildings

Letter to Miss Annie Sharp, West Port

Dear Madam,

With reference to your sister's call here on Saturday evening I have now to say that on behalf of Lord Ninian Crichton-Stuart I am prepared to let to you the house in Bruce Buildings, as presently occupied by Mr David Crichton, from year to year as from Whitsunday first. Your sister indicated that you might be willing to pay some portion of the cost of the necessary papering and painting, which would be required, but on consideration I think it better to increase the rent to £6 10s. per annum, and the proprietor will wholly defray the cost of doing what is necessary to the house. Kindly let us know that you agree to this.

Yours faithfully, George Gavin. (FEP)

17 April 1909

The light railway

A meeting of the Working Committee in connection with the above undertaking was held on Tuesday night at which the various members handed in their reports. The various reports indicate that the desire for a railway is unanimous, and it is encouraging to find that considerable promise to active support in the taking up of share capital exists among the merchants, traders, and others in Falkland and district generally. The tone of the meeting showed clearly that Falkland folks regard the future welfare and prosperity of the village as bound up in being provided with railway facilities. (FN)

17 April 1909

Lord and Lady Ninian Crichton-Stuart

Lord and Lady Ninian Crichton-Stuart returned to Falkland House last week after an absence of about two months.[1] (FN)

17 April 1909

Visitors

Monday being the Glasgow, Dundee and Perth Spring holiday,[2] there were a considerable number of visitors in the town over the week-end. (FN)

17 April 1909

Golf

The golfers played their first match on Saturday last at Markinch, but were defeated by 5 matches to 3. (FN)

24 April 1909

Circus

Pinders famous circus[3] visited the town on Tuesday, and there was a large attendance at the performance. (FN)

24 April 1909

Cricket Club

The Cricket Club have commenced practice for the season, and the first fixture falls to be played tomorrow (Saturday) at Kirkcaldy.

---

[1] Lord and Lady Ninian had intended to travel to Ceylon, but she had caught enteric dysentery in Egypt and they came back early.

[2] Easter Monday (12 April in 1909) is a public holiday in various parts of Scotland.

[3] Thomas, Ord, born 1784, the son of Rev. Selby Ord, ran away from home aged around 14 and joined the circus. By 1812 he had started his own circus, which became the most famous circus of the early 19th century. After Thomas Ord died in 1859 his daughter Selina Ord carried on with the circus. In 1861 she married Edwin Pinder whose uncles, George and William Pinder, had founded Pinders circus in 1854. Edwin left his uncles and he and Selina continued with Ord Pinders circus in Scotland.

There is every prospect of the season being a successful one. (FN)

1 May 1909
Telephone exchange
Efforts are at present being made with considerable success to obtain a sufficient number of subscribers so as arrangements can be completed for the installation of a telephone exchange at the Post Office. (FN)

8 May 1909
Cricket
The Cricket Club played off their second fixture on Saturday last at Kirkcaldy against Kirkcaldy 2nd XI, the result being a draw. Tomorrow (Saturday) they travel to Cupar to meet Cupar 2nd XI. (FN)

8 May 1909
Communion
Communion services were held in the Parish and United Free Church Churches on Sunday. In the evening, the Rev. William Porter, Cults, preached in the Parish Church, while the Rev. W. L. Craig, Kettle, occupied the pulpit of the United Free Church. (FN)

14 May 1909
Curling Club
Dear Mr Gavin,

The curling committee of management will meet in the shop of Mr Williamson, Saddler, High Street on Tuesday evening 18 inst at 8 o'clock to sign lease of ground for artificial rink. Please attend.

Yours faithfully, John Sheriff, secretary. (FEP)

22 May 1909
Brass Band
Falkland Brass Band is making considerable progress. After parading the streets last Saturday evening, they rendered a programme in the East Loan. (FN)

22 May 1909

Mrs Lucinda Campbell

Mrs Lucinda Wilson, or Campbell, High Street, died on Saturday last in her 94th year. Mrs Campbell, who was the oldest inhabitant of Falkland, was a daughter of the late Major Wilson of Ballo. (FN)

22 May 1909

Headmastership

The short list of candidates for the position of headmaster in the Public School here has been reduced to three, viz:

Mr Dunbar, Saltcoats; Mr Thomson, Glasgow; and Mr Young, Elphinstone, Tranent.

These gentlemen will be interviewed by the School Board on Monday first, after which the appointment will be made. (FN)

29 May 1909

School Board

At a meeting of the School Board held on Monday, Mr J. Dunbar MA, BSc, Saltcoats, was appointed to the headmastership of the Public School at a salary of £180 with a free house. Mr Dunbar commences his duties about the 16th of August. (FN)

29 May 1909

Cricket – Falkland v. Craighall

Falkland had Craighall (Dundee) as visitors on Saturday at Scroggie Park on a good wicket.

The home captain won the toss, and elected to bat, sending in Robinson and Michie to the bowling of McKay and Bruce. The opening was disastrous as the first wicket fell without any runs being scored and the second and third falling at 5, matters were beginning to look serious for the homesters. Before the fourth wicket fell, however, the total had been raised to 33, the Hon. F. H. Tracy being the retiring batsman with 16 to his credit, got by excellent cricket. The score mounted steadily up only Venters of the succeeding batsmen failing to augment to the total, and when the last wicket fell, the board showed 85.

The Dundee men started none too well either, the second wicket falling with only 1 run scored. McKay and Robertson, however, carried the score to 17 before a separation was effected. The fourth and fifth wickets also fell at this figure. Coxon and Robertson added 17 for the sixth wicket, but the remainder didn't offer much resistance and the whole side was out for 43.

Bowling for Craighall, Robertson had 2 wickets for 8 runs, Stratton 3 for 14, McKay 3 for 18. Donald 2 for 25 and Bruce 0 for 15. For Falkland, Grieve secured 3 for 12, and Michie 6 for 25. (FN)

5 June 1909

Shepherd assaults cattleman

George Donald, shepherd, Woodmill Farm, when charged at Cupar Sheriff Court today with having, on 29th May, at Moonzie Farm, assaulted Robert Barry, cattleman, tendered a plea of guilty. He pleaded for leniency on the ground that he had a guid few bairns. Sentence was passed by Sheriff Armour of a fine of 10s, or ten days imprisonment. (DET)

11 June 1909

Pond at Lodge Gate

My Lord,

I shall have the wire netting required to keep in the cranes and ducks erected without delay, and write your Lordship as soon as it is ready for the reception of the birds. I shall see they are met and taken care of.

Your obedient servant, George Gavin. (FEP)

12 June 1909

Falkland Brass Band

The Falkland Brass Band fulfilled their first engagements on Saturday last when they attended the annual market at Star, Markinch. They have been engaged for the local market and games, which take place to-morrow (Saturday). (FN)

19 June 1909

Menagerie

On the evening of Thursday, the 10th inst., Sedgewick's menagerie

38. Sedgwick's Menagerie, about 1909

visited the town with their excellent collection of animals, which
included 15 lions. [1] Four of the lions reflected great credit on their

---

[1] In the 1900s William Sedgewick's menagerie was one of the biggest on the
road. Oldham-based Sedgewick originally entered show business with a
photographic studio and by 1860 was travelling a waxworks show. He then
moved into the menagerie business and by 1869 was running a group of per-
forming lions. Sedgewick was a great breeder of lions, boasting that he had
more than any other showman. With the better documented shows of the
19th century the usual configuration was an open square, three sides of
which were composed of wagons containing the beasts, and the fourth of a
"walk-up", or steps leading to a platform on which was a paybox and a balcony. On the balcony was a band that performed popular music, while the
animal trainers strutted about and the "spieler" harangued the crowd with
stories of the dangers of wild animal training and begged the public to come
and judge for themselves. There were steps down into the show on the other
side and the whole outfit was covered by an awning of canvas tied off on
each side to the tops of the beast wagons. The front was very often a big
affair, consisting of wooden columns to represent marble, much gilt carving
and many pictures of wild beasts fighting, being hunted and captured, and
living in their native jungle. The main show took place in the beast wagons
themselves, where the trainers did most of their work. (www.fairground-
heritage.org.uk).

trainer by their clever performances. The special feature of the evening was the tug-of-war between the elephants and 30 local men. The result was a win for the men, who were presented with a silver cup, which, after a draw taking place among the competitors, fell to the possession of Mr William Stark Jnr, Newton of Falkland. (FN)

26 June 1909

Market and games

The annual market and games were held on Saturday last, when there was a record attendance. The games were specially well competed for, and a splendid exhibition of dancing was given by the troupe in attendance. There were the usual shows, etc. The local Brass Band played various selections during the games and also the music for the dancing, which was engaged in for four or five hours. (FN)

3 July 1909

Sunday School picnics

On Saturday last, both the Parish Church and United Free Sunday Schools held their annual picnics. The former chose for their destination this year Pitlour, by Strathmiglo, and the latter spent the afternoon at Balbirnie, near Markinch. Both parties enjoyed the outing very much. (FN)

10 July 1909

Golf

The Lathrisk Cup competition resulted in the Rev. A. Lyon Johnston winning the cup by beating Mr J. O. Levack. This is the third time Mr Johnston has been custodian of the trophy. (FN)

24 July 1909

Drive to Elie

The choirs of the United Free Church and a few friends enjoyed a splendid drive to Elie on Saturday last. There were some showers in the forepart of the day, but everyone was highly pleased with the outing. (FN)

29 July 1909

Inn-keeper fined

James Weepers, Stag Inn, admitted at Cupar Sheriff Court this afternoon having, on 10th June, sold two half glasses of whisky to the Cupar district sanitary inspector under the legal strength of 25 per cent, fixed by the Sale of Food and Drugs Act.

Mr G. E. B. Osborne, in extenuation stated that Mr Weepers was 72 years of age, and had been 36 years in business, and never had any complaint against him before. The whisky was .7 under the strength fixed by the Act.

Sheriff Shennan: That is very weak whisky.

Mr Osborne: I presume this.

The Sheriff: I suppose it will be better for you. How did it come to be so weak?

Mr Osbourne: He put too much water in it.

The Sheriff: I know that; but why did he put too much water in it?

Mr Osborne: It was due to his rough and ready way of reduction. He had three qualities of whisky. It was his second quality he was endeavouring to make equal to the third. He thought it could stand a little more.

The Sheriff: What is the penalty?

The Fiscal: £20.

The Sheriff: I think a nominal penalty will be sufficient here. You will be fined £1. (ET)

9 August 1909

Mr Charles Gulland's death

Mr Charles Gulland died with startling suddenness late on Friday evening.

Mr Gulland was at his office on Friday forenoon, and partook of lunch at his residence at Millfield. He had an appointment with Lord Ninian Crichton-Stuart and his factor for the afternoon, and when he did not put in an appearance a message was sent to Millfield to inquire if he was there. The response was that he had gone to his office, but as inquires there were without avail calls were made at various places in the hope of finding him.

On Mrs Gulland being notified that her husband could not be

found she instituted a search of
the house, and he was discovered in an unconscious condition
lying on the bathroom floor. He
was removed to his room, and Dr
Jack was soon in attendance. A
specialist was wired for from
Edinburgh, and he arrived before the end came, but all that
could be done had been done,
and no human skill could aid
him. Death was due to apoplexy.

Deceased, who was about sev-
enty years of age, came of a nota-
ble Fife family. His grandfather
was a medical practitioner in
Falkland for fully sixty years,
and his father was Town Clerk of
the Burgh for sixty-nine years.
Born in Falkland, and educated

39. Charles Gulland

at Edinburgh Academy and Edinburgh University, Mr Gulland
entered his father's office. The business then, as now, albeit the
factorship of the Lathrisk estates has passed into other hands, was an
extensive one, and to gain further experience Mr Gulland proceeded
to London, and spent some time in an office there.

Shortly after his return he succeeded his father as Town Clerk. That
was in 1865. He subsequently on the death of his father became agent
of the British Linen Company's Bank at Falkland, Clerk to the
Heritors, and factor for estates, and agent and adviser for many families, all of which positions, save the Lathrisk factorship, he retained
to the end.

Every project that tended to the prosperity of the old burgh
received Mr Gulland's warm support, and in connection with the
proposed light railway from Falkland Road Station to Falkland he
acted as secretary to the promoters. He was a fine type of the old
country lawyer-banker-factor, and was universally respected and
esteemed.

A few years ago he published a volume of verse running over 900 pages, which was very favourably reviewed.

In politics he was a staunch Unionist, and rendered good service to the party in his district. He is survived by his widow and four daughters. His only son Rowland, who was joint agent of the bank, and assistant and successor to his father in the office of Town Clerk, died after a brief illness in 1903. The death of his son was a sore blow to Mr Gulland. (DC)

11 August 1909
Charles Gulland's funeral

Amid many manifestations of sorrow the remains of Mr Charles Gulland, town clerk, were laid to rest yesterday in the New Cemetery. The old burgh was in mourning, and business for a period was suspended.

The officiating clergymen were the Rev. A. Lyon Johnston, parish minister; the Rev. J. H. Morrison, U.F. Church; and the Rev. A. E. Gordon, Kettle. There was a large company of mourners, including the Town Council, members of other public bodies, and most of the towns-people.

The pallbearers were: Dr McIntosh, Edinburgh; Mr H. O. Tarbolton, Edinburgh; Dr Howell, London (sons-in-law); Mr George Ballingall WS, Edinburgh, and Mr David Ballingall (nephews); Lord Ninian Crichton-Stuart, Mr Alex. Anderson and Provost Miller.

Among others present were: Mr Rae Arnot of Lochieheads; the Hon. Felix Hanbury-Tracy, Lathrisk; Captain R. C. Slacke, Mr F. Gordon Brown, British Linen Company's Bank, Edinburgh; Mr R. Osborne Pagan, Cupar; Mr Thomas McIntosh WS, Edinburgh; Dr Mackay, Leith; Mr Charles Wood, solicitor, Kirkcaldy;[1] Mr James Tod, Cash; Mr George Dun, Woodmill; the Rev. Charles Fraser, Freuchie; Mr J. O. Levack, Falkland; Mr Anderson, Falkland; Mr W. Tod, Brackly; Mr Tod, Pardovan; Mr John Lawson of Carriston; Mr Reid VS, Auchtermuchty; Mr D. S. Reid VS; Mr D. Carswell, Ladybank; Mr J. L. Lumsden, Eden Valley House, Freuchie; Mr R. Tullis, Strathendry; Mr R. Russell, Cadham; Mr George Gavin, Falkland Palace; Mr D. Scott, Kilwhiss; Mr Barry Ogilvie, Westfield; Mr Thomas

---

[1] Charles Wood was the son of Major William Wood, the former factor.

Arnot, Newton of Lathrisk; Mr John Sheriff; Mr John W. Jackson, Dunshalt; Mr Jackson, Lomond-Vale; ex Provost Bonthrone, Auchtermuchty; Mr Charles Welch, Cupar; Mr George Burton, Falkland; and Mr George Maxwell, Barrington. (DC)

21 August 1909

The late Mr Gulland

As both ministers are on holiday at present, there were no pulpit references last Sunday to the death of Mr Gulland, but the Town Council attended Church in their official capacity out of respect for their late Town Clerk. (FN)

28 August 1909

Bicycle thefts

John Balfour, floorcloth worker, Well Brae was charged at Cupar court on Monday with having on 20th June 1908 at the Bruce Arms, Hotel, stolen a bicycle, and on 19th July at the Market Green Auchtermuchty, stolen a bicycle.

He pleaded guilty, and in extenuation Mr D. Carswell, solicitor, Ladybank, stated in regard to the first charge that a man under the influence of drink gave him the bicycle, saying at the time that it was damaged and of no use to him, and in regard to the second charge that he had bought the bicycle for 12s 6d. The fiscal said he was not inclined to accept the statement. The first bicycle was lifted from the door of the hotel on the Falkland Games day of last year, and no trace of it was found of it until the police were making inquiries in connection with the second case. He passed sentence of twenty-one days imprisonment. (FFP)

19 September 1909

Coach and cart for Ladybank

Letter to Lord Ninian, Dumfries House

Dear Lord Ninian,

I have instructed Barnstaple to be at Ladybank on Saturday at 1.26. p.m. with the Victoria if fine and the Brougham if wet. Birrell will also be there with the luggage cart. [1]

I have arranged with the coachman for the cleaning of the peram-
bulator and impressed upon him the necessity of extreme care being
taken to avoid scratching.

Your obedient servant, George Gavin. (FEP)

21 September 1909
House sale
To be sold by public roup. within the Bruce Arms, Hotel, on Saturday
the 2nd of October, 1909, at 3 o'clock Afternoon.
(1) That Two-story Dwelling-house (with Small Dwelling-house on
north end thereof), known as Juniper Villa, the ground floor of
which was occupied by the late Mrs Menzies.
Assessed Rental £19. Ground Rental 18s 8¾d. Upset Price £375.
(2) That Two-story Dwelling-house adjoining the above on the north,
occupied by Mr Livingston and Mrs Stewart.
Assessed Rental £9 10s. No Feu-duty or Ground Annual. Upset
Price £200.
For further particulars apply to Alex. Wallace, Solicitor, Kirkcaldy,
who will exhibit the Title Deeds and Articles of Roup. (DC)

25 September 1909
British Linen Bank
Mr James Donaldson, British Linen Bank, Edinburgh, and Mr
Alexander Anderson, solicitor, have been appointed joint agents of
the British Linen Bank here. (FN)

25 September 1909
Poaching on Lathrisk estate
At Cupar Sheriff Court on Thursday – before Sheriff Armour –
George Page, joiner, Falkland, was charged with having on 20th July
trespassed in pursuit of game on the Lathrisk estate. He pleaded
guilty, and Mr David Robertson, solicitor, Markinch, who appeared

---

[1] A victoria was an elegant open carriage with seats for a coachman and two
passengers; a brougham (pronounced "broom") had an enclosed body, like
the rear section of a coach.

on his behalf, said that the case was more in the nature of a frolic than a serious poaching expedition. Page had been at Auchtermuchty, and after he went home he got a gun and went out with it. He did not fire any shots, however, and no game was killed. Mr A. E. Grosset, solicitor, Cupar, who prosecuted, said there were shots fired, for it was the sounds of shooting that attracted the attention of the game-keeper. There had been a good many complaints about poaching on the Lathrisk estate lately. A fine of 5s with 15s modified expenses, or ten days imprisonment was imposed. (FN)

2 October 1909
Y.M.C.A
The annual business meeting of the Young Men's Christian Associa-tion was held in the Town Hall on Tuesday. Mr Grieve, Treasurer, submitted his report, and also gave an interesting account of the National Conference held at Paisley. Office bearers were appointed as follows: Mr Walter Peggie, President; Mr C. C. Brunton, Vice-President; Mr George Robertson, Secretary; Mr Alexander Grieve, Treasurer; Mr William Dowie, Harmoniumist. (FN)

9 October 1909
Lecture Committee
The Popular Lecture Committee have again resolved to carry on another course during the coming winter, and a programme, which should prove very interesting, is being arranged. Dr Jack has been appointed president, and Mr Alexander Anderson and Mr James Peggie continue to be secretary and treasurer, respectively. (FN)

16 October 1909
Lecture
On Sunday evening, the Rev. J. H. Morrison, U.F. Church, delivered a very interesting lecture on "A year's mission work on the Canadian Prairie". There was a good attendance, despite the inclemency of the weather. (FN)

16 October 1909

Town Council

At a meeting of the Town Council held on Monday evening, Mr Alexander Anderson, solicitor, Falkland, was appointed Town Clerk and Treasurer, in place of the late Mr Gulland.

The burgh assessments for the current year have been fixed as follows: Lunacy etc., 2d per £1; roads and bridges, 9d per £1; public health, 1d per £1; water supply, 4d per £1; sewerage, 1s 5d per £1; and burgh general, 1s 1d per £1, the owners' proportion being 1s 4½d per £1 and the occupiers 2s 3½d per £1 – an increase of ½d per £1 on each, as compared with last year.

The members of the Council who fall to retire at this time are: Provost Miller, Councillors Angus and Williamson, and another. (FN)

30 October 1909

Ordination of elders

At the forenoon service in the United Free Church, Messrs Robert Hill, William Horne, and Christopher C. Brunton were ordained elders. (FN)

27 October 1909

Land for Meadowfield House

Letter to John Anderson, Kingskettle

Dear Sir,

Mr John W. Jackson, manufacturer, here, intends to build a house [1] adjoining that of his father, Mr Charles Jackson, on a piece of ground lying to the east of his father's house, and belonging to Dr Wallace of Liverpool, that piece of ground being too narrow on which to build the kind of house proposed. Mr Jackson approached Lord Ninian Crichton-Stuart with the view of his leasing to him a strip of ground about 10 or 12 yards in breadth, off the piece of land belonging to his Lordship and let to you. His Lordship has consented to lease this strip, and I now write to say that this strip will be resumed bye and

---

[1] Meadowfield House. Charles Jackson's house was Lomond View (now replaced by a care home). The open space between the two houses has since been filled up by new developments (Southfield and Liquorstane).

bye, and a deduction allowed to you in terms of your lease.

Yours faithfully, George Gavin. (FEP)

30 October 1909

Social meeting

On Friday the 22nd inst. the annual social meeting of the Established Church Guild was held in the school, when there was a large turn-out, and a very enjoyable evening was spent. During the course of the social, an address was delivered on "Mission Work", and several anthems were sung by the members of the choir. (FN)

30 October 1909

Lecture

On Wednesday evening, a lecture was delivered in the United Free Church by the Rev. John Lindsay, Bathgate. The subject was "Mission Work in Old Calabar, West Africa", to which place the Rev. Mr Lindsay recently paid a visit. The lecture was illustrated by splendid limelight views, which were explained in a very interesting and instructive manner. There was a good attendance, and before the lecture commenced, three anthems were rendered by the choir. The meeting closed with votes of thanks to the lecturer and to Mr Arch. Aitken, Freuchie, who worked the lantern. (FN)

6 November 1909

Municipal election

The annual election of Town Councillors took place on Tuesday. There were six candidates for four vacancies, and the result of the poll was as follows: Successful – Robert Ness, John Angus, George Robertson and Thomas Williamson. Unsuccessful – William Horne and James Peggie. Provost Miller, who fell to retire by rotation at this time, did not seek re-election. He has occupied a seat in the Town Council for almost 30 years, and has proved himself to be a very worthy servant of the Royal and ancient burgh. (FN)

13 November 1909

Lord's Supper

The sacrament of the Lord's Supper was celebrated in both churches

40. The Town Council, 1910

Back row: Christopher Campbell Brunton – George Robertson – Michael
Reekie – Thomas Williamson – John Walker Jackson – William Alexander
Mason – unidentified
Front row: Andrew Lister – Robert Drysdale (Junior Bailie) – Charles Jackson
Jnr (Provost) – Thomas Sutherland (Senior Bailie) – John Angus

on Sunday last. In the evening, the Rev. W. M. Tocher, Dunbog,
occupied the pulpit of the Established Church, and the Rev. J. M.
Richardson, Freuchie, preached in the United Free Church.[1] (FN)

13 November 1909

Town Council

At the first meeting of the Town Council held on Friday last, Bailie
Charles Jackson was elected Provost of the burgh, in place of Mr
Robert Miller, who has retired from the Council. [2]Councillor Robert
Drysdale was chosen Junior Bailie. Bailie Sutherland continues in the

---

[1] John Walker, Church Officer, annual allowance for looking after family
pew in Parish Church. £1.

[2] Robert Miller's death, less than three years later, seems to have escaped the
notice of the local papers. However his tombstone in Falkland Cemetery
records that he died on 19 April 1913 aged 67.

office of Senior Bailie. (FN)

13 November 1909

Malicious mischief

At Cupar on Tuesday, Robert Craig jnr, baker, Royal Terrace, Falkland, was fined 10s or five days imprisonment, for having on 9th October, maliciously thrown a stone at, and broken a spar off a gate at the dwelling-house in Victoria Place, occupied by Robert Strachan, tailor. (FN)

17 November 1909

West Loan

Letter to Alexander Anderson, Town Clerk

Dear Mr Anderson,

In the summer of this year I had occasion to complain to the police about a number of boys who had practically taken possession of the West Loan, and had erected tents and lit fires on it. I also asked the Provost to assist in protecting the interests of the grazing tenant, as it was manifest that the Loan was being used simply as a public playground. I have now received a letter from the tenant giving up his occupation of the West Loan on account of the amount of golf playing, cricket, and all sorts of enjoyment by the inhabitants and visitors. I believe that the public of Falkland have certain rights in the Loan, but I cannot conceive that they amount to its being used in the way indicated. Will you kindly bring this matter before an early meeting of your council, and let me know what steps the council are prepared to take to protect the interests of the proprietor and his tenant.

Yours faithfully, George Gavin. (FEP)

20 November 1909

Curling

The artificial curling pond, which has been in the course of construction during the summer, has now been completed, and the first game was played on Monday evening. This is the first time for many years that the Club has enjoyed a game in the month of November. (FN)

41. The new curling pond
Now the bowling green

22 November 1909

Dovecot Farm sale

Speedie Brothers, auctioneers, Cupar, conducted on Saturday a displenishing sale at the farm of Mr Henry Duncan having relinquished his tenancy.

As has been the case at most sales this season the attendance of the general public was gratifyingly large, attracted no doubt by the large herd of dairy cows exposed by Mr Duncan. The sale started at 11 am with barn things and harness and these went well. Implements had seen considerable service, and were sold for as much as they were worth. The chief centre of interest was the cows, and there was no lack of bidders when these were brought out. Cows in full milk and also those near the calving realised very satisfactory prices, but the best demand prevailed for Early spring calvers. Horses sold moderately well. Mr Duncan's crop was in fair order, and met with good competition, but there have been dearer stacks sold this season. Turnips will be extremely dear per acre.

The following is a note of the principal prices.

Implements: Milk cart and cans, £10; corn carts, £4 10s; coup carts, £5

5s; Massey-Harris binder, £12; reaper, £1 12s 6d; drill ploughs, £2
5s; common ploughs 17s 6d; harrows 10s; metal roller, £2; turnip
sewing machine, £2; steelyard, £3 5s; turnip slicer 12s 6d; ladders
15s; barrows 17s; engine, mill and shed, £50.
Live Stock: 12 milk cows to £18 5s and from £11 10s to £18; calving
heifers to £8 5s; cross hogs to 26s; cross ewes to 18s; half-bred ewes
to 30s; tup 29s; work horses from £17 to £27 10s.
Crop: Oat stacks from £7 5s to £9; barley straw to £2 10s; wheat straw
to £2; rye straw to £1 15s, all per small rick; Swedes from 7s 6d to
8s 3d per drill. (DC)

25 November 1909

Children's Christmas presents

My Lord,
I had a meeting with the two ministers and the schoolmaster on
Tuesday evening, and on Wednesday devoted the forenoon to
purchasing the toys at Maules.[1] There were somewhat over 200
children, and as there will be a few stragglers, I purchased 250
articles.
Your obedient servant, George Gavin. (FEP)

18 December 1909

Telephone exchange

The work is being proceeded with, of introducing the telephone into
the burgh, where there is to be an exchange in future. The exchange
is to be in the new Post Office premises in the shop below the Town
Hall. (FN)

18 December 1909

Lecture

On the evening of Friday last, a very interesting and instructive lecture on "Campaigning Experiences in South Africa" was delivered in
the Drill Hall by Mr James Donaldson, bank agent, Falkland. Mr Donaldson was at the front during the last South African War, and he is

---

[1] Maules was a large department store on the corner at the west end of
Princes Street, Edinburgh.

42. The Town Hall, including Middleton's shop and Post Office
A sign outside says "Post Office – Public Telephone".The United Free
Church is the prominent building at the far end of the High Street.

well qualified to give such a lecture, as his regiment of the Royal Scots
acquitted themselves very creditably. The lecture was illustrated by
limelight views, many of which were taken by comrades of Mr Donaldson while on the march. It was very appropriate that he should
have as his Chairman, Mr David Bonthrone, who also passed through
the Boer War with the Fife and Forfar Imperial Yeomanry. (FN)

27 December 1909

Children's party

A sumptuous treat was given on Christmas Eve by Lord Ninian
Crichton-Stuart to the school children of Falkland. The children, to
the number of 224, were dismissed for the Christmas holidays at
noon, and reassembling at the school later in the day marched along
with their teachers to the Drill Hall where an abundance of tea and
cake awaited them.

A Christmas tree laden with presents filled one end of the hall. Lord

Ninian Crichton-Stuart with his secretary, Captain Slacke, Mr and Mrs Gavin, and other ladies and gentlemen along with the teachers assisted the little ones to the tea and good things. Lord Ninian distributed the gifts off the Christmas tree to the children. The Rev. A. L. Johnston proposed a vote of thanks to Lord Ninian, and the Rev. J. H. Morrison proposed a vote of thanks to Mr Gavin and those who had so kindly assisted to make the evening enjoyable. Each child on leaving was presented with a box of sweets and an orange. (DC)

30 December 1909
Sunday drinking
Richard Hargraves, shoemaker, and James Miller, tailor, both of Freuchie, admitted at a JP Court at Cupar yesterday having, on Sunday, December 12, obtained by wilful and false representation whisky and beer at the Bruce Arms, Hotel. [1]

The Fiscal said his information was that the accused were addicted to drink, and that that was not the first occasion on which they had obtained liquor in like manner. Hargraves was found drunk in High Street, Falkland, on the Sunday night in question.

Hargraves said they had been having a walk round by Kinross, and they were entitled to a drink.

The Fiscal: Why did you say you came from Markinch?

Hargraves: If we had said we had come from Freuchie the hotel-keeper would not have let us in.

Hon. Sheriff Thomson: This appears to be quite a deliberate case of imposing upon a license-holder who is entitled to be protected by the Court. You will be fined £1, or ten days. (DC)

Estate office wages, 1909
George Gavin, salary per month, £29 3s 4d.
Robert Thomson, estate clerk, salary per month, £5.
Alan Marshall, junior clerk, salary per month, £4 11s 8d. (FEP)

---

[1] Under the Licensing (Scotland) Act, 1903, public houses were closed on Sunday, but hotels were allowed to sell drink to "travellers" i.e. those who had come from some distance.

1910

Lecture

On Thursday, the 23rd December 1909, the fourth lecture in connection with the course of popular lectures was held in the Drill Hall, when Mr Alexander Johnstone, Edinburgh, entertained a large and appreciative audience to a most instructive and enjoyable lecture on "The Flora of Burns". Mr Johnstone was in his element when describing the numerous and varied specimens of flowers and trees made use of by the National Bard in his poems and songs, and displayed the greatest zeal for, and a most thorough knowledge of "Rabbie's" works. Miss Dun, Woodmill, rendered with splendid effect a few of the poet's well-known songs, and four members of the Edinburgh Highland Reel and Strathspey Society entertained the audience to a selection of their popular pieces. (FN)

8 January 1910

Birth of Lord and Lady Ninian's daughter

A little daughter[1] has been born to Lady Ninian Crichton-Stuart. She was Miss Ismay Preston, and her marriage with Lord Bute's next brother made a union between Scotland and Ireland.

---

[1] Ismay Catherine Crichton-Stuart, born 23 December 1909. Lord Ninian missed the birth, as he was on his way back from electioneering in Cardiff, but he did make the children's party on 24 December. Estate men were given an extra day's pay in celebration of the birth.

284

The Prestons and Crichtons have always been friends, and as a girl she acted as one of Lady Bute's bridesmaids. Lady Ninian is pretty, slight, and dark haired, and with a keen, bright expression. Her talents are far above the average. She reads a great deal, sings, plays the violin, and also acts cleverly. … Although so young, she has come out as a hostess and given a dance and a concert in London.

Lord Ninian Crichton-Stuart was once in the Scots Guards, but is now a landowner in Fifeshire. He motors and shoots, has of late gone on the Turf, and is as fond of dancing and society as his elder brother is the reverse. His home in Scotland is known as House of Falkland. It is very ancient, and contains a chapel royal, which was restored by the late Lord Bute. This chapel is now hung with splendid pieces of "verdure" tapestry that came from an old house in Marrsen, Holland, said to have been built in 1400. (TQ)

8 January 1910
Social at House of Falkland
On the evening of Friday last, Lord Ninian Crichton-Stuart entertained the house servants, employees, and a few of their friends at a most enjoyable dance at House of Falkland. His Lordship paid a visit to the hall in which the company was gathered, and, in his usual genial manner, wished them all a bright and happy New Year. Hearty cheers were given for Lord and Lady Ninian and family on the call of Mr Liptrott, his Lordship's butler. The dance, which continued into the New Year, was varied by the rendering of songs, etc., by members of the company, and at the close the unanimous verdict was that a most pleasant evening had been spent. (FN)

15 January 1910
New store manager
On Tuesday evening, a meeting of the members of Falkland Equitable Co-operative Society was held in the Society's rooms for the purpose of electing a new manager in place of Mr Robert Sharp. Mr J. Speed, Freuchie, was, by a majority, appointed to the post. (FN)

43. Bryce's shop (left) and the Co-op store (right)

The whole building is often referred to, for instance in *The Buildings of Scotland*, as "The Old Town House", a term that has more recently been applied to the Town Hall.

15 January 1910

Liberal meeting

On Monday evening, a meeting in support of Mr Asquith was held in the Drill Hall.[1] The Rev. J. H. Morrison presided over a large audience, in the absence of Major Cusin, through illness. The speakers, Mr Drummond, Mr Thom, and Mr Leng Sturrock dealt principally with the House of Lords, the Budget, and Free Trade. A resolution in favour of Mr Asquith was passed unanimously, and on the call of Mr William Meiklejohn, a hearty vote of thanks was accorded to the speakers. The meeting closed with a vote of thanks to the Chairman. (FN)

---

[1] This was part of the General election campaign – the first of the two general elections in 1910.

24 January 1910

Death of Major Cusin

Major James Cusin JP, linen manufacturer, who died at Chapelyard, Falkland, yesterday, in his 79th year, was one of the best known business men in the Howe of Fife. He was a pioneer of the volunteer movement in Fife, and for many years commanded a company of the 6th V.B.R.H., which had its headquarters at Falkland. He recruited his men from Falkland, Strathmiglo, Freuchie, Auchtermuchty, and the surrounding villages, and was an officer of great experience. Possessed of a striking personality and genial manners, his keen interest in the service brought many young men into the ranks. He retired full of honours about fifteen years ago. In the public affairs of the Royal burgh of Falkland he bore his full share, and served on all the public boards. Politically he was a keen Liberal, and an ardent supporter of the Prime Minister. Indeed, it was in large measure due to his influence that Mr Asquith was adopted as the Liberal candidate for East Fife, twenty four years ago. He was a ready speaker, and did yeoman service on the Executive of the East Fife Liberal Association. (DC)

26 January 1910

The Eastern Division of Fife: election

Plague on the Peers! why do they throw out Budgets and cause a General Election in the "dead" of winter?[1] Yesterday was polling day in the Eastern Division of Fife. Fortunately it was a dry day above, but from three inches to a foot of snow lay on the public highways throughout the division, and the snow impeded vehicular traffic to such an extent as to make things perplexing for many men who were in "the thick of the fight". Snow operates sadly against motor cars, and as early as nine o'clock there were several motors lying "by the way side" out of action. "Motor doctors" were soon on the scenes of the obstruction, however, and in most cases they had the vehicles flying throughout the Division as if on the "wings of the wind" in a comparatively short time. As is well known the candidates were the Prime Minister and Colonel Sprot of Stravithie.

Both candidates visited the polling booths during the course of the

---

[1] The Prime Minister, H. H. Asquith, held the East Fife seat for the Liberals.

day. Time was when it was not possible to visit the whole of the stations in one day. With the motor the whole constituency can be overtaken with comparative ease. The following is the Prime Minister's timetable of yesterday:

1	Falkland, 9.15.	12	Bow of Fife, 12 50.
2	Strathmiglo, 9 35.	13	Rathillet, 2.25.
3	Auchtermuchty, 9.45.	14	Newport, 2.50.
4	Newburgh, 10 5.	15	Tayport, 3 15.
5	Ladybank, 10.40.	16	Leuchars, 3 35.
6	Kingskettle, 10 50.	17	St Andrews, 4.
7	Kennoway, 11 5.	18	Crail, 5.30.
8	Leven 11 15.	19	8t Monans, 6.
9	Largoward, 11.45.	20	Elie, 6.30.
10	Ceres, 12 10.	21	Largo, 7.
11	Cupar, 12 20.	22	Leven, 7.30.

In the forenoon the Prime Minister and Mrs Asquith reached Leven quite up to time and had a cordial reception at the polling booth, the schoolroom in Mitchell Street. The Prime Minister's motor was followed by a motor in which Sergeant Cumming, Cupar, and another officer were seated, and the two cars had just entered Mitchell Street when a suffragettes' car made its appearance. The suffragettes seemed "out for the polling day," and on the Prime Minister driving off they followed up. Fortunately the Prime Minister had the more powerful car, and it was pleasant he was able to out-distance his "militant" pursuers, and ultimately "jink" them. (LAWG)

29 January 1910

Lord Ninian defeated in Cardiff

Mr D. A. Thomas, after representing Merthyr Tydfil for a score of years, has succeeded in winning Cardiff against Lord Ninian Crichton-Stuart, who is brother of the Marquess of Bute, the over-lord of the town and port and of Cardiff Castle.[1] (SAC)

---

[1] D. A. Thomas held the seat for the Liberals.

5 February 1910

Estate of the late Mr Gulland

Mr Charles Gulland, Falkland, banker and lawyer, who died on 6th August last, aged 68, left, in addition to real estate of the estimated capital value of over £5,500, personal estate in the United Kingdom valued at £14,442 11s 9d, of which £14,428 15s 1d is Scottish estate, and the sole executrix of his will is his widow, Mrs Mary Rowland Halley Gulland of Millfield. (FN)

5 February 1910

Death of young Ninian

Ninian Patrick, aged two years and ten months only son of Lord and Lady Ninian Crichton-Stuart, died yesterday at House of Falkland. The child caught a chill whilst driving on the day of the election round Cardiff, where his father was a Unionist candidate. On the back of the motor car was a banner inscribed "Please vote for daddy." (DC)

12 February 1910

Death of heir of Falkland

A great sorrow possessed every dweller of the Royal and ancient Burgh of Falkland last Friday, when it became known that Ninian Patrick Crichton-Stuart, the only son of Lord and Lady Ninian Crichton-Stuart of Falkland had died early that morning.

High hopes had been centred in the bright little boy. He had reached the most interesting age of childhood – all but three years – and with his white and golden curls was a general favourite in Falkland town whose inhabitants he had been brought up by his father and mother to regard as his friends, and with whom he had frequent intercourse. So recently as the last General Election, he was at Cardiff with his parents, and went through the streets of that town, holding a bannerette upon which was inscribed – "Please vote for my daddy."

The illness which terminated fatally did not assume a serious aspect until a few days before death. Lord Ninian, as our readers are aware, presided at the annual business meeting and dinner of the Fife Agricultural Society at Kirkcaldy on Saturday, 29th ult., and it was only when his Lordship returned home to Falkland House that evening that he found his boy's illness had developed grave symptoms. A change for the better set in in the beginning of the week and on Tuesday Lord Ninian was again able to leave home and attend to public business in Cupar, where he spoke of going with Lady Ninian to the Continent for a short rest as soon as their son had sufficiently recovered. This hope was not to be realised; the illness once more became acute, and the patient's weakened strength gave out on Friday morning, as stated.

The funeral took place at 11.30 a.m. on Monday. Mass was said in the private chapel at Falkland House in the morning, after which the remains, enclosed in a plain, oak coffin, with silver mountings, made in Falkland, was carried by four of the estate keepers down the private walk to the restored Chapel Royal of Falkland Palace. Here, where Scottish kings and queens had bowed the knee in worship in bygone centuries, and where the original pulpit, a magnificent screen in oak and a decorated panelled roof still remain to attest the chapel's ancient beauty, a religious service was conducted, according to the rites of the Church of Rome, by the Bishop of Galloway, assisted by Lord Ninian's private chaplain, the Rev. Father Henry Woods. The Dowager Marchioness of Bute and Lady Ninian were present at this service. On its conclusion, a long procession, preceded by acolytes bearing the cross, was formed, and, slowly emerging from the Palace gates, wended its way through Falkland town to the House of Falkland avenue. Turning sharply in this avenue to the left, and crossing a turbulent stream by a strong stone bridge, the company arrived at a spot to the south-east of the Mansion where a grave had been prepared, and which is hereafter to be set apart as a private cemetery.[1] The remains, borne shoulder-high by the keepers in Highland garb, were followed by Lord Ninian (his head uncovered), and by the Marquis of Bute, both of whom were also attired in the Highland costume of the Stuarts, the Marquis carrying his brother's bonnet. Lord Ninian's younger brother, Lord Colum Crichton-Stuart, was also present, and at the grave another religious service was conducted by the clergymen named. The prayers were said in Latin, and were followed by the burning of incense and the sprinkling of hyssop.

The pall-bearers were: Lord Ninian Crichton-Stuart, the Marquis of

---

[1] The grave was later incorporated into what was planned as the Catholic parish church and is now the Crichton-Stuart Memorial Chapel.

Bute, Lord Colum Crichton-Stuart, Mr Thomas Preston, London; Captain Slacke, Mr Archibald Pitman WS, Edinburgh; and Mr George Gavin, factor on the estate.

Among those attending the funeral were: The Hon. Felix Hanbury-Tracy, Mr Alex. Lawson of Annfield, Mr Pat J. Home Rigg of Tarvit, Mr Cathcart of Pitcairlie, the Provost, Magistrates and Town Councillors of Falkland, Mr William D. Patrick, county clerk; Hon. Sheriff Wm. Thomson, Cupar; Mr J. E. Grosset, solicitor, Cupar; Mr F. W. Christie, Dairsie Mains; Mr George Dun, Woodmill; Mr James Tod, Easter Cash; Mr J. Ogilvie Fairlie, Myres Castle; Mr Alex Anderson, town clerk, Falkland; the Rev. A, Lyon Johnston, the Manse, Falkland; the Rev. J. H. Morrison, U.F. Manse, Falkland; Dr Jack, Falkland; Mr J. W. Jackson, manufacturer, Falkland; Mr Dykes, Drumdreel; Mr Calder, Corston Mill; Mr Philip, Wester Cash; Mr Morgan, Kilgour; Mr David Bonthrone, Newton of Falkland; Mr Wm. Duncan, Falkland; Mr Alex. Shanks, Falkland Wood; Mr Wm. S. Henderson, Reedieleys; Mr Arch. Ness, Cash Mill; Mr Robert Pringle, Nether Myres; Mr Wm. Ritchie, Plains; Bailie Muir, Auchtermuchty; ex-Provost Bonthrone, Auchtermuchty; Mr Lawrence Reid, Registrar, Falkland; Mr Baker, excise officer, Auchtermuchty, etc.

The funeral was a very large one, and the evidence of public sympathy was noticeable in the drawn blinds of the houses in Falkland and in the silent respectful attitude of groups of women and children who looked on from different points of vantage. Snow fell softly during the whole ceremony, and mantled the trees and grounds in white. Many beautiful wreaths were sent from Cardiff, including one from the Cardiff Conservative Association, another from the members of the Coal Exchange, and a number from friends belonging to all sides of politics.

Lord and Lady Ninian Crichton-Stuart have one other child – a baby daughter. (FN)

12 February 1910

Bruce Arms Hotel

James Forsyth. Estimate for building piggery, £3 17s.
For repairs to entrance gate to garden, £1 17s 3d. (FEP)

19 February 1910

Presentation

Mr George Smith, who has acted as post-runner here for the last 12 years, has been transferred to Kingskettle to take charge of a delivery there, and as a mark of the esteem of his many friends and well-wishers in the town and neighbourhood, he has been presented with a handsome gold watch. The presentation was made on the evening of Saturday last when Mr John Sheriff, on behalf of the subscribers, and with a few well-chosen and appropriate remarks, handed over the watch. Mr Smith suitably replied. (FN)

26 February 1910

Cricket Club dance

The annual assembly of Falkland Cricket Club was held on Friday last, when there was a splendid gathering in the Drill Hall. The dance commenced at nine o'clock, and continued until early morning. During the interval, songs were contributed by Miss Beveridge, Kingskettle, and the Messrs Andrew Melville, Glasgow and George Gardner, Falkland.

The dance was a great success, both socially and financially, and the tasteful way in which the hall was decorated and the manner in which the arrangements were carried out reflected great credit on the Committee. Mr Adamson, Kettle, supplied the music, and Messrs Alexander Grieve and Peter Robertson acted efficiently as MCs. (FN)

2 March 1910

New Town Clerk

Dear Captain Slacke,

I heard the other evening a rumour that Mrs Campbell's house has been taken by Anderson, Mr Gulland's successor. On seeing him today I gather that it is true, but it seems that he must do so in order to provide additional accommodation for storing papers as the bank are to make alterations on the existing buildings and take off two rooms. I would advise you to write to Mrs Gulland direct and you will get at the truth of the matter. The weather is still vile.

Yours faithfully, George Gavin. (FEP)

5 March 1910

Public roup

To be sold by Public Roup within the Bruce Arms, Hotel on Saturday 12th March at 3p.m. That two storey dwelling house known as Juniper Villa. The house on the ground floor was occupied by the late Mrs Menzies; and the first floor is occupied by Mr Skinner. Rental when fully let £18 10s. Ground Annual 18s 9d. Reduced upset price, to ensure competition £300. For further particulars apply to Alex Wallace, solicitor Kirkcaldy. (FFP)

5 March 1910

Presentation

On Sunday morning at a meeting of the Falkland Y.M.C.A., Mr Robert T. Thomson was presented by his fellow members with a handsome Bible on the occasion of his leaving Falkland Estate Office where he has been employed for the last two and a half years. Mr Thomson was also the recipient on Friday last of a Swan fountain pen as a parting gift from his companions. (FN)

8 March 1910

Falkland Heritors

My Lord,

There was a larger attendance than usual at the meeting of Heritors yesterday. By a majority it was decided to agree to the request for the erection of a mural tablet to Dr Barrack, son of a former minister, who was killed in the Malay Peninsula while defending the life of a companion against Chinese robbers, provided there was nothing contained in the Deed of Gift of the Church to stop the Heritors preventing the erection of such tablets on the walls. [1]

Your obedient servant, George Gavin. (FEP)

19 March 1910

Boys' training

A commencement was made on Monday evening, with the training

---

[1] In the Parish Church: the memorial was to Rev. John Barrack.

of the boys of the town in connection with the formation of a Boys' Brigade, or Boy Scouts, when over 50 boys mustered together in the Drill Hall. Mr Donaldson, bank agent, has undertaken the work of drilling the boys. (FN)

19 March 1910
Curling Club dinner
The annual dinner of the Curling Club was held on Wednesday evening last week in the Town Hall, when a large number of members were present. The purveying was in the capable hands of Mr and Mrs Angus of the Commercial Hotel. A number of new members were initiated. (FN)

19 March 1910
Recital
On Friday, the Band of Hope[1] in connection with the Established Church gave their annual recital, the piece chosen being "The Shadow of a Life". The story was ably read by the Rev. A. Lyon Johnston, and beautifully illustrated with lime-light views. The children acquitted themselves splendidly, and reflected great credit on the conductor, Mr George Spence. (FN)

19 March 1910
Concert
On Saturday Falkland Brass Band held a concert in the Drill Hall, in aid of their funds. Provost Jackson presided. A long and varied programme was sustained by the following artistes from the "Lang Toon": Misses Jessie Melville (soprano) and Aggie Reid (contralto), Messrs D. Thomson (tenor), W. Leitch (bass), J. Keddie (baritone), and W. Smart (comedian). The marked ability with which these ladies and gentlemen rendered the various items evoked the greatest enthusiasm from a "house" crowded in every part. The band, who made their first appearance in their new uniforms, also rendered in a very creditable manner various selections during the evening. (FN)

---

[1] The Band of Hope (now Hope UK) was set up to provide activities for young people and encourage total abstinence from alcohol.

31 March 1910

Memorial tablet and window for Church

Letter to Alex Anderson, Town Clerk

Dear Sir,

When Lord Ninian Crichton-Stuart came here the other day, he handed to me a letter sent to him by Mrs Barrack asking him as one of the principal Heritors to support the proposal to erect the mural tablet and also the insertion of the stained glass window in the Parish Church. I have informed him that the erection of the tablet has been agreed to, but that the matter of the stained glass window was left over in order to ascertain the views of the Kirk Session. His Lordship wishes to support Mrs Barrack and her daughter in their desire to have the stained glass window inserted in the Church.

Yours faithfully, George Gavin. (FEP)

2 April 1910

School boy's prize

Master Robert L. Hamilton, a pupil in the senior division of Public School, carried off the first prize in Messrs Carr & Co's painting competition open to school boys over 11 years of age in the counties of Fife, Kinross, Clackmannan, and Stirling. The prize takes the form of a complete Boy Scout outfit. (FN)

16 April 1910

The Glebe

My Lord,

We had a meeting of the Works Committee yesterday evening at the Glebe, with reference to the water supply to the Manse and Chapelyard.[1] The present old horseshoe pipes conducting the water from a spring in the Glebe to a tank at the bottom of it have become defective and choked up.

Your obedient servant, George Gavin. (FEP)

---

[1] The then Manse (now Ladywell House) and Chapelyard House, are well outside the village to the south-east. Chapelyard takes its name from a chapel which was there in the middle ages.

30 April 1910
Biddall Bros. Circus
Biddall Bros.[1] visited the town on Wednesday with their circus and cinematograph exhibition. (FN)

30 April 1910
Golf
The Golf Club played their first match on Saturday last, when they travelled to Markinch and enjoyed an excellent game. The match ended in a win for Markinch by seven matches to three. (FN)

10 May 1910
Heritors of Falkland
My Lord,

The meeting called to consider the minister's proposal to light the Manse by electricity was held yesterday. After discussing the details in the minister's scheme it was unanimously resolved that, while the heritors would place no obstacle in the way of his introducing electric light into the Manse, they could not agree to his request to take the plant over from him on his leaving the parish. Messrs Jackson and Bonthrone were there to support the minister in his endeavour to get the heritors to take over the plant for him, in the end they fell in line with the majority and the resolution, accordingly became unanimous.

The matter of the stained glass window regarding which Mrs Barrack wrote you was again before the meeting. You will recollect that when it was considered at a previous meeting it was thought well that the Kirk Session should be consulted as it was stated that the introduction of stained glass might have the effect of darkening the Church at that particular place. A letter was read yesterday from the Kirk Session to the effect that they quite approved to the introduction of the window provided it was not to darken the church. Yesterday the Heritors, accordingly, resolved to thank Mrs Barrack and her daughter for their kind offer and to ask them to submit a design of

---

[1] Biddall's circus travelled the country and the most famous part of their show was "Biddall's Ghost Illusion", which gave the impression of pictures moving.

the window, suggesting at the same time that there is not much light where it is to be put and the colouring of the glass should be light. Messrs Jackson and Bonthrone strongly opposed the introduction of the window and actually went to the length of making a motion that the window be declined, but it was, of course, defeated. They bluntly gave us their reason that they were opposed to any stained glass or ornamentation in the church of any kind, and as they were the only two heritors present who attended the parish church. One can only marvel at men who could possibly take up such an attitude as regards their place of worship.

Your obedient servant, George Gavin. (FEP)

14 May 1910
Death of King Edward VII
The death of King Edward evoked widespread feelings of sorrow and regret within the burgh of Falkland when it was received last Saturday morning, the unexpectedness of the sad event making it all the more startling. The bells were tolled at noon and the Town Council in their official capacity attended divine service in the Parish Church on Sabbath forenoon, the Council pew being draped in black. (FN)

15 May 1910
House of Falkland drawing room floor
My Lord,

I was at the house yesterday to see how Miller's men were proceeding with the work on the inlaid floor of the Drawing-room. I found that the work was being done thoroughly and satisfactory. The pieces of maple after the decayed parts were removed, are hammered in tightly and then planed flush with the polished floor.

Your obedient servant, George Gavin. (FEP)

21 May 1910
Bruce Arms Hotel
James Forsyth. Lifting causeway and putting drain in close to prevent water gathering under pantry floor. £3.2s.4d. (FEP)

May 1910

Butcher shop

Mr C. C. Brunton paid £8 10s. per annum for renting shop in Bruce Arms Hotel building. (FEP)

23 May 1910

Sugar Acre

Letter to Alex Anderson, Town Clerk

Dear Sir,

I have a complaint from the tenant of the Sugar Acre Field as to rubbish from the gardens adjoining being thrown into the field. If this is a matter which falls within the province of your sanitary committee to deal with, I shall be glad of their help in stopping the practise.

Yours faithfully, George Gavin. (FEP)

1 June 1910

Work on House of Falkland

Letter to Lord Ninian

My Lord,

The oak panelling in the Billiard Room is being completely finished. The scoring board is a piece of beautiful workmanship, the figures being inlaid with bog oak and I am sure you will like it very much. The chairs and sofa will all be here within the next few days, and the red pile carpet which I ordered in Perth for your study is to be laid on Friday. The restoration of the inlaid floor in the Drawing Room will also be finished and the room put in order before you and Lady Ninian's arrival.

Your obedient servant, George Gavin. (FEP)

11 June 1910

Problems with workmen

Dear Captain Slacke,

I have had the utmost difficulty in arranging for a post boy and while I am sorry to take Smith off his work I am doing so until the school holidays, a fortnight hence when I can get a boy to do the work for six weeks at least. Smith has been so constantly employed at

Payments at Whitsun for Alterations to Brunton House

Feb. 19th. James Forsyth, mason, work in connection with fitting up new w. c. £3.10s. 8d.

March 23rd. Thomas Ross, papering and painting house for occupation of chaplain. £18.7s.8d.

April 2nd. A. Hillock, wages for men reforming paths in garden and laying out ground at back. £4

April 6th. Walter Peggie, for repairs to plaster and roofs, new chimney cans etc. £2.6s.1d.

April 6th. Alex Fraser, for joinery work of repairs, forming partition in school room for maid's room, new outside back door. £9.9s.11d.

April 6th. William Lawrie, for plumber work, new w. c., fitting up gas stove and incandescent fittings on all gas brackets. £7.4s.11d.

June 23rd. Thomson Bros, Kirkcaldy, two grates for chaplain's house. £4.12s.

Above outlay incurred in order to make house sufficient for occupation of Lord Ninian's chaplain.

March 23rd. Thomas Ross. (FEP)

House of Falkland that the work on the walks is falling behind and they must be put in order now and kept in order. The other trouble about taking Smith away is that the other two men are no use without him to direct the work. One being blind as you know and the other very old and stupid.[1]

Yours faithfully, George Gavin. (FEP)

---

[1] Smith was probably William Smith from Key House. The blind man possibly John Hay, who was shown on the 1911 census as living in Royal Terrace, aged 35, an Estate Labourer, blind, married for 14 years with 3 children. He must have gone partially sighted as in the 1891 census he is an apprentice, son of James and Margaret Hay, one of 8 children. Not to be confused with John Hay the pauper.

44. Falkland Cricket Club, 1910

Back row: T. Grant (umpire) – James Craig – George Gardner (Hon. Sec.) –
R. Craig – H. Robinson (Vice Captain) – A. Grieve (Captain) – J. Venters –
T. Y. Mackenzie

Middle Row: P. Robertson – Hon. F. Hanbury-Tracy – H. D. Michie –
Dr J. G. Jack (President) – John Reekie – Duncan. C. Bryce (Vice President) –
T. Robertson

Front Row: W. Traill – T. C Schofield (scorer) – W. M. Venters

18 June 1910

Golf

The first two rounds of the Lathrisk Cup tournament have been completed and the members who play in the third round are as follows: David Bonthrone and James Cochrane, George Anderson and John Levack, George Robertson and James Peggie, Thomas Williamson and D. A. Robertson. (FN)

18 June 1910

Cricket

A fairly strong eleven of Cupar entertained Falkland at Bonvil, Cupar, last (Thursday) night. Falkland batted first, and ran up a total of 69. Things were proceeding quite well until Stark went on to bowl, and the amateur finished up with the fine analysis of 5 wickets for 7 runs.

For Falkland, Traill gave a good display. Cupar soon passed their opponents' total, and won comfortably. The feature of the game was the display of W. G. Innes, who played faultlessly for 51. In his score were no fewer than nine boundaries. (FN)

18 June 1910

A cowardly assault

At Cupar Sheriff Court on Tuesday – before Sheriff Armour Hannay – Alex Davie (17), farm servant, Newton of Falkland, pleaded guilty to having on 1st June, assaulted Alex. Watson, six years of age, by tying his hands with a rope drawn tight round his body, whereby he was put into a state of great fear. The Fiscal said there were two or three boys involved in the affair, which, he believed, was intended as a joke.

The Sheriff: You have pleaded guilty to what, in the eyes of the law, is a cowardly assault on this little boy, six years old, but I am quite willing to accept the statement that you are a well-behaved boy; that you will be punished by your father; that you probably did not intend to hurt the little boy, and did not realise what you were doing. You are, therefore, dismissed with an admonition, and I hope it will be a warning to you. (FN)

27 June 1910

Maspie Den

Letter to J. & F. Anderson

Dear Sir,

Recently a representation was made by the Town Council of Falkland to Lord Ninian Crichton-Stuart to have Maspie Den opened to the public. His Lordship has agreed to do so on the afternoons of Saturday during the Summer months. It is proposed that the admission should be by ticket obtained at the Palace Guides Room. It has just occurred to me, however, that his Lordship may run some risk in admitting the public to the Den. As you are aware the Maspie Burn is crossed at several places by wooden bridges of a not particularly substantial nature, the sides of the stream are, at a good many places, precipitous and the paths are narrow necessitating wooden guards at certain points. In the event of any member of the public being injured through the defect in the bridges or by falling into the stream would his Lordship be in any way liable to a claim of damage? If he opens the Den as proposed, can any liability for an accident be guarded against by its being so stated on the ticket of admission. Perhaps you will kindly write me as to this matter by an early post as it was proposed to open the Den on Saturday first.

P.S. If a sentence to the following effect be added to the ticket of admission, which I have omitted to say is free, would it safeguard the proprietor against risk: "The Den is open to the public on the distinct understanding that the proprietor will not be responsible for any accident which might occur in any way whatsoever to any member of the public visiting the Den."

Yours faithfully, George Gavin. (FEP.)

29 June 1910

Maspie Den

Dear Mr Gavin,

We do not think there is much probability of any risk to His Lordship through admitting the public to the Den. They will be there by toleration not by invitation, and in a recent case against the Corporation of Glasgow arising over a fatal accident at the Botanic Gardens, Lord Kinnear stated, "There is nothing unlawful in making a public garden or in opening a garden to the public in a place where there are streams or ponds, and if the place is made safe for persons of average intelligence I know of no rule of law which requires the proprietor to take further precautions, unless, therefore, there is some danger known to the proprietor which would not be apparent to the public." We cannot think there would be any liability, but of course in the event of an accident there is nothing to prevent the injured person making a claim.

The sentence you propose to add to the ticket of admission would be to some extent a safeguard though not necessarily conclusive.

Yours faithfully, J. & F. Anderson. (FEP)

1 July 1910

Telephones

Letter to Post Office Ladybank

Dear Sir,

I put on a call this forenoon on the telephone to Auchtermuchty and after waiting half an hour for the call I had to cancel it as I had to go out. I find that it takes invariably, a very long time to get a call to Auchtermuchty. As one could walk from here to Auchtermuchty in the time taken to get a call. You will quite see that as regards Auchtermuchty, at least, the telephone is of no use to us here. I have been particularly annoyed, recently, having to wait long intervals for calls when I ought to have been out. Will you kindly bring this representation under the notice of those responsible for this state of affairs.

Yours faithfully, George Gavin. (FEP)

2 July 1910

Telphones

Dear Mr Gavin,

There was heavy delay on most of the telephone calls which were sent over the Auchtermuchty and Ladybank circuit yesterday forenoon, and your calls would be one of the delayed calls. As to the calls which you have made previous to yesterday which you complain of, the wires would also be busy at these times. It is regretted those delays have occurred and every effort will be made at this office that no unnecessary delay takes place.

Your obedient servant, M. Crombie for Postmaster. (FEP)

2 July 1910

Boy Scouts

The local corps of the Boy Scouts was inspected by Major Lumsden on Wednesday evening. The Town Band was in attendance. (FN)

2 July 1910

Sunday School picnics

The annual picnics of the Sunday Schools of the Parish and United Free Churches here were held last Saturday. Although cloudy in the morning, the day turned out splendidly, and the weather was all that could be desired. The destination of the Parish Church party was Ramornie, and that of the United Free Church, Pitcairlie. Both companies spent a very enjoyable day, and arrived home about nine o'clock. (FN)

9 July 1910

Prospects of electricity

Application has been made to the local authorities by the Fife Tramway and Electric Power Company for consent to granting of provisional Order to authorise production, supply and distribution of electricity for lighting within Falkland parish. (FN)

9 July 1910

Choir picnic

The choir of the Parish Church here held their annual picnic on Saturday last. Leaving at seven o'clock in the morning, they drove via Kinross to Dunfermline, where they spent the day most enjoyably. The Carnegie baths were visited by the party, but the special attraction was Pittencrieff Glen, where excellent music by the Trust Band was heard. The excursionists returned by the route taken in the morning, and arrived home about ten o'clock. (FN)

23 July 1910

St John's Lodge of Free Masons

On Monday evening, at a meeting of St John's Lodge of Free Masons, Bro. Robert Miller[1] was presented with a very handsome marble timepiece by the brethren of the Lodge on the occasion of his marriage with Miss Jenny Richardson, late of the Schoolhouse, Falkland, which takes place in Edinburgh on Saturday first. The presentation was made by Brother Jackson, RWM, and Brother Miller suitably replied. A happy evening was thereafter spent. (FN)

---

[1] This is of course Robert Miller *Jnr*.

23 July 1910
Sudden death at picnic

A party from Cowdenbeath visited the town on Wednesday, and were proceeding to the Hill by the Leslie Road when a sad calamity overtook them. Mr George Watson, pitheadman, Broad Street, Cowdenbeath, had gone on the road so far with the brake, and was, along with others, walking up a part of the road near Hillfoot Cottage, when he complained of feeling faint and sat down at the roadside. He was suddenly seen to collapse, and on examination it was found he had died from heart failure. It is understood he had been troubled with heart disease for the past four years. (FN)

23 July 1910
Boy Scouts

The corps of Boy Scouts went into camp for the first time on Saturday afternoon under the command of Mr Donaldson. The camping ground is on the Lomond Hill in the "Triangle Park", kindly granted by Lord Ninian Crichton-Stuart. Four bell tents have been put up to accommodate the boys, who number over 30. The Scouts are enjoying the experience, and will no doubt be greatly benefited by their holiday under canvas. The Rev. J. H. Morrison MA conducted a service at the camp on Sunday evening, which was very largely attended by those interested in the boys, and by a large number of the visitors who are spending their holidays in the town. (FN)

30 July 1910
Boy Scouts

The week's camping of the Falkland Boy Scouts came to an end on Saturday, the boys having enjoyed their holiday under canvas very much. Their Scout-master, Mr Donaldson, bank agent, was married on Wednesday 20th inst., when the following congratulatory telegram was sent from the Scout camp: "Your matrimonial scouting done, May happiness bless the life begun."

There are three Companies of Scouts camping in the locality just now, viz. Leven, Wemyss and Dysart, and they, together with the Falkland corps, attended the morning service in the Parish Church. (FN)

45. Ye Klub members

Back row: Thomas Myles – Duncan Bryce – Tom Robertson
Middle row: Robert Miller Jnr – Peter Robertson – John Kish
– Jim Grieve – Rex Grieve
Front row: Robert B. Bryce – H. D. Michie – Miss Byre
"Miss Byre" is possibly a mistake for "Miss Bryce" i.e. Duncan Bryce's
daughter Elizabeth A. Bryce, six years older than her brother Robert B.
Bryce

30 July 1910

Presentation

At a special meeting of "Ye Klub", held on the evening of Thursday
last week, Mr Robert Miller jnr, was presented by his fellow members
with a handsome fumed oak bureau on the occasion of his marriage.
Mr Peter Robertson, in making the presentation on behalf of the
members, expressed their regret at losing him as a member of "Ye
Klub", but wished him happiness in his new sphere. He asked Mr
Miller to accept the bureau as a token of the respect and esteem in
which he was held by every member. Mr Miller fittingly replied. Mr

Bryce thereafter echoed the sentiments of the meeting when he said that he hoped Mr Miller and the future Mrs Miller would have a very happy and prosperous married life. A most enjoyable evening was spent, songs being contributed by a number of those present. (FN)

2 August 1910

Three Parish Councils and a pauper

Sheriff Armour Hannay at Cupar has given a decision in a poor law case in which the question between the parties was whether John Hay, a pauper, was of unsound mind or a lunatic during the six years he was boarded in the parish of Falkland.

During his stay in Falkland Hay's board was paid by his brother. On 15th May 1909, he was removed to Arngask, where he became chargeable to the parish. £12 12s 6d was paid out by the Parish Council of Arngask, and the body sought to recover from Edinburgh, where the pauper was born and had stayed with his parents for over thirty years. Edinburgh refused, replying that Hay had acquired a qualification in Falkland parish. Falkland in turn refused to pay, holding that Hay was of unsound mind, and therefore could not acquire a settlement there.

The case then came into court for a decision upon whom the responsibility rested. Sheriff Armour Hannay holds that Falkland parish is liable. His Lordship in the course of a lengthy note states that by a series of recent decisions it had been held that practically no form of weak mindedness, however exaggerated, would prevent a person acquiring a residential settlement. Idiocy or unsoundness of mind (to adopt the recent report of the Royal Commission on the care and control of the feeble minded) would do so, however. The pauper, John Hay, admittedly was not an idiot, and accordingly the only question between the parties was whether he was of unsound mind or a lunatic during the time he resided in the parish of Falkland. On the evidence he had come to the conclusion, without much difficulty, that he was not. The principal evidence that John Hay was a lunatic was the expert testimony of Dr Bruce of Murthly Asylum, and Dr Ferguson of the Fife and Kinross Asylum. Their view was that he had been from birth weak minded or imbecile, but that at some period of his life, which they were unable to specify, progressive brain disease or dementia supervened and from that period he fell to be classified as insane. The symptoms of that progressive brain disease were said to be facility and lack of initiative. It was unfortunate that Dr Carswell, Glasgow, the chief expert witness on the other side, was not asked to give his views upon that point, for one would imagine that facility and lack of initiative were quite as much symptoms of weak mindedness as of dementia. If these were the only criterion for distinguishing between the two, it must be a matter of considerable difficulty, not to say risk, to say when a man was to be classed as of unsound mind. In the present case he could find no satisfactory evidence of any material change in John Hay's mental condition, at all events before he left Falkland. There was no sufficient evidence that he was facile to any marked degree, and there was a considerable body of evidence that he had at least a certain amount of initiative. The fact, if indeed it be a fact that he wrote imperfect letters at the instigation of other pauper patients boarded along with him at Arngask seemed rather thin evidence of facility, especially keeping in view the length of time involved.

It was suggestive that the medical experts would not give any indication of when John Hay became insane, and that they admitted that cases of that kind usually landed in an asylum by reason of an accident, taking drink, stealing. Nothing of that kind had happened in John Hay's life as yet, and till it did occur there seemed no sufficient reason for certifying him as a lunatic. An attempt had been made to show that John Hay was subject to delusions. Only two instances were given, (1) that he was frightened at his own shadow, and (2) that he thought his brother Tom was dead, the fact being that he was still alive. To his mind it showed the hopelessness of the case if these were the only delusions that could be proved.

For Edinburgh Parish Council, Mr Alfred Carlisle, solicitor, Dundee; for Falkland Parish Council, Mr Osborne Pagan, Cupar. (DC)

13 August 1910
Falkland lad steals a bicycle
At a Children's Court in Cupar on Tuesday, before Hon. Sheriff Thomson, a young lad named William Clark, linoleum worker, South Street, Falkland, admitted having on 23rd July, stolen a bicycle in the

public park at Springfield. The Fiscal said the bicycle had been leaning against a dyke in the park on the afternoon of the annual sports at Springfield, when apparently the temptation to take it away had overcome this lad. He was in the employment of Messrs Jackson, Falkland, and they were anxious that he should get a chance. He was a promising boy, and they were willing to keep him on in their service. He had no parents, and was living in lodgings. The Hon. Sheriff said that taking these circumstances into consideration, he would dismiss accused with an admonition, and he ordered him to be put under probation for six months. (FN)

20 August 1910
Falkland Equitable Co-operative Society
The half-yearly meeting of the Falkland Equitable Co-operative Society (Ltd) was held in the Society's rooms on Saturday, 6th inst. The report showed that the sales for the half-year had exceeded those for the corresponding period last year by over £200, and the profits had considerably increased. This state of affairs reflects great credit on Mr Speed, the manager and salesman, who entered the Society's employment in the end of last year. (FN)

10 September 1910
Farm fire
An outbreak of fire occurred at the farm of Falkland Wood on Wednesday afternoon at two o'clock, which resulted in the loss of a large stack of hay. Auchtermuchty Fire Brigade was soon on the ground, and in the meantime the farm servants prevented the flames from spreading to the adjoining stacks. After an hour or two, the fire was completely under control and further damage averted. (FN)

24 September 1910
First Falkland Boy Scouts
During last week-end, a party of about twenty of the 1st Falkland Boy Scouts encamped about a mile out of the town on the Hill side. Practice in cookery was the main object, and a thoroughly enjoyable week-end was spent by all. Assistant Scoutmaster Gardner was in command. On Saturday the whole troop marched to Lathrisk House

under the command of Scoutmaster Donaldson. Here they were treated to a substantial tea by the Hon. F. Hanbury-Tracy.

After tea, various sports were indulged in, and the following were a few of the principal prize-winners: Race open to all Scouts – W. M. Venters (over 12), Andrew Page (under 12); Donkey Race – 1. W. M. Venters and Eben Allan; 2. Frank Dingwall and Ewan McMaster; Three-legged Race – W. M. Venters and R. S. Hamilton; Boot Race – Andrew Grant; Obstacle Race – 1. James Hay; 2. Robert Butters; Long Jump – 1. W. M. Venters; 2. J. Hay; 3. R. Kennedy.

On Sunday, a church parade was held in the Parish Church. (FN)

8 October 1910
Lodging without permission
At Cupar Sheriff Court on Wednesday, Daniel Sullivan, labourer, of no fixed residence, was charged with having on the previous day, lodged in a straw-house at Millfield Cottage, Falkland, the property of William Grant, butcher, without the permission of the owner. He pleaded guilty, and the sentence imposed by Hon. Sheriff Substitute Bruce was 10s or five days. (FN)

8 October 1910
Concert
A concert in aid of the Falkland Girls Club, which has been opened this week, was held in the Drill Hall on the evening of Saturday last. Provost Jackson presided over a good audience, and the entertainment was very enjoyable.

The programme was sustained by Lady Ninian Crichton-Stuart, House of Falkland; Miss Skene, Pitlour; Miss McLaren, Kirkcaldy; Capt. R. C. Slacke, Falkland; and Messrs Christie, Orr, and Hunter, Glasgow. On the call of the Chairman, three hearty cheers were given to those who had so ably contributed to the evening's enjoyment. (FN)

15 October 1910
Presentation
On Tuesday evening, the 1st Falkland Troop of Boy Scouts, under the command of Assistant Scout-master Gardner, met in their headquarters in High Street, Falkland, and presented their Scout-master,

Mr Donaldson, with a handsome barometer as a marriage gift.

The following members of the Scout Committee were also present: The Rev. A. L. Johnston, the Rev. J. H. Morrison and Messrs J. B. Ogilvie, D. Bonthrone and G. Robertson. Mr Johnston presided over the gathering, and called upon Patrol Leader William Burgon to make the presentation, who, on behalf of the 1st Falkland Boy Scouts, requested Scout-master Donaldson to accept the barometer as a marriage gift in token of their appreciation of the strenuous and wholehearted manner in which he had worked for the improvement of the Troop, and he expressed the hope that Mr and Mrs Donaldson would have a long and prosperous married life, and also that their interest for the welfare of the Troop would be continued in years to come.

Mr Donaldson thanked the Scouts for the beautiful gift they had presented to him, and said that he appreciated very much the spirit which had prompted them to do him such an honour. The Proceedings terminated with a vote of thanks to Mr Johnston for presiding. The Troop have been busy practicing for the concert and display which is to be held tonight (Friday). (FN)

22 October 1910

Concert

On the evening of Friday last, a concert was held in the Drill Hall in aid of the funds of the local troop of Boy Scouts. Scout-master Donaldson presided over a very large audience, and in his opening remarks he gave a report of the work that was being carried on amongst the boys. The programme which was submitted proved a very excellent and enjoyable one, and was ably sustained by the following ladies and gentlemen: Miss Margaret Pirie ARMC, and Miss Templeton, Dundee; Miss Lumsden, Eden Valley House, Freuchie; Miss Dun, Woodmill; Dr William Kinnear, Dundee; and Mr George Gardner, Falkland. Miss Pirie also acted very efficiently as accompanist.

The Scouts themselves contributed to the entertainment by rendering two choruses, "Marching through Georgia" and "The Maple Leaf", and a number of the Scouts took part in a sketch entitled "Kidnapped", which they carried through in a very acceptable manner. On the call of Lord Ninian Crichton-Stuart, a very hearty vote of thanks was accorded to those who had taken part in the evening's entertainment, which had been thoroughly enjoyed by all. The concert was brought to a close with the singing of "God save the King". (FN)

29 October 1910

Charges against hotel-keeper dropped

At a JP Court, held at Cupar on Wednesday – Hon. Sheriff Bruce and Colonel Campbell on the bench – a charge was to have been brought against William Alexander Mason, Bruce Arms Hotel, Falkland, for having on 3rd October – the autumn holiday in Falkland – a day on which, under the licensing by-laws the Magistrates ordered the closing of all licensed premises within the burgh, sold whisky, port wine and champagne in quantities to the prosecutor unknown, to or for the consumption of an assistant farmer then residing at Falkland Wood, an engineer from Toronto, and a professional golfer from Melbourne, Australia.

Mr J. L. Anderson, solicitor, who appeared for Mr Mason, tendered a plea of not guilty. Mr J. K. Tasker, the JP Fiscal, explained that proceedings had been taken against the license-holder for the alleged sale of liquor on a holiday, but as the by-law under which the complaint was made had been abolished at a meeting of the District Licensing Court the previous day, he was not sure, as Prosecutor, if the Justices would find that he was altogether justified in insisting on prosecuting under this by-law, in which a man might be punished today for what was apparently to be no offence tomorrow. If their Honours agreed with him, he proposed to withdraw the prosecution.

Mr J. L. Anderson said he was glad that the Fiscal had mentioned the point, because if he had not, he (Mr Anderson) intended bringing it up. The course the Fiscal proposed, he thought, was the right one in the circumstances. From the proceedings at the Licensing Court the previous day they must take it that the by-law in question had been found to be inexpedient and unnecessary, and that the closing of licensed premises in burghs, while public houses in the neighbourhood, perhaps only a mile or two distant, were allowed to remain open, was a mistaken policy. No doubt when the by-law was enacted it was thought a right policy, but after the experience of a year or two it was found to be a mistake. He fully expected that Mr Tasker would take the course he had proposed, and he felt the Bench would allow the prosecution to be withdrawn.

The Justices having consulted, Hon. Sheriff Bruce said they found that the constables had been justified in reporting the case, but under the circumstances related by the Fiscal and the action of the Licensing Court the previous day, they had decided to allow the charge to drop. Mr Anderson stated that it had been a bona-fide transaction as far as his client was concerned. (FN)

5 November 1910

Minister's stipend increased

In the Teind Court in Edinburgh on Friday, application was made on behalf of the minister of Falkland for an augmentation of three chalders, to raise the stipend to 26 chalders.[1] The last augmentation, it was stated, was in 1887. The heritors agreed to the augmentation asked. The application was granted. (FN)

5 November 1910

The elections

There was no poll in either the municipal election or Parish Council election, and the members were elected as follows:
Town Council – Robert Drysdale, William Horne, John Leaburn, and Andrew Lister.

Parish Council – Alexander Fraser, Robert Miller, Walter Peggie, and John Sheriff.

Messrs Horne and Leaburn are new members of the Town Council, in place of Bailie Thomas Sutherland and Councillor Michael Reekie. Bailie Sutherland has served on the Council for the past 30 years. (FN)

5 November 1910

Golf

The annual meeting of the Falkland Golf Club was held in the Club-

---

[1] A minister's stipend was paid by the heritors and calculated in chalders, one chalder being about a ton of grain converted to monetary terms.

house on Thursday last week, when Mr Cochrane was re-appointed Captain of the Club. (FN)

8 November 1910

Coal stealing

Walter Bonthrone Dick and Andrew Lawson, carters, Falkland, at Cupar today, admitted stealing a quantity of coal belonging to Messrs Jackson, manufacturers, Falkland. In extenuation Mr J. K. Tasker, Cupar, pointed out that the men looked upon the coal they took as their perquisite.

They went to Falkland Road Station for the coal and what they took for themselves was what was over the weight. The Fiscal said that coals were sold at Falkland Road, and it was difficult to detect thefts of that kind. Mr Jackson on several occasions saw a bag of coal on the top of the carts, and his suspicions having been aroused, a watch was kept. Lawson, on being challenged at Falkland, said he gathered the coal off the ground. The case had been brought forward to put an end to that sort of procedure.

Sheriff Armour Hannay said after what he had heard he thought he might deal with the case leniently and gave them an opportunity of paying a fine. Dick was fined 10s, or five days imprisonment and Lawson 5s, or three days imprisonment. (FFP)

11 November 1910

Success at Kirkcaldy

Mr W. Young, Palace Gardens was awarded first prize, the Nairn Challenge Cup for chrysanthemums.[1] This the second year in succession that he has won this cup. He also carried off the other principle trophy of the exhibition, the Kirkcaldy Corporation Gold Medal. (DET)

12 November 1910

Town Council

At a special meeting of Council on Friday, Mr Robert Drysdale was appointed Senior Bailie and Mr Andrew Lister Junior Bailie. (FN)

---

[1] Presumably presented by the Nairn family, owners of the linoleum factories in Kirkcaldy and donor of the Memorial Library near Kirkcaldy station.

19 November 1910

Conduit on the Myre

Letter to Alex Anderson, Town Clerk

Dear Sir,

I have had the conduit at the Myre cleared today. While the practice may have been different in past years the cleaning of this burn is manifestly a piece of work to be done by the Burgh Officer who already sees to the cleaning of the burn. In future, accordingly, the work will not be performed by the proprietor of Falkland Estate, and perhaps, accordingly, you will kindly give the Town Officer instructions to attend to the conduit as well as the other portions of the burn, which he already cleans out.

Yours Faithfully, George Gavin. (FEP)

19 November 1910

Kirkin of the Council

The Kirkin of the Council took place on Sunday, when the members attended the Parish Church in the forenoon and the United Free Church in the afternoon. (FN)

19 November 1910

Chrysanthemum show

At the chrysanthemum show held in Edinburgh on Wednesday, Mr William Young, head gardener to Lord Ninian Crichton-Stuart, at Falkland Palace Gardens, had the distinction of winning the Scottish Cup. (FN)

19 November 1910

Town Councillors entertained

On Saturday evening, the members of the Town Council and their officials, along with a few friends, were entertained to supper in the Commercial Hotel on the kind invitation of Provost Jackson. After the excellent supper, purveyed by Mr and Mrs Angus, a toast-list was gone through, and with songs rendered by members of the company, a very pleasant and enjoyable evening was spent. (FN)

24 November 1910

Conduit at the Myre

Dear Sir,

I duly received your letter of the 19th inst and I beg to inform you that Councillor Angus, the Convener of the Sanitary Committee, has been asked to look into the matter.

Yours faithfully, Alexander Anderson. (FEP)

26 November 1910

Presentation

On Wednesday evening, Miss Barbara Paterson, South Street (East), Falkland, was presented by her fellow workers at Pleasance Works, with a silver teapot, jelly dish and tray. Mr William Paton, yarn ware-houseman, handed over the gifts, and conveyed to Miss Paterson the good wishes of those with whom she had been associated in her work. Miss Paterson suitably replied. She sails shortly to Mexico to be married there. (FN)

26 November 1910

Y.M.C.A. presentation

A special meeting of the Young Men's Christian Association was held in the Town Hall on Tuesday evening at eight o'clock, when Mr George Robertson, secretary of the Association, was presented with a handsome green onyx eight day French striking clock, on the occasion of his marriage which takes place on Saturday first. Mr Walter Peggie, president, stated that Mr Robertson was one of the original members of the Association, which was commenced 13 years ago, and during that time he had fulfilled the duties of Secretary in a very efficient manner. On behalf of the Falkland Y.M.C.A., Mr Peggie requested Mr Robertson to accept the clock as a token of the respect in which he was held by his fellow members and as an expression of their best wishes for long life and prosperity. He wished him and his future wife, every happiness during their married life. Mr Robertson, in his reply, thanked the members very cordially for the beautiful gift they had presented to him, and said that it would be greatly appreciated by him as long as he lived. (FN)

2 December 1910

Bailie Lister versus Colonel Sprot

A Bailie of the Royal Burgh of Falkland was a persistent interrupter of Colonel Sprot's[1] meeting at Falkland last night, and the Chairman called upon the local police constable to eject him.

The Drill Hall was filled, and the junior section of the audience seemed strong supporters of Mr Asquith. Mr David Bonthrone, Newton of Falkland presided.

Colonel Sprot was speaking of Mr Asquith being under the domination of Mr Redmond[2] at the present juncture, when Bailie Lister rose and said "I do not consider it just to insult any man. (Applause) The Prime Minister is game for anything. (Noise)

The Chairman "I am chairman of this meeting, and I call upon you to keep your seat and hold your tongue, otherwise I will have to ask you to leave the hall. (Hear, hear and voices of "Sit Down")

Bailie Lister. "I am the hall keeper here, and you cannot put me to the door."

Cries of "Out with him."

The Chairman, "I like a bit of fun myself but,"

Bailie Lister, "I do not think that is justice to say the Prime Minister is not game to face that; I say he was game."

The Chairman, "Are you prepared to keep your seat and hold your tongue?"

Bailie Lister, "I will please myself."

Cries of "Sit down."

The Chairman, "Constable, will you be good enough to remove this man from the hall?"

Cries of "You canna dae that."

Bailie Lister, "I am the hall keeper."

A voice. "Colonel Sprot is paying for the hall, and you have no right here unless you conduct yourself properly."

Colonel Sprot, after quietness had been restored, said he would not

---

[1] Alexander Sprot was the Unionist candidate for East Fife in the two 1910 general elections, standing against the Prime Minister, H. H. Asquith.

[2] John Redmond was the leader of the Irish parliamentary party, which supported Asquith's Liberal government.

take back a single word he had said.

Bailie Lister, "Would the Colonel tell me who have been the bosses under our Constitution for the past six years?"

Colonel Sprot, "We have no bosses, and we don't want bosses. We don't want Mr Asquith or any of those people from Ireland to be bosses over us. We want to be independent men, with our free Constitution, which gives an appeal to the country."

Mr John Sheriff moved, and Mr George Dun, Woodmill, seconded, a vote of confidence in Colonel Sprot.

Bailie Lister moved that the Prime Minister was a more fit person to represent East Fife, and Mr John Methven seconded.

There was a good deal of noise during the taking of the vote, which was announced to be in favour of the amendment. (DC)

3 December 1910

Temperance lecture

Mr William Blackwood of the Scottish Permissive Bill Association[1] gave a lecture on "Home, Land and Liquor", on Thursday last week in the Drill Hall. The Rev. J. H. Morrison MA presided. (FN)

3 December 1910

Mr John Reekie

Mr John Reekie, who recently went to Manchester to take up duties in the Post Office there, has been transferred to Aberdeen. (FN)

3 December 1910

Lectures

The second of the course of popular lectures was held last Friday in the Drill Hall, when Mr A. Mackie MA, Aberdeen, delivered a very interesting and entertaining lecture on *Johnny Gibb o' Gushetneuk*.[2] Mr Mackie, who showed a very intimate knowledge of his subject, gave

---

[1] This was a Glasgow-based temperance organization. There had been several attempts in Parliament to pass a "Permissive Bill" which would have allowed a parish or town to prohibit the local sale of alcohol following a vote by its ratepayers.

[2] *Johnny Gibb o' Gushetneuk* is a novel by William Alexander, published 1871.

46. Lord Ninian arriving home after being elected MP for
Cardiff

excellent descriptions of the various characters in the story, and his
rendering of the passages illustrating the old Aberdeenshire dialect
was highly appreciated. On the motion of the Rev. Mr Morrison, the
chairman of the meeting, a very hearty vote of thanks was accorded
to Mr Mackie. (FN)

7 December 1910
Lord Ninian Crichton-Stuart MP
Lord Ninian Crichton-Stuart is the second son of the late Marquis of
Bute, and since he entered into possession of his estate of Falkland in
May 1904, he has nobly discharged the responsibilities of his position.
He has been well called the "Farmers' Friend", for every movement
designed to advance the farmers' interests in Fife receives invaluable
support at his hands. As President of the Fife Farmers' Club during
two terms of office, he has exceeded the highest expectations, not only
in placing the resources of his establishment at the officials' service
when opportunity offers, and doing generous deeds for the good of
all the members, but in personally assisting in the management of the

Society's affairs, and directing its summer show with the greatest zeal and enthusiasm. To the same characteristics and his capabilities as a public speaker is undoubtedly due the memorable decision of the Highlands and Agricultural Society of Scotland to hold its 1912 show in Fife or Kinross.

At the General Election in January 1910 Lord Ninian also made a great impression as the Unionist candidate in one of the divisions of Glamorganshire. On December 7th, 1910, he captured the Cardiff seat by a majority of 299. In Lady Ninian, he has an able helpmeet, and with energy, ability and youth on his side, he may be relied on to make his mark on the history of both our county and our country. (FN)

14 December 1910

General election: East Fife

Friday was the polling day in the Eastern Division of the county. [1] In the morning and forenoon the weather was all that could be desired for a December day, but in the afternoon the wind suddenly veered to the east, and for hours a drenching rain was experienced. Between 4 and 8 o'clock a pitch darkness was the rule, and in some of the villages and hamlets in rural Fife the meteorological circumstances had the effect of reducing the number of voters who would otherwise have exercised the franchise.

there was an entire absence, on Friday, of the enthusiasm exhibited in January. The only literature to be seen on the Liberal side was a placard appealing to the electors to "Vote for Asquith," while the gallant Colonel practically ignored the issue of the contest, the House of Lords Veto, and asked the Unionists to negative "Home Rule, and vote for Sprot." (LAWG)

---

[1] This was the second general election that year. Voting took place of different days in different constituencies.
Results for the Eastern Division of Fife:
- H. H. Asquith, Liberal 5,149
- Col. A. Sprot, Unionist 3,350
- Liberal majority 1,799. Liberal hold.

Results for the Cardiff Boroughs constituency:
- Lord Ninian Crichton-Stuart, Conservative 12,181 (50.6%, + 3.7%)
- Sir Clarendon Hyde, Liberal, 11,882 (49.4%, –3.7%)
- Turnout 83.8%, swing of 3.7%, Conservative gain from Liberal.

17 December 1910

Presentation

During the evening of the Falkland Cricket Club dance, held on Friday 2nd December, Mr H. D. Michie, who acted as Secretary of the Club for many years, was presented with a fountain pen and cigar case on the occasion of his leaving for a situation in Dundee. Dr J. G. Jack, president of the Club, handed over the gifts, and Mr Michie suitably returned thanks. (FN)

17 December 1910

Lecture

On Friday last, the third lecture of the course was held in the Drill Hall, when Mrs Donaldson, Bank House, entertained a large audience to a very interesting and instructive lecture on "A Tour through Belgium and South Germany". The lecture was splendidly illustrated with lime-light views. On the call of Dr Jack, a very hearty vote of thanks was accorded to Mrs Donaldson for her excellent lecture. (FN)

20 December 1910

200 torch Bearers light the scene

Lord Ninian Crichton-Stuart, MP for Cardiff, and the Lady Ninian Crichton-Stuart, last night were accorded an enthusiastic welcome home by the Town Council, the tenantry of the estate, and the towns-people of Falkland and the surrounding district.

On arrival at Liquorstane, at the entrance to the burgh, Lord and Lady Ninian Crichton-Stuart were received with loud and prolonged cheers. Miss Hilda Ogilvie, daughter of Mr J. B. Ogilvie, Westfield, presented the Lady Ninian, on behalf of the tenantry, with a beautiful bouquet of flowers.

It was a picturesque scene. There were 200 torch bearers, and lights, many of them coloured, were displayed in numerous houses in the burgh. The Town Band headed the procession. Lord and Lady Ninian left their motor car and occupied seats in their private Victoria carriage. The carriage was drawn by the kilted gamekeepers and other estate servants, and was flanked on either side by Mr James Tod, Easter Cash; Mr George Dun, Woodmill; Mr Alex Shanks, Falkland Wood; and Mr J. B. Ogilvie, four of the principal farm tenants, each bearing a flaming torch.

Cheers were raised at intervals as the imposing procession passed by the Palace and through the town to the House of Falkland. A dozen torches erected in a circle opposite the front door of the mansion house threw a bright light over the assembly when the proper welcome home took place.

Speaking from the steps of the front door, Provost Jackson said Falkland in the past had doubtless been the scene of many brilliant pageants, but he ventured to say that never before had she witnessed a more brilliant or more enthusiastic gathering than they had there that night. (Cheers) That great assembly was entirely free from political significance. (Hear, hear) All shades of political opinion were present, and were vying one with another in welcoming them home. (Cheers)

We welcome you home, sir, not as the mere victor of a great political fight, but we welcome you home as a fellow citizen and brother Scot. (Cheers)

His Lordship, having the honest conviction of his opinions, had gone forth against what appeared to be overwhelming odds, and he had fought with dourness and determination, such as only Scotsmen were capable of exercising, and had carried his flag to victory. (Loud cheers) He had followed the campaign at Cardiff with interest, and had observed that the Lady Ninian, after expressing her regret that her husband was not an Irishman, (Laughter) had said that he had done the next best thing in marrying an Irish lady. (Cheers) He rather thought the result of the campaign had been due to the happy combination of the Scotsman and the Irish lady, the dour determination of the Scot and the vivacity and brightness of the Irish lady. (Cheers) Her Ladyship, when her husband's voice failed on the last day of the election, had taken up the flag and spoken even more brilliantly for the Unionist cause than Lord Ninian, so that the victory was due as much to her Ladyship's efforts as to those of Lord Ninian himself. (Cheers)

"Let me express the hope," the Provost concluded, "that the great interest you have taken in our county in the past will in no wise be diminished by this new avenue you have carved out for yourself. I wish you a long and prosperous career. I wish to assure you, whether prosperity or adversity may be your future lot, that you will find nowhere more true friends or more loving hearts than in this good town of Falkland. My Lord, I have pleasure in welcoming you home."

Lord Ninian, who had an enthusiastic reception, said he had not very much voice left, as they could hear, for he had left it down South. (Laughter) He thanked the Provost very much for his kind words and them all for the spontaneous sportsmanship they had shown. He was glad to see all his friends of both shades of political opinion. (Cheers) He had gone to Cardiff with certain fixed political opinions, and he had come back with these opinions unaltered; indeed, they had been strengthened, but he valued that splendid welcome home more than the political honour they had secured. (Cheers) The Provost had referred to his work in the town and county, and he could only say that he would endeavour to work harder for the county than he had done before. (Cheers).

He had been given a certain amount of notoriety in public, and he only hoped it would stimulate him to do his little bit for the burgh and the county in which he loved to live. (Cheers)

Mr James Tod, Easter Cash, on behalf of the tenantry, extended a cordial welcome home. He referred to his Lordship's fight in Cardiff, and mentioned that Lord Lansdowne complimented Lady Ninian, and said that the candidate did not require any outside help so long as he had Lady Ninian beside him. (Cheers)

That you will be long spared to one another, to help each other, is the earnest wish of everyone of us. (Cheers)

Lady Ninian, who was requested to reply by Lord Ninian, thanked them for that splendid homecoming, and the tenants for the beautiful bouquet they had given her. Nowhere had they enjoyed a reception like what they had had there, it really did go to one's heart. Their ideas had been broadened by what they had gone through, and if they had any regrets at all it was that they were not representing a seat in Scotland. (Cheers).

In spite of their victory and all the kindness they had received at Cardiff, their hearts really were and always would be in Falkland. (Cheers)

Cheers having been raised for Lord and Lady Ninian, Lord Ninian said, in conclusion, that their politics might be down in Cardiff, but their hearts were in Scotland.

"He's a jolly good fellow" having been sung, his Lordship said, "Once more, goodnight, and thank you very much indeed." The band played the National Anthem, and the gathering dispersed. (DC)

24 December 1910

Boy Scouts

On Saturday last, the local troop of Scouts, under Scoutmaster Donaldson and Assistant Scoutmaster Gardner, marched to Auchtermuchty, to take part in the rally which was held there during the afternoon. On arrival at Auchtermuchty, they were met by the troop recently formed there, and also by the troops from Strathmiglo and Newburgh. The whole Company then proceeded to the Cross, where a photograph was taken by Mr Frank Findlay, and after this was done, they marched to the Victoria Hall, where they were addressed by Mr Herbert Pullar, of Bridge of Earn, Scout Commissioner for Perthshire. He gave the boys a very practical and instructive address on the principles of the Scouting movement, and after having demonstrated how to dress a wound when rendering first aid, he presented each of the troops with a very neat and compact ambulance outfit. After partaking of tea, the various troops returned home. (FN)

31 December 1910

Christmas service

A special service of praise was held in the Parish Church on Sunday evening, when several anthems were rendered by members of the choir. Solos were also sung by Miss Agnes Forsyth and Mr George Spence. (FN)

31 December 1910

Christmas treat

In the Drill Hall on Monday, Lord and Lady Ninian Crichton-Stuart entertained the whole of the school children of Falkland, numbering about 240, to a Christmas treat, consisting of tea and a gift from a Christmas tree to each child. On the call of the Rev. A. Lyon Johnston, a hearty vote of thanks was given to the noble host and hostess for their kindness. The purveying was in the capable hands of Mr Mason of the Bruce Arms. (FN)

47. Falkland Boy Scouts, 1911

Back row: Tom Drysdale, Bob Hamilton David Sturrock, Andrew Page,
Andrew Collins, Jim Ross, George McHardie, Ambrose Reekie
Middle row: Walter Venters, Mr Gardner (teacher), Capt. Donaldson, John
Venters, Peter Walker, Eben Allan, Smith (Westfield)
Front row: Bob Anderson, Andrew Grant, Bob Kennedy, Willy Anderson,
Andrew Ross, David Lister, Smith (Westfield), Kenny Calder

31 December 1910

Masonic

The brethren of St John's Lodge (No. 35) held their annual St John's festival in the Bruce Arms, Hotel on Monday evening. A very enjoyable evening was spent with song and sentiment. The IPM, Bro. James Jackson, was presented with a handsome P.M. jewel. The RWM, Bro. Alex Grieve, made the presentation in a neat speech. IPM Bro. Jackson suitable replied. Bro. Mason purveyed in his well-known and up-to-date style. The following are the office-bearers for the ensuing year: RWM, Alex Grieve; SW, P. Robertson; JW, Wm. Reid; SD, J. Donaldson; JD, D. Munro; IG, H. W. Skinner; OG, J. Walker. (FN)

31 December 1910

Historical tableaux

A unique entertainment took place yesterday afternoon at the House of Falkland, the home of Lord and Lady Ninian Crichton-Stuart., when there was presented a series of historical tableaux illustrative of the period from 1436 to 1651, when Falkland Palace was a Royal residence.[1]

The stage, handsomely draped with old gold plush, was erected in the spacious dining room, which was crowded with appreciative spectators, among whom were: The Lady Ninian Crichton-Stuart; the Dowager Lady Bute; Lord and Lady Glamis; Lady Anstruther and Miss Anstruther; Major Anstruther Gray and Mrs Anstruther Gray; Colonel and Mrs and Misses Sprot; the Hon. F. Hanbury-Tracy; Col. and Mrs Anstruther of Charleton; Col. And Miss Oswald of Dunnikier; Mrs Balfour of Balbirnie and party; Sir Charles Bruce of Arnot Towers; Mr J. L. Lumsden Freuchie; Miss Lawson Forfar; Misses Osborne Belmore; Mr R. Tullis of Strathendry and party; Dr and Mrs Jack; Mr and Mrs Gavin Falkland Palace; Mrs Walker Auchtermuchty; Mr Jackson Lomondvale; Mr and Mrs Dickie Devon; Mr and Mrs Melville Rumdewan; Mr F. W. Christie Castlefield.

Antique French tapestry and crimson and gold embroidered curtains formed a suitable background for the pictures. An exceedingly brilliant effect was produced when the limelight shone on the gorgeous costumes of the medieval age worn by the ladies and gentlemen personating the historic characters who played so large a part in the history of their troubled times.

The costumes and accessories closely followed in every detail the customs of the various periods, and, apart from the interest attaching to the famous personages portrayed, furnished a striking study of the transition of dress from the days when it showed the exact rank, social position, or avocation of the wearer.

The first tableau revealed James I, the poet King, well impersonated by Lord Ninian, in black velvet mantle and gold tunic with purple

---

[1] The proceeds of the three performances was £70, which went to "providing and maintaining a club for the young factory girls in Falkland that can meet daily for reading and recreation".

48. Tableau of King James I of Scotland
Hon. Bernard Howard (gentleman-in-waiting), Lord Ninian (King James I),
Hon. Mrs C. Hanbury-Tracy (Queen Joan), Miss Lane Fox and Mr Alex.
Rawlinson (lady and gentleman-in-waiting)

hose and jewelled crown. By his side was seated his consort Queen
Joan Beaufort, in milk-white dove of poetic story, the Hon. Mrs C.
Hanbury-Tracy. She wore a flowing robe of yellow and white brocade, with richly jewelled stomacher, over this a royal blue velvet
sleeved mantle bordered with ermine. Her rich auburn hair, worn in
two long braids was surmounted by a gold jewel-studded crown. On
either side stood the Ladies-in-Waiting, Miss Lane Fox, a charming
figure in crimson velvet gown, banded with gold embroidery, large
white satin collar, and lace covered steeple headgear, from which
floated a white veil. She also wore a ruby necklace and ear-rings; a
contrasting toilet of emerald green velvet, bordered with ermine, was
worn by Miss Osborne, her companion, whose triple pointed headdress was of white sequined net. The Lords-in-Waiting, the Hon. Bernard Howard and Mr Alex Rawlinson, were splendid figures in their

fur trimmed velvet mantles and rich tunics of brocaded silk.

In Tableau II, Lord Colum Crichton-Stuart was seen as King James II, who succeeded to the throne as a boy. He was attired in black and gold embroidered mantle and black silk hose. Queen Mary of Guildres was represented in stately fashion by the Hon. Ethel Stourton. Her exquisite white silk dress was strewn with glittering sequins in blue and gold, a stomacher of gold tissue being worn over a pale blue satin bodice, adorned with large pearls. Over this was thrown a magnificent amethyst velvet mantle edged with ermine, and her long fair hair was crowned by a glittering gold and silver headdress and white veil. Two Ladies-in Waiting attended the Queen, Miss Kenny, who favoured gold brocade with pale blue revers, old rose kirtle and gleaming silver steeple hat with white veil, and Miss O'Hara, radiant in sage green satin which had an appliquéd design of white satin on skirt and white soft collar and cuffs. A very long tissue veil hung from her silver headdress.

James III and the Queen Mother were represented in Tableau III. The boy king's part, in the unavoidable absence of Lord Leslie,[1] was filled by Master W. Mason. In this effective group the widowed Queen Mother, holding her small son, is attired in gown and headdress of black velvet, lavishly trimmed with ermine, glittering diamond ornaments and long rope of pearls. The young king's suit of green velvet was slashed with gold satin, and he wore a scarlet velvet cap. In the background were Miss O'Hara in a lovely gown of petunia satin, headdress to match edged with ermine and veil of golden tissue, and Miss Kenny in grey brocade, embroidered in silver, and wearing pearl ornaments.

A splendid group formed the fourth tableau, consisting of Queen Mary of Guildres, who along with her children receives the fugitive Queen of England, Margaret of Anjou, the beautiful and high-spirited daughter of King René of Anjou, and her son Prince Edward of England. Queen Margaret was personated by Miss Grizel Anstruther, wearing a black velvet mantle, with deep ermine cape over her pale yellow kirtle, while her Ladies-in Waiting were Miss Anstruther Gray, gowned in soft grey brocade with facings and kirtle of rose and

---

[1] Posibly John Leslie (1902 – 1975) who succeeded his father as Earl of Rothes in 1974.

silver headdress and veil. Miss Osborne in terra velvet, with panel and waist band of bright green satin powered with bronze sequins. Her pointed headgear was of gold tissue from which hung a white veil. As Prince Edward of England, Master Aeneas Gavin wore a green velvet cloak over a green silk suit and red velvet cap adorned with a white plume. Little Miss Gavin was Princess Mary and wore a trailing gown of dull blue velvet with a touch of ermine. The vest and kirtle were of canary silk and a gold filet surrounded her dark hair.

In tableau V the youthful Prince Edward is seen with Princess Mary.

In the next tableau Mr Reginald Fairlie, in crimson velvet mantle and deep ermine cape, personated James III, while his Queen, Margaret of Denmark, had a charming representative in Miss M. Fairlie. Her kirtle of rich black velvet was worn with a bodice of crimson and gold brocade, while on her fair hair she wore a gold circlet and coif of gold net and pearls. The attendant Ladies were Miss M. Anstruther and Miss Marjory Dalrymple in purple and gold brocade and pink satin respectively. Two Gentlemen-in Waiting and the Myres Macer,[1] Mr J. Fairlie, a gorgeous figure, completed this fine group.

An interesting tableau was No VII, when King James IV receives Perkin Warbeck[2] with Royal honours. The Earl Rothes was a dignified personage in his fur-trimmed, silver brocaded mantle and trunk hose, while Lord Colum Crichton-Stuart, as Perkin Warbeck, was resplendent in purple velvet and orange. As a Lord-in Waiting Lord Ninian looked handsome in dark blue tunic slashed with black silk and black plumed bonnet.

The meeting of Perkin Warbeck and Lady Catherine Gordon (who afterwards married him) at the Court of James IV, was the subject of the eighth tableau. Miss Freda Villiers was Lady Catherine, and

---

[1] The proprietors of the Myres estate anciently had the right to appoint one of the four macers (court officials) to the Court of Session. The Myres Macer is now an honorary title of the Laird of Falkland.

[2] Perkin Warbeck (c. 1474–1499) claimed to be one of the "princes in the Tower" and thus heir to the throne of England. He was supported for political reasons by James IV, who mounted a brief invasion of England with him.

looked charming in her gown of dark blue brocade, brightened with terra velvet. The flowing sleeves were lined with gold tissue, and her white and gold headgear had a broad border of black velvet. Her ladies were Miss Balfour, in pink and white silk brocade, pearl trimmed coif and white veil; and Miss Eva Balfour, in pale green and white silk, gold jewelled girdle and necklet, and becoming pearl net coif.

A pretty tableau was No IX, when James IV was portrayed by the Earl of Rothes and his Queen, Margaret Tudor, by the Countess of Rothes,[1] attended by the Ladies Mildred and Eleanor Leslie as Maids of Honour. The Queen was daintily gowned in silver brocade embroidered with pearls. Her long crimson velvet train was ermine trimmed, and on her dark hair rested a glittering crown of jewels. Lady Mildred Leslie's green robe had sable fur edgings and head-dress to match while Lady Eleanor Leslie was becomingly robed in rose pink with pale pink velvet and pearl embroidered coif.

Tableau X to XI showed James V's escape from Falkland Palace and subsequent discovery, the part of the King being taken by the Lord Kinross dressed in the picturesque uniform of a Yeoman of the Guard. King James V, and his Queen, Mary of Guise, figured in Tableau XII. Miss Dorothy Cochrane, as the Queen, was a graceful figure attired in heavy dark blue and gold brocade, panelled with black velvet and bordered with sable; she wore strings of pearls and pearl trimmed blue velvet cap. Her Lady-in-Waiting was her sister, Miss K. Cochrane, in sage green cloth with gold embroideries, the sleeves being slashed with cream satin. This pretty toilet was completed by a pearl coif, from which depended a yellow veil.

An impressive scene was presented in Tableau XIII showing the death of King James V at Falkland Palace. On his death bed he is surrounded by cardinal Beaton (Mr Stanley Cary) in scarlet robe and ivory prayer book in hand; Kirkcaldy of the Grange (Captain Slacke) and Sir David Lindsey (Lord Ninian) displaying on his tabard the Scottish Lion Rampant, scarlet on white ground.

Perhaps the prettiest picture was Tableau XIV, when a hunting scene at Falkland Palace was depicted. The central figure is Mary

---

[1] The following year, the Countess of Rothes (Noël Leslie) was to survive the sinking of the Titanic.

Queen of Scots, most delightfully represented by the Lady Kinross. Her lovely gown of emerald velvet was richly braided in gold, the bodice being slashed with pale blue satin and draped with white lace. A becoming green velvet cap to match with white ostrich plume was worn on her lovely auburn hair. The parts of the four Marys were filled by Mrs Slacke, as Mary Beton, in pale grey gown banded with grey velvet, short cloak, with neck ruffle, and cap with long pink and white shaded feather; Miss Lane Fox, as Mary Livingston, in bright green velvet, the shoulder cloak being lined with golden silk, and a green cap ornamented with upright green plume; Miss Bellew as Mary Seton, in pale green and sable, white neck ruffle, and green cap with white plume; and Miss Farrell, as Mary Fleming, also wore green brocaded with gold, and hat to harmonise.

A charming scene was next presented, where Rizzio, in sable suit and cap, is entertaining the Queen and her ladies with music while they are engaged at their broidery frames winding wool. Queen Mary is now gowned in black velvet with characteristic cap, and wearing ropes of pearls.

The next picture shows Queen Mary, in dazzling white satin, with Lord Darnley, Captain Slacke, and her Lords and Ladies-in-Waiting.

In Tableau XVII, we see James VI, Captain Moncrieff Skene, and his Queen, Ann of Denmark. Mrs M. Skene, who looked lovely, wore a handsome pink velvet and silver brocaded gown, with pearl headdress and white veil. The Misses Skene and Miss Nancy Dewar were Ladies-in-attendance. Very pretty they looked in their quaint distended gowns, upstanding square collars, and becoming pearl and sequin coifs. Miss Ruth Skene was in cream and blue brocade, richly embroidered in blue sequins and pearl shells; Miss Hilda Skene in green and gold brocade having a panel of sequins and pearls, and wearing a black velvet cap with white lace; and Miss Nancy Dewar who looked sweet in cream brocade striped with pink rosebuds, lace coil adorned with gold balls and pearl embroidery. The two Lords-in-Waiting were Mr James Cathcart and Mr Archie Middleton.

The Gowrie Conspiracy in six scenes was next presented, with Captain Skene as King James VI; the Master of Ruthven, Lord Colum Crichton-Stuart; the Earl of Mar, Mr James Cathcart; the Earl Lennox, Mr Archie Middleton; the Earl of Gowrie, Mr R Anstruther, all in brave attire.

The nineteenth Tableau depicted Charles I, Mr Percy Guthin,[1] en route to Edinburgh, knighting county gentlemen, the Hon. B. Howard and Captain Meldon, and formed a brilliant spectacle. In the rear stood two soldiers, Mr Anstruther and Mr R. Anstruther.

Extremely interesting was the last Tableau, when the Earl of Rothes posed as his ancestor, the Duke of Rothes, the favourite courtier and statesman of Charles II, who had obtained for his house the highest rank of nobility. The present holder of almost the oldest honour of Scotland, in his splendid suit of velvet and silk, looked well as the gay gallant who was Fife's greatest magnate of his time. The scene shows Charles II, Mr Alex. Rawlinson, receiving homage at Falkland.

The Rev. A. Lyon Johnston, parish minister gave short historical surveys explanatory of the tableaux.

Lady Ninian Crichton-Stuart, with whom the idea of the tableaux originated, and who was instrumental in establishing the Falkland Girls Club, for whose benefit the proceeds of the entertainment will be given, wore a charming gown of black satin trimmed with silver and lace. (DC)

HOUSE OF FALKLAND

Friday 30 December and 31st December 1910

Tickets: Second seats 5 shillings, Third Seats 1 shilling

Proceeds to the Falkland Girls Club

20 scenes from 1436/60 up until 1651 and Charles II receiving homage at Falkland.

---

[1] Apparently a typo for Gethin: Percy Francis Gethin (1874–1916) was a quite well known artist, teacher and etcher – he had works in an exhibition of Irish painter-etchers in the National Gallery of Ireland in Dublin in 2018. He was killed on the Somme in WWI serving with the 8th Bn Devonshires, aged 42.

1911

Fife C.C. – Cupar District Committee

Balmblae water supply and drainage

Lord Ninian Crichton-Stuart said the sub-committee appointed in connection with the Balmblae water and drainage supply had gone into the matter very thoroughly, and had come to the conclusion, so far as the drainage part was concerned, that owing to the situation of Balmblae it would be necessary to form it into a special drainage district if anything was going to be done. The sub-committee felt they would be exceeding the powers given to them if they took any steps towards the formation of a special district, and therefore on that question they asked to be relieved of their labours. When they went into the water question they had found a curious state of affairs, in so far as the users of water in Balmblae had to pay double the water rate those in the burgh were paying. The sub-committee had gone into the question of whether another water supply could be got, and they found it quite impossible. Mr Galloway, who had the right of the water at the mill dam at the west end of Falkland, would, he was sure, grant them every facility in his power to get the water.

The Chairman: Do you move that the sub-committee be reappointed?

Lord Ninian: No. I move that the present sub-committee be released from their labours.

Mr James Cathcart of Pitcairlie: Reappoint the sub-committee as it stands with fresh powers to go into the matter of water and drainage and report. – Agreed.

Falkland and Auchtermuchty Hospital

A letter was submitted from the Town Clerk of Falkland intimating that the Town Council was to withdraw from the agreement regarding Auchtermuchty Hospital [1] at Whitsunday first. Mr Jackson, Falkland, stated that an agreement was entered upon four or five years ago, and at that time the rate was something like £8 a year. The rate had steadily risen, and it was now £40, and the Town Council considered the amount charged out of all proportion to the benefits received. They would be quite willing to go into a new arrangement, and pay a fixed annual sum.

Provost Ferlie, Auchtermuchty, said he would like to know how many patients had come from the four burghs, and also the number of patients that had been treated in the hospital. He understood Falkland had only three patients in the hospital in five years.

The Clerk pointed out that if the burghs had not joined with the county they would have had to provide hospital accommodation for themselves, and the expense would have been far greater than at present.

On the recommendation of the Medical Officer it was agreed to refund the cost of antitoxin administered to diphtheria patients before removal to hospital if their circumstances were such that it was considered they could ill afford to pay. (DC)

7 January 1911

Bird show

The fifty-first annual show of the Falkland and District Ornithological Society held in the Drill and Town Halls on Tuesday was a gratifying success. The entry was one of the largest in the history of the Society, and the quality of the exhibits was of a high order. The judging, which was by no means an easy task, was well accomplished by Mr Wm. Morgan, Windygates (soft feathers); Councillor George White, Cupar (game and game bantams); Mr A. Anderson, Edinburgh (pigeons); and Mr George Arnott, Kirkcaldy (cage birds). (FN)

---

[1] Southfield House, Auchtermuchty, was used as the local authority infectious diseases hospital from about 1895

14 January 1911

Mr R. Cameron

Mr R. Cameron,[1] who has been for the past four years in the British Linen Co's Bank in Cupar, was met by a few friends on Thursday evening last week, and presented with a handsome Gladstone bag and a volume of Burns on his leaving Cupar to take up the appointment of teller in the Company's Bank, Falkland. (FN)

21 January 1911

House of Falkland staff dance

The annual staff dance took place at Falkland House on Friday night of last week, when the servants, estate workers, and a few friends assembled together and took part in a very enjoyable dance. On the call of Mr Liptrott,[2] three hearty cheers were given for Lord and Lady Ninian Crichton-Stuart for having provided such an entertainment. (FFP)

28 January 1911

Dance at stables

Captain Slacke entertained the servants at Falkland House, the employees on the estate, and a few friends to a supper and dance on Tuesday evening at the stables, when a most enjoyable time was spent. In an appropriate manner Mr Liptrott, on behalf of the company, proposed "The health of Captain Slacke and Mrs Slacke", and wished them long life and prosperity, which was responded to with three hearty cheers.

Captain Slacke suitably acknowledged the toast. The purveying was in the capable hands of Mr Mason, Bruce Arms, and a quadrille band from Kirkcaldy supplied the music for the dancing. (FN)

---

[1] Randolph Cameron had lodged with the Hardies at the Temperance Hotel, He later went to work in the Northern Crown bank of Winnipeg in Canada. He served with the 16th Bn Canadian Army in WWI, and made a short visit to Falkland in 1917 whilst on leave. He survived the war.

[2] Mr Liptrott was the butler. He lived with his family at the Lodge.

11 February 1911

Lady Ninian

Lady Ninian Crichton-Stuart will be confined to the House of Falkland for some time, her physicians having ordered her a spell of complete rest. (FN)

11 February 1911

Political meeting

On Wednesday evening, a meeting was held in the Drill Hall under the auspices of the Women's Unionist Association, when an address was delivered by Mr W. C. Ritchie on Tariff Reform. Provost Jackson presided. (FN)

11 February 1911

Y.M.C.A.

The Rev. J. H. Morrison addressed the morning meeting on Sunday last. He delivered an excellent address his subject being "The Conversion of Saul". A fortnightly mission was also begun on Sunday evening in the Town Hall by Mr Baird of Dundee. (FN)

11 February 1911

Masonic dance

The annual assembly of Lodge St John No 35, was held in the Drill Hall on the evening of Friday last week, when a very pleasant and enjoyable dance was engaged in. The music was supplied by Adamson's Quadrille band, and the catering was in the hands of Mrs Hardie, Temperance Hotel. (FN)

18 February 1911

Lecture

The last of the course of popular lectures was given in the Drill Hall on Friday last when the Rev. Mackintosh Mackay, Glasgow, delivered a very interesting and instructive lecture on a "Trip from Liverpool to the Rocky Mountains", which was beautifully illustrated with lime-light views.

49. Mrs Hardie's Temperance Hotel, High Street

The pictures is marked GWW, for George Washington Wilson, a pioneering
Scottish photographer. He later set up a company that took photographs
throughout Britain and elsewhere. The firm took 44 photographs of Falkland
and Estate.

On the call of Mr James Jackson, Lomondvale, who occupied the
chair, a very hearty vote of thanks was accorded Mr Mackay. The Rev.
Johnston stated that the course which had just finished had proved
most successful in every way. (FN)

18 February 1911

Cessio

Thomas H. Forbes, farmer and mill-owner, Falkland, was to have been examined in connection with cessio[1] proceedings at Cupar Sheriff Court on Thursday, but Mr A. E. Grosset, solicitor, Cupar, explained that Forbes had met with an accident at the railway station and would not be able to attend. Mr Grosset asked for an adjournment of a fortnight, and this was agreed to. (FN)

25 February 1911

Sale of Juniper Villa

Juniper Villa, Pleasance, Falkland, was exposed to sale in the Bruce Arms, Hotel on Saturday last, and was purchased by Mr James Clark, Edinburgh. (FN)

4 March 1911

Property to let

To Let, on Lease for 3 or 5 years. Lomondside House, as presently occupied by Mr James Cochrane, containing handsome Dining-Room and Drawing-Room, 4 Bedrooms, Bathroom (H. & C.), Kitchen, Scullery, Servants Bedroom and Lavatory, ample Press Accommodation, also Washing-House, Coal House; and Cottage of 3 Apartments used for storage, with excellent Walled Garden, productive and well stocked, and Poultry Run. Rent £35. Entry Whitsunday 1911. The House may be viewed on Mondays, Wednesdays, and Saturdays from 2.30 p.m. to 4.30 p.m. Apply to Alex Anderson, Solicitor, Falkland. (FN)

18 March 1911

School Board

A meeting of the ratepayers was held in the Town Hall on Monday evening in view of the forthcoming School Board election, which takes place on April 8th, when the retiring members gave an account of their stewardship. The members present were Mr J. L. Lumsden,

---

[1] See Glossary.

the Chairman, the Rev. A. L. Johnston, Mr David Bonthrone, ex-Provost Miller, and Mr William Horne. Mr Lumsden explained fully the work of the Board under the Education Act of 1908, and after several questions were asked, nominations were made as follows: The five retiring members, and Mr George Gavin, Councillor J. W. Jackson, and Dr J. G. Jack. The proceedings terminated with a vote of thanks to Provost Jackson, who presided. (FN)

22 March 1911

Falkland hen raiders

William Barr, carter, Victoria Place, the raider of a Newton of Falkland hen-roost, was smartly spotted by Police Constable Calder.

It was reported to the constable that half a dozen hens had been stolen from the lock fast henhouse of Alex. Adams, cattleman, Newton of Falkland, early on Sunday morning 17th February. He learned from Robert Jackson, who resided at the east side of Adams' henhouse, that he was awakened by the barking of his dog, and that he heard a footstep about one o'clock in the morning. He next traced the feathers from Newton to Falkland, and thereafter discovered that James Lister, baker, when walking along South Street shortly after one o'clock, hears footsteps and the flapping of hens' wings and cackling. The last he heard of the hens was about the foot of Victoria Place, about thirty yards from the accuser's house. The constable visited accused's premises on Wednesday, and found half a dozen hens which answered the description of the missing birds.

The accused at Cupar Sheriff Court yesterday, said he got the hens about eleven o'clock on Saturday night from a man going to Leslie. He did not know the man. He paid 1s 6d apiece for the hens.

Sheriff Armour Hannay said it was a clear case, and after hearing the accuser's story it became still clearer. If the hens were stolen at one o'clock in the morning it was clear accused could not buy them from that alleged individual he had met on the road at eleven o'clock. The sentence would be twenty-one days imprisonment. (DC)

25 March 1911

Falkland Light Railway

Substantial help has been given to the Falkland Light Railway undertaking through the generosity of Lord Ninian Crichton-Stuart MP. As will be seen from the subjoined letter he has addressed to Provost Jackson, Falkland, he has offered to take up shares in the Company to the value of £1,000, on the condition that the rest of the £10,000 capital required is raised before the promoters' powers under the Railway Commission expire, and that work is immediately commenced. With equal public spirit, his Lordship agrees to take in shares of the Company any compensation that may be awarded him for land taken from him or for severance and other damages. The terms of his letter are:

House of Falkland, Falkland, Fife. 11th February 1911.
Falkland Light Railway
    Dear Mr Provost,
    I have now most carefully gone into the whole question of the Falkland Light Railway, and especially taking into consideration the convenience and position of the inhabitants in the burgh, I have come to the conclusion that the Railway will be to their very great advantage. I have, therefore, the pleasure of advising you that I am about to apply for shares in the Railway to the value of one thousand pounds sterling (£1,000) on the condition that the rest of the £10,000 etc., required is raised before your powers under the Railway Commission expire, and that work is immediately commenced. I beg to add that I shall take in shares of the Light Railway any sum which may be given to me as compensation for land taken from me or as compensation for severance and other damages.
    Believe me, Dear Mr Provost, yours most faithfully, Ninian Crichton-Stuart.

Meeting of Town Council

The above letter was read at a meeting of Falkland Town Council on Wednesday evening. Provost Jackson said Lord Ninian had been good enough to tell him he had discussed the scheme with financial experts and those who were well able to advise him as to its feasibility, and the words he had used to him were:

"While it will never pay an enormous dividend, it will give a modest return for the capital invested, and to those residing in the district who are to have the use of the railway, it will form a very handsome investment." (Applause)

They should now make an effort to get the scheme carried through. He moved that the Town Clerk be instructed to accord Lord Ninian their hearty thanks for his generous offer. (Applause) Mr William A. Mason seconded.

Messrs Jackson's offer

Mr John W. Jackson said it was perfectly true that the railway would come as a considerable advantage to the firm to which he belonged, but there was not a single individual from the humblest to the highest that would not receive direct and permanent advantage from the railway. They would observe in Lord Ninian's letter there were two main points he laid down as the basis of his support:

(1) The great advantage it would be to the town of Falkland; and

(2) that the necessary capital would require to be raised before the powers under the Railway Order expired.

They were in this position with the railway that the compulsory powers for the acquisition of ground expired in the month of October of this year. If they were to renew these powers they had to give six months' notice. His firm was prepared to give a sum not exceeding £1,000 in addition to the £1,000 they had already subscribed, so that they were in the position now that if they could get a sum of something like £1,500 the railway would go through. (Applause) Mr John Angus said he was a shareholder, and he would be very proud to see the railway into Falkland. There was no fear of it paying.

Bailie Drysdale expressed the opinion that, while he had no doubt that the inhabitants would like to see the railway introduced, they might not be prepared to invest in it to any great extent. This view was also expressed by Councillor Williamson. The Provost said as a Town Council they could not commit the ratepayers to anything, but individually he thought it was their duty to do all they could to help forward the interests of the burgh. (Hear, hear)

The place that would benefit most

Mr J. W. Jackson spoke of the saving that would be effected to householders in the price of coals and all kinds of foodstuffs by the introduction of the railway. He had been over the length and breadth of the land trying to get support. He had got it in London, Birmingham and Manchester, but the place he had received the least support was the place that would benefit most. It was agreed to call a public meeting with the view of securing financial support for the undertaking. An arrangement has already been made with the North British Railway Company to work the line upon stated terms. (FN)

25 March 1911

Soirée

The annual social meeting in connection with the United Free Church took place in the church, which has been beautifully redecorated, on the evening of Friday last, when the Rev. Morrison presided over a large attendance. A new departure was made in doing away with the usual soirée tea and the programme was commenced straight away by a few introductory remarks by the Chairman. The speeches of the evening were made by the Rev. Craig, Balmalcolm; the Rev. Frances, Raith Parish Church, Kirkcaldy, and the Rev. Johnston, Falkland, all of whom gave very eloquent and able addresses. An excellent musical programme was also carried through. Solos were sung by the following ladies and gentlemen: Miss Daisy Cochrane, Lomondside, gave an excellent rendering of "Sleep and Forget", Miss Mary Macdonald, Montrose, enraptured the audience by the manner in which she sang "The Gleaner's Slumber Song" and she was prevailed upon to sing a second time in response to a hearty encore; Miss Euphemia Duncan, Dunshalt, sang "God Shall Wipe Away All tears" very beautifully, and the gentlemen soloists were Mr Robert Morgan, Freuchie, and Mr James Menzies, Leslie, who contributed "Remember thy Creator" and "Galilee" respectively. The choir under the leadership of Mr William Burgon rendered four anthems, and a juvenile choir sang a hymn. Miss Bryce presided at the organ. At the close of the meeting, the Chairman called for a vote of thanks to all who had so ably contributed to the programme, and this was heartily responded to. (FN)

1 April 1911

Social

Under the auspices of the Falkland Women's Unionist Association, a social and dance were held in the Drill Hall on Friday night, when there was a very large attendance. In the early part of the meeting, tea was served, and an address was delivered by Miss Collum. An enjoyable dance followed. During the evening songs were contributed by a number of ladies and gentlemen. (FN)

1 April 1911

Lord Ninian Crichton-Stuart

The *Daily Sketch* of Tuesday publishes a portrait of Lord Ninian Crichton-Stuart in its "Social and Personal" columns, and says of his Lordship:

"Lord Ninian Crichton-Stuart, brother of the Marquis of Bute, has been appointed to command the 6th Battalion of the Welch Regiment.[1] Born in 1883, Lord Ninian was the second son of the third Marquis of Bute, and received his education at Harrow and Oxford. After six months' travel, he joined the Scots Guards in 1905, and served with them for two years. Retiring, he began to interest himself in politics and agriculture, and most of his time was taken up in looking after his estate in Fife, and his mineral mines in Durham. A Conservative in politics, Lord Ninian contested Cardiff in January last year, but was not returned to Westminster until the December election. As a speaker he has plenty of dash and fire, and is a keen judge of human nature. He takes great interest in the improvement of the breed of Hungarian partridges, of which he places fifty brace on his estates every year." (FN)

15 April 1911

School Board election

Polling took place on Saturday, and the result was declared at eleven o'clock as follows.

Rev. J. Morrison, 433; Rev. J. Richardson, 421; Mr Gavin, 396; Mr Lumsden, 330; Mr Bonthrone, 309; Mr Horn, 172; Rev. Johnston, 148.

Unsuccessful: Mr Millar, 147; Mr Jackson, 125; Mr Rymer, 114. (FN)

---

[1] The 6th Battalion was a territorial one. Lord Ninian obtained the rank of Lieutentant-Colonel.

22 April 1911

Dispute between ministers

At the first meeting of the Falkland School Board the Rev. Mr Lyon Johnston moved that the standing orders be suspended in order that he might bring forward a personal matter.

Mr Bonthrone, acting chairman, asked him to indicate the nature of the question he wished to raise.

The Rev. Mr Johnston said he took exception to the Rev. Mr Morrison's statement that Lord Ninian Crichton-Stuart paid more in stipend to him than he paid in school rates.

The Rev. Mr Morrison objected to the question. It was out of order. Subject to certain qualifications, he admitted having made the statement.

Mr George Gavin said the only persons who knew the exact amount Lord Ninian paid in stipend were himself and Mr Johnston's agent.

Mr Morrison: You seem to have in your mind I received the information from a source from which I ought not to have received it. As a matter of fact I received no specific information.

Mr Gavin: In that case, it appears you made a random statement for electioneering purposes.

The Rev. Lyon Johnston said he would not pursue this matter further, and Mr Gavin said he would also allow the question to drop in the meantime.

Mr David Bonthrone gave notice of motion to the effect that at the next meeting he would call upon the Rev. Morrison to substantiate certain statements he made regarding the actions of the old Board, and of individual members thereof.

The Rev. Mr Morrison objected to that motion on the ground that Mr Bonthrone had made no specific charge. After discussion the notice of motion was minuted. (FFP)

22 April 1911

Brass Band

The Brass Band progresses amazingly under its new conductor, Mr Briggs, Kirkcaldy. Any one hearing it today, and comparing its performances with its former efforts of, say, 12 months ago, could not

50. Falkland Town Band, about 1910
Variously described as a brass band or a silver band.

fail to be struck with the great advance.

The members are enthusiastic and determined to excel. With such a unanimous and praiseworthy spirit of cohesion animating the bandsmen, it is highly desirable that a full measure of practical support should be forthcoming at the bazaar which is being organised for June 10th, in order to strengthen the funds. May we not look forward to a date not far distant, when there shall be a crack brass band in Falkland rivalling in excellence to other Fife prize bands whose beginnings were as humble as our own. (FN)

22 April 1911
Falkland Light Railway
Under the auspices of the Provost, Magistrates, and Town Council of Falkland, a well-attended meeting of the inhabitants was held in the Town Hall on Friday night. Various prominent citizens warmly supported the railway scheme in view of the proved advantages it holds for the whole district through which the line will pass. A strong Committee was formed for the purpose of canvassing the town of Falkland and district so that the comparatively small balance of capital required may be obtained as speedily as possible, and the

necessity of applying for any further extension of time avoided. The feeling of the meeting was that no one ought to withhold his support from the railway, and when it does come, step forward and take full advantage of the facilities provided by it. (FN)

22 April 1911

Golf

Mr James Cochrane, Lomondside, who has been Captain of the Club for the past season, has presented to the Club a beautiful silver medal for monthly competition on the occasion of his leaving Falkland for Glenfarg. Mr Cochrane is a keen golfer himself, and has done a great deal in the interests of the Club and for the advancement of the game. (FN)

29 April 1911

Cricket

The Falkland C.C. have commenced practice at the nets in preparation for the first match of the season which takes place tomorrow (Saturday) against Cupar 2nd XI, at Bonvil, Cupar. (FN)

29 April 1911

Coronation celebrations

At a public meeting held on Friday last in the Town Hall, a large and representative committee was appointed to act in co-operation with the Provost, Magistrates and Councillors, with a view to making the necessary arrangements for the celebration of the Coronation. It is proposed that there should be a public service in the Parish Church, a treat and games for the children, and a distribution of gifts to the old folks, on the Coronation day, and the committee will also take over the management of Falkland Market and Games, which will be postponed for one week from the usual date so as to be held on the Saturday after the Coronation. (FN)

6 May 1911

Glasgow exhibition

Of special interest to Fifers is Falkland Palace, in which the floral decorations are in keeping with the historic memories associated with the building. Only flowers that are admittedly old, such as wallflower and pansies, have been selected. The Bruce Shield and the Stuart Shield have been worked out very prettily and artistically in the floral design. [1] (FFP)

6 May 1911

Falkland Light Railway

The scheme of the introduction of a light railway between Falkland Road Station on the Dundee to Edinburgh line and Falkland has advanced another step and it is probable that the work will be commenced this year.

The movement, which began five or six years ago it may be remembered, got a push forward recently by an offer from Lord Ninian Crichton-Stuart MP of Falkland, who stated he would subscribe £1,000 if the rest of the capital was forthcoming, and also by the Messrs Jackson, manufacturers, who offered to take another £1,000 of shares. This substantial help reduced the amount of capital required to launch an undertaking to £1,500, and, as the result of a canvas of the district made by the Committee appointed at a public meeting, this amount has been further reduced, £600 being subscribed. Thus £900 of the necessary capital is still required, and the promoters are confident that this sum will be forthcoming within the next week or two, in order to avoid the necessity of a further extension order, which would involve more expenses, and application for which would have to be made by May.

The Light Railways Commissioners Order expires in October, and in order that there may be no delay in getting a start made with the work, negotiations are at present taking place with regard to the taking over the ground, over which the railway will travel. The line will be about 2½ miles long, and will link up Freuchie and Newton of Falkland, each place having a station. The cost of the undertaking is £20,000, and the commencing capital £10,000. The promoters have

---

[1] This is probably the Scottish Exhibition of National History, Art and Industry held between 3 May and 4 November 1911 in Kelvingrove Park. Attendance 9,369,375. Buildings were baronial in style and segmented into structures for "History" (modelled after Falkland Palace and built around the remains of the Kelvingrove Mansion).

powers to borrow £6,600. (FN)

13 May 1911

Memorial tablet in U.F. Church

A marble tablet has been erected this week in the vestibule of Falkland United Free Church in memory of the founders of the congregation. The tablet, which is inscribed with the names of the Rev. Thomas Burnside, Dr and Mrs Lyell, and twenty others, was a gift of Mr John Ronaldson Lyell of the Home Office, London, son of the late Dr Lyell, surgeon, Falkland. Mr Lyell, at the same time defrayed the cost of having the whole church redecorated.

A pathetic circumstance with the erection of the tablet is the fact that the original tablet was broken on the way from Italy, and ere the second was completed, there occurred the sudden death of the donor. In consequence of this, the arrangements for a formal unveiling ceremony have been cancelled at the request of Mr Lyell's family, but suitable reference to the event will be made at the forenoon service on Sunday first by the Rev. William Affleck, Auchtermuchty. (FN)

20 May 1911

U.F. Church memorial tablet

At the forenoon service on Sunday last the Rev. William Affleck MA, Auchtermuchty, occupied the pulpit of the United Free Church, and delivered a discourse with special reference to the memorial tablet which has been erected in the vestibule of the Church. He traced the history of the Scottish Church up to the time of the Disruption, and concluded by dealing more closely with the course of events at that period in the immediate neighbourhood, and the part played by those in whose memory the tablet is erected. The tablet, which is of Carrara marble, surrounded by a background of dove marble, is of a plain, but substantial design, and bears [*the inscription shown opposite*], the letters of which are inlaid with lead.

The work was executed by Mr Alexander Ramsay, monumental sculptor, Cupar. As will be seen from the inscription, the Rev. Thomas Burnside was minister of the congregation for 22 years. Dr Lyell, the father of the donor, was for many years surgeon in the parish, and by his kindly and genial manner endeared himself to his patients and the

IN MEMORIAM.

REVERED BRETHREN, WHO NOT POSSESSING MUCH OF THIS WORLD'S GOODS WERE
RICHLY ENDOWED WITH THE GRACE OF GOD, AND WERE ENABLED BY THE PRACTICE, AND
THROUGH THE POWER OF PRAYER NOBLY TO SHARE IN FOUNDING THE FREE CHURCH, FALKLAND,
AND MAINTAINING FOR YEARS THE ORDINANCES OF GOD'S HOUSE IN THIS SANCTUARY.
THE REV. THOMAS BURNSIDE, M.A., A DEVOUT PREACHER AND FAITHFUL PASTOR,
1845-1867, AND JANET ISDALE, HIS SPOUSE, A TRUE HELP-MEET.
JAMES LYELL, "THE BELOVED PHYSICIAN," AND ELIZABETH RONALDSON, HIS SPOUSE,
OF BLESSED MEMORY, AND HER BROTHER, JOHN RONALDSON, ADVOCATE.

MARGARET MOYES or DEAS.	WILLIAM KILGOUR.	JAMES REID.
PETER DICK.	RACHEL BROWN or MENZIES.	JAMES ROBERTSON.
HENRY DOWNIE.	WILLIAM PEGGIE.	MARGARET ROBERTSON.
ANDREW DUNCAN.	MARGARET GARDINER or PRESTON.	ROBERT STEVENS.
JOHN HENDERSON.	HELEN YOUNG or REEKIE.	DAVID WALLACE.
ROBERT JACKSON.	JOHN REEKIE.	JAMES WHYTE.

"LORD, I HAVE LOVED THE HABITATION OF THY HOUSE, AND THE PLACE WHERE THINE HONOUR DWELLETH"
IN CHRISTIAN REVERENCE, AND FILIAL PIETY, THIS TABLET IS ERECTED A.D. 1911, BY
JOHN RONALDSON LYELL, M.A., LONDON.

51. Memorial Tablet in the United Free Church

inhabitants in general; while Margaret Moyes or Deas was the mother of Lord Deas, the famous Scottish Judge, and of Sir David Deas, of the Indian Medical Service. The other names are mainly those of men and women in humble life, and it is as beautiful as it is rare to have such a memorial erected to commemorate their virtues. (FN)

26 May 1911

Accident at Falkland House

Dear Slacke,

I regret to have to write you about a most regrettable occurrence which took place last night at House of Falkland about 11 p.m., Duggan[1], the house joiner, after having had some supper, thought he would go to the engine house and see how the petrol stood, and while proceeding to do so he heard a crash as of something breaking about the basement. On making a search he first discovered a slipper and on proceeding further along, to his dismay, he found the house-

---

[1] The 1911 census records Jeremiah Duggan, Welsh-born carpenter and joiner, as living at the House of Falkland.

keeper, Mrs Birmingham, lying at the bottom of the basement stair where it emerges in the sub-basement near the joiner's shop. She was unconscious and was bleeding profusely from the head. I am sorry to say that lying beside her was a brandy bottle which was smashed in the fall. Andrew Toole was at once sent for Dr Jack, but owing to the condition of the woman and her weight it was most difficult to lift her, and Birrel and Pat Shields were sent for. Ultimately Dr Jack had to put five or six stitches in her head. She has a very severe scalp wound, but Dr Jack at first thought her injuries were very serious.

Duggan was in Falkland during the whole evening assisting with the *Cinderella* performance at the Girls Club, and he had no opportunity of seeing Mrs Birmingham after tea-time. I gather from him, however, that he saw her about supper time on his returning home about 10 o'clock. Duggan states that he never before observed her showing signs of liquor hitherto. In any case the truth must be told that when the accident occurred she was intoxicated. There can be no doubt that in going up to bed she had mistaken the turning at the foot of the chapel staircase and fallen right down the basement stairs. I have seen Dr Jack who says he will send the district nurse to call and dress the wound and that he sees no reason why the three maids in the house should not attend to her in the meantime. I am going up to the house after lunch when I shall ask the girls to do the best they can in the circumstances until I hear from you what is to be done.

Yours faithfully, George Gavin. (FEP)

27 May 1911

Things not going smoothly

With the School Board of Falkland, which includes three clerical members, things are not running smoothly, and a repetition of the scenes which characterised the first meeting was on Monday night only prevented by the timely intervention of Mr Lumsden, the Chairman, who appealed to the Board to co-operate in helping him to carry out the work in a smooth and harmonious manner.

The teaching of Roman Catholicism in the Public School is to a large extent responsible for the trouble, and more is likely to be heard of it at the next meeting of the Board. Rev. J. Morrison, at the close of Monday night's meeting, gave notice that he would move "that the

52. Falkland Public School
Photograph from the 1960s, but still showing the Victorian school building.

facilities granted by the late Board for the teaching of Roman Catholic doctrine in Falkland Public School be not continued after the summer holidays."

The minute of the last meeting bore that Mr David Bonthrone gave notice that at next meeting he would move that the Rev. Mr Morrison be asked to withdraw certain statements he made at public meetings, reflecting upon the work of the late Board and on individual members of the Board.

Rev. J. H. Morrison said he would like it made clear in the minutes that Mr Bonthrone's motion arose out of a statement Mr Johnston made, because when Mr Johnston and Mr Gavin said they would proceed with the matter Mr Bonthrone said he would do so.

Mr Bonthrone moved the adoption of the minutes, and Mr Gavin seconded. The motion was agreed to.

Mr Lumsden said the work of the last Board would bear inspection as well as that of the previous Board, and if any member had a personal grudge he had the civil courts to take action against Mr Morrison.

The Chairman appealed to Mr Bonthrone, who withdrew his motion.

Rev. Mr Morrison said he wished it to be distinctly understood that he did not for one moment admit that what he said in criticising the action of the Board or otherwise was improper.

Mr Bonthrone: Mr Morrison is just re-opening the discussion.

The Chairman: We don't consider it worthwhile going into the matter.

Mr Morrison: I am simply in the position as having been brought before the public as running amok. At the meetings, (he added) he spoke with care and consideration, and as the matter was to drop he was pleased to acquiesce. If any one had anything against him let him approach him, and he would meet him in a gentlemanly way.

The Chairman then proceeded with the ordinary business, which was disposed of without friction. (FFP)

29 May 1911

More problems at House of Falkland

Dear Captain Slacke,

I am afraid that matters at House of Falkland cannot go on long as they are. While Duggan and the Still Room maid told me after I had written you, that Mrs Birmingham had been taking drink on the two days previous to the accident, and that on the night before the Still Room maid had put her to bed, they did not tell me what I now hear, that tippling had been going on for about three weeks.

In any case the matter is now public talk and as Mrs Birmingham's influence or control over any maid servant is now gone it will be necessary to replace her at the earliest possible moment, or make some other arrangement. Duggan, I know, is not to be depended upon in the least and there is consequently no responsible person in charge of the house or of the maids. I do not know if Father Woods has written Lord Ninian about the chapel, as you know very strict regulations as to the care of the blessed sacrament were laid down when his Lordship got permission to reserve it and one of the important conditions is that a responsible Catholic housekeeper should be in the house to undertake this important duty. There is no such person and if Father Woods is worrying very much over the state of matters perhaps you could come here sooner than you intended and make arrangements for the proper charge of the house.

Yours faithfully, George Gavin. (FEP)

1 June 1911

New housekeeper

Dear Mr Gavin,

Thanks for letter of yesterday. I am sorry to inform you Lady Ninian has got English measles.

I am sorry I don't quite agree with you with regard to Mrs Liptrott, at any rate as a temporary measure. I particularly did not want to get an elderly responsible woman because, 1. It would mean getting a stranger, as I certainly would not have a local person, and 2. Because when the house was opened again she would be invidious. It is quite decided that when the house is opened again to have a cook/housekeeper instead of two people, as it is both cheaper and more satisfactory.

Yours Faithfully, Slacke. (FEP)

3 June 1911

Girls' Social Club: *Cinderella*

The first session of this Club was brought to a close on Thursday evening last week by a very successful performance of *Cinderella* by about twenty of the girls. The Club was instituted in the autumn of last year, largely through the efforts of Lady Ninian Crichton-Stuart, in order to provide a place of leisure for factory girls, where they might not only be taught to sew, but where amusement will be provided. The Club-rooms have been open every night during the winter months, and much good must have resulted to the girls. The committee of ladies, one of whom in turn was responsible for one night per week for the work of the Club, are to be congratulated on the quality of the work of the first season of the Club. The *Cinderella* performance, which took place in the Drill Hall, was witnessed by a large audience, and the performers acquitted with much credit to themselves, and to Miss Hilda Skene, Pitlour House, who trained them, and who personally superintended the staging and production of the piece. The performance showed that there is talent and ability, if properly directed, to produce something more pretentious next season.

At the close of the performance, prizes for sewing were distributed to a number of the girls by Mrs Livingstone, Lomondvale. An adjournment was then made to the Club-rooms where the girls were entertained at tea by Mrs Livingstone, the tables being nicely decorated with pot plants and cut flowers. That the President of the Ladies' Committee, Lady Ninian Crichton-Stuart, could not, on account of her absence in London, be present at the final meeting of the Club, was greatly regretted, but it is satisfactory to know that much good work has been achieved during the session of the Club. (FN)

3 June 1911

Brass Band bazaar

The astonishing progress which Falkland Brass Band has made since the advent of its new conductor, Mr Briggs, Kirkcaldy, not only demonstrates an ambition to procure for this band one day an honourable place in the final of the Scottish prize bands, but displays an inherent musical talent among its members which ought to find expression to its fullest limits, assisted and encouraged by the combined efforts of the entire community. Conceived in order to variegate the somewhat leaden outlook of a people condemned by their enforced isolation to all its accompanying disadvantages and inconveniences, and born amid the derision of many evil prophets who now enjoy its well-executed programmes, the band has, step by step, and after much labour and many discouragements, now reached that stage at which, through the medium of a bazaar to be held in the Public School on Saturday, 10th inst., future progress which lack of funds has placed in its way, has been removed. From reliable sources, information comes to hand that a large amount of valuable assistance in the shape of work and other donations has been obtained through the kindness of various ladies in Falkland. (FN)

3 June 1911

Cricket – Falkland v. Freuchie

Teams representing the above Clubs met at Falkland on Saturday. The home team ultimately ran out comfortable winners, though only by 19 runs. Falkland were sent in to bat on a bowler's wicket, and two good wickets were soon down when the score stood at six. Walter Venters, a lad of barely sixteen years, stopped the rot, and played the attack splendidly. H. Robinson and Hon. F. H. Tracy had both double figures. Freuchie opened disastrously, five wickets being down for 12 runs. W. Stark came to the rescue with his characteristic hard hitting, and played well for his 22, although he gave two possible chances before he had scored many. J. S. Allan, for Falkland, had the splendid analysis of six for 12, while W. M. Venters had two for 4. (FN)

Falkland
BRUCE ARMS, HOTEL.
(OPPOSITE PALACE)
BREAKFASTS DINNERS TEAS
At Moderate Charges.
Picnic Parties Catered For.
GARAGE, STABLING, CYCLES STORED.
Marquee can be erected for Large Parties
Phone No 8. W. Mason, Proprietor.

10 June 1911 (FN)

---

13 June 1911
Catholic teaching in the school
Letter to the Editor of Dundee Courier

Sir,

Be so good as allow me a few words on the extraordinary discussion on the 7th inst. at a meeting of the Falkland School Board anent granting the use of a school room to a Popish priest to teach Popery to Popish children.

The two U.F. ministers, Mr Morrison, Falkland, and Mr Richardson, Freuchie, deserve all praise for the stand they took in defence of our public schools not being invaded by Popish priests, and that for sectarian purposes.

Now, Rome condemns our public schools, and forbids her children attending them. She demands schools of her own, and that they be supported at the expense of the nation. She allows no public control or interference in any way, even to see His Majesty's Inspector's report, by School Boards.

Why, then, should this School Board grant permission to a Popish priest to invade the Public School, and thus interfere with the teaching staff, and become virtually one of the staff and teach what he pleases, and that independent of the School Board? And why do they not allow all different sects to invade the school with teachers of their own?

The chairman, Mr J. Lumsden, Freuchie, professes to be a Protestant, yet he declared Popery to be "a Christian religion as well as their own." Well, "by their fruits ye shall know them." Mr Lyon Johnston, declaring that to refuse permission to the Popish priest to teach in the Public School his children "would be one of the first steps towards the general secularising of the teaching of the Board schools of that parish," and that the spirit shown by the objectors savoured of medieval intolerance.

After that, Mr Editor, what are we coming to?

I am, Jacob Primmer,[1] The Manse, Kingseathill, Dunfermline. (DC)

17 June 1911
New assistant teacher
Miss Falconer, Blairgowrie, has been appointed assistant teacher in the Public School here. Her duties, which include the tasks of cookery and laundry work, will commence on the 1st of August. (FN)

17 June 1911
Golf
The final of the Lathrisk cup tournament was played off on Wednesday evening, between Mr Walter Peggie and Mr A. N. Fraser. After a close game, Mr Peggie proved to be the winner of the trophy by a margin of two holes. (FN)

17 June 1911
Help for band funds
The bazaar which was held in the Public School on Saturday in aid of the Falkland Brass Band was very successful in all respects. The

---

[1] Jacob Rimmer is described in a newspaper obituary as "a leader of the Protestant crusade against Romanism and Ritualism, a zealous advocate of Total Abstinence, and on all these subjects an incisive speaker."

weather was excellent, and there was a very large gathering of ladies and gentlemen who patronised the stalls and amusements to such a purpose that when the drawings came to be counted, it was found that the handsome sum of £92 12s 11d had been realised, and with subscriptions received brings to total amount to over £100.

No little disappointment and regret was expressed when the company gathered at the opening of the bazaar learned of the indisposition of Lady Ninian Crichton-Stuart, whose charming and gracious manner has endeared her to the good folks of Falkland. She intended being present with Lord Ninian who opened the bazaar. Three large stalls completely filled the school-room, and the display of goods and useful and ornamental articles would have done credit to a larger hall. The ladies had worked assiduously for the success of the band, and the substantial sum drawn was very gratifying. The bandsmen looked very smart in their gold embroidered tunics, and their selections during the afternoon in front of the building, and later in the playground at the back, where al fresco tea was served, were very pleasing.

Opening ceremony

Provost Jackson presided, and, in introducing Lord Ninian Crichton-Stuart, said they were all very sorry that her Ladyship had been unable to be present through indisposition. He was very pleased to be informed by Lord Ninian that her Ladyship was very much better and now making a rapid recovery. (Applause) He voiced the wish of everyone present when he expressed the hope that Lady Ninian would soon be restored to good health. (Applause) Lord Ninian, who was greeted with enthusiasm, expressed grateful thanks for the kind sentiments expressed by the Provost. He expected that her Ladyship would be able to come north by the month of August, and he was sure that the quiet of the country would make her all right again in a very short time. (Applause) He had every sympathy with the object of the bazaar.

A band was one of the best things a community could possess, and he was very glad that Falkland had such a good band. They had come up to his house and played one day, and he enjoyed it very much – so much that he hoped they would come soon again, and often. (Applause) He sincerely hoped that the bazaar would be a success, and that it would bring in a sufficiency of money, a thing which none of them could do without. (Laughter and applause) Dr Jack, in proposing a vote of thanks to Lord Ninian, said it had been a great trouble to his Lordship to come all the way from London, a distance, he believed, of 430 miles. And they all knew that just now Lord Ninian was very busy. They all knew him as a soldier, and he was now a legislator, having been elected Member of Parliament for Cardiff. They all congratulated him upon qualifying for the salary of £400 per annum which MPs were about to receive. (Laughter and applause) His Lordship, he noticed, had lately received another appointment, that of President of the Highland and Agricultural Society.

All these things made him a very busy man, but they knew that no matter how numerous and complex his duties were, Lord Ninian was always ready and willing to do what he could for the community of Falkland.

He therefore had much pleasure in calling upon the company to accord Lord Ninian a very hearty vote of thanks. (Applause)

Lord Ninian, in returning thanks, said Dr Jack's calculation was scarcely correct; it was 432 miles from London. (Laughter) Distance, however, made no difference to him, for he was always glad to be in Falkland. (Applause) (FN)

24 June 1911

Coronation celebrations

For some considerable time past, Falkland Town Council, along with a large representative Committee, made the necessary arrangements for a fitting celebration of the Coronation of King George the Fifth. These arrangements were successfully carried out. At 11.30 a.m. a procession was formed at the Public School, comprising the members of the Town Council and officials, the Parish Councillors and members of School Board, the brethren of St John's Lodge of Freemasons and of "Lomond Oak" Lodge of Free Gardeners, the Territorials and Boy Scouts, and the school children. The procession was marshalled by Messrs Dunbar and Gardner. As noon approached, the procession moved off, and proceeded by way of Pleasance and High Street to the Parish Church, where a joint service conducted by the Revs. A. L. Johnston and J. H. Morrison was held.

At 1.15 p.m. the children re-assembled in the school play-ground, when they were pre-sented with Coronation mugs, kindly provided by Mr J. L. Lumsden, Eden Valley House, Freuchie, and Chairman of the School Board. Thereafter the pro-cession re-formed and, headed by Falkland Brass Band, the com-pany marched to the Myre of Falkland, where the sports ground was situated. On arrival there, the children were pro-vided with pies and lemonade prior to the commencement of the games. A long list of events was gone through, there being keen competition in most of the

53. King George V and Queen Mary

Queen Mary made a long-remembered visit to Falkland in 1923.

items, which included: For the boys – Dispatch race, running long leap, 3-legged race, tug-of-war, wheelbarrow race, sack race, hop, step and leap, high jump, coat and boot race etc. For the girls – Skipping rope race, throwing ball, threading needle race, semi-circle ball race, egg and spoon race, hat trimming competition etc. The prizes were awarded to the winners at the close of the games.

At 5 o'clock the children partook of a sumptuous tea, and on dis-persing each one was made the recipient of a bag of sweets. In the evening, dancing was engaged in in the Myre to music supplied by the Town Band, and at 10.30 p.m. the bonfire, which had been erected on the top of the East Lomond by Mr Alex Fraser, joiner, was lit.

Provost Jackson acted as Convenor of the General Committee, and the secretarial duties were performed by Mr Alexander Anderson, Town Clerk, with Mr James Peggie as his assistant. The town was decorated with flags and bunting. (FN)

23 June 1911

Pleurisy

Letter to Lord Ninian

My Lord,

Yesterday morning, somewhat to my dismay I need not say, I read in the *Scotsman* that you were suffering from pleurisy. I immediately wrote a telegram of enquiry but found at the Post Office that, being Coronation Day, no telegraphic business was being done. On my way to the Post Office early this morning with the wire I received your Lordship's telegram to me from which I was sorry to learn that the newspaper paragraph was correct. I hope however, that the pleurisy is of a mild type and that you are not suffering from a serious form of it. I should very much like to know how you are keeping before I leave on Sunday evening and would be very greatly pleased to receive a wire either late on Saturday night or before 10 o'clock on Sunday morning.

Your obedient servant, George Gavin. (FEP) [1]

24 June 1911

Falkland fairness

The *Catholic Herald* of last Saturday, in an article on the recent discussion at Falkland School Board on the question of allowing Roman Catholic children the use of an unoccupied school-room during the religious instruction hour, says, under the heading of "Falkland Fairness":

"It was surprising to find the Rev. J. H. Morrison saying that the Roman Catholic children were not taught to think for themselves and that the Roman Catholic Church was opposed to modern education. Had Mr Morrison visited any of their Roman Catholic schools? If he had, he would not have made the statements he did make… The only proof the Rev. Mr Morrison could adduce for his statement regarding the influence of the priest on education was something that appeared in the *Encyclopaedia Britannica*. If this is the extent of the U.F. minister's knowledge concerning religion and education, we respectfully

---

[1] Gavin to reach London on Wednesday night or Thursday Morning. He took a room at the Westminster Palace Hotel, Victoria Street.

suggest that he has mistaken his vocation.

The decision of the Board shows the fair-minded spirit of the Falkland Board. The *Catholic Times* of the 16th inst. also refers to the incident and reports a reply made to Mr Morrison by the Rev. Father Henry Woods at a service in the chapel of Falkland Palace the previous Sunday, at which Lord Ninian Crichton-Stuart was present. The Catholic Church, he said, not only taught but insisted on the development of the mental faculties, and, in addition, she insisted on the development of all the faculties of our nature. ... That the Church was not opposed to modern education was shown by the fact that lately one of the Government Inspectors of a neighbouring county – Dr Dunn – stated that of the schools he had examined, the Catholic school revealed the highest tone, and likewise Mr Waddell, Government Inspector for Stirlingshire, incurred displeasure among some of the School Board teachers by praising the Catholic schools for their superior tone, discipline and general efficiency. Father Woods concluded with a quotation from the late Dr Carr, Head Inspector of Schools for Scotland, who, referring to the Notre Dame Training College in Glasgow, had said it was second to none in Scotland, and he was ashamed and sorry to admit that there was not even any second to compete with it. (FN)

1 July 1911
Coronation day
On the evening of the Coronation day, Provost Jackson entertained the members of the Town Council and others at a cake and wine banquet in the Bruce Arms, Hotel, at which the usual loyal toasts were heartily honoured.

Songs were contributed by members of the company, and altogether a very happy evening was spent.

In the burgh, which has a population of 830, there are no fewer than thirteen of the residents, natives of the town, who remember the celebration of the Coronation of Queen Victoria. (FN)

Juy 1st 1911
Market and games
Under the management of the Coronation Committee, the annual

market and games were held on Saturday afternoon. Falkland Brass Band was in attendance. Despite the inclemency of the weather, the sports were proceeded with, and the following is a list of prize-winners:

Open Events

Half-mile Race – J. Lister, Falkland; Ballantyne, Gateside; G. Fernie, Falkland.

Hop, Step and Leap – H. Black, Dundee; J. Craig, Falkland; G. Inglis, Edinburgh.

Vaulting – P. Rutherford, Strathmiglo; J. Lister; Henderson.

One Mile Race – Ballantyne; J. Lister; Ness, Leslie.

Putting the Ball – Watson, Ladybank; G. Inglis; D. McDonald, Cupar.

High Leap – H. Black; P. Rutherford; J. Craig.

100 Yards Race – G. Inglis; W. Middleton, Falkland; A. Dalrymple.

Local Events

Boys' Race (under 12) – R. Kennedy; T. Drysdale; D. Lister.

Girls' Race – M. Robertson; Alice Finnis; Mary Fleming.

Half-mile Race – G. Fernie; J. Lister; P. Robertson.

Boys' Race (under 16) – R. Kennedy; T. Drysdale; A. Smith.

Scouts' Race – A. Smith; A. Page; K. Calder.

Dancing Competition

Highland Fling – D. McLennan, Dundee; T. Dawson, Stirling; R. Condie, Cowdenbeath.

Sword Dance – D. McLennan; W. S. Mearns, Lochore; R. Condie.

Sailors' Hornpipe – W. S. Mearns; J. Roy; W. T. Lindsay, Dunfermline.

Irish Jig – W. T. Lindsay; W. S. Mearns; J. Roy. (FN)

2 August 1911

Lord and Lady Ninian returning

Dear Mr Gavin,

Lord and Lady Ninian are returning to Falkland by day on Wednesday 16th. On the night train of Monday 14th I am sending up Fisher with the Daimler Car and also the second footman, in order to start getting the place ready. On Tuesday night Liptrott, the odd man, Mrs Drysdale and the two maids from the kitchen will be going up with all the luggage, silver etc by the night train to Falkland Road

Station. I shall try and get the train stopped there, but I doubt if they will do it as there is a slow train just following the fast from Kirkcaldy. I am taking a railway van for the luggage. Mrs Slacke and myself will also go north by the same train. Would you please arrange that two large lorries of Ness's meet the 9.18 at Falkland Road on Wednesday morning and also Birrel's cart. If Ness has not got two large lorries we will have to have a large one, a small one, and also a farm cart, as there is a devil of an amount of luggage, also can you arrange that there are two extra men at the station with the lorries as the station staff is not enough to move all that heavy silver. I shall be sending up my clerk and a servant also by the same train. Unless they stop the express at Falkland Road Mrs Slacke and myself will get out at Kirkcaldy and motor from there.

Will you please see Mrs Liptrott and ask her to arrange that there is some breakfast for the servants when they arrive. That is for two men and three women. I shall arrange for breakfast for my own people at my own house. Would you please see what coal and wood there is in the house. I think it would be far the best plan to get the coal cellar filled before they return, and also to have both kinds of wood in the wood cellar, that is the long logs for the smoking room and the others.

Yours faithfully, Slacke (FEP)

14 August 1911

Flower show

The Falkland show was held, through the kindness of Lord Ninian Crichton-Stuart, within the charming grounds of the House of Falkland. Taken all over the show was the best that has ever been held at the historic burgh. The local brass band discoursed pleasant music during the afternoon.

Mr John Steedman gained the challenge bowl for the most points, and he also carried off the Mason Cup for the best basket of vegetables. Mr Macpherson, Milnathort, won the open rose competition, while Mr Lawrence Black was second. Mr William Young, Falkland Palace, carried off the first prize in the open sweet peas competition, and Mr Thomas Christie, Kinglassie was second.

The leading prize winners were: A. Bisset, John Fernie, John Steedman, Thomas Page, James Fleming, David Lawrie. Mrs Thomson, Freuchie; Miss Jeannie Smith and Miss Moyes.

The judges were: Messrs Laing, Pitlour; McNaughton, Leslie House; Dudgeon, Inchdairnie, and Grieve. Industrial work: Mrs Livingstone, Mrs John Jackson, Mrs Gavin and Miss Morgan.

The features were a fancy cycle parade and a marathon race to the top of the East Lomond Hill. The winners of the first and second prizes of the cycle parade were Master Aeneas Gavin and Miss Margaret Gavin, Falkland Palace respectively.

For the Lomond Marathon race eight started. The hill is 1,471 feet high, and the course was marked by Boy Scouts who were stationed at intervals from the show park to the summit. George Fernie won the race in the splendid time of twenty-one minutes. (DC)

15 August 1911
Baby Ismay falls from window
Letter from 32 Trevor Square, London[1]
Dear Mr Gavin,

Yesterday morning when they were loading the baggage on the van, the nurse had tied the baby in the long chair while she went into the next room about the packing. The baby wriggled out of the chair, climbed up on the windowsill and fell out from the upstairs window. The doctor was called at once and proclaimed that as far as he could see there was no serious damage done, but of course it will be impossible to tell for certain for two days. The baby has slight concussion.

Yours Faithfully, Capt. Slacke. (FEP)

19 August 1911
Accident to Lord Ninian's daughter
As reported in the Morning Post

While looking out of the window of an upstairs apartment at Beechgrove, Sunninghill, on Monday morning, Lord and Lady Ninian Crichton-Stuart's daughter, about eighteen months old, fell out, and was picked up severely bruised but otherwise apparently

---

[1] 32 Trevor Square was Captain Slacke's London home. While in Falkland he and his wife stayed at a house in the Stables.

unhurt. She fell a distance of from 15 to 17 feet. (FN)

26 August 1911

Illness of Lord Ninian Crichton-Stuart

Lord Ninian Crichton-Stuart MP, who has suffered another relapse, was stated to be rather better on Wednesday morning. His doctors have ordered him to undergo a period abroad, and it is expected that he will be leaving for the Continent in about a week's time.[1] (FN)

16 September 1911

Popular lectures

On Monday evening a meeting of Falkland Popular Lecture Committee was held in the Liquorstone Temperance Hotel, when it was resolved to proceed with another course of lectures during the coming winter. A provisional list of entertainments and lectures was drawn up, and the session promises to be up to the usual standard. (FN)

16 September 1911

Presentation

On the occasion of his leaving Falkland Public School, where he has been assistant master for the past two years, to take up his new duties at Gorebridge, Mid-Lothian, Mr George Gardner was made the recipient of a handsome dressing-case, travelling bag, and walking stick as a farewell gift from the members of Falkland Cricket Club, of which he was the energetic Hon. Secretary and Treasurer. Dr J. G. Jack, President of the Cricket Club, made the presentation, and in a few appropriate and well-chosen words, referred to the very cordial relationship which had existed between the members of the Club and Mr Gardner, whose genial disposition and force of character had made him many friends in Falkland and district. Dr Jack expressed the hope that continued success and prosperity would attend him, and that he would yet attain a high position in his profession.

Mr Gardner, in returning thanks for the beautiful presents with which he had been honoured, said that he felt very much the severing of his connection with Falkland in view of the many friendships he

---

[1] Lord Ninian went to a spa in Normandy with thermal baths.

had made in the place. He hoped these would be continued, as, although he was removing to another sphere of activity, he would always cherish pleasant memories of his stay in the Royal and ancient burgh. Mr Gardner also received, as a parting gift from the Falkland Troop of Boy Scouts, of which he was assistant Scout Master, a framed photographic enlargement of a group of the Scouts taken recently. Mr Deas, who was appointed in room of Mr Gardner, commenced duty in the school on Monday. (FN)

14 October 1911

Sermon

Owing to the indisposition of the Rev. A. Lyon Johnston, the pulpit of the Parish Church was occupied by the Rev. J. H. Morrison of the U.F. Church on the evening of Sunday last. (FN)

14 October 1911

Golf

The monthly medal was won on Saturday afternoon by Mr George Robertson, and as this was the last competition for the season, Mr Robertson will be custodian of the trophy during the winter. (FN)

14 October 1911

Y.M.C.A.

The winter session of the Y.M.C.A.was commenced in the Town Hall on Sabbath morning when a report of the Conference recently held in Arbroath was given by Mr Alexander Anderson, who attended as delegate from the Falkland Association. (FN)

14 October 1911

Concert

The concert arranged in aid of the Falkland Girl's Club was held in the Drill Hall on Saturday evening when there was a very good turn-out. The audience was treated to a very fine programme ably sustained by The Lady Ninian Crichton-Stuart, Mrs R. C. Slacke, Falkland; Miss A. Beveridge, Kettle; Miss Biggar, Edinburgh; Mlle. Yvonne Descamps, Kirkcaldy; Mrs Farquharson, Edinburgh; Captain R. C. Slacke, Mr A. J. Christie, Glasgow; Dr Farquharson, Edinburgh;

and Mr R. Taylor, Auchtermuchty. (FN)

21 October 1911

Social

Under the auspices of the Falkland Parish Church Women's Guild, a very enjoyable social meeting was held in the Drill Hall on Friday evening. The Rev. Charles Fraser, Freuchie, occupied the chair in the absence of the Rev. A. L. Johnston, and addresses were given by Miss Wingate, Edinburgh, a member of the Committee of the Women's Missionary Association, Mrs Kinnear, Dundee, the Rev. Hugh Brown, Strathmiglo Parish Church, and Mr James Donaldson, banker. Various solos were contributed during the evening, and two anthems were rendered by the choir. (FN)

27 October 1911

Funeral of Rev. Johnston

Falkland mourns the death of the minister of the parish, the Rev. A, Lyon Johnston The sad event took place on Sunday after a fortnight's illness, and his remains were laid to rest yesterday in the New Cemetery.

It is thirteen years ago since Mr Johnston came to Falkland as colleague and successor to the late Rev. John Barrack. He was a kindly and broad-minded minister, and the esteem in which he was held was demonstrated by the huge concourse of people who attended the obsequies. He was only forty-nine years of age.

The service at the manse, attended by his relatives, was conducted by the Rev. Charles Fraser, Freuchie, and the Rev. W. H. Porter, Cults.

About half-past one o'clock the oaken casket containing the remains of the deceased was conveyed to the church. As it was borne to the front of the pulpit the large congregation, which included many members of the Presbytery of Cupar, and all the public bodies of the Royal Burgh, remained upstanding. The service was brief but impressive, and was conducted by the Rev. W. J. Jamieson, Logie, moderator of the Presbytery, assisted by the Rev. A. E. Gordon, Kettle, and the Rev. J. H. Morrison, U.F. Church, Falkland.

It included the singing of the hymn, "Now the labourer's task is o'er," and the playing on the organ of the "Dead March" from *Saul*.

The funeral cortege was the largest ever seen in Falkland. Immediately following the hearse was a car laden with floral tributes. At the graveside the Rev. Alex Alison, Abdie, performed the committal service.

The pall-bearers were: Mr Andrew Johnston, Selkirk (brother); Mr Currie, Cambusnethan (father in law); Mr John Mason, Alloa (brother in law); Dr William Currie, Edinburgh; Mr D. Tinto, Cambusnethan; Mr Robert Millar, Falkland; and Mr Brown, Edinburgh. (DC)

28 October 1911

Lord Ninian Crichton-Stuart

Lord Ninian Crichton-Stuart MP, who is on a visit to his constituency at Cardiff, has had a return of illness, and was unable to attend a meeting under the auspices of the Cardiff Branch of the Navy League. He caught a chill on his way South and has had a recurrence of his former trouble, pleurisy. Latest accounts bear that he is showing signs of improvement. (FN)

28 October 1911

School Board officer resigns

A meeting of Falkland School Board was called for on Wednesday night to receive the resignation of the attendance officer, Mr Baxter, who has performed the duties for the past sixteen years. Mr Baxter, the chairman (Mr J. L. Lumsden) explained, was retiring on account of ill health. It was agreed to advertise for a successor. (FN)

1 November 1911

Lord Ninian's health

Dear Mr Gavin,

I am sorry to inform you that Lord Ninian has had rather a set back. He was very seedy all day yesterday and had a great deal of pain, which has pulled him down a lot. She, however, is worrying a lot about him and cannot sleep at night.

Yours faithfully, Slacke. (FEP)

1 November 1911

Lord Ninian's health

Dear Captain Slacke,

Many thanks for sending me so many wires with the latest news as to his Lordship's condition.

I am sending round these bulletins by telephone and by messenger to all interested daily. There is, as you can imagine intense anxiety here to know the latest bulletins, and I hear that his Lordship's illness was the sole topic of conversation at Cupar Market yesterday.

From the letter that my wife has from Mrs Slacke I gather that the crisis will pass today.

Yours faithfully, George Gavin. (FEP)

4 November 1911

Illness of Lord Ninian Crichton-Stuart

It was stated at Cardiff Castle on Tuesday night that Lord Ninian Crichton-Stuart MP, after a restless night on Monday, had had a good sleep, and during the day an improvement set in, which was being well maintained. (FN)

11 November 1911

Lord Ninian Crichton-Stuart

The news concerning Lord Ninian Crichton-Stuart's health continues favourable. He is still, however, far from well and complete recovery will, it is expected, take a considerable time.

11 November 1911

Trees blown down at House of Falkland

Sunday's storm has left sad traces in the wooded grounds surrounding the House of Falkland. Not only have many ornamental trees been laid low, but a most regrettable loss has been sustained in the complete destruction of one of the fine old lime trees forming the beautiful line on the north side of the approach to the house. (FN)

18 November 1911

Concert

Falkland Popular Lecture Committee opened the session with a splendid concert by members of the Choral Society and arranged for by Mr R. Douglas, Cupar. The chair was occupied by the Rev. J. H. Morrison, and there was a large and appreciative audience. A very full and entertaining programme was given. On the motion of Mr Morrison, a very hearty vote of thanks was accorded to the ladies and gentlemen who had so willingly come from Cupar and given such a fine entertainment. (FN)

18 November 1911

Town Council supper

On Saturday evening, Provost Jackson entertained the members of the Town Council, officials, and a few friends at supper in the Bruce Arms, Hotel. Mr Mason provided an excellent spread, to which full justice was done. Thereafter the toast-list was gone through, the loyal toasts, "The King and Queen", and "The members of the Royal Family" were proposed by the Provost and were heartily responded to. The other toasts were: "Town Council", proposed by Mr J. Dunbar and replied to by the Provost; "The New Councillors", proposed by Bailie Drysdale and responded to by Councillor J. W. Jackson; "The Convenors of Committees" by the Provost and replied to by Councillor Angus; "The Outside Friends", proposed by Councillor Jackson and replied to by George Gavin; and "Provost Jackson" by Councillor Robertson. During the evening songs, recitations etc., were given by members of the company, Councillor Ness acting as accompanist. Altogether a very enjoyable time was spent and the Provost was heartily thanked for the splendid manner in which he had entertained those present. (FN)

22 November 1911

Lord Ninian's health

Dear Mr Gavin,

I am glad to say that Lord Ninian had a good night last night and I think is a bit better. It is really very hard to say from day to day how he is. The lungs are still far from being all right, but one hopes they are really improving.

He has moved this afternoon into another room, which I trust will do him some good, as this one he was in was very bad for him. The roof goes into a point like a tent, which was very bad for him as one cannot ventilate it, and it has three outside walls also, so when the windows were all open he was almost blown out of bed.

Yours faithfully, Slacke. (FEP)

25 November 1911

Lecture

On Wednesday evening, the Rev. J. H. Morrison delivered a missionary lecture on "Jamaica" in the United Free Church. The attendance was very good, and the lecture, which was beautifully illustrated with lime-light views, was interesting and instructive. The meeting closed with votes of thanks to Mr Morrison and to Messrs Grieve and Miller for manipulating the lantern. (FN)

28 November 1911

Lord Ninian's health

Dear Mr Gavin,

I think on the whole, now that we may say Lord Ninian is getting on pretty well, and although his progress is slow, I hope that means it is all the more permanent.

Of course, it is impossible yet to say whether his lungs will be permanently affected, but personally I think from what they tell me he will be none the worse in that respect once he is really over this illness. The doctors say however that probably for the rest of his life he will be troubled a bit with phlebitis, as there is such a lot of it his mother's family.

Yours faithfully, Slacke (FEP)

2 December 1911

Parish Church vacancy

On Monday evening, a meeting of the congregation of the Parish Church was held when a Committee was elected to deal with the applications for the vacant charge. Provost Jackson was appointed convenor. (FN)

2 December 1911

Lecture

On Friday evening, the second lecture of this winter's course was given in the Drill Hall by Mr J. Armstrong Barry, Dundee, his subject being "Alexander Smith, Poet and Essayist." Mr Donaldson, Bank House, was in the chair. (FN)

16 December 1911

Whist

On the evening of Wednesday last week, a match was engaged in between the Falkland and Markinch Clubs, and resulted in a win for the former by six points. (FN)

16 December 1911

Literary Society

A meeting convened by Miss Anderson was held at Allan Park on Thursday evening last week, when it was decided to form a Literary Society. A full and varied programme was drawn up, and the session should prove interesting and instructive. (FN)

16 December 1911

Lectures

On Friday evening, the third lecture of this winter's course was given in the Drill Hall by Mr Robert Kinmont MA, FEIS, Tullibody, his subject being "A short ramble on the Continent", which he treated in a racy and enjoyable manner. Mr Alexander Anderson occupied the chair, and his motion for a vote of thanks to the lecturer was heartily responded to. (FN)

23 December 1911

Political meeting

On Wednesday evening, Colonel Sprot addressed a public meeting held in the Drill Hall, when he dealt with the Insurance Bill. (FN)

23 December 1911

Boy Scouts

On Saturday, the members of the local troop of Boy Scouts, who attend the Y.M.C.A. were entertained at tea at Bank House by Scoutmaster and Mrs Donaldson. During the evening, each of the boys was presented with a copy of "Tom Brown's Schooldays" for regular attendance at the Y.M.C.A. morning meeting. On the motion of Assistant Scoutmaster Venters, a very hearty vote of thanks was accorded to the host and hostess. (FN)

30 December 1911

Concert

In connection with the popular lecture course, a splendid concert was held in the Drill Hall on Friday evening, when the Misses Mather from Edinburgh, submitted one of their now famous programmes to a large and appreciative audience. Mr J. G. Simpson, also from Edinburgh, rendered a number of songs in a very efficient manner. On the motion of Provost Jackson, who occupied the chair, a very hearty vote of thanks was accorded to the artistes for the excellent entertainment. (FN)

1912

6 January 1912

Falkland Light Railway Orders

There was issued on Monday night an Order made by the Light Railway Commissioners and confirmed by the Board of Trade extending the period limited by the Falkland Light Railway Orders, 1906 and 1909, for the compulsory purchase of land and for the completion of the railway and works thereby authorised. (FN)

27 January 1912

New shepherd on Falkland Estate

Mr David Weir, who for the past few years has been shepherd at Galalaw, and received so much credit for the way in which he brought forward Mr Smith's sheep for the record sale in September last, has been engaged to take charge of Lord Ninian Crichton-Stuart's choicely bred young flock at Falkland.

Lord Ninian has only been a Border Leicester breeder for little more than eighteen months, but in that time he has laid the foundation of what ought in time to be a high-class and even famous flock. It will be remembered that he was the purchaser at Galalaw of the famous ram His Majesty, the price being the big one of £140 for a sheep in his fourth year. He has also some very worthy representatives of other strains in his flock. Mr Weir is well-known to be one of the most expert hands at bringing out sheep in the trade. He has had a first-class training at Galalaw, and under his management it will be a wonder if the Falkland estate flock does not go steadily ahead and

374

become widely known. Mr Gavin, Lord Ninian Crichton-Stuart's factor at Falkland and all concerned are to be congratulated on an engagement which is so promising and so interesting from the point of view of the breed. (FN)

3 February 1912

Assault on Mr Bonthrone

At Cupar Sheriff Court on Thursday, three young men hailing from Falkland – Henry Birrell, Alex. Hamilton,[1] and Mungo Robertson – appeared before Sheriff Armour Hannay, charged with having on 27th January, assaulted Mr David Bonthrone, Newton of Falkland, on the public road near the school at Falkland. Each pleaded guilty, but denied having kicked Mr Bonthrone.

Mr A. E. Grosset, solicitor, Cupar, appeared on behalf of the accused, and stated that on the occasion on which the incident occurred, a friend of these young men was going away to New Zealand, and they had been having a farewell spree, and a good deal more drink than was good for them, when they unfortunately came across Mr Bonthrone. One of them in a more or less playful manner, tripped him, and then there was more or less a fight between Mr Bonthrone and the lad, Mr Bonthrone naturally retorting and the lads going to the assistance of their comrade.

The Fiscal stated that Mr Bonthrone was returning home from Falkland. He tried to pass them on the road, when one of the three kicked him from behind. He observed that the action was a very cowardly thing to do whereupon they fell upon him. The scuffle continued for about one hundred and so yards along the road, until Mr Bonthrone pulled into Dr Jack's premises. Sheriff Armour Hannay stated he regarded the case an exaggerated case of hooliganism. That sort of thing must be put down with a firm hand, and they would be fined £2 or twenty days imprisonment. (FN)

---

[1] Alex Hamilton lived in Cross Wynd, and had worked for Chris Brunton the butcher. He emigrated to New Zealand aged 19. In WWI he enlisted in the Canterbury Regiment of the NZ Expeditionary Force and was killed in France on 14 July 1916. He is commemorated on the Falkland memorial.

3 February 1912

Cantata

On Saturday evening, this choir of the United Free Church rendered the cantata *The Shepherd King* in the church to a large and appreciative audience. The solos were beautifully sung by Miss Horne, Miss Duncan, Dunshalt, and Mr Robert Morgan, and a duet by Miss Duncan and Mr Morgan was very well done. Quartets were sung by members of the choir, and these along with the choruses reflected great credit on the conductor, Mr William Burgon. Miss Bryce officiated at the organ in her usual efficient manner.

On the call of the Rev. J. H. Morrison, a very cordial vote of thanks was given. (FN)

3 February 1912

Curling

The members of the Club have enjoyed a few days curling both on the artificial and deep water ponds. A match was arranged with Stratheden Club for Wednesday, but before the game had proceeded very far, it had to be abandoned owing to the ice giving way. (FN)

February 3rd 1912

Falkland Band

Falkland band, under the very able supervision of Messrs Schofield and Briggs, respectively Secretary and bandmaster, are assiduously running a series of Saturday evening dances that are providing a great gain to the funds. Mr Briggs is making a vast difference in the young players, and when summer arrives Falkland Burgh Band will be able to hold their own with any engagement band. (FFP)

10 February 1912

The late Mr John Sheriff

It was with great regret that many here and elsewhere heard in the beginning of the week that Mr John Sheriff, writer, had died at a nursing home in Dundee on Sunday morning. Of a kindly disposition, Mr Sheriff was long a faithful assistant in the office of the late Mr Charles Gulland, Town Clerk, and was the trusted adviser of many clients in need of legal counsel. He was unmarried, and has died at the age of

64. A sister, Miss Euphemia Sheriff, Bruce Buildings, survives him.
(FN)

10 February 1912
At Home
An "At Home" was held at Bank House on Saturday evening, when Mr and Mrs Donaldson entertained the choir of the United Free Church. After tea was served, songs and recitations were given by members of the company, and games were engaged in. A most enjoyable evening was brought to a close by according a hearty vote of thanks to the host and hostess for their kindness and by the singing of "Auld Lang Syne". (FN)

10 February 1912
Curling
The competitions for the Club trophies were played off on Saturday last and resulted as follows:

First Points Competition – 1st medal, Walter Peggie; 2nd medal, Gordon Sturrock; 3rd medal, David Bonthrone; 4th medal, George J. Lumsden.

Second Points Competition – Biscuit box, David Bonthrone; mug, Gordon Sturrock.

The drawing medal was won by William Bonthrone after a tie with Walter Peggie, who won the Lathrisk Bowl for the best aggregate. (FN)

27 February 1912
To let
Commodious House, in High Street, Falkland, with Stable, Outhouses and Large Garden. Apply Alex. Anderson, Solicitor, Falkland.
(FN)

17 February 1912
Entertainment
The course of lectures was brought to a successful close on Friday last, when a cinematograph exhibition was given in the Drill Hall. The special feature was the "Courierscope" which gave the audience an idea of the work entailed in the production of a daily newspaper. (FN)

17 February 1912

Entertainment for School Children

On Thursday evening last week, the children attending the Public School at Falkland were entertained to a treat which but for an epidemic of whooping cough would have taken place at Christmas. It was only last week that the children could return to school in sufficient number to enable the entertainment to be given.

To the number of 230, they marshalled at the school, and under the direction of the teacher marched to the Drill Hall where a sumptuous tea was served. Besides the children, there was a representative gathering of people interested in the school, among those present being: Mr J. L. Lumsden, Eden Valley House, Freuchie, chairman of the School Board; Rev. Henry Woods, Falkland; Rev. Charles Fraser, Freuchie; Mr and Mrs Gavin, Falkland Palace; Mr and Mrs Dunbar, the School House, Falkland; Mr and Mrs Donaldson, Bank House, Falkland; Mrs Robertson; Mrs O'Flahertie; Miss Cochrane; Mrs Falconer; Mr Alan Marshall; Mr David Deas etc.

After grace by the Rev. Charles Fraser, and the children had done every justice to the purveying of Mr Mason of the Bruce Arms, whose tastefully decorated tables were much admired, Mrs Gavin caused a thrill of amusing entertainment among the little folks by lighting the Christmas tree which was laden with handsome toys and otherwise beautifully adorned, and by handing a gift to every child present. Provost Jackson, in a few remarks at the close, said that when Lord Ninian was lying seriously ill at Christmas, he had not forgotten the children of Falkland, and they (the children) were not to forget him. (Applause) He asked them to give three cheers for his Lordship and let them be as loud as they might be heard in Ceylon[1] (Laughter and loud cheers) On leaving the Hall, each child was presented with a packet of sweets and an orange. (FN)

24 February 1912

New minister

Voting took place on Wednesday for a minister for the Parish of Falkland, with the following results.

---

[1] Lord and Lady Ninian had planned to be in Ceylon, but didn't get there.

Rev. J. K. Russell: 204.

Rev. A. F. Scott: 62.

Rev. Hugh Shirlaw: 43.

Mr Russell, who had a clear majority over the other candidates, was declared elected.

The new minister is the son of Mr Russell, schoolmaster, Glendevon, and is a graduate of St Andrews University, where he had a brilliant career. He took his MA degree with first class honours in economic science, in April 1904, and his BD with distinction in divinity, Dutch history, Hebrew, and Biblical criticism, in 1907. He was also awarded the Barry Scholarship, which is the highest prize St Andrews gives.

54. Rev. J. K. Russell

He was licensed by the Auchterarder Presbytery in April 1908 and acted as assistant to the Rev. A. M. McLean, Peebles, until the end of 1911. (FFP)

24 February 1912

Literary Club

At a meeting of the Literary Club, held at Allan Park on Saturday evening, Miss Anderson read an excellent paper on "Side Lights, or Life in the Highlands". (FN)

24 February 1912

Dance

The annual assembly of the "Lomond Oak" Lodge B.O.A.F.G. was held in the Drill Hall on Friday, when there was a good turn-out of the brethren and friends. A cordial welcome was extended to those present by Brother Geo. Hardie, WM, and dancing was engaged in from 9.00 p.m. till the small hours of Saturday morning, and altogether a very enjoyable time was spent. (FN)

2 March 1912

School Board

At a meeting of the School Board of the parish, held on Monday evening, Mr Alexander Anderson, solicitor, was appointed Clerk and Treasurer in succession to the late Mr John Sheriff. (FN)

16 March 1912

Cricket Club dance

On the evening of Friday last, the members of the village Cricket Club held their annual dance in the Drill Hall. There was a very good turnout. To excellent music supplied by Messrs Richardson and Berry, the "Grand March" commenced at 8.30 p.m., and thereafter a splendid programme of dances was engaged in. During the evening, songs were sung by Miss Beveridge, Kingskettle; and Messrs A. Grieve and J. Venters.[1] The purveying was in the hands of Mrs Hardie. (FN)

30 March 1912

Whist

Cupar whist players paid a visit to Falkland Club on Thursday of last week when the home players won by 9 points. (FN)

30 March 1912

Town Council

At a meeting of the Town Council on Tuesday, it was resolved to adopt the section of the Burgh Police (Scotland) Acts dealing with places of public refreshment.[2] (FN)

30 March 1912

Literary Society

The last meeting of the session was held at Allan Park on Monday evening, when Mr Robert McHarg submitted the manuscript maga-

---

[1] The Venters family, stalwarts of the Cricket Club, had a grocer's and photographer's shop in Horsemarket.

[2] The Burgh Police (Scotland) Act, 1911 allowed for the regulation of hours when "places of public refreshment" could be open.

zine of which he was Editor. The contributions by the members were very good, and were thoroughly enjoyed by those present. The Society has carried through the first winter's programme very successfully, and such a result is in a great measure, due to the efforts of Miss Anderson, the secretary. (FN)

6 April 1912
Presentation
On the occasion of leaving to take up a situation in Edinburgh, Mr John Collins jnr, who for the past years has been in the Town Clerk's Office, was presented with a handsome Gladstone bag and a letter wallet as a parting gift from his fellow clerks in the office, and the staff of British Linen Bank, Falkland, as a token of their good wishes for his future success. (FN)

17 April 1912
Minister ordained
Cupar Presbytery met in Falkland Parish Church today, and ordained and inducted the Rev. G. K. Russell[1] MA, BD, assistant, Hamilton, to be minister of Falkland Parish in succession to the late Rev. Lyon Johnston.

The service was conducted by the Rev. Hugh Brown, Strathmiglo, and the Rev. Robert Frizelle, Cupar, delivered the addresses to the minister and congregation. The settlement of the Rev. Mr Russell was a most harmonious one. (DET)

20 April 1912
Y.M.C.A. presentation
At the morning meeting on Sunday, Mr John Collins was the recipient of a beautiful fountain pen as a token of the best wishes of his fellow-members on the occasion of his leaving for Edinburgh. Mr Walter Peggie, president, made the presentation, and Mr Collins suitably acknowledged the gift. (FN)

---

[1] Other sources give him as "J. K. Russell".

20 April 1912
Concert
An entertainment in aid of the funds of the local Troop of Boy Scouts was held in the Drill Hall on Saturday – the Rev. J. H. Morrison in the chair. Scoutmaster Donaldson gave a report of the year's work, and a long and varied programme was thereafter proceeded with. Songs were contributed by Miss Horne, Miss Auchterlonie, St Andrews, and Mr J. Venters, Miss Pirie, Dundee, acting as accompanist. Displays of ambulance work, semaphore signalling, and physical drill were given by the boys and an exhibition of Indian club swinging by Mr T. Watson, Freuchie. An interesting feature of the evening was the presentation of prizes to the Scouts for regular attendance and ambulance work. Mr T. Watson was made the recipient of a set of brushes in recognition of his training the boys in the physical drill. On the call of the Chairman, a hearty vote of thanks was given to all who had contributed to the evening's enjoyment. (FN)

11 May 1912
Cricket
Members of the cricket team travelled to Kinross on Saturday, and after a slow game on the part of the home team, the result was a draw, viz.: Kinross, 69; Falkland, 33 for 5 wickets. Springfield XI pay their first visit to Scroggie tomorrow (Saturday). (FN)

11 May 1912
Communion
The half-yearly communion was celebrated in both Parish and United Free Churches on Sunday. Preparatory services were held in both churches on Friday, with the Rev. J. K. Russell and the Rev. Mr Wilson of Rathillet, occupied the respective pulpits. At the thanksgiving services on the Sunday evening, the Rev. A. O. Taylor, Glendevon, preached in the Parish Church, while the Rev. J. P. Berry, Ceres, officiated in the United Free Church. (FN)

11 May 1912
Golf
The monthly medal competition took place on Saturday afternoon,

and for the second time this season, Mr Alex. Anderson proved the successful competitor. After the first round, tea was tastefully served in the Clubhouse by Mrs Donaldson, assisted by Misses Cochrane and Falconer. (FN)

1 June 1912

Band of Hope

The usual treat given to the members of the Band of Hope in connection with the Parish Church, took place on Friday last in the Drill Hall. The Rev. J. K. Russell BD presided, and after a sumptuous tea, a programme of songs and recitations were gone through. The children enjoyed the evening's entertainment very much (FN)

8 June 1912

Police-Constable William Calder

Police-Constable William Calder, who has been stationed at Falkland for the past five years, has been promoted to be Acting Sergeant at Leven. (FN)

6 July 1912

Prizes

On Sabbath, at the close of the afternoon service, the children attending the Parish Church Sunday School, who had regularly attended during the past year, were presented with book prizes. (FN)

6 July 1912

Picnics

The Sunday schools of the Church and United Free Churches held their annual picnics on Saturday. The children were driven in carts as usual – the former to Wellfield and the latter to Pitlour. The weather conditions were very favourable during the afternoon, and with the accustomed games and races, a very happy and enjoyable afternoon was spent by both parties. (FN)

27 July 1912

Accident

As Robert Laing, son of Mr Robert Laing, ploughman, Falkland Wood, was turning into the Strathmiglo Road from the Castle-Shots Road, on his bicycle, he collided with a motor car belonging to Mr A. N. Thomson, manufacturer, Strathmiglo, and as a result, he sustained a fractured ankle. He was at once taken in the car to Dr Jack's and after the injured limb had been attended to, he was removed to his home at Falkland Wood. No blame is attributed either to the driver of the car or to the boy. (FN)

17 August 1912

Flower show

The annual exhibition and competition of Falkland and District Horticultural Society was held in the grounds of House of Falkland on Saturday.

Rain fell heavily just before two o'clock, and although the weather improved during the afternoon, there were some heavy showers, and the presence of so much dampness on the ground was against a large turnout. Yet it was an interesting little show, the quality of the exhibits being really good. The prize-winners last year were again well to the fore, and seemed to be quite determined to maintain the reputation already earned. Particularly was this noticeable in the case of Mr John Steedman, the winner of the Jackson challenge bowl last year, for he won it this year again with a comfortable margin. The Mason cup also fell to the same exhibitor for the best collection of vegetables, and he won the walking-stick for most points in pot plants.

Boy Scouts from Falkland, Freuchie, Auchtermuchty and Strathmiglo were present and gave numerous displays. A programme of sports were also carried through by them. The boys were inspected by the Hon. R. Preston,[1] Royal Artillery. Falkland Brass Band played selections during the afternoon. (FN)

---

[1] The Hon. R. Preston was Lady Ninian's brother, known as "Dick". He was to end WWI as a Lieut Col with DSO and Bar – he was recommended for the Victoria Cross.

24 August 1912

Co-operative Society

The half-yearly meeting of Falkland Equitable Co-operative Society was held in the Society's rooms on Saturday, when a very satisfactory report was submitted.

The sales for the half-year exceed those of the corresponding period last year by the sum of £200; and the profit for the period surpasses any former year.

The membership and the share capital also show a considerable increase. (FN)

14 September 1912

Fire

On Tuesday afternoon, an outbreak of fire occurred at the Bruce Arms, Hotel, as a result of which a stack of hay belonging to Mr W. A. Mason was destroyed. The fire is said to have been caused by a little boy who had been playing with matches in the neighbourhood of the stack. (FN)

14 September 1912

Unionist meeting

Under the auspices of the Unionist Association, a political meeting was held in the Drill Hall on Monday evening, when an address on current politics was delivered by Mrs Pierson, London. Lady Ninian Crichton-Stuart, House of Falkland, occupied the chair. (FN)

14 September 1912

Golf

The monthly medal competition took place on Saturday last when David Bonthrone, Captain of the Club, proved to be the winner. During the afternoon, tea was served in the Clubhouse by Misses D. and J. M. Cochrane and Miss Falconer. (FN)

21 September 1912

Whist Club

The first meeting of the Whist Club for this session was held in the

Liquorstane Temperance Hotel on Tuesday evening, when there was a good turnout of the members and a pleasant game was played. (FN)

21 September 1912

Excursion

The members of the Roman Catholic Church had their annual pic-nic on Saturday last, their destination this year being Kinghorn. The party drove to Falkland Road Station and journeyed to Kinghorn by train where a most enjoyable day was spent. (FN)

21 September 1912

Burgh rates

At a meeting of the Town Council held on Thursday of last week, the annual accounts were submitted and passed, and the assessments for the current year were fixed as follows: Burgh general, 10d per £1; sewerage, 1s 5d per £1. (FN)

21 September 1912

What's in a name?

At Cupar Sheriff Court on Tuesday, an elderly man was placed in the dock and the Sheriff Clerk read a charge against "William Reid", labourer, South Street, Falkland, of having on 26th July, maliciously knocked down stones and made holes in the dyke for a distance of 100 yards at Westfield Farm. Respondent strongly protested against being described "William Reid". "That's not my name, my Lord", he replied. "I object to that". The fiscal – "Well, what is your name? Respondent – "My name is William James Reid". The Fiscal was granted leave to amend the complaint by putting in the word "James", and a plea of not guilty being rendered, the case was continued till 30th for proof. (FN)

28 September 1912

Lecture

A meeting of the Falkland Popular Lecture Committee was held on Thursday last week, when a provisional programme was submitted. The course promises to be quite up to the standard of former years. (FN)

28 September 1912

Weekly half holiday

At a conference of the shopkeepers with the Provost and Magistrates on Friday with reference to fixing a suitable day for the weekly half-holiday under the Act, it was unanimously agreed to close on the afternoon of Thursday each week from October to May inclusive. As the Burgh is a holiday resort, the Town Council granted an order exempting the shopkeepers from the obligations under the Act for the four months of June, July, August and September. (FFP)

5 October 1912

Free rabbit shooting

Sheriff Armour Hannay, Cupar, was surprised when informed that the ratepayers of Falkland enjoy the privilege of free rabbit shooting.

The information came out in the course of the trial of William James Reid labourer, South Street, Falkland, on a charge of maliciously knocking holes in a stone dyke between a field on Westfield Farm and the road which leads to the Common. Accused denied making the holes, and said he shot rabbits on the Common. The ratepayers had a right to do so. The Sheriff remarked that he had heard it suggested that public shooting should be provided for those who wanted to shoot, but he was afraid it would be a dangerous sort of thing. It was rather interesting to know that the people of Falkland had such a right. His Lordship imposed a fine of 10s, or five days in prison. (FFP)

19 October 1912

Social meeting

As is customary, the Young Women's Guild, in connection with the Parish Church here, commenced their session by holding a social meeting in the Public School on the evening of Friday last. The Rev. J. K. Russell, BD, presided over a large attendance. Tea was served by ladies of the Guild, and thereafter the Chairman introduced the speaker of the evening, Miss Rettie, one of the Guild deputies, who, in a very interesting and instructive address, gave an account of the various departments of work undertaken by the Guild. During the evening solos were contributed by Miss Dun, Miss A. Forsyth and Messrs G. Spence, J. Venters, and J. Peggie. Several anthems were rendered by the choir. A very pleasant evening was brought to a close by the Chairman proposing a vote of thanks to Miss Rettie for her address, to the Ladies' Committee for providing the tea, and to all who had sustained the programme. The call was heartily responded to. (FN)

26 October 1912

Harvest thanksgiving

A special thanksgiving service was held in the Parish Church on Sunday afternoon. (FN)

26 October 1912

Dance

The "Harvest Home" was celebrated by the employees on the farms of Westfield and Kilgour by a dance in the Drill Hall on the Friday evening. The dance was well attended. (FN)

26 October 1912

Band meeting

The annual meeting of the Falkland Brass Band was held on Thursday evening last week, when it was reported that there was a balance of £11 at credit of the Band. During the evening, Mr D. Briggs, the conductor, was presented with a baton in recognition of the appreciation of the members of the Band Committee of Management. It was also arranged to hold a concert in aid of the funds. (FN)

26 October 1912

Municipal election meeting

On Wednesday evening, a meeting of the electors of the Burgh was held in the Town Hall when the retiring members of the Town Council, Provost Jackson, Councillors Angus, Brown, Ness and Robertson, gave an account of their stewardship. Bailie Drysdale, who presided, called for questions, as a result of which there was a heated discussion on the subject of the burgh boundaries. All five retiring Councillors were thereafter nominated for re-election, and the meeting terminated with a vote of thanks to the Chairman, on the call of Provost Jackson. (FN)

2 November 1912

Municipal election

The five retiring Councillors, Provost Jackson, Councillors Angus, Brown, Ness and Robertson are the only gentlemen nominated for election as Councillors, so there will be no poll. (FN)

16 November 1912

Town Council

At the meeting of the Town Council held on Friday, Mr Charles Jackson Jnr, was unanimously re-elected Provost of the Burgh. The annual "kirkin" took place on Sunday, when the Town Council and officials attended both the Parish and U.F. Churches. (FN)

23 November 1912

Y.M.C.A.

On Sunday morning, a deputation from Leslie Association paid a visit to Falkland, Messrs Jarvis and Stark being the representatives. Mr Jarvis read an essay on "John the Baptist" and an interesting discussion followed. (FN)

23 November 1912

Political meeting

A meeting under the auspices of the Liberal Association was held in the Drill Hall on Wednesday evening – Mr Walter Peggie, president, in the chair. Addresses on Home Rule for Ireland were given by Messrs Dick, Semple and Dack. (FN)

23 November 1912

Inspector of Poor

Mr George S. Hardie, Newton of Falkland, has commenced his duties as Inspector of Poor and Registrar of the parish in succession to Mr Lawrence Reid, who has resigned after a period of honourable and faithful service of over 30 years. (FN)

55. Charabanc in front of the Palace
Date unknown – possibly a church outing?
The railings were donated to the war effort in WWII
and have since been replaced by a hedge.

23 November 1912

Banquet

Provost Jackson, who has again been elected to the Civic Chair, entertained the members of the Town Council and officials and a few friends in the Commercial Hotel on Saturday evening. An excellent supper was provided by Mr John Angus, and thereafter a lengthy toast-list was gone through, various members of the company contributing to the musical part of the programme. As usual, a most enjoyable evening was spent, and after a toast to the Provost had been responded to in a right royal manner, the meeting was brought to a close by the singing of "Auld Lang Syne". (FN)

27 November 1912

Ice-cream man

An Italian fish and ice-cream restaurateur, bearing the picturesque name of Raphil Tarabella, who carries on business at the Palace Restaurant, Falkland, appeared before the Justices at Cupar today on a charge of having after ten o'clock on the night of 15th November permitted the consumption of excisable liquor. The accused pleaded guilty, and on his behalf Mr J. L. Anderson, Cupar, said the section under which the accused was prosecuted was very far-reaching. It would probably surprise them to know that after ten o'clock at a Hydro, if they sought to get a little "comfort" they would be contravening the law.

In this case Tarabella had had a drink with the gamekeeper in the hotel opposite his premises before ten o'clock, and the gamekeeper was about to return the compliment, when Tarabella saw someone enter his shop, and he went out. After ten o'clock the gamekeeper and another man entered the fish restaurant with two bottles of beer. They waited until the shop was cleared of customers before drawing the corks.

The police-constable saw the bottles on the shelf behind the counter. Mr Tasker, the fiscal, said the police-constable was attracted to the restaurant by the loud noise, and one of the men, when asked for a statement later, said he was so drunk that he did not remember anything about it. He might mention that the beer was put out in three tumblers. Tarabella got a share of it. Mr Anderson said that was not a case of surreptitious drinking. The bottles were open to the view of the police. Hon. Sheriff Thomson thought the ends of justice would be met by a fine of 10s, or three days. He cautioned Tarabella, however, to be more careful in future in allowing the consumption of liquor on his premises. (DET)

7 December 1912

Literary Society

The subject under discussion at the meeting of the society held on Monday evening was "The Situation in the Near East". The Rev. J. H. Morrison and Mr Andrew Venters were the leaders, and a general discussion followed. (FN)

7 December 1912

Curling

The members of the local club have enjoyed a spell at the "roarin" game on both the artificial and deep water ponds here. None of the club trophies have been competed for, but several keenly contested games have been played. (FN)

7 December 1912

Y.M.C.A.

At the morning meeting on Sunday last, the Rev. J. K. Russell delivered an interesting and instructing address on "Nature's Voices". On Monday evening at a general meeting of the Association, it was decided to form a recreation club under the auspices of the Association, and the first branch to be started is a football club. Mr Tom Schofield[1] was appointed captain and Mr Wm. Burgon Jnr, secretary and treasurer. (FN)

7 December 1912

Concert

In aid of the funds of the Falkland Brass Band, a concert was held in the Drill Hall on the evening of Friday last – Mr James Donaldson presiding. The programme submitted was thoroughly enjoyed by those present. It was worthy of a larger turnout.

The artistes were, Miss C. Waugh, Mrs C. A. Baird and Messrs Tawse and Baird, Edinburgh; Mr George Gardner and Mr D. Briggs Jnr. Miss Tawse, Edinburgh, acted very efficiently as accompanist. Two selections and a quartet were rendered by members of the band. A vote of thanks to all who had contributed to the evening's enjoyment was proposed by the Chairman, and heartily responded to, and a similar compliment was paid to Mr Donaldson for organising the concert, on the call of Provost Jackson. (FN)

14 December 1912

Parish Council

At the statutory meeting of the Parish Council on Monday evening, Mr J. L. Lumsden, Eden Valley House, Freuchie, was re-elected

---

[1] Kent-born Tom Schofield came to Falkland in 1907 to work in Messrs Jackson's Pleasance Linen Factory. In 1935, when the Scottish Co-operative Wholesale Society ran the factory, he was appointed Manager, a post he held until his retirement in 1959. He was known as "the man from Kent".

chairman. (FN)

14 December 1912

Y.M.C.A.

A special meeting of the Association was held in the Town Hall on Tuesday evening to meet Mr B. D. Kaye, travelling secretary of the Scottish National Council. Mr Kaye delivered an interesting and inspiring address on the work carried on by the Association, and at the close a general discussion took place as to the various means which might be used for the welfare of the youth of the town. (FN)

14 December 1912

Lecture

The second of the course of lectures was given in the Drill Hall on the evening of Saturday last – Provost Jackson in the chair.

The lecturer, Mr Edgar Bellingham, London, treated his subjects in a very interesting and instructive manner, and brought vividly before his audience, by means of beautiful lime-light views, the habits, customs and surroundings of "The People of the Desert". Mr Bellingham's lecture sparkled with humour. The usual votes of thanks brought the proceedings to an end. (FN)

1913

4 January 1913

Lecture

An interesting lecture was given in the Drill Hall by Colonel Harry Walker, Dundee. His subject, "Rocky Scrambles in Skye and Norway", was beautifully illustrated by lime-light views. On the call of Mr James Donaldson, who presided, the audience showed their appreciation of the lecture by according Colonel Walker a very hearty vote of thanks. (FN)

4 January 1913

Seasonable generosity

Following her usual custom, Lady Ninian Crichton-Stuart distributed to poor people in Falkland, Newton and Freuchie, parcels containing articles of clothing, blankets, and tea etc. The distribution was made by Mrs Stuart, the district nurse,[1] who, by her knowledge of the people, was well able to judge of the individual wants of the various recipients. (FN)

---

[1] In the 1911 census District Nurse Stephanie Stuart lived in Back Wynd, Falkand. Aged 39 and born in Bavaria, she had a daughter Stephanie, aged 15. Her son Louis was in Australia in 1915 aged 19 and joined the Australian army, winning the Military Medal, he survived the war. Nurse Stuart was probably Catholic.

4 January 1913

New Year

1913 was ushered in very quietly. A watch-night service was held in the Parish Church on Tuesday night from 11.15pm until the New Year was entered and an appropriate address was delivered by the Rev. J. K. Russell, BD. The public works have been shut down during the whole week and most of the shops were closed on Wednesday and Thursday. (FN)

4 January 1913

Song lecture

On Friday, 27th inst., a very enjoyable lecture was given by Miss Yule, of Edinburgh, on Burns' songs, and during the course of the lecture, selections from the bard's works were sung by a party of young ladies who accompanied Miss Yule. On the call of Mr James Jackson, who presided, a very hearty vote of thanks was accorded to Miss Yule and party for the very enjoyable entertainment. (FN)

4 January 1913

Presentation

On the occasion of Mr Lawrence Reid's[1] retiral from the office of Inspector of Poor and Registrar, which he has held for 26 years, the members of the Town and Parish Councils, and a few others thought it to be a fitting time to recognise his long connection with the work of the parish in a tangible form, and on the evening of Friday last, a meeting of the subscribers to the testimonial was held in The Bruce Arms, Hotel, when Mr J. L. Lumsden, Chairman of the Parish Council, presented Mr Reid with a purse of sovereigns and a silver salver, the latter bearing a suitable inscription. Mr Reid, in his reply, thanked them for their kind token of appreciation. (FN)

4 January 1913

Christmas treat to school children

On Thursday evening last week, the children attending the Public

---

[1] Lawrence Reid lived at Viewhill House.

School were entertained by Lord and Lady Ninian Crichton-Stuart. The gathering took place in the Drill Hall, which was packed by about 220 eager and happy children. This event, now an annual one, is looked forward to by the children with great expectancy, because not only are the "creature comforts" in the shape of tea and cakes provided, but there is the attraction of a Christmas tree laden with a gift for each child. Tea having been heartily partaken of, the Chairman of the School Board, Mr J. L. Lumsden, in a few well-chosen words, expressed on behalf of the children, their thanks to Lord and Lady Ninian Crichton-Stuart for their generosity in year after year providing this splendid treat for the children.

Lady Ninian Crichton-Stuart then proceeded to dismantle the tree, which was now ablaze with lights to the great delight of the children, and handed to each child the toy or other useful article assigned by the teachers. A short programme of music was performed by the children, the action songs of those in the infant department causing much amusement. Mr John Duncan MA, the headmaster, and his assistants, are to be heartily congratulated on the appearance of the children. (FN)

18 January 1913

B.O.A.F.G.

The annual general meeting of the "Lomond Oak" Lodge was held on Wednesday evening, when the Secretary submitted a very satisfactory report, which showed a large increase both in funds and membership. Office-bearers for the ensuing year were appointed as follows: WM, Bro. George S. Hardie; DM, Bro. P. Robertson; PM, Bro. James Oswald; SW, Bro. J. Skinner; JW, Bro. D. Lawrie; IG, Bro. P. Lawson; OG, Bro. J. Reekie; Chaplain, Bro. G. Fernie; Sick Stewards, Bro. James Lawson and J. Biggs; Secretary, Bro. Alexander Grieve Jnr; Treasurer, Bro. James Peggie. (FN)

18 January 1913

Literary Society

The members of the Society along with a few friends met in a social capacity at Allan Park on Monday evening. The proceedings opened with a sketch, entitled "Jessamy's Courtship", the various parts being sustained in a very entertaining manner by Miss Anderson, Miss P.

Cochrane, Miss S. Falconer, Dr Jack and Mr James Donaldson. Thereafter songs, etc., were rendered by members of the company and games engaged in. A very enjoyable evening was brought to a close by a vote of thanks to Mr and Miss Anderson for the hospitable way in which they had entertained those present, and by the singing of "Auld Lang Syne". (FN)

25 January 1913

Lecture

In connection with the course of Lectures, the Rev. J. K. Russell, BD, minister of the Parish Church, gave his contribution to the programme on Friday last in the Drill Hall. His subject was "Parodies and Parodists", and he treated it in a most instructive and enjoyable manner. On the call of Mr Alex. Anderson, who presided, a very hearty vote of thanks was accorded to Mr Russell. (FN)

8 February 1913

Curlers dinner

The members of the Falkland Curling Club held their annual dinner in the Bruce Arms, Hotel on Wednesday evening. Mr Gavin, president of the Club, occupied the chair. (FN)

8 February 1913

Literary Society

At the meeting of the Society held on Monday evening, an excellent paper was read by Mr James Donaldson, Bank House, on "The Clan System of Scotland". Miss Anderson led off the discussion which followed. (FN)

8 February 1913

Dramatic recital

In connection with the course of popular lectures, a dramatic recital was given in the Drill Hall on Friday evening by Mr J. Bruce Alston, lecturer on elocution, Glasgow and St Andrews Universities. The various selections, which included "The Election of a Minister", "Through the Flood", "The Raven", and "The Wooin' of Meg" were rendered in a very efficient manner, and were very favourably received by the audience. A very hearty vote of thanks was accorded to Mr Bruce Alston on the call of the Rev. J. K. Russell, who presided. (FN)

15 February 1913
Football
The Y.M.C.A. team played a friendly game with Freuchie Y.M.C.A. on Saturday afternoon, the visitors proving the winners by four goals to one. (FN)

15 February 1913
Continuation classes
These classes were concluded on Monday evening after a successful session. The members of the afternoon dress-making and millinery classes held a small social meeting at the close of the class, when the teachers, Misses Taylor and Forrester, were cordially thanked for the manner in which they had conducted the classes. (FN)

15 February 1913
Whist drive
On Friday evening, the members of the Falkland Whist Club and friends engaged in a very enjoyable whist drive in Ness's Temperance Hotel. There were seven tables in all and trump whist was the order of the evening. During an interval in the play, tea was served in a dainty manner by the ladies. At the close, the prize-winners were announced by Provost Jackson as follows: Ladies – Miss Sharpe and Miss Russell; Gentlemen – Dr Jack and Mr D. W. Deas. Thereafter songs etc., were contributed by members of the company and a very happy evening was brought to a close by a hearty vote of thanks to the ladies and the singing of "Auld Lang Syne". (FN)

22 February 1913
Missionary lecture
On Wednesday evening of last week in the U.F. Church, the Rev. J. H. Morrison delivered an interesting lecture on a tour round the Mission fields of the United Free Church in India. The lecture was beautifully illustrated by limelight views. (FN)

22 February 1913

Popular lecture

The last of the course of popular lectures was given in the Drill Hall on Friday evening, when Mr J. C. Adam, Portobello, read an account of the experiences of "a bird hunter at large". The lime-light views thrown on the screen numbered about 150, and illustrated different sections of bird life in a very interesting and instructive manner. On the call of Dr Jack who presided, Mr Adam was cordially thanked for his lecture. (FN)

22 February 1913

Literary Society

The meeting of the Society held on Monday evening took the form of a debate – "City Life v. Country Life". Miss Falconer and Mr W. D. Robertson advocated the advantages of the former, while Miss Cochrane and Mr D. A. Richardson[1] set forth the delights of the latter to an appreciative audience. An interesting discussion followed, and on a vote being taken, country life had the majority of supporters. (FN)

1 March 1913

Lomond Tavern

Desirable licensed premises for sale. These premises known as Lomond Tavern. All particulars can be obtained from Gibson & Spears, solicitors, Kirkcaldy. (FA)

8 March 1913

Y.M.C.A.

At the morning meeting on Sunday last, the Rev. J. H. Morrison delivered an address on "The Kingdom of God". There was a good attendance. (FN)

---

[1] David Alexander Richardson was the son of the former Head Teacher at Falkland School. His sister Janet was married to Robert Miller Jr. He worked for the Lumsdens in Freuchie. Commissioned in WWI, he was killed in 1918 and is on the Falkland War memorial.

8 March 1913

Literary Society

The meeting on Monday evening took the form of a *Scotsman* Night, when the leading articles of *The Scotsman* of 1st March were discussed. (FN)

8 March 1913

Concert

On Saturday evening, a concert in aid of the funds of the Falkland Brass Band was held in the Drill Hall – Mr A. Forrester, Lomondside,[1] presiding. The programme submitted was sustained by the members of Freuchie combined choir, and consisted chiefly of Scotch selections. The soloists were Misses E. Forsyth, E. Breingan, J. Swinton, and J. and M. Wallace, and Messrs J. Blyth and P. Breingan. The performance reflected great credit on Mr R.M. Bruce, the conductor of the choir. Miss Forsyth acted very efficiently as accompanist. On the call of the Chairman, a hearty vote of thanks was accorded to all who had contributed to the evening's entertainment. (FN)

15 March 1913

Recital

The annual recital in connection with the Parish Church Band of Hope was held in the Church on Friday evening, the title of the cantata being "Hump and All". The story was read by the Rev. J. K. Russell, and the various choruses, solos and duets were rendered in a manner which reflected great credit on the conductor, Mr George Spence. Mr John Venters presided at the organ, and Messrs R. Miller & A. Grieve manipulated the lantern for the lime-light views which illustrated the piece. On the call of Mr Russell, a hearty vote of thanks was accorded to the children and the others who had contributed to the evening's entertainment. On Saturday afternoon, the usual treat was held in the Drill Hall, when a very enjoyable time was spent. (FN)

---

[1] Mr Forrester was the works manager at Jackson's floorcloth factory in Falkland. His son Archibald is on the Falkland war memorial.

22 March 1913

To Let

To Let, with Entry at Whitsunday 1913, LICENSED GROCER'S SHOP
with DWELLING-HOUSE and other Premises attached in High Street,
Falkland, presently occupied by Mr Colin Herd.[1] For further Particu-
lars, apply to ALEXANDER ANDERSON, Solicitor, Falkland, with whom
Offers should be lodged not later than Wednesday, 26th March curt.
(FN)

22 March 1913

Y.M.C.A.

A deputation from Freuchie visited the Association on Sunday last.
Mr L. Rymer read an essay on "Character", which was much appre-
ciated. Mr D. A. Richardson expressed the good wishes of the
Freuchie Association to the Falkland Branch. (FN)

22 March 1913

Literary Society

On Monday evening, Dr Jack read an excellent paper on Shylock, the
famous Jew of the *Merchant of Venice*, the Rev. J. H. Morrison
following as critic. The subject was treated in a very interesting and
instructive manner, and a hearty vote of thanks was accorded to both
speakers on the call of Mr Donaldson, the Chairman. (FN)

22 March 1913

Dance

The annual assembly in connection with "Lomond Oak" Lodge
B.O.A.F.G. was held in the Drill Hall on Friday evening, when there
were 40 couples present.

Dancing to music supplied by Berry's Band was engaged in until
the small hours of the morning. Songs were sung by members of the
company at intervals and a very pleasant time was spent. Messrs G.
Fernie and G. Collier acted as MCs. (FN)

---

[1] Colin Herd's shop was one of the main suppliers to the House of Falkland.

56. Colin Herd's shop

22 March 1913

Livingstone centenary

A special joint service in commemoration of the birth of David Livingstone, Africa's great missionary explorer, was held in the Parish Church on Sunday evening. The Rev. J. K. Russell gave a sketch of Livingstone's life and his work in the "Dark Continent", and the Rev. J. H. Morrison followed with an account of the pathetic death scene and the results which have manifested themselves as a consequence of Livingstone's labours. (FN)

22 March 1913

Soirée

The annual social meeting of the United Free Church congregation took place on Thursday evening last week in the church, the Rev. J. H. Morrison presiding. Tea was served at 7.30 p.m., and thereafter the programme was proceeded with. The speakers were the Rev. S. Crabb, Cupar, D. W. Greenfield, Edenshead, and J. K. Russell, Falkland. Solos were sung by Miss Horne, Falkland; Miss Forsyth, Freuchie, and Messrs R. Morgan and J. Blyth, Freuchie. Anthems, Quartet tee etc., were rendered by the choir and the juvenile choir. In spite of the inclemency of the weather, a very enjoyable evening was spent. The usual votes of thanks proposed by the Chairman were heartily responded to. (FN)

22 March 1913

A serious offence

At Cupar Sheriff Court on Monday before Sheriff Armour-Hannay, Peter Spittal (44), general dealer, Falkland, pleaded guilty to an offence against a girl of fifteen years of age. The complaint was brought under the Criminal Law Amendment Act.

Mr A. E. Grosset, solicitor, Cupar, on behalf of the accused, said the latter's story was that the girl, although of tender years, made overtures to him. Of course, that was no excuse for the offence. Accused had been in business in the neighbourhood for the past twenty years, selling butter, eggs, and groceries from a cart, and he had always borne a good character. Mr Grosset read a large number of letters from residents in Freuchie, Markinch, and other places in which Spittal was given a good character. One said the accused led "an honest Christian life."

The Sheriff, in passing sentence, said that no doubt accused had a more or less unblemished record, but it was not only he who had to be considered, but his victim. His Lordship could pay no attention whatever to the suggestion that the girl made overtures to accused. Pursuer would go to prison for twelve months, with hard labour. (FN)

29 March 1913

Hope Trust lectures

Mr J. Lumsden and Mr Alex. Reid, under the auspices of the Hope Trust, delivered lectures in the Drill Hall on Friday evening. The subject at the meeting for adults was "Undoing the Reformation". [1]

---

[1] The Hope Trust is a charity supporting reformed religion and temperance.

Both lectures were beautifully illustrated by lime-light views. (FN)

29 March 1913

Social and dance

The first session of the Parish Church Bible class under the Rev. J. K. Russell, BD, was brought to a close on Sunday, and on Thursday last week, the members met in a social capacity in the Drill Hall. After partaking of an excellent tea, purveyed by Mr William Mason, dancing was engaged in for an hour or two, and a very enjoyable evening was spent. (FN)

5 April 1913

Subscription dance

A subscription dance was held in the Drill Hall, Falkland, on Friday night, and being somewhat of a novelty for the district, it excited considerable interest locally. The hall was prettily decorated for the occasion, and a goodly company assembled, largely recruited from neighbouring villages. Dancing began at 9.00 p.m., and a selection of the latest music was admirably rendered by Mr McPherson, Dundee. The catering was in the capable hands of Mr Mason, Bruce Arms, Falkland, while the duties of MCs were efficiently discharged by Messrs G. B. Morgan and Alex. Bonthrone. Dancing was carried on with great spirit until 3.00 a.m. when a pleasant evening came to a close, and wishes were generally expressed that the function would become an annual one.

The company comprised the following: Mrs Livingstone, Lomond-vale, black satin, with tunic of net, jet embroidered; Mrs Donaldson, Bank House, cream satin; Mrs Jack, Canonbury, gray satin charmeuse; Mrs Jackson, Meadowfield, pale blue taffetas with sequin trimmings; Mrs Brown, Falkland, meteor blue satin; Mrs Methven, Schoolhouse, Freuchie, reseda green voile with coloured embroidery; Mrs Bonthrone, Newton House, helio voile; Mrs Bonthrone, Kins-leith, black ninion over black silk; Miss Falconer, Falkland, fawn taffetas; Miss Richardson, Edinburgh, olive green poplin; Miss Cochrane, Glenfarg, cream lace over cream satin; Miss Thomson, Lochie, Strathmiglo, cream voile with forget-me-nots; Miss Honey-man, Kingskettle, sapphire blue accordion voile with lace coatee; Miss

McDonald, Perth, petunia satin; Miss Cochrane, Falkland, cream silk with net overdress in silver sequins; Miss Orchison, Denbrae, Cupar, lemon satin with tunic of pale green voile; Miss Maxwell, Auchtermuchty, pale blue satin with overdress of blue and white voile; Miss McLaren, Dalmeny, saxe blue satin with lace coatee.

Gentlemen: Provost Jackson, Falkland, Messrs A. Anderson, L. Granger, J. W. Jackson, J. Dunbar, G. Gavin, Dr Jack, J. Donaldson, G. B. Morgan, J. Brown, A. J. Christie, Glasgow; R. Ferlie, Auchtermuchty; A. Bonthrone, W. Henderson, J. Donaldson, C. McDonald, J. Keir, Eric Thomson, Strathmiglo; J. Methven, Freuchie; D. Richardson, Freuchie; J. H. Lawson, Edinburgh; W. McLellan, Kinsleith. (FN)

12 April 1913
Falkland Brass Band
Falkland Brass Band made its first appearance for the season on Saturday evening, and after a few selections had been rendered, dancing was engaged in for some time. (FN)

12 April 1913
Spring holiday
Monday of this week was observed in the Burgh as the annual Spring holiday. During the week-end a detachment of the Territorials[1] were stationed in the Drill Hall. The Company attended the forenoon service in the Parish Church on Sunday. (FN)

19 April 1913
Concert
A concert in aid of the funds of the Boy Scouts was held in the Drill Hall on the evening of Thursday last week. Provost Jackson occupied the chair.

The musical part of the programme was well sustained by Miss Dun, Woodmill; Miss Pirie, and Miss M. Gray, Dundee, Dr W. Graham Campbell, Dundee, and Mr John Venters, Falkland. A display of

---

[1] The Territorial Force (later the Territorial Army and since 2014 the Army Reserve) had been formed in 1908 by merging the Volunteers and the Yeomanry.

physical drill and Indian club swinging by the Scouts under Mr T. Watson was very credible. The special feature of the evening was the rendering of four scenes from *Hamlet* by some of the boys.

On the call of the Chairman, a very hearty vote of thanks was accorded to all who had contributed to the evening's entertainment. (FN)

19 April 1913

Licence for the Lomond Tavern

Falkland's Provost proposes Refusal

The next application was by Edward Herd, Lomond Tavern, Falkland, for transfer of the public-house certificate for these premises at present in the hands of Mrs Kennoway.[1]

The Chief Constable's report in this case stated that Falkland's population was 940, and in addition to the house concerned, there were in the burgh two full hotel licences, two public-house licences, and two grocer's licences.

Mr J. E. Grosset, for applicant, said this was an application of some importance. The Lomond Tavern had been very long licenced. At the death of Mr Kennoway in October last year, the certificate was transferred to his widow, and from that time the business had been managed by the applicant, Mr Herd, who was Mrs Kennoway's uncle. Mr Herd had been engaged in the trade all his life. He (Mr Grosset) would not have troubled the Court with many remarks on the case, had he not known that Provost Jackson did not see eye to eye with him in the matter. It was great consequence to his client whether the licence was renewed or not. Failure to renew it would render Mrs Kennoway bankrupt, and would deprive her of her sole means of livelihood. The reason suggested as to why the licence should not be renewed was that Falkland was said, like some other places, to be over-licensed. It would also be said that the trade done in that house was small. He admitted that, but it was good enough for the Kennoways. The late Mr Kennoway paid £950 for the house,

---

[1] Provost Jackson, who opposed the license, said that in In Falkland they had one license for every 120 of the population. The drawings of the Lomond Tavern were stated at £10 a week, and taking the other licensed places on the same basis that gave an expenditure of £4 10s per head of the population – ridiculous. (DC, 16 April)

and it kept him and would keep his widow in comfort. There had never been a complaint as to the way in which the house was conducted.

At the present moment the Legislature was endeavouring to pass an Act to meet cases of this kind to provide for compulsory insurance of licences so that when a reduction was declared necessary the affected parties could get compensation. It would be rather drastic to ask the Court, pending immediate legislation on the subject, to take away the licence and deprive Mrs Kennoway of any benefits she would derive under the statute. The population of the burgh of Falkland was 940 and of the parish 2,256. Falkland was one of the few parishes in Fife which showed an increase in population last census both in the rural and burghal parts, and he did not think it had yet reached the end of its prosperity.

Mr Wm. Guild, Lindores, proposed that the licence be granted.

Provost Jackson said the house was really only nominally owned by Mrs Kennoway. The late Mr Kennoway, a year before he died, was anxious to sell and came to him to consult him, and said he could not make a living out it. The people at the back of this licence had advertised in order to get someone to take it over, and it was only within fourteen hours of the expiry of the time for lodging applications that Mr Herd's name was put in.

Mr Grosset said it was not the case that this was not a genuine licence. Mr Kennoway bought the house for £950, and of that sum £600 was loaned by a private land-owner in Fife and £250 was got from a firm in Kirkcaldy. The Court would agree that that did not make it a tied house.

There was no support for Provost Jackson, and the Court granted the application. (SAC)

3 May 1913

Cricket – Falkland v. Kennoway

The match at Kennoway on Saturday had to be abandoned on account of the rain, and Falkland did not bat. Kennoway were dismissed for 32, J. Venters having the excellent analysis of 7 for 14, and W. Venters, 3 for 17. (FN)

10 May 1913

Communion

The half-yearly communion was celebrated in both churches on Sunday, when there were large attendances. On Friday evening, the usual preparatory services were held, the Rev. J. K. Russell preaching in the Parish Church, and the Rev. W. L. Craig, of Balmalcolm, in the United Free Church. On Sunday evening, the thanksgiving services were conducted by the Rev. Mr Cairns, Muckart, and the Rev. P. W. Lilley, Freuchie, in the respective churches. (FN)

17 May 1913

Light railway

Notice is hereby given that an ORDINARY GENERAL MEETING for the conduct of the Company's Affairs will be held in the Hall of the Royal Hotel, Cupar, on Monday 26th inst., at 3.30 p.m. A. E. GROSSET, Secy. (FN)

24 May 1913

Golf

A mixed foursome competition was held on Saturday afternoon between Mr D. Bonthrone (captain) and Mr A. Anderson (treasurer), and resulted as follows:

Captain

1. Miss Martyn and D. Bonthrone	0
2. Mrs Methven and F. Grainger	1
3. Mrs Bonthrone and G. Robertson	0
4. Mrs Fraser and Mr Lincoln	1
5. Miss Allan and J. Methven	1
Total	3

Treasurer

1. Miss Forsyth and A. Venters	1
2. Miss Falconer and A. Anderson	0
3. Miss D. Cochrane and Rev. J. K. Russell	0
4. Miss P. Cochrane and Rev. C. Fraser	0
5. Mrs Venters and W. Peggie	0
Total	1

31 May 1913

Falkland Light Railway

An Ordinary General Meeting of the Falkland Light Railway Company was held in the Royal Hotel, Cupar on Monday afternoon. Mr W. Jackson, Falkland, presided, and Lord Ninian Crichton-Stuart MP, House of Falkland, was amongst the shareholders present. On behalf of the Directors, Mr A. E. Grosset, Cupar, Secretary, presented a report upon the present position of the Company. The report showed that a considerable proportion of the capital had been taken up. The shareholders considered the report was satisfactory, and it was adopted unanimously. The auditors' report was also adopted. About fifteen minutes sufficed for the business of the meeting. (FN)

7 June 1913

Cricket – Falkland v. Freuchie

These near rivals met at Falkland and the home side won by 17 runs, chiefly through the bowling of Messrs W. and J. Venters. Bowling for Freuchie, Croall took six wickets for 32 runs. Rymer had three for one, and Spence one for 11. Scores:

Falkland

W. M. Venters b. Croall	22
J. Reekie b. Croall	28
J. Venters c. Stark, b. Spence	6
G. Thomson b. Croall	2
R. Craig b. Croall	0
T. C. Schofield b. Rymer	4
M. Robertson b. Croall	0
T. Drysdale c. D. Duncan, b. Rymer	0
P. Robertson b. Croall	7
F. Grainger c. J. Jack, b. Rymer	0
A. Gavin not out	0
Extras	5
Total	**74**

Freuchie

J. Jack Jnr b. J. Venters	3
D. Duncan b. W. Venters	0

J. Morrison b. J. Venters	2
W. Stark c. Reekie, b. W. Venters	0
J. W. Leishman b. W. Venters	1
L. Rymer c. W. Venters, b. J. Venters	1
J. Duncan b. W. Venters	0
E. Croall b. P. Robertson	17
A. Spence b. W. Venters	1
R. Jack not out	20
W. Simpson b. P. Robertson	1
Extras	11
Total	**57**

24 June 1913

£100,000 paid for Fife estates

Messrs Young & Kennaway WS, Auchterarder, have purchased, on behalf of clients, from Mr J. C. Makgill Crichton, through his agent, Mr J. E. Grosset, writer, Cupar, the estates of Lathrisk and Rossie, in the county of Fife. The price has not transpired, but it is understood to be about £100,000. Mr Crichton sold recently the farms of Drumley and Caldwells, which formed part of these estates. Mr Crichton has purchased a ranch in California which he proposes developing.

The estate of Lathrisk extends to between 6000 and 7000 acres, and includes the summits of the two highest points in Fife – namely, the East and West Lomonds.[1] On the property there are twenty considerable farms and various holdings of a smaller kind, and also a good deal of valuable timber. Mr Crichton succeeded to the property in 1900, on the death of the late Mr George Johnston of Lathrisk. It is understood that the estates will now be divided into smaller lots. (DET)

27 June 1913

Interdict against a farmer

In the Court of Session today Lord Hunter gave judgment in a note for Lord Ninian Crichton-Stuart of Falkland for interdict against John

---

[1] "The rental is £6,000, and the purchase price is stated to be £100,000. Mr Makgill-Crichton still owns the Perthshire estate of Monzie, and the Largo estate in Fife." (FA, 28 June)

Barrie Ogilvie, farmer, Westfield Farm, Falkland.

Complainer sought to have the respondent interdicted from trespassing upon and from grazing live stock in the Mansion House Park. The park in question was let to the respondent for grazing purposes, with power to the complainer to resume the land let for any purpose except that of letting to another agricultural tenant on giving a month's notice, the tenant to be entitled to compensation for any loss or damage sustained by such resumption. At Martinmas complainer's factor intimated to respondent that the park would be required by the complainer in the spring of 1913 for the grazing of pedigree sheep belonging to him.

Respondent refused to recognise the right of the complainer to resume possession of the park. The complainer had the respondent ejected from the park and his stock removed. Respondent replaced the stock in the park and they were again removed. Respondent maintained that the clause in the lease founded on had no binding effect in respect that it was an attempt to qualify the provisions of the Agricultural Holdings Act, 1908, and that the tenant was entitled to six months notice before the termination of the lease.

In granting interdict as craved, Lord Hunter found that after 31st March 1913, the respondent had no right to possession and therefore was not entitled to replace cattle on the field in question. (DET)

28 June 1913
To let – Chapelyard House
To Let, with Entry at Martinmas or sooner, if desired. Chapelyard House, with large Garden and small Paddock adjoining. The House, which is beautifully situated overlooking the town of Falkland, consists of 3 Public Rooms, 3 Bedrooms, Dressing Room and Kitchen etc. The outhouses contain Stabling and other usual accommodation.

For particulars, apply to George Gavin, Estate Office, Falkland Palace, Falkland, Fife. (FN)

28 June 1913
Daughter for Lady Ninian
Lady Ninian Crichton-Stuart gave birth to a daughter on Tuesday morning at House of Falkland. The event caused much rejoicing in

Falkland and all over the estate, and flags and other decorations were displayed at many places. (FN) [1]

28 June 1913
School Board
Dr J. G. Jack has been appointed a member of the School Board in room of the late ex-Provost Miller. (FN)

28 June 1913
Market and games
The annual market and games were held on Saturday last in the Myre, and the weather being very favourable, there was a good turn out of the public. The Town Band rendered selections during the afternoon, and played dance music in the evening. The sports were well contested.

The following were the principal prize-winners: Half-mile (open) – Ross, Bowhill; hop, step and leap (open) – McPherson, Blackford; boys' race (under 12, local) – C. Drysdale; running high leap (open) – McPherson; wheelbarrow race (local) – T. Drysdale and J. Hay; one mile (open) – Ross, Bowhill; potato and bucket race (local) – J. Hay; boys' race (under 16, local – R. Kennedy; half-mile (local) – G. Fernie; girls' race (local) – C. Duncan; cigarette race (open) – McPherson; sack race (local) – J. Hay; 100 yards (open) – Clark, Thornton; long jump (open) – McPherson; putting ball (open) – Walton, Magask. (FN)

5 July 1913
Services
On Sunday forenoon, the Rev. J. H. Morrison, and the Rev. P. W. Lilley, Freuchie, exchanged pulpits, and Mr Morrison conducted the afternoon service in the open air. (FN)

5 July 1913
Cricket
On Thursday evening of last week, an XI visited Strathmiglo, but

---

[1] Claudia Miriam Joanna Crichton-Stuart, born 24 June 1913

sustained a defeat by 51 runs to 35. On Tuesday evening, however, at Auchtermuchty, they proved the winners, the score being 26 runs to 45 for 5 wickets. St Andrews are the visitors at Scroggie to-morrow (Saturday). (FN)

5 July 1913

Picnics

The Sunday Schools of both the Parish and U.F. Churches held their annual picnics on Saturday, when they were favoured with delightful weather. As usual, the journey was made in carts, the respective destinations being Pitcairlie and Ramornie. On arriving home about nine o'clock, the general verdict was that a very enjoyable day had been spent. (FN)

7 July 1913

New Catholic chapel

The corner stone of the new Roman Catholic Church, built by Lord Ninian Crichton-Stuart, to the memory of his son, who died when only three years old, was laid on Saturday afternoon by the Very Rev. the Bishop of Galway in presence of a large attendance of the congregation. It is interesting to note that the whole of the stones and wood for the building was hewn and cut on the estate, and that the church is being entirely built by local tradesmen.

The architect is Mr Reginald Fairlie Edinburgh,[1] and the structure is in the Scottish style, being a modification of St Leonard's Chapel, St Andrews. It is expected the church will be finished and open for service in 1916. (DC)

12 July 1913

Lecture Committee

This Committee met on Monday evening, when it was agreed to suspend the course for the coming winter session in the hope that a greater interest may be created in the lectures after the absence of a year. (FN)

---

[1] Reginald Fairlie was a Catholic neighbour and family friend, brought up at Myres Castle.

57. The Memorial Chapel

The planned church was never actually finished. Following Lord Ninian's death in 1915 it remains a roofless Memorial Chapel.

12 July 1913

Choir picnics

The annual drives in connection with both the Parish and U.F. Church choirs took place on Saturday, the former going to Aberdour and the latter to St Andrews. The weather on the whole was favourable, and a very enjoyable day was spent by both parties. (FN)

12 July 1913

Falkland Palace closed to visitors

Falkland Palace has been closed from Monday last week until further notice. This will be disappointing to visitors to the town during the holiday season. It is understood that the Palace is closed owing to fear that damage may be done by militant suffragists. This is another instance of the inconvenience that the public are put to by the ruthless acts of the "votes for women" fanatics.[1] (FN)

---

[1] Mr Gavin later announced with an advertisement on the front page of the *Fife News* that Falkland Palace would be re-opened to the public on and after Monday 28 July 1913.

12 July 1913

Cricket – Falkland v. St Andrews

Falkland entertained St Andrews on Saturday. The home side had first lease of the wicket, and after registering 58 runs at a loss of six wickets declared. St Andrews gave a display of batting that surprised their hosts, winning the match by scoring 71 for three wickets. Falkland 58 (J. Venters 31); St Andrews 71 (J. Smith 34 not out). (FN)

2 August 1913

Public address

Mr T. Byars from County Tyrone delivered an address at the fountain on Tuesday evening on Irish Home Rule. There was a fair attendance. (FFP)

23 August 1913

Y.M.C.A.

The annual general meeting of Falkland Y.M.C.A. was held in the Town Hall on Tuesday evening, when reports were given by the Treasurer and Secretary of the Recreation Committee, and found to be satisfactory. Office-bearers for the following year were appointed as follows: President, Mr Walter Peggie; Vice-Presidents, Messrs C. C. Brunton and George Robertson; Secretary, Mr James Donaldson; and Treasurer, Mr Alex. Grieve. It was decided to carry on the Football Club during the season now started, and to allow all young men to join whether members of the Y.M.C.A. or not. Mr Donaldson was elected Captain of the Club, and Mr William Burgon Jnr, secretary and treasurer. (FN)

13 September 1913

Book by U.F. Church minister

The Scotsman, in reviewing *On the Trail of the Pioneers* (2s), London: Hodder and Stoughton, says the book is a sketch of the missions of the United Free Church of Scotland. It has been written mainly for the youth of the Church. The author has stories to tell of many wonderful experiences of missionaries and others, which give his narrative all the charm of romance. So much, indeed, is this the case that the volume can scarcely fail to prove popular with youthful readers and with older people too. It gives what may be described as a "bird's eye view" of what the Church has accomplished in the mission field. The volume has a number of beautiful illustrations. The following paragraph appeared in the September issue of the *Missionary Record* of the United Free Church:

"A book will shortly be issued which has a peculiar and even romantic interest. It is written by the Rev. J. H. Morrison MA, our minister at Falkland, who has had an experience with it that recalls more than one famous incident in literary history. The volume is a brilliant sketch of the Missions of the United Free Church, and was originally finished a year ago. Consigned to the care of a well-known man-of-letters, it was placed in a bag which was stolen during a railway journey and never recovered. After the first shock of the loss, Mr Morrison set to and re-wrote the work, and it will shortly be published by Messrs Hodder & Stoughton. *On the Trail of the Pioneers* is original in conception and style, and will catch the popular fancy, and especially the fancy of the young. The opening chapter describes Foreign Mission night at the Assembly Hall, and readers are then taken on an imaginative voyage round the world." (FN)

27 September 1913

Lord and Lady Ninian's house party

Lord and Lady Ninian Crichton-Stuart are at present at House of Falkland where they are this week entertaining the following ladies and gentlemen: Mr and Lady Beatrice Kerr Clerk; Countess of Abingdon; Lady Betty Bertie; Hon. Bernard Howard; Mr Montague Wood; Lord Colin [sic] Crichton-Stuart; Viscount and Viscountess Gormanston; Miss Enid Campbell; Hon. Hubert Preston; Miss Marguerite Connellan; and Miss Sybil Williams. (FN)

27 September 1913

Football

The Y.M.C.A. Football Club played their first match of the season on Saturday afternoon, with Denside Thistle, but were defeated by 6 goals to 3. To-morrow (Saturday) afternoon, they meet Ladybank. (FN)

27 September 1913

Burgh rates

The Town Council have fixed the burgh assessments for the current year to 15th May 1914 as follows: burgh general, 10d per £1, sewerage 1s 4d, water supply 5d, roads & bridges 9d, public health 2d, and lunacy, registration etc., 2d – in all 3s 8d per £1 of which 1s 5d is payable by owners and 2s 3d by occupiers. There is no change in the total rate from last year. (FN)

4 October 1913

Football

On Saturday afternoon, the Y.M.C.A. team met Ladybank on the home ground but suffered defeat at the hands of the visitors by 8 goals to 6. The junior team played Kettle, and won by 8 goals to 1. (FN)

4 October 1913

Cricket

The annual meeting of the Cricket Club was held in the Town Hall on Monday evening, when a satisfactory report was submitted by the Secretary and Treasurer. Mr W. M. Venters won the prize presented by Mr D. Bonthrone, Newton House, for the best all round player for the season, his batting and bowling averages being 24 and 40 wickets for 240 runs, respectively. It was agreed to arrange for holding a dance on the 12th of December. (FN)

11 October 1913

Holiday

The annual autumn holiday was observed in the burgh on Monday last. (FN)

11 October 1913

Church elders

On Sunday forenoon it was intimated from the pulpit of the Parish Church that Messrs George Robertson and David W. Chisholm had been elected elders of the church. (FN)

11 October 1913

Cantata

The members of the U.F. Church Junior Christian Endeavour Society rendered the cantata, *In the King's Garden*, in the church on Friday evening last week, when there was a good turnout to hear the performance. The "Model Garden" was composed of a beautiful array of flowers with five arches, and a small fountain played in the centre. The cantata was arranged by the Rev. J. H. Morrison, minister of the church, and he also conducted the singing. The reading was beautifully done by Miss Jeannie Smith, and the various hymns, solos, choruses, and recitations were admirably carried through. Mr Walter Peggie Jnr, officiated at the organ. On the call of Mr Walter Peggie, a very hearty vote of thanks was accorded to all who had contributed to the entertainment, which proved to be most interesting and instructive. The flowers were afterwards sent off to be distributed amongst some of the poor and sick of Glasgow. (FN)

11 October 1913

Golf

The monthly medal competition was held on Saturday afternoon, when Mr Walter Venters was the winner. Tea was provided during the afternoon by Mrs Venters and Mrs Peggie. (FN)

18 October 1913

Football

The Y.M.C.A. team played an eleven from Auchtermuchty on Saturday afternoon, and won by 4 goals to nil. (FN)

18 October 1913

Y.M.C.A.

The first meeting of the Y.M.C.A. for the session was held in the Town Hall on Sunday morning when there was a good turnout of the young men. Mr Walter Peggie, president, addressed the meeting. (FN)

18 October 1913

Motor cycle up East Lomond Hill

Mr T. R. Inglis Melville, Kettle, with Mr Forsyth, teacher, Kettle, in his side car, drove a 3½ h.p. Triumph motor cycle on Wednesday to the top of the East Lomond Hill, a height of 1,500 feet. The route was by way of Purin Den, Falkland, and the journey was accomplished in less than three-quarters of an hour, including two stops. The side car was detached forty yards from the top. This is the first time a motor climb of "The Lomond" has been attempted. (FN)

18 October 1913

Curling Club

The annual meeting of this Club was held in the Town Hall – Mr David Bonthrone presiding –

58. The Fountain, with the East Lomond Hill behind

when the following appointments were made: Patron – Lord Ninian Crichton-Stuart MP; Patroness – Lady Ninian Crichton-Stuart; President – David Bonthrone; vice-President – Thomas Williamson; Rep. Members – David Bonthrone and George B. Morgan; Chaplain – The Rev. J. K. Russell, BD; Secretary and Treasurer – James Donaldson; Committee – John Angus, Alex. Shanks, Wm. Horne, Wm. Mason, Walter Peggie and Thomas Ross.

The Treasurer's statement showed a balance in hand of £10 9s 6½d. It was agreed to enter two rinks for the grand match at Carsebreck or Edinburgh. Entries for the ice rink trophies at Edinburgh were left to be arranged by the skips. (FN)

27 October 1913

Westfield sale

Messrs Macdonald, Fraser & Co, auctioneers, Perth, conducted an extensive displenishment sale at Westfield, the home farm on the Falkland Estate, on behalf of the outgoing tenant, Mr Ogilvie. The farm, which is beautifully situated at the foot of the East Lomond Hill, is being operated by the proprietor, Lord Ninian Stuart, and he was a very large purchaser.

The implements and stock were of superior quality, and good prices were realised. Carts sold to £11; Massey-Harris binders to £18 10s; reapers to £2 10s; rollers to £3 5s; turnip slicers to £3 5s; turnip sowing machines to £4; grain sowing machines to £9; manure distributors to £2 5s; thistle cutter £6 10s; horse rakes to £7 5s; ploughs to £2 7s 6d; diamond harrows to £2 2s 6d; cultivators to £2 7s 6d; circle harrows to £1 2s 6d; potato diggers to £7 5s; bruisers to £1 10s; steelyard £1 15s; fanners £5; sheep shearing machine £2; horses brought £63, £44, £36, £33, £51, £33, £43 10s, £13 10s and £32; crossed lambs sold to 29s 6d, and two crop ewes to 38s; pigs (five weeks old) from 20s to 22s each; and sows to £6 10s; milch cows sold to £19 15s; bulls to £26; bullocks made up to £15. The stack-yard sold dear, oat stacks in particular being much in demand. (DC)

1 November 1913

Elections

The following five candidates for the four vacant seats in the Town Council have been nominated: Messrs Robert Drysdale, Andrew Lister, William Horne, and Thomas Williamson, who are the retiring members, and Mr James McCall.

The four retiring members representing the burgh on the Parish Council have been re-elected, namely: Messrs James Donaldson, Alexander Fraser, Charles Jackson Jnr, and Walter Peggie. (FN)

1 November 1913

Social meeting

The annual social meeting of the Women's Guild of the Parish Church was held in the school on Friday evening, when the Rev. J. K. Russell presided over a good audience. Tea was served by members of the

Guild, and thereafter an interesting address was given by Miss Scott from Daska, North India, on her work there as one of the Guild Missionaries. During the evening, the choir rendered several anthems, and songs and recitations were contributed by Miss Jessie Anderson and Messrs George Spence and William Burgon. The meeting was brought to a close with the usual votes of thanks. (FN)

1 November 1913

Golf

The annual general meeting of Falkland Golf Club was held in the Clubhouse on Monday evening, when a satisfactory statement was submitted by Mr Anderson, treasurer.

Office-bearers were appointed as follows: Patron – Lord Ninian Crichton-Stuart MP; President – Mr J. L. Lumsden; vice-President – Mr George Gavin; Captain – Mr D. Bonthrone; Secretary and Treasurer – Mr James Peggie. (FN)

8 November 1913

School

The Public School was re-opened on Monday morning after having been closed for three weeks during the potato-lifting season. (FN)

8 November 1913

Literary Society

The first meeting of the Literary Society was held at Allan Park on Monday evening, when an inaugural address was delivered by Mr James Donaldson. (FN)

8 November 1913

Presentation

At the meeting of the Whist Club on Tuesday last week, Mr J. Barry Ogilvie was presented with a handsome pipe and tobacco pouch as a token of the respect and esteem of his fellow members on the occasion of his leaving Westfield Farm, of which he has been the tenant for the past seven years. Dr Jack made the presentation, and Mr Ogilvie suitably replied. (FN)

8 November 1913

Communion

The half-yearly communion was celebrated in both churches on Sunday. Preparatory services were held on the preceding Friday evening, when the Rev. J. K. Russell officiated in the Parish Church, and the Rev. J. M. Munro, Strathmiglo, in the United Free. At the thanksgiving services on Sunday evening, the Rev. A. O. Taylor, Glen Devon, and the Rev. W. D. Beattie, Monimail, preached in the respective churches. (FN)

15 November 1913

Town Council

At a meeting of the Town Council held on Friday, Councillors Angus and Robertson were appointed Senior and Junior Bailies, respectively, in place of Bailies Drysdale and Lister. Mr W. D. Robertson was appointed Procurator Fiscal for the burgh in room of Mr James Reekie. The Council attended both the Parish and the U.F. Churches on Sunday in their official capacity. (FN)

18 November 1913

Breach of the peace

Amusing evidence was led in Cupar Sheriff Court, in the trial for breach of the peace of Andrew Lister, baker, Town Councillor and ex-Magistrate of the burgh of Falkland. Mr J. L. Anderson, Town Clerk, Cupar, appeared for the accused.

William Duncan, the complainer, stated that 22nd September, he was out in one of his fields at Backdykes taking a look at his wheat sheaves when he saw the accused and his son in the field. The son was flying a kite, the kite was resting on one of his stooks. He spoke to Lister quite civilly and the latter told him he had no right to put him out of the field and that he would let him know the law of the country.

Lister called him "all the names", and when Duncan took hold of the kite, Lister let bang at him. Lister cursed and swore and challenged him to fight.

Mrs Lister, who was at the foot of her garden, cried out "Dinna strike him, Andrew."

Charles Smith, James Lawson and Police Constable Pratt gave further evidence for the prosecution.

Accused, who was the first witness for the defence, said for some years he had been a magistrate, and at present he was a town councillor of the burgh of Falkland. His dwelling house was 150 yards distant from the place where the alleged disturbance took place.

Mr Anderson: You have the reputation in Falkland of being an expert in flying and making kites? – Yes.

Mr Anderson: is it the case that until recently, for almost 25 years past, either your boys or yourself have, without objection, used that field for flying your kites? – Yes.

Lister: On the day in question my eldest boy was out flying a kite which had been lying in the house for months waiting until the field was in stubble, and I went out to give him a hand when it came down. He was only about a minute or half a minute there when Mr Duncan came on the scene. He was very angry looking. He had his sleeves rolled up and his hat off. He said "I have got you now." I said "I am sorry if I have done any damage. I am quite willing to pay for it."

He said to me "How are you able to pay damages?" I said "I am as able to pay as a Duncan." Then we got into a pickle words, just like a couple of school laddies. Duncan took hold of the kite and at the same time I took hold of it, and it got torn for which I was very sorry. I told him if it had not been for the laws of the country there would have been a wap.

Mr Anderson: What's that?

Accused: You ken what that is.

The Fiscal: Did you lay down the law to Duncan?

Lister: I did I think I was a sort of correct. He never put his hands on Duncan.

The Fiscal: Did your wife call to you to keep down your hands?- yes. Why did she do that if you didn't put your hands upon him?

Answer: She knows the sort of gentleman I am. I will fight at once for my rights. There was no swearing or anything of that sort.

Mrs Lister in the witness box stated that her husband and Duncan were both swearing.

The Sheriff stated that one regretted to see a town councillor in that position, but after hearing the evidence he had no hesitation whatever in holding the charge proved. There was a good deal to be said in mitigation and at best it was a very trumpery case. He was very unwilling that a conviction should be recorded against him, but he was afraid he had no alternative. He did not think it was a case for a fine, but he ordered Lister to find caution for £1 for six months that he would not repeat that conduct. (DET)

20 November 1913

Grocer Bankrupt

Peter Reid Baxter, grocer, Falkland, examined in cessio at Cupar Sheriff Court today by Mr A. E. Grosset, Cupar, who appeared for the petitioning creditors, Messrs Thomson & Porteous, Edinburgh, stated that he began business as a grocer in Falkland four years ago with £25 of borrowed capital. That sum figured in the state of affairs he had lodged as being still due.

What caused the fall off in your business?

Well, opposition, of course, and bad trade and co-operation.

Did the Co-Operative Store take away a number of your customers? – Yes.

I think they increased the dividend they paid shortly after you began? – That is true, and things have gone worse since then.

The state of affairs showed liabilities, £108; assets, £35. Mr P. Craig, C.A., Edinburgh, was appointed trustee. (DET)

22 November 1913

B.O.A.F.G.

At a meeting of the "Lomond Oak" Lodge held on Thursday evening last week, Mr T. D. Hopkins was appointed Secretary in place of Mr Alex. Grieve, who has resigned. (FN)

22 November 1913

Literary Society

The topic of Monday evening's meeting of the Society was "Holiday Reminiscences". The various contributions were very interesting, and an enjoyable evening was spent. (FN)

29 November 1913

The Rev. J. H. Morrison

The Rev. J. H. Morrison announced from the pulpit of the United Free Church on Sunday last that he had been appointed to visit the Livingstonia Mission Field[1] in Central Africa, and that he would probably be leaving for this purpose about March next. The duration of his absence from Falkland will be six months. (FN)

29 November 1913

Banquet

On Saturday evening, Provost Jackson entertained the members of the Town Council, along with the officials and a few friends, at supper in the Bruce Arms, Hotel. After an excellent repast, purveyed by Mr Mason in his usual efficient manner, the customary loyal toasts were pledged, and with songs, recitations etc., a most enjoyable time was spent. On the call of Bailie Angus, a hearty vote of thanks was accorded to Provost Jackson for his kind hospitality, and with the singing of "Auld Lang Syne" the proceedings were brought to a close. (FN)

29 November 1913

Lodge St John, No 35

The under-noted brethren of this Lodge have been nominated as office-bearers for the ensuing year, viz.: RWM, Bro. Robert Craig; JPM, Bro. Alex Grieve; DM, Bro. Jas. Jackson; SM, Bro. Jas. Weepers; SW, Bro. Jas. Donaldson; JW, Bro. T. D. Hopkins; Secretary, Bro. David Campbell; Treasurer, Bro. Andrew Venters; Chaplain, Bro. William Lawrie; SD, Bro. Jas. Speed; JD, Bro. David Munro; architect, Bro. Alex. Fraser; BB, Bro. John Traill; SB, Bro. Henry Skinner; Stewards, Bros. John Angus and William Mason; IG, Bro. John Drysdale; OG, Bro. John Walker. (FN)

---

[1] Livingstonia was founded as a mission village in 1894 by the then Free Church of Scotland in a remote area of Nyasaland (now Malawi).

29 November 1913

Women's Unionist Association meeting

A very successful public social under the auspices of the local branch of the East Fife Women's Unionist Association was held in the Drill Hall on Friday night. There was a crowded attendance, over which Lady Ninian Crichton-Stuart presided.

The first part of the programme consisted of a concert. Lady Ninian, Miss H. Sprot, and Miss Christian Page contributed songs; Mr Dudgeon played a violin solo, and Mr Normand and Mr Bateman kindly came over from Leven and sang. A farce by Mrs Hammond and Mr Toole proved very amusing.

Mrs Pierson then spoke on the Home Rule Bill, its effects upon the people of Great Britain, and the determination of the Ulster people to die for their principles. Mrs Pierson concluded a splendid address by proposing a resolution of sympathy with the Ulster loyalists in their determination to resist Home Rule. Colonel Sprot, prospective Unionist candidate for East Fife, seconded in a rousing speech, and the resolution, having been put to the meeting, was carried by acclamation. An enjoyable dance followed. (FN)

6 December 1913

Public meeting

A Public Meeting will be held in the Town Hall on Monday evening, 8th inst., at 8 p.m., for the purpose of enrolling recruits for the Highland Cyclist Battalion.[1] In the unavoidable absence of Lord Ninian Crichton-Stuart MP, George Gavin Esq., will preside. (FN)

6 December 1913

Falkland people's right to take rabbits

The question of the right of the people of Falkland and district to take game from a portion of the East Lomond Hill was argued at considerable length in Cupar Sheriff Court on Tuesday before Sheriff Armour-Hannay.

Wm. James Reid, residing at South Street, Falkland, was charged with having on 26th August, trespassed in pursuit of game in a lime

---

[1] Part of the British Army's Territorial Force.

quarry situated in the East Lomond Hill, Falkland, in a portion which forms part of the estate of Lathrisk, which Mr J. C. Makgill-Crichton recently sold to a syndicate.

Mr J. Kerr Tasker, Cupar, for the respondent, held that the proceedings were incompetent in two respects. (1) That the complainer had no title to prosecute, as he was not, either at the date of the alleged offence, or at the date of the institution of the present proceedings, either the owner or the occupier within the meaning of the Trespass (Scotland) Act 1832, or game tenant of the lime quarry mentioned in the complaint, and (2) that the charge involved a question of civil right.

Mr A. E. Grosset, Cupar, who appeared for the complainer, said that the case had been adjourned in order that he might produce his title to prosecute. His title to the land in question was really founded upon a private Act of Parliament dated 1815, which dealt with the division and allotment of the commonty on the Lomond Hills at Falkland and Strathmiglo, in the parish of Strathmiglo. A commissioner (Sir William Rae) was appointed to carry out the division, and he was directed, in section 14 of the Act, to make up plans of the whole commonty, and to mark in the plans all parts which had been allocated to each proprietor. He produced the plans. The lime quarry in question, together with ten acres of land around it, had been allocated to the proprietor of Lathrisk. This also applied to two other quarries in the neighbourhood.

Mr Tasker said that the people of Falkland had taken game from the quarry for the last 100 years. When the commonty was divided, he stated, the proprietor of Lathrisk got no higher right than the Magistrates and Town Council of Falkland, acting on behalf of the inhabitants. If the proprietor of Lathrisk had any right at all to this lime quarry and the ten acres around it, it was a right in common with others. Lathrisk had been sold, and the present proprietors claimed the ownership of the quarry. They entered on 15th August, and the alleged offence took place on 26th August when the complainer's ownership was gone. Therefore, he held that they had no title to prosecute.

Mr Grosset said it was quite true that the estate was sold on 15th August, but as a matter of fact, the price was not paid until 5th September, and it was not till then that their deed was put upon record.

Mr Tasker – "I think that all this discloses a very healthy question of civil right."

Mr Grosset – "What is the civil right? You have been talking of this civil right, but I have yet to learn what it is."

Mr Tasker – "All right, I will tell you now. The civil right the Provost and Magistrates of Falkland claim is exactly the right which they possessed before the Act of 1815, and prior to the award of 1818, which included the right of the people of Falkland and the neighbourhood to take rabbits. They have exercised that right for the last 100 years."

Mr Grosset said that all the right they ever had was to "take, win, burn and carry away limestone." His point was that the quarry formed part of the commonty and the solum had been allotted to him.

The Sheriff, after listening to protracted arguments, said that the only question he had any interest in was what was to be done with the case. It had to be either dismissed or sisted.

Mr Tasker moved that it be dismissed, and Mr Grosset moved that it be sisted.

The Sheriff said he had come to the conclusion after hearing the arguments that the case must be dismissed. It was perfectly clear that the prosecution was really raised with an ulterior object, namely to get a decision as to the ownership of this quarry. And two points of apparently no inconsiderable difficulty were raised:

(1) as to the interpretation of this private Act of 1815, with the accompanying award of 1818, and

(2) to have a proper principle established in law as to who could prosecute in that particular case, when the alleged poaching offence was committed on 26th August, when the property changed hands on 5th September, and the prosecution was raised on 14th November.

All these matters raised the question of civil right, and accordingly his Lordship thought that the proper course under the circumstances was to dismiss the prosecution. Mr Tasker said that he was instructed to move for expenses. The Sheriff allowed £1 1s expenses. (FN)

13 December 1913

Sale of Work

The Falkland U.F. Church Sale of Work is to be held in the Public

School, Falkland, on Saturday 13th December, to be opened at 2.30 p.m. by Mrs Black, of Chapel. Admission: Adults 2d; Children 1d. (FN)

20 December 1913

Lecture Committee

At a meeting of the Committee held on Monday evening, it was decided to have a special entertainment during the New Year holidays, and a concert is being arranged. (FN)

20 December 1913

Literary Society

At a meeting of the Society held on Monday evening, Miss Anderson read an excellent paper on Shakespeare's *Midsummer Night's Dream*. Mrs Donaldson led off the discussion with an able criticism, and the subject proved both interesting and instructive. (FN)

20 December 1913

Cricket Club dance

The annual assembly of the Falkland Cricket Club was held in the Drill Hall on Friday evening. An enjoyable programme was gone through to music supplied by Mr G. Berry's Quadrille Band, Auchtermuchty. Messrs A. Grieve Jnr, and W. M. Venters acted as MCs.

An interesting part of the proceedings was the presentation of a gold badge to Mr W. M. Venters as the best all-round cricketer in the Club last season. Mr James Donaldson, in the absence of Mr David Bonthrone, the donor of the badge, handed over the prize, and Mr Venters suitably replied.

The following ladies and gentlemen were present: Mrs Liptrott, Mrs Mason, Mrs Robertson and Mrs Venters and Misses J. Anderson, Angus, Burgess, Chisholm, D. and P. Cochrane, R. Falconer, S. Falconer, C. & J. Fernie, Henderson, McCall, Milne, Mora, Morton, Page, E. Page, Reid, Robertson, M. & L. Smith, Steedman, K. Venters, Walker and Wallace. Messrs Allan, Donaldson, Dunbar, Fernie, J. and A. Grieve, Keddie, Kidd, Liptrott, Mason, Ness, Oswald, Peggie, Schofield, Skinner, Steedman, Toole, J. and W. Venters. (FN)

20 December 1913

Falkland Sale of Work

A Sale of Work, organised in connection with Falkland U.F. Church, for the purpose of building a wall round the Manse garden and Manse renovation generally, was held in the Public School, Falkland, on Saturday, the Rev. J. H. Morrison, minister of the congregation, presided over a large gathering which included the Rev. J. K. Russell, Falkland Parish Church, the Rev. Philip Lilley, Freuchie U.F. Church; Mr and Mrs J. W. Jackson, Meadowfield; and Mrs Black of Chapel, who performed the opening ceremony.

In introducing Mrs Black, the Rev. J. H. Morrison said that she was well-known and respected in Falkland, not only for the sake of her father (Sir Michael Nairn), but for her own association with the community, and so needed no introduction. Mrs Black had always taken a deep interest in the affairs of the church and every good cause, and the cause of temperance in particular, had her whole-hearted sympathy and support. (Applause) Mrs Black, in a few well-chosen words, declared the sale open, remarking that one who had written such a splendid book as Mr Morrison had done, was deserving of every encouragement. *On the Trail of the Pioneers*, she said, did its author the greatest credit. (Applause)

The stalls and stall-holders were as follows: Work Stall No. 1 – Mrs Donaldson, Mrs White, Mrs Bisset, and Mrs Graham.Work Stall No. 2 – Mrs Morrison, Mrs Burgen, Miss Hay and Miss Page. Provision Stall – Mrs Trail, Mrs Ross, Miss Hill, Miss M. Page, and Miss A. Peggie. Hoop-la – Miss Isa Hill and Miss M. Peggie. Refreshment Stall – Mrs Walter Peggie and Miss Horn.

A miniature shooting range was under the charge of Messrs Wm. Peggie and James Donaldson. £100 proceeds were aimed at, but when the takings were counted, it was found that no less a sum than £136 had been realised.

The shooting competition at Saturday's Sale of Work resulted as follows: 1st prize (silver cup) – Miss P. Cochrane; 2nd prize (timepiece) – Mr W. Horne; Ladies' prize – Miss R. Falconer; Boys' prize – Mr David Sturrock. (FN)

27 December 1913

Co-operative Society

The year ended 9th December last has been a very prosperous one for the Society, and a dividend of 3s 2d per £1 for members and 1s 7d per £1 for non-members has been declared. (FN)

27 December 1913

Y.M.C.A.

On Sunday morning, the meeting was addressed by Mr Guthrie from Edinburgh. The football team met Kelty Queens Park on Saturday afternoon, but suffered defeat at their hands by 4 goals to nil. (FN)

27 December 1913

Lecture

On Saturday evening a very interesting and instructive lecture was given by the Rev. J. H. Morrison in the Drill Hall. His subject, "Summer and Winter on the Canadian Prairies" was beautifully illustrated by lime-light views. Provost Jackson presided. (FN)

27 December 1913

Treat to school children

The school children of Falkland on Wednesday night were entertained by Lord and Lady Ninian Crichton-Stuart in the Drill Hall. Among those present were: Lord and Lady Ninian Crichton-Stuart; the Rev. J. K. Russell, Parish Church; Mr George Gavin, Falkland Palace; Provost Jackson; Dr Jack; Mr J. Donaldson, banker, etc. The gifts from the heavily laden and beautifully decorated tree were given out by Lady Ninian, who wished all the children a happy Christmas. Tea was served, and a programme of music was sustained by the children. (FN)

59. Lord and Lady Ninian's Christmas card for 1913.
Standing outside the House of Falkland with little Ismay
and baby Claudia

After 1913 life in Falkland would never be the same again.

Falkland's People

Falkland's people in 1901

The 1901 census gives the population for the Parish of Falkland as 2,231 including 809 for the Royal Burgh. Families were large and households often consisted of several generations. There were still some handloom weavers, but the linen factory employed people as yarn dressers, twisters, warehouse men and weavers.

There is no census listing for the House of Falkland, but the Palace was occupied by Major Wood and ten members of his family and lodgers.

Falkland was a place of shopkeepers (grocers, butchers, bakers), craftsmen (joiners, plasterers, slaters, painters, masons, dykers) many of whom had worked on the Palace and House of Falkland. There was the rise of white-collar workers as clerks in banks and factory offices. There were still home-based workers such as John Brown, Horse-market, a self-employed umbrella manufacturer; dress makers, shoe makers. Many men were labourers, work which may often have been seasonal. In transport there were carters and an occasional mechanic.

Some men of the village worked on the estate as labourers, gardeners, ploughmen, foresters.

Falkland's people in 1911

By the 1911 census the population for the Parish had gone up to 2,356, including 830 for the Royal Burgh.

The population had been boosted by the influx of factory workers, many of whom lodged in the town – a widow in Westport described her occupation as Boarding House Keeper. There are instances of apprentices for plumbers and joiners, but some of the youth of the village were starting to seek employment in towns, joining the army and some even emigrating, while some found work outside Falkland on the railways.

There must have been a sizeable child population, as 244 attended a Christmas party in 1909.

There was now the Pleasance Linen Works and the St John's floor-cloth factory, both owned by the Jackson family, who started building substantial houses for themselves. Employment was found in both factories for men and women. The floorcloth factory employed warehouse hands, block cutters, hand printers, lino painters and a fireman, while the linen factory had tenters, bobbin winders, card cutters, machinists, weavers, croppers, lappers and mechanics.

The professional classes were represented by bank staff, Registrar, teachers, and typists in law offices. The retail trade was represented by drapers, publicans, the hotel keeper at the Commercial Hotel, grocers, bakers, a china merchant in the Cross Wynd, and confectioners. Traditional craftsmen still survived such as Alexander Galloway, wood turner, a saddler, a tailoress, and a watchmaker in Brunton Street.

For the service industry there were laundresses and housekeepers.

The House of Falkland is listed as having 50 rooms with 24 residents, nearly 20 of whom were servants. Estate staff were living in both the village and tied houses and the farms tenanted. With the move to the motor car there was a chauffeur.

The Bruces

PROFESSOR JOHN BRUCE (1745–1826) bought land around Falkland from 1821 onwards, building up the Falkland Estate. On his death the estate passed to his niece MARGARET BRUCE (c 1781–1869) from India,

60. The third Marquess of Bute's four children
Depicted on cupboard doors in Falkland Palace
Lady Margaret, John (later fourth Marquess), Lord Ninian, Lord Colum

who in 1828 married the barrister **ONESIPHORUS TYNDALL** (1790–
1855), changing the family name to **TYNDALL BRUCE**. The Tyndall
Bruces commissioned the building of the House of Falkland (replacing Nuthill) and the Temple of Decision (now sadly ruined) and
funded the Parish Church and the Fountain. The statue of
Onesiphorus now stands near the Kirk, and he is also commemorated
by the Tyndall Bruce Monument on the Black Hill.

The Crichton-Stuarts

THE THIRD MARQUESS OF BUTE (John Patrick Crichton-Stuart, 1847–
1900) converted to Roman Catholicism aged 21. He had extensive
properties in South Wales, where he commissioned the restoration on
a magnificent scale of Cardiff Castle and Castell Coch. In 1887 he
purchased the Falkland Estate, becoming Laird of Falkland and
hereditary keeper of Falkland Palace, where he initiated major
restoration works. He and his wife had four children, Lady Margaret,
John (Fourth Marquess), Lord Ninian and Lord Colum. He left the
Falkland Estate to his second son, Lord Ninian.

After Lord Bute's death, his widow, née Gwendolen Fitzalan-

Howard, referred to (strictly speaking only after the fourth Marquess's marriage) as the **DOWAGER MARCHIONESS**, continued to take an interest in Falkland, particularly St Andrew's House (a home for Roman Catholic orphan boys) and the declining handloom weaving trade.

LORD NINIAN CRICHTON-STUART (Ninian Edward Crichton-Stuart, 1883–1915) was intended to enter the diplomatic service, and was studying in Kiev when he fell ill with typhus and returned home, to study at Christ Church, Oxford. In 1903 he was commissioned into the Queen's Own Cameron Highlanders and later served in the Scots Guards. He inherited the Falkland Estate on his 21st birthday in 1904. After his marriage in 1906, Lord Ninian transferred into the Army Reserve and took up politics, serving on Fife County Council. In 1910 he was elected as MP for Cardiff Boroughs. In 1912 he became lieutenant-colonel of the 6th battalion, the Welsh Regiment.[1] At the outbreak of war in 1914 the battalion was shipped to France, and in 1915 he was killed at the Battle of Loos.

In 1906 Lord Ninian married the **HON. ISMAY LUCRETIA MARY PRESTON** (1882–1955), thereafter referred to as **LADY NINIAN**: she was the daughter of Viscount Gormanston, and the wedding was held at Gormanston Castle estate in Ireland. Lord and Lady Ninian had four children: Ninian Patrick (1907–1910), Ismay Catherine (1909–1989), Claudia Miriam Joanna (1913–1985), and Michael Duncan David (1915–1981). After Lord Ninian's death Lady Ninian married Archibald Henry Maule Ramsay.

Lady Ninian's cousin **CAPTAIN SLACKE** (Roger Cecil Slacke, known as Rory) became Lord Ninian's secretary. Like many others he was killed in action in 1915.

The Jacksons

CHARLES JACKSON (1837–1914) founded the firm that became a major employer in Falkland. Originally from Kent, he lived in London and Birmingham, but in 1861 he moved to Strathmiglo for health reasons and fathered a child there – Albert James Jackson. In 1863 he moved

---

[1] Renamed "the Welch Regiment" in 1920.

61. Three Jacksons
John Walker Jackson – Charles Jackson – Charles Jackson Jnr

to Falkland and married Janet Walker; they had five children: Euphemia, Thomas, John, James Walker, and Charles Jnr. Janet died in June 1878.

Trained as a draper, Charles started a handloom weaving business, and in 1871 built the linen factory, followed in 1901 by the floorcloth factory. The firm of Charles Jackson & Sons was registered in 1905. By the time of his death the business employed 200 people. He was also chairman of the Falkland Light Railway Company.

Charles Jackson was elected Provost of Falkland in 1873 and re-elected in 1876, but resigned before the end of his term in May 1879; possible reasons for his resignation could have been the death of another son Ernest Edward in February of that year aged 8 months, and the birth of his son William (by Janet's sister Euphemia) in April. William was described as illegitimate on his birth registration form, but later seems to have the surname Jackson. By the 1881 census Euphemia was described as Charles Jackson's wife, although there seems to be no record of a marriage.

CHARLES JACKSON JNR (c. 1860–1937) ran the family firm, with his brothers James Jackson and John Walker Jackson, after his father's death, retiring when the firm was sold to the Scottish Co-operative Wholesale Society in 1919. He was Provost of Falkland from 1909 to

1921. He never married. In 1930 he donated a pipe organ to the Falkland Kirk in memory of his parents and of his sister Euphemia (Mrs Birrel Livingston, died 1917).

JOHN WALKER JACKSON was a Town Councillor and a JP. He married Janet (Hettie) Wilson, youngest daughter of the late George Wilson, Cranchie, Prestonkirk and Mrs Wilson, Rosenheir, Perth. Their daughter was born on 2 March 1910 at their rented home at Viewfield, Dunshalt. In 1909 John Walker employed the architectural firm Gillespie & Scott for his new house, Meadowfield in Falkland.

John Walker's son, another John Walker, died in Cupar in 1950, and there are now no Jacksons left to carry the family name forward.

The Kentish connection

With the growth of the Jackson factories, workers were recruited from Kirkcaldy and elsewhere, but these proved insufficient to meet the demand. Charles Jackson turned to his Kentish roots and formed a connection with the Medway Guardians who ran children's homes near Chatham. Some children were orphans, others had been placed in residential care by parents who couldn't cope.

The homes provided a ready source of cheap labour with boys and girls aged 14 or over being sent up by train to Falkland Road station and often then having to walk to Falkland. The 1911 census lists 32 of them working as machinists, lappers, croppers and card cutters in the linen factory, and handprinters, lino painters, block cutters and warehouse hands in the floorcloth factory. They were housed in a hostel, but many lodged in homes throughout Falkland. Some served in the army during the Great War, several are commemorated on Falkland's war memorial while others such as ALF BURGESS, DICK HOMDEN and HARRY LEE returned from the war, married and became Fifers. One of Dick's descendants lives in Falkland to this day.

The Lawsons

WILLIAM LAWSON, a labourer, served as a sergeant in the Boer War, having taken part in "many striking episodes". In his absence three of his eight sons, HERIOT BAIN LAWSON, sometimes known as Harriott, and the twins ALEXANDER and WILLIAM JNR, were several times convicted of minor burglaries. Heriot Lawson was killed in World War One serving with the Cameron Highlanders as was a much younger brother Stephen who is commemorated on the Falkland War Memorial.

Several other, apparently unrelated, Lawsons appear in these pages, including JOHN LAWSON, the "respected tenant of Falkland Wood Farm", and ALEXANDER LAWSON of Annfield and Burnturk,

The Bonthrones

ALEXANDER BONTHRONE (1832–1906) was the head of a very long-established brewing company, which was the main industry in Newton of Falkland. The Bonthrones had begun brewing there in 1600 and stopped in 1916, to concentrate on malting and bottling.

Alexander's son DAVID BONTHRONE was wounded in the Boer War, and later served, like his father, on the county council, eventually becoming chairman of the Cupar District Committee. He was a member of the School Board and a keen sportsman.

Another member of the family, JOHN BONTHRONE, was Provost of Auchtermuchty.

The Johnstons of Lathrisk

GEORGE JOHNSTON (died 1900) had built up the Lathrisk Estate, and was rumoured, probably without much foundation, to be an eccentric recluse. His ancestors are buried in the Johnston family enclosure in the old burying ground in Falkland, and he himself is commemorated on the stone he erected there.

On George's death the estate passed to a distant relative, CHARLES JULIAN MAITLAND-MAKGILL-CRICHTON (1880–1915), whose name was reported inconsistently in newspaper reports, sometimes with Johnston added at the end. He was the elder son of David Maitland-Makgill-Crichton, of Rankeillor, near Cupar. On 15 February 1902 he married Sybil Twynihoe Erle, of Craigentor, Crieff, Perthshire, the daughter of a former Master of the Supreme Court.

Charles took on the role of Laird of Lathrisk until 1908, when he moved to Monzie Castle, Perthshire (which was severely damaged by fire the next month), and Lathrisk House was leased for five years to

Hon. Felix Hanbury-Tracy.

At the expiry of the lease, the estate was sold to a syndicate, and Charles Julian bought a ranch in California. On the outbreak of war he volunteered for service, and was killed at the Battle of Loos.[1]

The County Council

In 1913 Lord Ninian Crichton-Stuart succeeded Major Maitland-Makgill-Crichton of Lathrisk as the Falkland Landward representative[2] on Fife County Council when the Major parted with Lathrisk Estate to go to America. Alexander Bonthrone had also represented the Falkland Landward.

Falkland Burgh was represented by John Walker Jackson of Lomondvale.

The Provosts

1879–1903: **WILLIAM PAGE**, builder, died 1903. In his youth he had spent some time as a "digger" in Australia. He was in charge of much of the masonry work on the restoration of Falkland Palace. He was elected Provost in November 1879, having acted as interim Provost since Charles Jackson's resignation in May.

1903–1909: **ROBERT MILLER**, joiner, sometimes spelt "Millar". His son, ROBERT MILLER JNR was also a joiner, and worked in the Palace after WWII. He died in the 1950s and was reputed to be one of the most miserly men in Falkland.

1909–1921: **CHARLES JACKSON JNR** (see above). His father, also Charles Jackson, had been Provost in the previous century.

---

[1] www.winchestercollegeatwa+om/archive/charles-julian-maitland-makgill-crichton/

[2] Lord Ninian's home, the House of Falkland, was not in the Royal Burgh, so it was Falkland Landward that he represented, in other words the part of the parish outwith the Royal Burgh. His son, Major Michael Crichton Stuart, registered as a voter in the Royal Burgh and was thus able to act as Provost.

The Councillors

The following served on the Council at some time during the period:

62. The Provost's Lamp, with
the arms of Falkland
Now located outside the Palace, it
was formerly outside the home of
the current Provost.

- John Angus (innkeeper; Bailie)
- Brown
- Christopher Campbell Brunton (butcher)
- Robert Drysdale (Bailie)
- James Forsyth (building and masonry work)
- Alex Fraser (joiner)
- George Hardie
- Harvie (Bailie)
- William Horne
- Charles Jackson Jnr (manufacturer; Bailie, then Provost)
- John Walker Jackson
- William Lawrie (Bailie)
- John Leaburn
- Andrew Lister (baker; Bailie)
- Lornie (Bailie)
- William Alexander Mason (Bruce Arms)
- Robert Miller (master joiner; Bailie, then Provost)
- Robert Ness (proprietor of a Temperance Hotel; he also ran a cartage and bus service)
- William Page (builder; Provost)
- Michael Reekie (farmer)
- David Reid (shoemaker)
- George Robertson (Bailie)
- Thomas Sutherland (tailor; Bailie)
- Thomas Williamson (saddler)

The Town Clerk

The Town Clerk was a key figure in running the affairs of the Burgh Council. From 1819 until 1865 this post was held by **CHARLES GULLAND SNR** (died 1886) who was succeeded by his son, another **CHARLES GULLAND** (from 1865 till his death in 1909. Both Gullands were lawyers, factors of the Lathrisk Estate, and Agents at the British Linen Bank. Charles's son **ROWLAND GULLAND** also acted briefly as Town Clerk, probably jointly with his father, until his untimely death in 1903. The family lived at Millfield House. The younger Charles was a published poet.[1]

The solicitor **ALEXANDER ANDERSON** was appointed Town Clerk on Charles Guilland's death in 1909. In 1912 he was also appointed clerk and treasurer of the School Board, replacing the late **JOHN SHERIFF**.

The bank agents

The bank agents with the British Linen Bank were significant figures in local society. Charles and Rowland Gulland (see above) were both bank agents until their deaths. Charles ("CG") is commemorated by a plaque on the extension to Bank House in Back Wynd.

In 1909, following Charles Gulland's death, Alexander Anderson (see above) and Captain **JAMES DONALDSON** from Edinburgh, who had served in the Boer War, were appointed joint bank agents. Mr Donaldson thereafter took an active part in Falkland life, serving on the Parish Council, chairing various meetings, reading a paper at the Literary Society and acting as Scoutmaster, secretary of the Curling Club and captain of the Y.M.C.A. Football Club.

The factors

MAJOR WILLIAM WOOD was factor of the Falkland estate for more than 30 years. He died on 14 February 1902.

He was succeeded by **GEORGE GAVIN** (officially appointed December 1904, having acted as administrator of the estate since Major

---

[1] *An Alphabet of Falkland Folk*, page 10.

Wood's death). Major Wood was a Protestant, but it was an important factor in the appointment of Mr Gavin that he was a Catholic; he became very involved in dealings with the priest and in the arrangements for the Chapel Royal in the Palace. George and his wife are both buried inside the Memorial Chapel.

The architects

ROBERT WEIR SCHULTZ (1860–1951) worked extensively for the third Marquess of Bute, including work on the House of Falkland. Within the Palace he designed the fittings for the Chapel Royal, which were made by Robert Miller and paid for by Lady Bute. He restored Brunton House, and in 1898 he had advised on the lowering of the street level in Brunton Street.

HAROLD OGLE TARBOLTON (1869–1947; nicknamed Tarrybreeks) was based in Edinburgh. In Falkland he designed the Town Clerk's office, and made some of the plasterwork for the House of Falkland. His wife Beatrice Gulland was the daughter of Charles Gulland Snr.

REGINALD FAIRLIE (1883–1952) was the son of J. Ogilvy Fairlie of Myres Castle and Jane Mary Fairlie. He was educated at the Oratory School in Birmingham, his father having been a Catholic convert. He was apprenticed to Robert Lorimer in 1901 and much of his style echoes that of Lorimer. He is best known for the National Library of Scotland. In Falkland, he designed the new Catholic Church in memory of young Ninian Crichton-Stuart, which was left unroofed as a memorial chapel.

The politicians

Falkland, throughout our period, was represented in Parliament by H. H. ASQUITH (1852–1928) as member for East Fife. He was born in Yorkshire and educated at the City of London School and Balliol College, Oxford. He was elected for East Fife as a Liberal in 1886, and while in opposition became a successful barrister. He was Home Secretary in the 1892–5 Liberal Government. When the Liberals returned to power in 1905 he became Chancellor of the Exchequer, and from 1908 to 1914 he was leader of the Liberal Party and Prime Minister. With homes in London and Surrey, he seems to have been little involved in the daily life of Fife.

Asquith's Conservative opponent at the 1906 General Election was a local man, JOHN GILMOUR (born in Montrave in 1876). He was elected as MP for East Renfrewshire in 1910, and for Glasgow Pollok in 1918. From 1924 onwards he held several government posts, including Secretary of State for Scotland and Home Secretary.

In the two general elections in 1910 Asquith was opposed by COLONEL ALEXANDER SPROT, originally from Lanarkshire, who lived at Strathvithie near St Andrews. He went on to win the East Fife seat in 1918. He lost it in 1922, but became MP for North Lanarkshire from 1924.

The clergy

The ministers of both the Established Church and the United Free Church took a prominent part in local affairs.

For the Established Church, REV. A. LYON JOHNSTON, originally from Cambusnethan, was minister from 1898 until his death in 1911 aged 49. He was succeeded in 1912 by REV. J. K. RUSSELL, who is commemorated by a memorial window in the kirk.

For the United Free Church, REV. JAMES HORNE MORRISON served as minister from about 1901 In 1913 he published a book about U.F. missions, and in 1914 he left for a mission in central Africa.

Rev. Johnston and Rev. Morrison were both members of the Falkland School Board, and a dispute arose between them at a School Board meeting in 1911.

The small Roman Catholic community was (and still is) centred on the Chapel Royal in Falkland Palace. FR DE STOOP was employed as Lord Ninian's chaplain, but dismissed in 1905, possibly on account of financial irregularity. He was in due course replaced by FR HENRY WOODS, for whom accommodation was provided not in the Palace but in Brunton House, which had been used as a Roman Catholic school. Following the closure of the Brunton House school, Catholic children had their own religious instruction in the public school, a practice that was roundly condemned by Rev. Morrison.

The solicitors

Solicitors were an essential element in Edwardian Scotland and, with Cupar having been the seat of justice since mediaeval times, eastern Fife had many. Until the middle of the twentieth century, many solicitors were "men of business" who, as well as the core duties of prosecuting and defending in the courts, acted as factors to estates whose scale or wealth did not justify a resident one, and operated in partnership with the resident factors of those which did. Solicitors organised the purchase and sale of land and property, sometimes by roup (auction), as well as dealing with the legal transfer of title (conveyancing). Most branches of banks outside the largest towns and cities had solicitors as their "bank agents", as with the British Linen Company's branch in Falkland.

Fife's solicitors were town clerks, secretaries of committees, company secretaries, and agents for private Acts of Parliament (as for the Falkland Light Railway Company), and generally helped the wheels of society to turn smoothly by taking an active part in local organisations and social events. Cupar, being the county town and the seat of the Sheriff Court, hosted several firms of solicitors, including Mr **GROSSET,** and the Pagans and Osbornes of their family firm of **OSBORNE PAGAN**, which had opened in Cupar in 1770 and survived until 2017.

In Edinburgh, the firm of **J. & F. ANDERSON** at 48 Castle Street were the Crichton-Stuart family solicitors, the main partners being the Andersons and the Pitmans. In 1992 J. & F. Anderson merged with Strathern and Blair to form Anderson Strathern LLP. Both firms had been in practice for over 200 years. Francis Anderson, Lord Bute's private secretary, was a member of the family.

Places and People

We list below over 300 places (cities, towns, villages, houses, most but not all in Scotland) that are mentioned in this book, with the people who lived there or were associated with the place in another way. For each place we generally avoid listing multiple people with the same surname, to avoid making this chapter even longer. County names are the traditional names, as used at the time of the events.

Places in the parish or royal burgh of Falkland, and a few in the rest of Fife, are shown on the maps on pages 467 onwards, and marked below as follows:

ⓟ   on the parish map on page 467.

ⓑ   on the burgh map on page 468.

① to ㊿   on the detailed map on page 469 (and listed in the index on page 464).

Abdie (Fife)
  Rev. Alex Alison
Aberdeen
  Benjamin Reid & Co.
  A. Mackie
  Nazareth House
  John Reekie
  George Gavin working there

Aberdour (Fife)
  Seaside resort; venue for choir excursion.
Abernethy (Perthshire)
  Mrs Davidson
Addiewell / West Calder (Midlothian)
  Edwin Justice

Allan Park Ⓑ

House in woodland above Falkland.

Rev. John Wilson Thomson
Alexander Anderson
Literary Society

Alloa (Clackmannanshire)

John Mason

Annfield Farm Ⓟ

Andrew Morgan (forester)

Annfield House (Kettle) Ⓟ

*Large mansion up the hill opposite
    Kettle cemetery, now demolished.*

Alexander Lawson (Annfield and
    Burnturk)

Arbroath (Angus)

Keith & Blackman Co.
Y.M.C.A. Conference, 1911

Arngask (Fife)

John Hay

Arnot Tower (Fife)

House with ruined tower near Leslie.

Sir Charles Bruce

Auchtermuchty Ⓟ

Rev. William Affleck
Mr Baker (Excise Officer)
G. Berry (music)
John Bett (thatcher)
James Bonthrone
John Bonthrone (Provost)
Mr Cant (councillor)
Mr Clark (Bailie)
Robert Ferlie (Provost)
Rev. D. N. Hogg
Thomas Hutchison
John Laing
Mr Leven
Mrs Maitland
Miss Maxwell
Mr Muir (Bailie)
J. R. Oliphant
George Page
J. Peters
D. S. Reid VS

Mrs Shearer
Dr Shearer
Mr Simpson (councillor)
C. G Simpson
J. Simpson
R. Simpson
Mr Stocks (postmaster)
R. Suttie
R. Taylor
Archibald Walker
Mr Walker (Town Clerk)
Auchtermuchty Brass Band
Auchtermuchty Hospital

Back Wynd ㊿

David Anderson
Alexander Lawson
Thomas Ross

Balbirnie (Fife)

Charles Henderson
Mrs Balfour

Balgonie (Fife)

Henry Hood
Henry Laird

Ballo Ⓟ

Major Wilson

Balmalcolm (Fife)

Rev. W. L. Craig

Balmblae ⑥ Ⓑ

*To the north of the Maspie Burn and
    thus outside the Burgh. Many
    houses since demolished.*

Mrs Agnes Birrell (loom shop)
James Galloway (mill)
Lawson family
Peter Robinson

Balmblae Burn ⑫

Boundary of the Royal Burgh.

Balmumgo (Fife)

Henry Maitland
Henry Murray

Barrington Ⓟ

Part of the Falkland Estate.

George Maxwell

Bathgate (West Lothian)
Rev. John Lindsay
Bavelaw (Midlothian)
Belfast
Mr Russell (Station Master)
Belmore (near Cupar, Fife)
Small "Gentleman's Estate" just outside Cupar.
David Osborne WS (Pagan & Osborne)
Blackford (Perthshire)
Mr McPherson
Blairgowrie (Perthshire)
Miss Falconer
Bluebrae Plantation Ⓑ Ⓟ
Wooded area south of the Leslie Road.
Boarhills (Fife)
Ada Bain (Burnside Farm)
Bonvil (Cupar)
Cricket ground.
Bowhill (Selkirkshire)
Mr Ross
Brechin (Angus)
James Clark
Bridgend Quarry (on the Lathrisk estate)
Source of road-building material.
Bridge of Allan (Stirlingshire)
Dr A. Macintosh
Bridge of Earn (Perthshire)
Herbert Pullar
Briggs Plantation (on the Falkland estate)
Theft of lead piping.
British Linen Bank and Bank House ㉖
Mr Davison
Agents:
Charles Gulland
Rowland Gulland
James Donaldson (1909)
Alexander Anderson (1909)
Employees:

Francis Henderson
Alexander Sutherland
Randolph Cameron (teller)
Bank House:
Mrs Gulland
James Donaldson
Bruce Arms ㉗
Later called the Falkland Arms Hotel, then the Hunting Lodge Hotel, now reverted to the Bruce. Two previous tenants bankrupt.
Thomas Hardie
William Alexander Mason
Mrs Swanson
Bruce Arms, butcher shop
Christopher Campbell Brunton
Bruce Buildings ⑦
David Crichton
Annie Sharp
John Sheriff
Brunton House ㊺
(Brunton Street)
Lady Bute's Catholic School; Altered 1910 for Lord Ninian's chaplain
Romond Aboad de Lazeu (teacher)
Rachel Graham
Annie and Sarah Higgins
Agnes O'Brien
George Lumsden
Mrs O'Connor
Brunton Street ㊻
Re-paved in 1901.
Mrs George Ramsay (next door)
Bryce's shop ⑯
Now the Violin Shop.
Duncan C. Bryce
Buckhaven (Fife)
D. Brown
Burnturk (Fife)
Alexander Lawson (Annfield and Burnturk)
Burying ground (old cemetery)

ⓐ
Cadham (Fife)
R. Russell
Caldwells Farm (Fife)
Cambusnethan (Lanarkshire)
Mr Currie
D. Tinto
Canada
Thomas Myles emigrating
Canonbury (Newton Road) Ⓑ
Later became the Manse.
Dr J. G. Jack
Carlisle (Cumberland)
Sister Ethelburga (Durranhill
House)
Francis Henderson
Carluke (Lanarkshire)
Francis Henderson moving there
Carriston (Fife ?)
John Lawson
Cash Mill Ⓟ
Arch. Ness
Mr Ritchie
Mr Todd
Castell Coch (near Cardiff)
Castlefield (near Cupar)
F. W. Christie
Castle-Shots Road ⑭ Ⓑ
*Running north from Falkland. Motor
accident*
Cemetery Ⓑ
*New cemetery on Newton Road.
Burial place of many people mentioned
in this book.*
Ceres (Fife)
Rev. J. P. Berry
Ceylon
Now Sri Lanka
Lord and Lady Ninian intending to
go there
Chancefield Ⓟ
Joseph McKay (gamekeeper)
Gordon Sturrock (gamekeeper)

Chapel (Fife)
Mrs Black
Chapel Royal (Falkland Palace)
*The Chapel Royal became the Catholic
parish church for the area.*
Chapelyard House Ⓑ
*High up to the south of the town, next
to the Manse.*
Major James Cusin
Chatham (Kent)
Children's homes
Colin Herd's Shop ㊹
Now a private house
Commercial Hotel ㉑
Now the Covenanter Hotel.
John and George Angus
Co-op store ⑰
Now Campbell's coffee house.
Corston Mill Ⓟ
W. Calder
Couston (Fife)
Andrew Whitton (factor)
Cowdenbeath (Fife)
George Watson (Broad Street)
R. Condie
Crackland Hillpark ㊿ Ⓑ
Rubbish being left there
Crawford Priory *(Fife)*
*Country house near Springfield. Now
in ruins.*
Hon. Thomas Cochrane MP
Craigeach School (Galloway)
Walter Wilson and James David to
be sent there
Cross Wynd ㊴
Charles Birrell
Mr (?) Gallon
Jane Hamilton
Elizabeth Hyslop
John Lawson
John Mackenzie (flesher)
James Page
Mrs L. Reekie

Cults (Fife)
Rev William H. Porter
See also Priestfield.
Cupar (Fife)
The county town of Fife at this period.
H. Adamson (jeweller)
Thomas Aitken MICE
J. R. Baillie (vet)
Mr Bonthrone (Cupar District
  Committee)
Mrs Bonthrone (Kinsleith)
Randolph Cameron (bank teller)
James Carmichael
Conservative Club
D. Cooper
Rev. S. Crabb
Police Sergeant Cumming
H. Diggle
R. Douglas
Rev. Robert Frizelle
John Gilmour (photographer, 94
  Bonnygate)
D. Gordon & Son (Photographer,
  The County Studio)
Herd & Robertson
George Innes (*Fife Herald*)
J. & G. Innes (printers)
A. B. Keddie (Bonnygate)
David G. Maule (bandmaster,
  Provost Wynd)
D. McDonald
Miss McGregor
W. McLellan (Kinsleith)
Miss Orchison (Denbrae)
Outhwaite (car hire)
William D. Patrick (County Clerk)
Alexander Ramsay (sculptor)
Royal Hotel (auction, meetings)
Miss Sharp
Speedie Bros. (auctioneers)
Robert Spence
W. Stark
W. Stewart (plumber)
George White

Sheriffs:
  Sheriff Armour-Hannay
  Sheriff Gillespie
  Sheriff Substitute Gray
  Sheriff William Thomson
Solicitors:
  J. L. Anderson (Town Clerk)
  A. E. Grosset
  J. E. Grosset
  G. E. B. Osborne
  R. Osborne Pagan
  J. Kerr Tasker
  James Welch
Curling ponds
Old curling pond near the Golf
  Course Ⓑ
New curling pond near the
  Strathmiglo Road Ⓑ
now the bowling green
Dairsie Mains (Fife)
F. W. Christie
Dalmeny (West Lothian)
Miss McLaren
Demperston Ⓟ
Mr Walker
Denside Farm (in Falkland; not
  located)
William Dowie
Dovecot Farm (Pleasance) ㊲
House c. 1835.
Henry and William Duncan
Drill Hall ㊹
*Originally a Burgher chapel (a
  Presbyterian denomination
  originating in the 18th century).
  Now two private houses.*
Treasurer: Andrew Lister.
Drumdreel Ⓟ
Mr Amos
Mr Dykes
Drumley Farm (Fife)
C. J. Maitland Makgill Crichton

Drums ℗
Mr Barclay
Dublin
Rev. W. Delaney
Gresham Hotel
Dumfries
A. C. Penman, Motor Carriage
Works
Dumfries House (Ayrshire)
Lord Ninian born there
Dunblane (Perthshire)
J. W. Barty, Factor
Dunbog (Fife)
Rev. W. M. Tocher
Dundee (Angus)
J. Barry Armstrong
Mr Baird
H. Black
Dr W. Graham Campbell
Carnegie baths
Miss M. Gray
J. M. Haynes (telephone express
office)
Mr Hook (Post Office)
Dr William Kinnear
D. McLennan
Mr McPherson
H. D. Michie (moving there)
Miss Pirie
John Sheriff (solicitor: died there)
Miss Templeton
Col. Harry Walker
Dunfermline (Fife)
R. T. Lindsay
Rev. Jacob Primmer (Kingseathill)
Dunnikier (Fife)
Colonel Oswald
Dunshalt ℗
A. Duncan
John W. Jackson
William Malloch
Mr Ritchie
Mr Smith

John Steedman
Henry Suttie
Janet Wilson (Mrs John Walker
Jackson) born at Viewfield
Durham (County)
Mistakenly quoted as "Duraway"
Lord Ninians' estates:
Bryan's Leap
Burnopfield
Tanfield
East Brackley (Kinross-shire)
W. Todd
East Conland ℗
Andrew McQueen (gamekeeper)
Easter Cash ℗
James Tod
East Loan ㊿
Grassy area to the south of the Burgh.
East Lodge
See Lodge Gate.
East Lomond Hill ‡ ℗
At one time part of the Lathrisk estate.
Scout camp (Triangle Park)
East Port ㉛
William Burgon (fish dealer)
East Wemyss (Fife)
John Kennoway
Edenshead (Fife)
Rev. D. W. Greenfield
Edinburgh: firms and organi-
sations
J. & F. Anderson (48 Castle Street,
solicitors):
J. Anderson
Archibald Pitman
John S. Pitman
British Linen Bank:
F. Gordon Brown
James Donaldson
Alfred Carlisle (Solicitor, Edinburgh
Parish Council)
Catholic Boys home (Lauriston
Place)

Deaconess Hospital
Hamilton & Inches (jewellers, 47
  George Street)
Cockburn Campbell (wine mer-
  chant, 32 St Andrews Square)
Edinburgh College of Agriculture:
  J. G. Stewart
Edinburgh Highland Reel and
  Strathspey Society
Edinburgh Public Library:
  Hew Morrison
  Edinburgh Royal Infirmary
Maule & Sons (department store,
  Princes Street)
Melville & Lindsay (110 George
  Street)
Roxburgh Hotel
Teind Court
Thomson & Porteus

Edinburgh: individuals

A. Anderson
George Ballingall (solicitor)
J. Augustus Beddie
Mr Baird
Miss Biggar
J. H. Bonnar (interior decorator)
Mr Brown
G. Somervel Carfrae (engineer)
James Clark
Rev. W. W. Clark
John Collins Jnr
P. Craig (accountant)
Dr William Currie
Mr Dandie
Reginald Fairlie (architect)
Dr Farquharson
R. W. Forsyth (kilt maker)
William Alexander Glass
Mr Guthrie
G. Inglis
Alexander Johnstone
J. H. Lawson
W. H. Massey
Misses Mather

D. McGregor
Dr McIntosh
Thomas McIntosh (solicitor)
John Methven
C. Miller
Mr Rennie
Miss Richardson
Miss Robertson
J. G. Simpson
Misses Smith
Harold O. Tarbolton (architect)
Mr Tawse
Miss Wingate
Miss Yule

Egypt
Lord and Lady Ninian staying in
  Cairo

Elgin (Moray)
A. F. MacDonald (Solicitor)

Elie (Fife)

Elphinstone, Tranent (East
Lothian)
Mr Young

Falkland Cross ⑲
*A small cross made of cobbles near the
  fountain, marking the site of the
  former Mercat Cross.*

Falkland Islands
Mail misdirected to.

Falkland Palace ㉜ Ⓑ
*Built for James IV on the site of a
  mediaeval castle, and extended
  under James V. Later fell into ruin
  and was restored by the third
  Marquess of Bute.*
Factors:
  Major William Wood
  George Gavin
Chaplains:
  Fr de Stoop
  Fr Henry Woods
Guides:
  D. Campbell

Andrew Hillock
Michael Reekie
Gardeners:
William Young
Denson
George Galloway

Falkland Road Station P

About 2½ miles from Falkland.
Mr Nichol (stationmaster)

Falkland Wood P

Robert Laing (ploughman)
John Lawson and Misses Lawson
Alex Shanks

Fettykil (Fife)

Mr Wallace

Fiddlehall B

Site for Golf Club
James Clark

Forfar (Angus)

Miss Lawson

Fountain ⑳

By Alexander Roos, 1856.

Freuchie P

Arch. Aitken
J. Blyth
Alexander Bonthrone
R. M. Bruce at al. (choir)
E. Croall
D. and J. Duncan
Eden Valley Factory
Miss Forsyth
Rev. Charles Fraser
Richard Hargraves
D. Inglis
R. Jack
James W. Leishman
Rev. Philip W. Lilley
Rev. George Lowe
J. L. Lumsden (Eden Valley House)
Constable Lumsden
Jane Middleton (Lomond Hotel)
J. Methven
James Miller
Robert Morgan

J. Morrison
James Philp
Rev. J. M. Richardson
L. Rymer
J. Robertson
W. Simpson
J. Speed
A. Spence
W. Stark
Mrs A. Thomson
T. Watson

Gallatown (Fife)

Mr Collins

Gas Works ⑬

Now a private house

Gateside (Fife)

Between Strathmiglo and Burnside;
there is another Gateside between
the New Inn and Markinch. P
Miss Lily Leburn
Mr Ballantyne

Glasgow

J. Bruce Alston
Dr Carswell
A. H. Charteris (Glasgow Archae-
ological Society, 79 West Regent
Street)
A. J. Christie
John Drake
Mr Hunter
Rev. Mackintosh Mackay
Andrew Melville
Agnes O'Brien
Mr Orr
Page & Sandeman (wine merchants,
Buchanan Street)
Mr Thomson

Glendevon (Perthshire)

Rev. J. K. Russell
Rev. A. O. Taylor

Glenfarg (Perthshire)

Miss Cochrane

Golf Course B

On the Myre

Gormanston Castle (County Meath, Ireland)
Sold in 1950; now a school
Viscount and Viscountess Gormanston, and their daughter, Hon. Ismay Preston, until she became Lady Ninian.

Guardbridge (Fife)
Mrs Lucinda Campbell

Hamilton (Lanarkshire)
Rev. J. K. Russell

Hawick (Roxburghshire)
Annie and Sarah Higgins
Mr Smith (Galalaw)

High Street ㉘
Also referred to as High Street East. See also individual houses.
William Duncan
Mrs Garland
David Lumsden (publican)
William James Ried

High Street West ⑧
Heriot, Alexander and William Lawson
Andrew Wallace

Hillfoot Cottage [B]
On the Leslie Road.

Horsemarket (52)
John Brown (umbrella maker)
John Chisholm (baker's shop)
Alex Douglas
Isabella Glendenning
James Forsyth
William Lamb
Venters family shop
Watterson's Palace Bakery

House of Falkland [B]
Onesiphorus and Margaret Tyndall Bruce
Sir John and Lady Murray (1905 to 1907)
Lord and Lady Ninian Crichton-Stuart (from 1907)
Butler:
Ainslie
Liptrott
Gardener:
Ewan Macpherson
Carpenter:
Jeremiah Duggan
Housekeepers:
Mrs Mullins
Mrs Birmingham
Stillroom maid:
Mary Ryan
Laundry maid
Mary Dickson
Secretary to Lord Ninian:
Captain R. C. Slacke
Houseboy:
Andrew Toole

House of Falkland Stables [B]
Now headquarters of the Falkland Stewardship Trust
Birrell (Coachman /chauffeur)

Houston (Renfrewshire)
George Galloway

Inchdairsie (Fife)
Mr Dudgeon

India
Margaret Bruce
Miss Scott (Daska, North India)

Juniper Villa (Pleasance) ㊶
Mrs Menzies (ground floor)
Mr Skinner (first floor)
James Clark (from 1911)
Mr Livingston; Mrs Stuart (house next door)

Kent
Charles Jackson
Alf Burgess
Dick Homden
Harry Lee
Tom Schofield

Kettle / Kingskettle / [P]
Mr Adamson
John Anderson

Dr Bell
Mr Beveridge
R. W. Forsyth
Rev. A. E. Gordon
Miss Honeyman
Charles Jackson
George Lindsay
James Maxwell
T. R. Inglis Melvile
George Smith

Kettlehills Ⓟ

A. Mitchell

Key House ⑥④

*Between St Andrew's House and the
Palace.*

William Smith

Kilgour Ⓟ

*Old settlement; gave its name to what
became the parish of Falkland.*

John Morgan

Kilgowrieknowe Ⓟ

William Duncan

Kilwhiss (Fife)

D. Scott

Kinghorn (Fife)

Mr Taylor
Rev. Thomson

Kinnes Cottage (New Road) ③④

*Wrongly called Kinross Cottage in a
newspaper report.*

Isabella and Susan Henderson

Kinross

Kirkcaldy (Fife)

George Arnott
Barry, Ostlere & Shepherd Band
D. Briggs
John Burnett
Mr Collins (Gallatown)
James Craw
Messrs Descamps (car hire)
Rev. Frances (Raith Parish Church)
Gibson & Spears (solicitors)
Robert Grubb

Thomas Jackson (52 Glebe Park)
T. & T. Johnston (solicitors, 180
High Street)
J. Keddie
William Lawson
W. Leitch
Alexander Lumsden (Gallatown)
Miss McLaren
Oliver Melville (engineer)
R. Milliken (photographer)
A. Murdoch (sculptor)
Nairn family
Paterson & Cooper (electricians)
Aggie Reid
W. Smart
David Thomson (Sang & Sons)
Joseph Thomson
Thomson Bros (Ironmongers)
Alex. Wallace (solicitor)
Charles Wood (solicitor)

Kirkcowan (Wigtownshire)

Local station for Mochrum

Ladybank Ⓟ

R. Boucher
D. Carswell (solicitor)
Fife & Forfar Imperial Yeomanry
(Ansmuir Camp)
Fifeshire Auction Co. Ltd
Post Office:
M. Crombie
Mr Scott (postmaster)
Mr Watson

Largo (Fife)

Mr Carr

Lathrisk Ⓟ

Nearest substantial estate to Falkland.

George Johnston
C. J. Maitland Makgill Crichton
Hon. Felix Hanbury-Tracy
Jean Douglas
Captain Wemyss
Arthur Ross (gardener)
Factors:
Charles Gulland

James Carr

Lauder Light Railway (Berwickshire)
Opened 1901.

Laurencekirk (Kincardineshire)
Train ordered to stop there

Leith (Midlothian)
Dr Mackay

Leslie (Fife)
David Clement
Mr Jarvis
James Menzies
Mr Ness
Mr Stark

Leslie House
Mr McNaughton

Leslie Road ⑥② Ⓑ
*Running south from Falkland, with a
gate to the House of Falkland park.*

Letham (Angus)
Peter Kinnear

Leven (Fife)
Mr Bateman
Police-Constable William Calder
(going to Leven on promotion)
Kate H. Carswell (Blacketyside)
John Lumsden (Burn Mill)
Mr Normand

Lindores (Fife)
William Guild
F. L. Maitland

Linen factory
See Pleasance Works

Liquorstane
*See Temperance Hotel. The house has
given its name to a new residential
road.*

Livingstonia (Africa)
Rev. J. H. Morrison

Liverpool
Dr Wallace

Loanfoot (Kingskettle)
James Smart

Mr Taylor

Lochgelly (Fife)
Lochgelly Brass Band or Temperance Band

Lochieheads (Fife)
Rae Arnot

Lochore (Fife)
W. S. Mearns

Lodge Gate Ⓑ
*Main entrance to the House of Falkland
Park, at west end of the Burgh, with
lodge and pond.*
Access severely restricted.
John Drake drowned in pond.

Logie (Fife)
Rev. W. J. Jamieson

Lomond Cottage ④
William Duncan

Lomondside House ㊻
Substantial house off Back Wynd
Charles Fernie a widower aged 91
Barbara Jane Hardie
Previously Dr Mackay
George Gavin (until he moved into
the Palace on being confirmed as
Factor).
James and Daisy Cochrane
A, Forrester
*In 1920 Mrs Gulland of Millfield sold
it to the War Memorial Committee
to be converted to an institute, with
reading-room and billiard-room. It
later became the Y.M.C.A.,
thenFalkland Backpackers and now
the Smart Cookies nursery.*
*Not to be confused with another
Lomondside, high above the East
Loan.* Ⓑ

Lomond Tavern ㊼
John Kennoway
Edward Herd

Lomondvale Ⓑ
Since replaced with the residential

home of the same name.
Charles Jackson Jnr
Mrs Livingstone

London
Edgar Bellingham
A Brown (St John's Lodge, Regents Park)
Henry Burgess (W. D. Hodge & Co. Ltd, Brompton Road)
Rev. John Barrack (Maida Hill)
Miss Collum
Lady Margaret Crichton-Stuart (St John's Lodge, Regents Park)
Lord and Lady Ninian Crichton-Stuart (Beechgrove, Sunninghill)
Ninian Patrick Crichton-Stuart (born at Ovington House)
Howard & Co. (patent agents,
Dr Howell
John Robertson Lyell (Home Office)
R. E. Noble (barrister)
Mrs Pierson
Thomas Preston
Mr Robb
Robert Weir Schultz (architect, 14 Gray's Inn Square)
Captain Slacke (32 Trevor Square)
Strum & Knight (67 South Audley Street)
Westminster Palace Hotel
Mrs Wilson (Housekeeper, Ovington House)

Lundie Mill (Fife)
Mr Bell

Magask (Fife)
Mr Walton

Mairsland (Fife)
Farm near Auchtermuchty.

Manse [B]
Outside the Burgh to the south. Now self-catering holiday accommodation called Ladywell House. Listed in Gifford as Glebelands.

Markinch (Fife)
James Philp
David Robertson (solicitor)
J. C. Rolland and Sons (decorators)
Mr Scott (Markinch Marquee Co.)

Maspie Den [P]
Local beauty spot

Maspie House ㉔
Present-day name of a building for many years used as the post office. Now a shop.

Maspie Burn [B]
Alex Adams
Alex Davie
George S. Hardie
Robert Jackson

Meadowfield [B]
House in a secluded position to the south of the town, built for J. W. Jackson. A panel on the front of the house has the date '1910' and the initials 'JWJ'.
John Walker Jackson

Memorial Chapel [A]
Lord Ninian planned a new Catholic church on the Falkland Estate, as a memorial to his eldest son, also called Ninian, who died in 1910, but the church was uncompleted at Lord Ninian's death and is now a roofless memorial chapel.

Mexico
Barbara Paterson

Mill
See "turning Mill".

Mill Burn [B]
Burn leading to the mill pond, now diverted into the Maspie Burn

Millfield House (61) [B]
Inside the Burgh at one time, later excluded from it.
Charles Gulland
Mrs Howell

Millfield Cottage (unidentified)
William Grant (butcher)

Mill Green
Green space on the side of the old
turning mill.

Mill Lade ⑤
*Channel leading from the mill-pond to
the Turning Mill, partly in tunnel.
Now diverted into the Maspie Burn.*

Mill Quarry (unidentified)
Source of stones for building a wall

Mill Wynd ⑪
Rachel Thomson
Alex Reid
Henry Wright

Milnathort (Kinross-shire)
Mr Macpherson
Andrew Ramsay (3 Viewlands
Terrace)

Mochrum (Galloway)
Lord and Lady Ninian Crichton-
Stuart staying at Old Place of
Mochrum
Rev. Andrew Robertson

Moncreiffe Estate (near Bridge of
Earn, Perthshire)
George Gavin (former factor)

Monifieth (Fife)
Christopher Morrison

Monimail (Fife)
Rev. W. D. Beattie

Montrose (Angus)
Mary Macdonald
Rossie Reformatory

Monzie Castle (Perthshire)
Charles Julian Maitland Makgill
Crichton Johnston movied there
1908; the house then burnt down

Moonzie Farm (Fife)
Near Cupar.

Mount Stuart (Bute)
*Ancestral home of the Marquesses of
Bute*

Muckart (Perthshire)
Rev. Cairns

Muirhead (Fife)
David Bonthrone

Muirkirk (Ayrshire)
Andrew Brunton to be sent there

Murthly Asylum (Perthshire)
Dr Bruce

The Myre Ⓑ
Golf course
Market and games

Myres Castle (Fife)
Bought by Professor Bruce. Later
sold to the Fairlie family but the
title of Myres Macer rests with
Falkland Estate.
J. Ogilvie Fairlie
Mr Coventry

Nether Myres (Dunshalt) Ⓟ
Robert Pringle

Newburgh (Fife)
Mr Edwards (Provost)
Miss A. Melville

New Inn Ⓟ
*Demolished but gave its name to the
New Inn Roundabout.*

New Road ㉟ Ⓑ

Newton of Falkland Ⓟ
Alexander Adams
David Bonthrone (Newton House)
Alexander Davie
George S. Hardie
Robert Jackson
George Knox (van driver)
William Meiklejohn (Glen Newton)
D. McMillan
H. D. Michie
James Paterson
William Stark Jnr

Newton of Lathrisk Ⓟ
Thomas Arnot

Newton Stewart (Galloway)
Mr Maxwell (Galloway Arms)

Newtyle (Strathmore, Forfarshire)
 George Gavin working there
Nisbetfield (Monimail; Fife)
 Mrs Webster
Nochnarie Ⓟ
 George Morgan
Normandy (France)
 Lord Ninian recuperating at a spa
Nuthill
 Replaced by House of Falkland
Old house opposite Palace ㉚
Orchard Park Ⓑ
 Rubbish being left there
Oxford
 Lord Ninian studying at Christ
  Church
Palace Restaurant (probably in the
 High Street)
 Raphil Tarabella
Pardovan (West Lothian)
 Mr Tod
Parish Church ⑱
 Built 1848 at the expense of Ones-
 iphorus and Margaret Tyndall
 Bruce, replacing an older church on
 the site).
 Ministers:
  Rev. A. Lyon Johnston
  Rev. J. K. Russell
Peebles
 Rev. A. M. McLean
Perth
 Brady & Sons
 Rev. Walter F. Lee (East Parish)
 Macdonald, Fraser & Co, (auc-
  tioneers)
 Mr Glass (chemist)
 Joe Hunter
 Thomas Love (Lord Provost)
 Thomas Love & Sons (auctioneers,
  removers, antique dealers)
 William Alexander Mason (Hen-
  derson's Buildings; Victoria

 Hotel)
Miss McDonald
Macdonald, Fraser & Co. (auc-
 tioneers)
Rev. James Horne Morrison
Henry Jamison
J. Reid (40 Princes Street)
Robertson, Dempster & Co.
 (solicitors, Methven Street)
David Smart (architect)
David A. Stewart (architect, 8 High
 Street; 6 Rosemount Place)
Mrs Wilson (Rosenheir)
Pillars of Hercules Ⓟ
 Acquired by the Falkland Estate in the
 1820s.
Pitcairlie (Fife)
 Historic house near Newburgh. Now
 an hotel.
 James Cathcart
Pitlour (Fife)
 Mr Laing
 Miss Skene
 Mr Utterson
Pittencrieff (Fife)
 Public park in Dunfermline, donated by
 Andrew Carnegie in 1902
Plains Ⓟ
 William Ritchie
Pleasance ㊳
 Miss C. Bisset
 George Hardie
 Mr Howe
Pleasance Works Ⓑ
 Linen factory
Pluscarden Priory (Moray)
 Bought by the 3ʳᵈ Marquess for Lord
 Colum, who gave it to a Benedictine
 community in 1943.
Police Station (Falkland) ⑨
Portobello (Midlothian)
 J. C. Adam

Post Office (Falkland):
- Previously next to the Old House opposite the palace ㉚
- Then on the corner of High Street and Cross Wynd (57)
- Later in Maspie House ㉔
- Then in the ground floor of the Town Hall ㉒
- Now back near its original location ㉚

Prestonkirk (East Lothian)
- George Wilson (Cranchie)

Priestfield (Fife)
- *Country house near Cults, now demolished.*
- Miss Martin

Public School / School House ㊵ [B]
- Mr Dunbar
- John Richardson
- *Since demolished and replaced with current Falkland Primary School*

Purin Den [P]
- *Local beauty spot.*

Purin Hill [P]
- *On the slopes of the East Lomond; Rifle range*

Ramornie (Fife)
- *Large country house near Ladybank, associated with Field Marshall Haig (since demolished)*

Rathillet (Fife)
- Rev. Wilson

Reading Room (59)
- *Later converted to an electricity substation*

Reedieleys [P]
- W. S. Henderson

Rossie Estate (Fife)

Rossie Reformatory (Forfarshire)
- Founded 1857, Later re-classified as an "approved school". Now Rossie Young People's Trust.

Rothes (Fife)
- Peter Whitecross

Rothesay, (Isle of Bute)
- John Dale

Royal Terrace [B]
- William Page
- Robert B. Bryce
- Robert Craig Jnr (baker)
- John Hay

Russia
- Lord Ninian ill with typhus in Kiev (now in Ukraine)

Saddlers House ㉓
- Robert and Thomas Williamson

Saltcoats (Ayrshire)
- J. Dunbar

Sauchie (Clackmannanshire)
- John Arnot

Scroggie Park [B]
- *Cricket pitch*

Selkirk
- Andrew Johnston
- Rev. J. Sharpe (Heatherlie)

Shields (Glasgow ?)
- George Brunton

Slaughter House (New Road) ㉝ [B]
- Christopher Campbell Brunton

South Street ㊸
- William Clark
- Barbara Paterson
- Michael Reekie
- Wiliam James Reid

Springfield (Fife)

St Andrews (Fife)
- J. Bruce Alston
- Miss Auchterlonie
- 3rd Marquess of Bute (St Andrews Priory)
- Isabel Johnston (Argyll House)
- Mr McMillan (Clifton Bank School)
- Walter Mitchell
- George B. Rodger (photographer)

J. Smith
John H. Wilson (St Andrew's
    University)
St Andrew's House ㉕
Mrs Gertrude Quiller (Matron)
Walter Wilson
James Davis
Robert Grubb
St John's Works ㊾ Ⓑ
Floorcloth and linoleum factory
Stag Inn ⑮
*The original inn is now a private house;
    the Stag Inn now occupies adjacent
    buildings opposite Mill Green.*
James Weepers
Stirling
T. Dawson
William Wood (artist)
Stratheden (Fife)
Dr Ferguson (Fife and Kinross
    Asylum – now Stratheden
    Hospital)
Strathendry (Fife)
Also spelt Strathenry.
R. Tullis (probably of Tullis Russel
    papermakers)
Strathmiglo Ⓟ
Rev. Hugh Brown
Rev. J. M. Munro
J. R. Oliphant
P. Rutherford
Thomson family (Lochie)
Strathmiglo road Ⓑ
Now the A912.
Stravithie (Fife)
Mrs Sprot
Sugar Acre Field ㊺
*Now used in part by the car park,
    village hall and library*
Tarvit (Fife)
Pat J. Home Rigg
Tayport (Fife)
E. J. Turner

Temperance Hotel (High Street)
㉙
Now the "Love Restored" shop
Mrs Hardie
Temperance Hotel (Liquorstane)
㊷
Robert and Catherine Ness
Templelands Ⓑ
On the slopes of East Lomond Hill.
Alexander Douglas occupying
    neighbouring land.
The Terrace
Another name for Royal Terrace.
Thornton (Fife)
Mr Clark
Town Hall ㉒
*Venue for Town Council meetings.
    Ground floor used as a shop and
    post office, now a delicatessen.*
William Middleton (sub-
    postmaster)
Trinity Gask Estate (Perthshire)
George Gavin former factor
Tullibody (Clackmannanshire)
Robert Kinmont
Turning Mill ⑩
*Since demolished and replaced by Mill
    Green*
David Galloway, wood turner
Tyrone (County)
T. Byars
Uddingston (Lanarkshire)
Mrs Davis
United Free Church ㊱ Ⓑ
*Built 1844. Later became the Parish
    Church Hall. Now a private house.*
Minister:
    Rev. J. H. Morrison.
United Free Manse ㊴ Ⓑ
Now Pleasance House.
Rev. James H. Morrison
Urquhart Ⓟ
Mr Rae

Valescure (South of France)
Lord Ninian staying there
Victoria Place ㊼ Ⓑ
William Barr
Andrew Lawson
Robert Strachan (tailor)
John Swinton
Viewhill House (West Port) ②
Lawrence Reid
Frank Henderson
Well Brae ㊽
John Balfour
William Skinner
Wellfield (Strathmiglo)
Historic house and grounds
West Conland Ⓟ
Wester Cash Ⓟ
Thomas Philp
Wester Kilwhiss Ⓟ
Westfield Ⓟ
John Barrie Ogilvie

Alex Nicoll
James Martin
Poaching (Greenhill Park)
A.Smith
West Loan ①
West Lomond Hill Ⓟ
West Mill (Fife)
J. M. Wilkie
West Port ③
Robert Sharpe
Mrs F. Kilgour
Miss Storrar
Annie Sharp
George Robertson
Mr Robb (loom shop)
Windygates (Fife)
William Morgan
Woodmill Ⓟ
George Dun
George Donald (Shepherd)

Index to numbered features on Map D

Maps

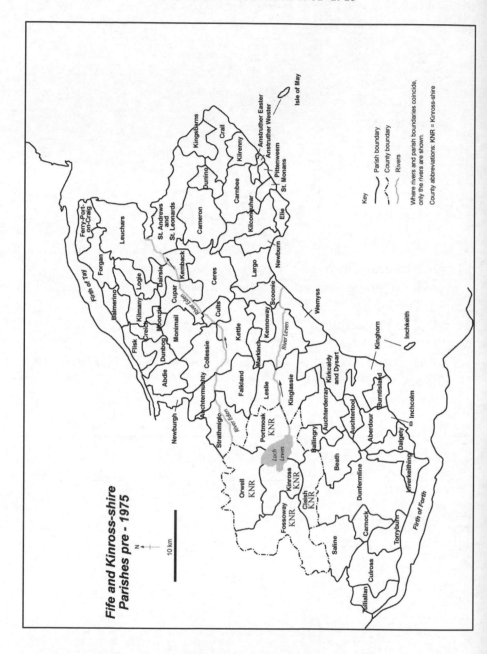

Fife and Kinross-shire Parishes pre - 1975

Key

— Parish boundary

—·—· County boundary

~~~ Rivers

Where rivers and parish boundaries coincide, only the rivers are shown.

County abbreviations: KNR = Kinross-shire

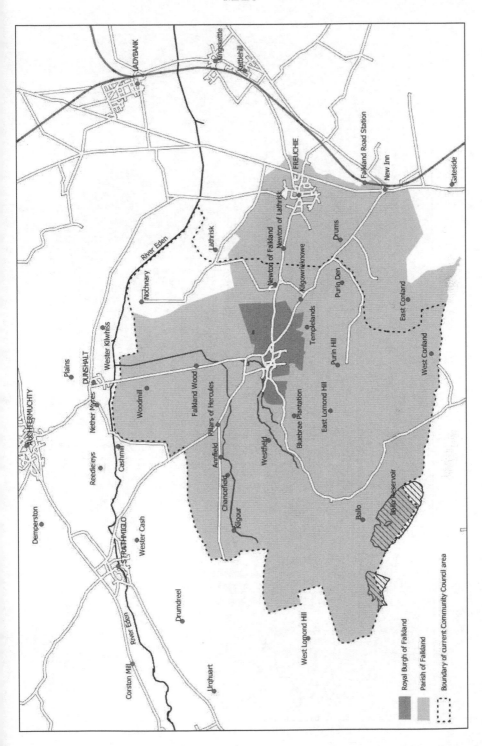

Royal Burgh of Falkland

Parish of Falkland

Boundary of current Community Council area

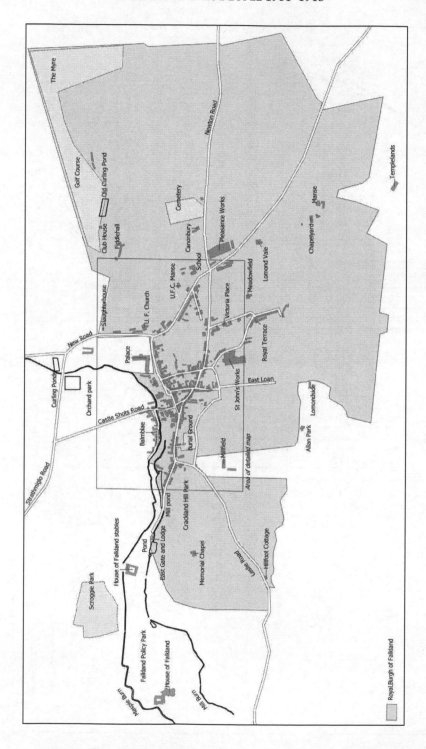

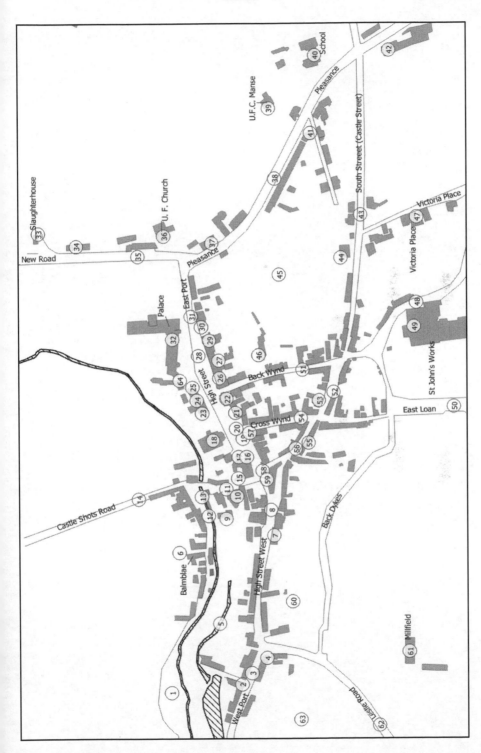

Timeline

1458   *Falkland becomes a Royal Burgh.*

1542   *King James V dies at Falkland Palace.*

1818   *Division of the Commonty of the Lomond Hills*

1843   *The Disruption: the Free Church of Scotland breaks away from the Established Church.*

1844   *Falkland Free Church built.*

1848   *Falkland Parish Church built (replacing an older church on the site).*

1871   *Charles Jackson Snr opens the linen factory in Falkland*

1872   *Education (Scotland) Act establishes a nationwide system of primary schools managed by elected School Boards.*

1886   *H. H. Asquith elected as Liberal MP for East Fife.*

1887   *The 3rd Marquess of Bute purchases the Falkland Estate and begins restoring the Palace.*

1890   *County Councils introduced in Scotland, including Fife.*

1900   *Death of the 3rd Marquess: he leaves the Falkland estate to his second son, Lord Ninian.*

1900   *The United Free Church of Scotland formed by a merger of the Free Church of Scotland and the United Presbyterian Church.*

Jan 1901   Death of Queen Victoria.

Feb 1902   Death of William Wood, factor to the Falkland Estate.

Feb 1902   Floorcloth factory (St John's Works) opened

May 1902   Treaty of Vereeniging: the end of the Boer War.

Jun 1902   Coming of age of the 4th Marquess.

Aug 1902   Delayed coronation of King Edward VII.

Nov 1903   Robert Miller elected Provost.

May 1904	Coming of age of Lord Ninian.
Dec 1904	George Gavin appointed factor to the Falkland Estate (acting in this role since Major Wood's death).
Jun 1905	House of Falkland leased to Sir John Murray.
Jan 1906	General Election: H. H. Asquith re-elected for East Fife.
Jun 1906	Lord Ninian married to Hon. Ismay Preston.
Jan 1907	Handloom weaving finally abandoned.
Apr 1907	Birth of Ninian Patrick Crichton-Stuart.
Aug 1907	Lord and Lady Ninian move into House of Falkland.
Apr 1908	H. H. Asquith becomes Prime Minister.
Aug 1909	Death of Charles Gulland, town clerk.
Nov 1909	Charles Jackson Jnr elected Provost.
Dec 1909	Birth of Ismay Catherine Crichton-Stuart
Feb 1910	Death of Ninian Patrick Crichton-Stuart.
May 1910	Death of King Edward VII.
Jan 1910	General Election: H. H. Asquith re-elected for East Fife; Lord Ninian unsuccessful for Cardiff.
Dec 1910	General Election: H. H. Asquith re-elected for East Fife; Lord Ninian elected Unionist MP for Cardiff.
Jun 1911	Coronation of King George V.
Apr 1912	Sinkjng of the *Titanic*.
Jun 1913	Birth of Claudia Miriam Joanna Crichton-Stuart.
Jul 1913	Memorial Chapel foundation stone laid.

1914	*Outbreak of the Great War.*
1915	*Battle of Loos: Lord Ninian killed.*
1929	*Most of the United Free Church absorbed into the Church of Scotland, removing the need for two separate church buildings in Falkland as elsewhere.*
1975	*Royal Burghs and County Councils abolished: Falkland absorbed into a new district of North East Fife within the Fife region.*
1978	*First meeting of the Royal Burgh of Falkland and Newton of Falkland Community Council.*
1994	*Fife region and its districts abolished and replaced by the current Fife Council.*

Glossary

agent (banking): part-time bank manager.

B.O.A.F.G.: British Order of Ancient Free Gardeners.

bailie: an honorary title for a senior town councillor, similar to an alderman: in Falkland there were two bailies, designated as Senior Bailie and Junior Bailie respectively.

burgh: (pronounced like "borough"): a municipal corporation with its own provost and councillors. Royal Burghs (such as Falkland) were founded by royal Charter. Falkland was one of the four "inactive Royal Burghs of Fife" - never represented in Parliament, or in the Convention of Royal Burghs until modern times. All burghs were abolished in 1973, however the title of "Royal Burgh" may be maintained for ceremonial purposes, as for instance in the 'Royal Burgh of Falkland and Newton of Falkland Community Council'.

burgh court: a court in which the provost and bailies acted as magistrates, dealing with minor criminal and civil matters, the equivalent of a JP court, but within a burgh.

causeway: (also "causey") paved area in front of a house.

cessio (in full, **cessio bonorum**, Latin for "surrender of goods") a form of bankruptcy (since abolished) by which a debtor could escape imprisonment for debt by surrendering all his possessions.

chalder: a measure of capacity for dry goods – about 2 or 3 cubic metres, depending on what was being measured.

common good: the land, property, etc., historically owned by a Scottish burgh.

commonty: property held by two or more people in common.

Court of Session: Scotland's highest civil court.

depot: a place for depositing dung.

displenishment: selling off the contents of a farm.

disposition: a deed for changing ownership of property.

divot: a thin piece of turf used in thatching.

DM: ? Deputy Master (B.O.A.F.G).

dyke: a wall (not a ditch as in England).

facile: weak-minded; easily influenced by others.

factor: the person who manages an estate on behalf of its owner.

feu: a form of land tenure (since abolished) in which the owner had to pay annual feu duties to a feudal superior.

fiscal: see **procurator fiscal.**

flesher: butcher.

glebe: land assigned to a parish minister.

grieve: overseer or head workman.

heritor: a major landowner, who had certain rights and duties in respect of the parish church.

homologation: the act of ratifying a deed that was not previously legally binding.

IG: Inner Guard (B.O.A.F.G. and Freemasons).

interdict: court order (injunction).

JD: Junior Deacon (Freemasons).

IPM: Immediate Past Master (Freemasons).

JP Court: a court presided over by lay magistrates, dealing with minor civil and criminal matters.

JW: Junior Warden (B.O.A.F.G. and) Freemasons).

kirkin: ceremonial attendance at church; the kirkin of the council is a long held custom to inaugurate the new term of a council.

lade: channel bringing water to a mill.

lair: a grave plot in a cemetery.

laird: the owner of an estate and recognised leader of the community, roughly equivalent to a squire or lord of the manor in England.

lint hole: a pond used for steeping lint (flax).

loan: a grassy track through arable land.

manse: parish minister's residence.

midden: dunghill or rubbish heap.

OG: Outer Guard (B.O.A.F.G. and Freemasons).

pendicle: piece of land subsidiary to a main estate.

PM: Past Master (B.O.A.F.G. and Freemasons).

policy: enclosed ornamental grounds.

poorhouse: an institution in which paupers were housed; equivalent to the English workhouse, except that in Scotland the residents were not required to work.

port (in street names): entrance to a town.

procurator fiscal: public prosecutor.

provost: the chief magistrate of a burgh, equivalent to a mayor.

public school: a state school, set up under the Education (Scotland) Act 1872 and managed by an elected School Board. No connection with the term "public school" as used in England to mean a major independent school.

reset: to receive stolen goods.

roup: an auction.

Royalty: the lands of the Royal Burgh.

RWM: Right Worshipful Master (Freemasons).

SD: Senior Deacon (Freemasons).

sheriff: a judge who presides over a sheriff court, dealing with most types of civil and criminal cases.

sist: to suspend a legal process.

solum: the ground on which a building stands.

steading: the buildings on a farm.

stance: site; **ground stance:** rubbish disposal site.

stirk: a young bullock or heifer.

SW: Senior Warden (B.O.A.F.G. and Freemasons).

teind: a charge payable by landowners for the upkeep of the Established Church, originally a tenth part (tithe) of the annual produce.

teind court: the body (part of the Court of Session) that administers teinds.

tup: ram (male sheep).

upset price: reserve price at an auction.

VS: Veterinary Surgeon

wap: a brawl.

whins: gorse.

WM: Worshipful master (B.O.A.F.G).

writer: a member of the Society of Writers to Her Majesty's Signet, an organisation of Scottish solicitors. Writers had the power to seal petitions, without which no action could be raised in the Court of

Session
WS: see **writer.**
wynd: narrow street or lane leading off a main street.

Names and titles

By convention, the daughters and the *younger* sons (and their wives) of marquesses and dukes use have the courtesy title "Lord / Lady (forename) (surname)" – hence "Lord Ninian Crichton-Stuart" – the usage "Lord Crichton-Stuart" occurs sometimes in the press articles, but is clearly wrong as it would imply he was a peer in his own right. The *eldest* sons of marquesses and dukes use one of their father's subsidiary titles – thus the eldest son of the Marquess of Bute is the Earl of Dumfries.[1]

The prefix "Honourable" (abbreviated "Hon.") is used for the sons and daughters of viscounts and barons – hence Lady Ninian before her marriage was the Hon. Ismay Preston, being the daughter of Viscount Gormanston, and the Hon. Felix Hanbury-Tracy was the son of Baron Sudely of Toddington.

Among ordinary people, "Miss Smith" normally indicates Mr and Mrs's Smith's *eldest* daughter, their *younger* daughters being distinguished as "Miss Mary Smith" etc.

In official contexts a married woman, Mrs Johnson (née Robinson) may be referred to as "Jane Robinson or Johnson", which seems to be a peculiarly Scottish usage.

£sd

Prior to decimalisation in 1971, the pound sterling (£) was divided into 20 shillings (s) and the shilling into 12 pence (d). So a 1910 penny would equate to just over 0.4p in today's terms; but in purchasing power would be more like 50p.

---

[1] The present Marquess was known as "Johnny Dumfries" during his motor-racing career

Bibliography

Sources for extracts

AJ	*Aberdeen Journal*
CFUK	*County Families of the United Kingdom*, 1919
DC	*Dundee Courier*
DEP	*Dundee Evening Post*
DET	*Dundee Evening Telegraph*
EEN	*Edinburgh Evening News*
FEson&P	Falkland Estate Papers
FFP	*Fife Free Press*
FH	*Fife Herald*
FNA	*Fife News Almanac*
FSC	Falkland Society Collection
FTCM	Falkland Town Council Minutes
LAWG	*Leven Advertiser & Wemyss Gazette*
LEP	*Lancashire Evening Post*
SAC	*St Andrews Citizen*
TQ	*The Queen*
TS	*The Scotsman*

Sources for illustrations

1 Drawing by Frances Crichton Stuart
2, 4, 6, 7, 8, 12, 15*, 16, 17, 18 20, 27, 28, 41, 42, 43, 44, 49, 50, 52, 54, 55; 56 Historic Images of Falkland
3, 5, 9, 22, 30, 38, 53 Wikimedia Commons

10, 14, 25, 35, 57, 62 Photos by Ross Burgess
11, 19 Fife News Almanac
13 Crichton Stuart family archives
21 Lamont-Brown and Adamson
23, 36, 37, 40, 45, 46, 47, 61 Falkland Society photo collection
24 Pinterest
26 From an old postcard
30 *Illustrated Guide to Falkland, Fife*
32, 39, source unknown
33, 60 Photos by Peter Burman
34 Petersham Remembers
48 DC
51 FN
59 Photo by Marietta Crichton Stuart

Other works consulted

ANON, *Illustrated Guide to Falkland, Fife: With story of its Royal Palace and notes on the district*, second edition, revised and enlarged (Cupar: J. & G. Innes, c.1915).

GIFFORD, John, *Fife*, the Buildings of Scotland Series (London: Penguin Books, 1988).

GILBERT, Christopher, James LOMAX and Anthony WELLS-COLE, *Country House Floors*, Temple Newsam Country Houses Studies (Leeds: Leeds City Art Galleries, 1987).

HUNTER BLAIR, Right Rev. Sir David Oswald, *John Patrick, Third Marquess of Bute, K.T. (1847–1900), a Memoir* (London: John Murray, 1921).

LAMONT-BROWN, Raymond and Peter ADAMSON, *Victorian and Edwardian Fife from Old Photographs* (Edinburgh: Ramsay Head, 1980).

TAYLOR, Simon, with Gilbert MÁRKUS, *The Place-Names of Fife, Volume Two: Central Fife between the Rivers Leven and Eden* (Donington: Shaun Tyas, 2008).

Index

Note: the source documents for this book refer to the same individual in different ways: John Smith, J Smith, Mr Smith, with or without a note of their occupation or where they live. An attempt has been made to bring together under one heading the references to a particular person, but it is impossible to do this entirely consistently; consequently it is possible that a single index heading below may refer to two or more different people, and almost certain that references to a single person may come under more than one heading.

The very large numbers of letters to or from George Gavin, factor, have not been separately indexed under his name.

References to illustrations are marked (*illus.*)

The Falkland Society
Scottish Registered Charity SC017201

For information about our monthly meetings and
other activities, how to join the society, and
details of our other publications, see
www.falklandsociety.org.uk

To view our online database of facts and pictures
about Falkland's historic buildings, and other
resources about Falkland's history, see
www.historicfalkland.scot